Contents

KT-526-594

A note about copyright

Dear Customer

What does the little © mean and why does it matter?

Your market-leading BPP books, course materials and e-learning materials do not write and update themselves. People write them: on their own behalf or as employees of an organisation that invests in this activity. Copyright law protects their livelihoods. It does so by creating rights over the use of the content.

Breach of copyright is a form of theft – as well as being a criminal offence in some jurisdictions, it is potentially a serious breach of professional ethics.

With current technology, things might seem a bit hazy but, basically, without the express permission of BPP Learning Media:

- Photocopying our materials is a breach of copyright
- Scanning, ripcasting or conversion of our digital materials into different file formats, uploading them to facebook or emailing them to your friends is a breach of copyright

You can, of course, sell your books, in the form in which you have bought them – once you have finished with them. (Is this fair to your fellow students? We update for a reason.) Please note the e-products are sold on a single user licence basis: we do not supply 'unlock' codes to people who have bought them second-hand.

And what about outside the UK? BPP Learning Media strives to make our materials available at prices students can afford by local printing arrangements, pricing policies and partnerships which are clearly listed on our website. A tiny minority ignore this and indulge in criminal activity by illegally photocopying our material or supporting organisations that do. If they act illegally and unethically in one area, can you really trust them?

Using your BPP Learning Media products

This Kit gives you the question practice and guidance you need in the exam. Our other products can also help you pass:

- **Learning to Learn Accountancy** gives further valuable advice on revision

- **Passcards** provide you with clear topic summaries and exam tips

- **Success CDs** help you revise on the move

- **i-Pass CDs** offer tests of knowledge against the clock

- **Underlying knowledge CD** offers guidance on assumed knowledge for Options papers P4, P5, P6, P7

You can purchase these products by visiting http://www.bpp.com/acca

ACCA

PAPER F7

FINANCIAL REPORTING (INTERNATIONAL AND UK STREAM)

PRACTICE & REVISION KIT

BPP Learning Media is the **sole ACCA Platinum Approved Learning Partner – content** for the ACCA Qualification. In this, **the only Paper F7 Practice and Revision Kit to be reviewed by the examiner:**

- We discuss the **best strategies** for revising and taking your ACCA exams

- We show you how to be **well prepared** for your exam

- We give you **lots of great guidance** on tackling questions

- We show you how you can **build your own exams**

- We provide you with **three** mock exams including the **December 2012 exam**

- We provide the **ACCA examiner's answers** as well as our own to the June and December 2012 exams as an additional revision aid

Our **Passcard** and **I-Pass** products also support this paper.

FOR EXAMS UP TO JUNE 2014

BPP
LEARNING MEDIA

First edition 2007
Seventh edition January 2013

ISBN 9781 44 53 6647 0
(previous ISBN 9781 4453 7996 8)

e-ISBN 9781 4453 6950 1

British Library Cataloguing-in-Publication Data
A catalogue record for this book
is available from the British Library

Published by

BPP Learning Media Ltd
BPP House, Aldine Place
London W12 8AA

www.bpp.com/learningmedia

Printed in the United Kingdom by Polestar Wheatons

Hennock Road
Marsh Barton
Exeter
EX2 8RP

All our rights reserved. No part of this publication may be
reproduced, stored in a retrieval system or transmitted, in
any form or by any means, electronic, mechanical,
photocopying, recording or otherwise, without the prior
written permission of BPP Learning Media Ltd.

We are grateful to the Association of Chartered Certified
Accountants for permission to reproduce past
examination questions. The suggested solutions in the
exam answer bank have been prepared by BPP Learning
Media Ltd, except where otherwise stated.

Your learning materials, published by BPP Learning
Media Ltd, are printed on paper sourced from
sustainable, managed forests.

©
BPP Learning Media Ltd
2013

Question index

The headings in this checklist/index indicate the main topics of questions, but questions are expected to cover several different topics. Questions marked 2.5 were examination questions under the previous syllabus.
Examiner's answers. For the June and December 2012 exams the examiner's answers can be found at the end of this Kit.

	Marks	Time allocation Mins	Page number Question	Page number Answer
Part 1: The conceptual framework				
1 Porto (Pilot paper amended)	13	23	3	83
2 Concepts (6/08 amended)	15	27	3	84
3 Baxen (6/12)	10	18	4	85
Part 2: The regulatory framework				
4 Regulatory framework (2.5 12/04)	25	45	4	86
5 *Preparation question: IFRS*	-	-	4	88
Part 3: Presentation of published financial statements				
6 Candel (12/08)	25	45	5	89
7 Pricewell (6/09)	25	45	6	92
8 Sandown (12/09)	25	45	8	95
9 Dune (6/10)	25	45	9	98
10 Cavern (12/10)	25	45	11	102
11 Keystone (12/11)	25	45	12	105
12 Fresco (6/12)	25	45	14	108
Part 4: Non-current assets				
13 *Preparation question: Plethora plc*	-	-	15	112
14 Elite Leisure (2.5 12/05 part)	12	22	16	112
15 Dearing (12/08)	10	18	16	113
16 Flightline (6/09)	10	18	17	114
17 Apex (6/10)	10	18	17	116
18 Derringdo II (2.5 6/03 part)	9	16	18	117
Part 5: Intangible assets				
19 Emerald (12/07)	10	18	18	119
20 Dexterity (2.5 6/04)	25	45	19	120
21 Darby (12/09)	15	27	20	122

BPP
LEARNING MEDIA

BPP
LEARNING MEDIA

Mock exam 3 (December 2012 paper)

Planning your question practice

Our guidance from page (xvii) shows you how to organise your question practice, either by attempting questions from each syllabus area or **by building your own exams** – tackling questions as a series of practice exams.

June and December 2013 exams

BPP's answers for these exams will be available for free after the exams on http://www.bpp.com/acca

Helping you with your revision – the ONLY F7 Practice and Revision Kit to be reviewed by the examiner!

BPP Learning Media – the sole Platinum Approved Learning Partner - content

As ACCA's **sole Platinum Approved Learning Partner – content**, BPP Learning Media gives you the **unique opportunity** to use **examiner-reviewed** revision materials for the 2013 and June 2014 exams. By incorporating the examiner's comments and suggestions regarding syllabus coverage, the BPP Learning Media Practice and Revision Kit provides excellent, **ACCA-approved** support for your revision.

Tackling revision and the exam

Using feedback obtained from ACCA examiners as part of their review:

- We look at the dos and don'ts of revising for, and taking, ACCA exams
- We focus on Paper F7; we discuss revising the syllabus, what to do (and what not to do) in the exam, how to approach different types of question and ways of obtaining easy marks

Selecting questions

We provide signposts to help you plan your revision.

- A full **question index**
- **BPP's question plan** highlighting the most important questions and explaining why you should attempt them
- **Build your own exams**, showing how you can practise questions in a series of exams

Making the most of question practice

At BPP Learning Media we realise that you need more than just questions and model answers to get the most from your question practice.

- Our **Top tips** included for certain questions provide essential advice on tackling questions, presenting answers and the key points that answers need to include
- We show you how you can pick up **Easy marks** on some questions, as we know that picking up all readily available marks often can make the difference between passing and failing
- We include **marking guides** to show you what the examiner rewards
- We include **examiners' comments** to show you where students struggled or performed well in the actual exam
- We refer to the **2012 BPP Study Text** (for exams up to June 2014) for detailed coverage of the topics covered in questions
- In a bank at the end of this Kit we include the **examiner's answers** to the June and December 2012 papers. Used in conjunction with our answers they provide an indication of all possible points that could be made, issues that could be covered and approaches to adopt.

Attempting mock exams

There are three mock exams that provide practice at coping with the pressures of the exam day. We strongly recommend that you attempt them under exam conditions. **Mock exams 1 and 2** reflect the question styles and syllabus coverage of the exam; **Mock exam 3** is the December 2012 paper.

Revising F7

If you are sitting the F7 UK paper, at least 90% of the marks on your paper will be for questions based on International Standards. For the remaining part, which can be up to10%, we are producing a supplement detailing areas of difference between International and UK standards on which you could be tested. This will be available free at: www.bpp.com. Follow links to Learning Media / Supplements. However, your first priority should be the 90%, so you should begin by working through this Kit.

Topics to revise

What we do know about F7 is that Question 1 will be a consolidation question. This can be a statement of financial position or statement of profit or loss or both, and it will probably include an associate, so be prepared for all of this. Therefore you must revise all the consolidation workings, and you must know how to account for an associate. All questions are compulsory.

Question 2 will be a single company accounts preparation question. This allows the examiner to bring in more complex issues that he would not test in the consolidation question. Make sure you can deal with finance leases, deferred tax, calculating finance costs using the effective interest rate, prior period adjustments, discontinued operations and construction contracts.

Question 3 will be on statements of cash flow or interpretation of accounts. You have studied both of these at F3/FFA, so make sure you can do them well. Other recent questions have involved non-current assets and impairment, intangible assets, EPS, provisions and regulatory issues. These are all likely topics for questions 4 and 5.

There will be a certain amount of discussion in some of the questions, so be prepared to write about financial reporting topics, such as the *Conceptual Framework* or specific accounting standards.

Question practice

This is the most important thing to do if you want to get through. All of the most up-to-date exam questions from the previous syllabus and all the F7 questions to date are in this Kit. Practise doing them under timed conditions, then go through the answers and go back to the Study Text for any topic you are really having trouble with. Come back to a question week later and try it again – you will be surprised at how much better you are getting. Be very ruthless with yourself at this stage – you have to do the question in the time, without looking at the answer. This will really sharpen your wits and make the exam experience less worrying. Just keep doing this and you will get better at doing questions and you will really find out what you know and what you don't know.

Passing the F7 exam

If you have honestly done your revision then you can pass this exam. What you must do is remain calm and tackle it in a professional manner. The examiner stresses a number of points which you should bear in mind.

- You must read the question properly. Students often fail to read the question properly and miss some of the information. Time spent reading the question a second time would be time well spent. Make yourself do this, don't just rush into it in a panic.

- Workings must be clear and cross-referenced. If the marker can read and understand your workings they can give you credit for using the right method, even if your answer is wrong. If your answer is wrong and there are no workings, or they are illegible and incomprehensible, you will get no marks for that part of the question.

- Stick to the timings and answer all questions. Do not spend too long on one question at the expense of others. The number of extra marks you will gain on that question will be minimal, and you could have at least obtained the easy marks on the next question.

- Do not neglect the short parts of the question. If you get a 20-mark consolidation with a 5-mark discussion topic at the end, leave time for that last part. You can't afford to throw away 5 marks.

- Make sure you get the easy marks. If an accounts preparation question contains something that you are unable to do, just ignore it and do the rest. You will probably only lose a few marks and if you start trying to puzzle it out you might waste a lot of minutes.

- Answer the question. In a discussion-type question you may be tempted to just write down everything you know about the topic. This will do you no good. The marking parameters for these questions are quite precise. You will only get marks for making points that answer the question exactly as it has been set. So don't waste your time waffling – you could be scoring marks somewhere else.

Note that you have 15 minutes reading time at the start of this exam, during which you are allowed to make notes on the question paper. Use this to read the questions carefully and underline important points. Make note of any points that occur to you which you may otherwise forget. Get really familiar with the paper and focus on what you can do, not the bits you think you can't do.

Gaining the easy marks

The first point to make is that you do not get any marks for just writing down the formats for a financial statement. But, once you have put the formats down, you are then in a position to start filling in the numbers and getting the easy marks. Also, correct formats will give you a guide so that you don't miss things. For instance, it's easy to forget about the non-controlling interest in a group statement of profit or loss. So that's a good place to start.

Having put down the formats, then go through the workings and slot in the figures. Make sure you get in all the ones you can do easily. Complicated parts are well worth doing if you are able to do them – there will be marks for those. Complicated parts which you don't know how to do are best left alone.

If you have an interpretation question, you will not get many marks for just producing lots of ratios or restating information you have already been given in the question. You have to be able to evaluate the information and see what judgements can be made. So go through the information critically and see which ratios are actually relevant. Then calculate them and say something sensible about them.

Exam information

Format of the exam

All questions are compulsory.

	Number of marks
Questions 1-3; 25 marks each	75
Question 4	15
Question 5	10
	100

Time allowed: 3 hours plus 15 minutes reading time

December 2012

		Marks
1	Goodwill calculation and consolidated statement of profit or loss – parent and subsidiary	25
2	Single company statement of comprehensive income, statement of changes in equity and statement of financial position	25
3	Analysis of financial performance including ratios	25
4	Scenario question on changes in accounting estimates and construction contract	15
5	Scenario question on environmental provisions	10
		100

June 2012

		Marks
1	Consolidated statement of financial position including associate	25
2	Single entity statement of comprehensive income, SOCIE and SFP	25
3	Statement of cash flows and analyse effect of new contract	25
4	Scenario question on impairment of assets	15
5	Rules and principles-based systems and advantages of IFRS adoption	10
		100

December 2011

		Marks
1	Consolidated statement of financial position including associate	25
2	Single entity statement of comprehensive income and SFP	25
3	Statement of cash flows and contrast with accruals-based accounting	25
4	Scenario question on provisions	15
5	Scenario question on accounting for convertible loan notes	10
		100

June 2011

		Marks
1	Consolidated statement of profit or loss and other comprehensive income, plus equity section from SFP	25
2	Single company statement of profit or loss and other comprehensive income, statement of changes in equity and statement of financial position	25
3	Statement of cash flows and comment on performance	25
4	IFRS discussion and diluted EPS	15
5	Scenario question on construction contract	10
		100

December 2010

		Marks
1	Consolidated statement of profit or loss and other comprehensive income and statement of financial position – parent and subsidiary	25
2	Single company statement of comprehensive income, statement of changes in equity and statement of financial position	25
3	Analysis of financial performance including ratios	25
4	Scenario question on changes in accounting policies	15
5	Scenario question on restructuring	10
		100

June 2010

		Marks
1	Consolidated statement of financial position including associate	25
2	Prepare statement of profit or loss and statement of financial position from trial balance	25
3	Statement of cash flows and comment on liquidity	25
4	Substance over form scenario question	15
5	Scenario question on borrowing costs	10
		100

December 2009

		Marks
1	Consolidated statement of profit or loss including associate	25
2	Single company statement of comprehensive income and statement of financial position	25
3	Mixed question on non-current assets, cash flows and ROCE	25
4	Scenario question on assets	15
5	Scenario question on EPS	10
		100

June 2009

		Marks
1	Consolidated statement of financial position including associate	25
2	Prepare statement of profit or loss and statement of financial position from trial balance	25
3	Statement of cash flows and comment on ratios	25
4	IAS 10 scenario question	15
5	Financial statement extracts for complex asset	10
		100

Examiner's comment. The overall performance of candidates in this paper was poor. A significant number of candidates did not attempt either or both of Questions 4 and 5. Answers to sections of the paper requiring written comment, interpretation or analysis were weak or non-existent.

December 2008

		Marks
1	Consolidated statement of profit or loss and statement of financial position	25
2	Single company statement of profit or loss and other comprehensive income, statement of changes in equity and statement of financial position	25
3	Ratio analysis and comparison of performance for two companies	25
4	Discussion and scenario on provisions	15
5	Non current asset and depreciation – financial statement extracts	10
		100

BPP
LEARNING MEDIA

June 2008

		Marks
1	Consolidated statement of profit or loss plus calculate goodwill on acquisition and discuss treatment of associate	25
2	Redraft financial statements	25
3	Statement of cash flows and comment on cash flow management	25
4	Explain qualitative characteristics and apply to inventory	15
5	Accounting for convertible loan note	10
		100

Examiner's comment. I am disappointed in the overall performance of candidates. Answers were weak in sections requiring written comment and analysis, which accounted for 33 marks. The first two questions were done quite well. In question 3 candidates often scored well on the cash flow statement but the interpretation was generally weak. Question 4 was mixed, Question 5 on the financial instrument was very badly answered by most candidates.

December 2007

		Marks
1	Consolidated statement of financial position including associate	25
2	Single company accounts preparation question	25
3	Performance appraisal including calculation of ratios	25
4	Discussion of 'faithful representation' and leasing scenario	15
5	Discussion and scenario on development expenditure	10
		100

Examiner's comments. The overall pass rate for this paper was disappointing. Performance was poor on questions requiring written comment and analysis. Many candidates did not answer the question that was asked. The first two questions were generally done well. Candidates did well on the ratios in Question 3, but their analysis was poor. Questions 4 and 5 were not well done.

Pilot paper

		Marks
1	Consolidated statement of financial position including associate	25
2	Single company accounts preparation question	25
3	Performance appraisal including calculation of ratios	25
4	Discursive question on qualitative characteristics of financial information including short scenario	15
5	Construction contract	10
		100

Analysis of past papers

The table below provides details of when each element of the syllabus has been examined and the question number and section in which each element appeared.

		June 2010	Dec 2010	June 2011	Dec 2011	June 2012	Dec 2012
A	**A CONCEPTUAL FRAMEWORK FOR FINANCIAL REPORTING**						
A1	The need for a conceptual framework						
A2							
	– Framework qualitative characteristics			Q4(a)			
	– Accounting policies, changes in accounting estimates and errors		Q4				Q4
A3	Recognition and measurement						
A4	The legal versus the commercial view of accounting	Q2, Q4		Q2	Q2		
A5	Alternative models and practices (accounting for inflation)						
A6	The concept of 'faithful representation' ('true and fair view')						
B	**A REGULATORY FRAMEWORK FOR FINANCIAL REPORTING**						
B1	Reasons for the existence of a regulatory framework					Q5	
B2	The standard setting process					Q5	
B3	Specialised, not-for-profit and public sector entities						
C	**FINANCIAL STATEMENTS**						
C1	Statements of cash flows	Q3(a)		Q3(a)	Q3	Q3	
C2	Tangible non-current assets	Q2, Q3	Q2, Q4	Q2	Q2	Q2	Q2
	– Property, plant and equipment						
	– Investment properties						
	– Government grants						
	– Borrowing costs	Q5					
C3	Intangible assets						
C4	Inventories and construction contracts	Q2	Q4(b)	Q2, Q5	Q2		Q4
C5	Financial assets and financial liabilities						
	– Fair value through profit or loss/OCI	Q2	Q2		Q2		
	– Amortised cost	Q2	Q2	Q2			Q2
	– Convertible debt				Q5		
C6	Leases	Q3(a)				Q2	

BPP LEARNING MEDIA

	June 2010	Dec 2010	June 2011	Dec 2011	June 2012	Dec 2012
C FINANCIAL STATEMENTS (CONT'D)						
C7 Provisions, contingent liabilities and contingent assets		Q2, Q5		Q4		Q5
C8 Impairment of assets						
– Group accounting	Q1(a)			Q1		
– Other					Q4	
C9 Taxation						
– Current tax	Q2	Q2	Q2	Q2	Q2	Q2
– Deferred tax	Q2	Q2	Q2	Q2	Q2	Q2
C10 Regulatory requirements relating to the preparation of financial statements						
– Statement of profit or loss	Q2(a)					
– Statement of profit or loss and other comprehensive income		Q2(a)	Q2 Q2	Q2	Q2	
– Statement of financial position	Q2(b)	Q2(c)	Q2	Q2	Q2	
– Statement of changes in equity		Q2(b)			Q2	
C11 Reporting financial performance						
– Discontinued operations		Q5	Q4(b)			
– Non-current assets held for sale	Q2	Q5				
– Earnings per share			Q4(b)			
D BUSINESS COMBINATIONS						
D1 The concept and principles of a group						
D2 The concept of consolidated financial statements	Q1(b)		Q1(b)			Q1
D3 Preparation of consolidated financial statements:						Q1
–Consolidated statement of profit or loss						
–Consolidated statement of profit or loss and OCI		Q1(a)	Qn1(a)			
–Consolidated statement of financial position	Q1(a)	Qn1(b)	Q1(a)	Q1	Q1	
–Associates	Q1(a)			Q1	Q1	
E ANALYSING AND INTERPRETING FINANCIAL STATEMENTS						
E1 Limitations of financial statements				Q3		
E2 Calculation and interpretation of accounting ratios and trends to address users' and stakeholders' needs	Q3(a)(b), Q4(c)	Q3	Q3(b)		Q3	Q3
E3 Limitations of interpretation techniques						Q3
E4 Specialised, not-for-profit and public sector entities	Q3(b)					

BPP
LEARNING MEDIA

Planning your question practice

We have already stressed that question practice should be right at the centre of your revision. Whilst you will spend some time looking at your notes and Paper F7 Passcards, you should spend the majority of your revision time practising questions.

We recommend two ways in which you can practise questions.

- Use **BPP Learning Media's question plan** to work systematically through the syllabus and attempt key and other questions on a section-by-section basis

- **Build your own exams** – attempt questions as a series of practice exams

These ways are suggestions and simply following them is no guarantee of success. You or your college may prefer an alternative but equally valid approach.

BPP Learning Media's question plan

The BPP Learning Media plan below requires you to devote a **minimum of 30 hours** to revision of Paper F7. Any time you can spend over and above this should only increase your chances of success.

Step 1   **Review your notes** and the chapter summaries in the Paper F7 **Passcards** for each section of the syllabus.

Step 2   **Answer the key questions** for that section. These questions have boxes round the question number in the table below and you should answer them in full. Even if you are short of time you must attempt these questions if you want to pass the exam. You should complete your answers without referring to our solutions.

Step 3   **Attempt the other questions** in that section.

Step 4   Attempt **Mock exams 1, 2 and 3** under strict exam conditions.

Syllabus section	2012 Passcards chapters	Questions in this Kit	Comments	Done ☑
The conceptual framework	1	1, 2, 3	Porto is a straightforward question on the *Conceptual Framework*. Make sure you do Baxen from the June 2012 paper.	☐
The regulatory framework	2	4,5	These questions cover a lot of material and are good revision.	☐
Presentation of published financial statements	3	11 12	All of these questions are good practice. Keystone and Fresco are the most recent.	☐
Non-current assets	4	15 16 17	Dearing and Flightline deal with the more complex aspects of IAS 16. Apex covers borrowing costs.	☐
Intangible assets	5	20, 21	Dexterity is a 25-mark on goodwill and intangible assets, so it covers a lot of ground. Darby is a recent question.	☐
Impairment of assets	6	24	Telepath is an excellent question on impairment. See if you can do it in the time.	☐
Reporting financial performance	7	27 28	Manco is a good question on discontinued operations and Tunshill deals with restructuring.	☐
Introduction to groups	8	29, 30	Question 29 is a good preparation question on the basics. Question 30 is a useful introduction to consolidation.	☐
The consolidated statement of financial position	9	32 33	Pedantic and Pyramid are both good practice for the key workings	☐
The consolidated statement of profit or loss and other comprehensive income	10	34, 36, 37	Start with the preparation question, and then do Premier and Prodigal, which are recent questions.	☐
Accounting for associates	11	43 44	Do the two preparation questions first and then Picant and Paladin, which are the latest exam questions.	☐
Inventories and construction contracts	12	45,46, 47	Start with the preparation question and make sure you also do Beetie and Mocca.	☐
Provisions, contingent liabilities and contingent assets	13	48 50	Make sure you do Bodyline, which is a full question on provisions. Borough is a good example of a 15-mark question from the December 2011 paper.	☐
Financial assets and financial liabilities	14	52 53	Both of these questions cover calculation of interest costs. Make sure you can do them.	☐
The legal versus the commercial view of accounting	15	55 56	These are good questions on the application of substance over form. Do both of them.	☐
Leasing	16	57,58, 59	These are all short questions. Do them all.	☐
Accounting for taxation	17	60 62	Do the preparation question. Question 62 is good practice for a question on deferred tax.	☐

Syllabus section	2012 Passcards chapters	Questions in this Kit	Comments	Done ✓
Earnings per share	18	64, 65	Question 65 is a recent exam question, so good practice.	☐
Analysing and interpreting financial statements	19	68 69	You must do Bengal and Tangier, which are recent questions.	☐
Limitations of financial statements and interpretation techniques	20	70 71	Waxwork and Hardy are the most recent questions.	☐
Statements of cash flows	21	72, 74 75	Do the preparation question and Deltoid and Mocha, which are the most recent questions.	☐
Alternative models and practices	22	77	Update is a typical question on this area.	☐
Specialised, not-for-profit and public sector entities	23	78	You will not get a full question on this. The examiner has stated that this part-question in the pilot paper is typical of how it will be examined.	☐

Build your own exams

Having revised your notes and the BPP Passcards, you can attempt the questions in the Kit as a series of practice exams. This is our suggestion:

Question	Practice exams					
	1	2	3	4	5	6
1	40	35	43	44	35	41
2	7	8	9	10	11	6
3	71	74	73	67	69	67
4	21	27	50	65	27	49
5	15	16	17	19	46	52

We have selected these questions on the following basis:

- Question 1 will be a consolidation
- Question 2 will be an accounts preparation question
- Question 3 will be a statement of cash flows or an interpretation of accounts question
- Questions 4 and 5 will test other areas of the syllabus

December 2011 Paper: 25, 44, 50, 53, 75
June 2012 Paper: 3, 12, 24, 33, 69

Questions

BPP
LEARNING MEDIA

1 Porto (pilot paper amended)

23 mins

(a)   The qualitative characteristics of relevance, faithful representation and comparability identified in the IASB's *Conceptual Framework for Financial Reporting* are some of the attributes that make financial information useful to the various users of financial statements.

Required

Explain what is meant by relevance, faithful representation and comparability and how they make financial information useful. **(9 marks)**

(b)   During the year ended 31 March 20X6, Porto experienced the following transactions or events:

(i)   Entered into a finance lease to rent an asset for substantially the whole of its useful economic life.

(ii)   The company's statement of profit or loss prepared using historical costs showed a loss from operating its hotels, but the company is aware that the increase in the value of its properties during the period far outweighed the operating loss.

Required

Explain how you would treat the items above in Porto's financial statements and indicate on which of the Conceptual Framework's qualitative characteristics your treatment is based. **(4 marks)**

(Total = 13 marks)

2 Concepts (6/08 amended)

27 mins

(a)   The IASB's *Conceptual Framework for Financial Reporting* requires financial statements to be prepared on the basis that they comply with certain accounting concepts, underlying assumptions and (qualitative) characteristics. Five of these are:

Matching/accruals
Going concern
Verifiability
Comparability
Materiality

Required

Briefly explain the meaning of each of the above concepts/assumptions. **(5 marks)**

(b)   For most entities, applying the appropriate concepts/assumptions in accounting for inventories is an important element in preparing their financial statements.

Required

Illustrate with examples how each of the concepts/assumptions in (a) may be applied to accounting for inventory. **(10 marks)**

(Total = 15 marks)

3 Baxen (6/12)

(a) The methods by which Accounting Standards are developed differ considerably throughout the world. It is often argued that there are two main systems of regulation that determine the nature of Accounting Standards: a rules-based system and a principles-based system.

Required:

Briefly explain the difference between the two systems and state which system you believe is most descriptive of International Financial Reporting Standards (IFRS). **(4 marks)**

(b) Baxen is a public listed company that currently uses local Accounting Standards for its financial reporting. The board of directors of Baxen is considering the adoption of International Financial Reporting Standards (IFRS) in the near future. The company has ambitious growth plans which involve extensive trading with many foreign companies and the possibility of acquiring at least one of its trading partners as a subsidiary in the near future.

Required:

Identify the advantages that Baxen could gain by adopting IFRS for its financial reporting purposes.

(6 marks)

(10 marks)

4 Regulatory framework (2.5 12/04 amended)

45 mins

Historically financial reporting throughout the world has differed widely. The IFRS Foundation (formerly the International Accounting Standards Committee Foundation (IASCF)) is committed to developing, in the public interest, a single set of high quality, understandable and enforceable global accounting standards that require transparent and comparable information in general purpose financial statements. The various pronouncements of the IFRS Foundation are sometimes collectively referred to as International Financial Reporting Standards (IFRS) GAAP.

Required

(a) Describe the functions of the various internal bodies of the IFRS Foundation, and how the IFRS Foundation interrelates with other national standard setters. **(10 marks)**

(b) Describe the IFRS Foundation's standard setting process including how standards are produced, enforced and occasionally supplemented. **(10 marks)**

(c) Comment on whether you feel the move to date towards global accounting standards has been successful.

(5 marks)

(Total = 25 marks)

5 Preparation question: IFRS

The US is currently contemplating the transition to IFRS. US GAAP is regarded by many in the US as the 'gold standard'. It is detailed and rules-based and in many cases industry-specific and there is a perception among some that the adoption of IFRS will compromise the quality of financial reporting.

Required

(a) Explain in what ways IFRS differs from US GAAP, as described above.

(b) Discuss the advantages that a country may gain from transitioning to IFRS.

BPP
LEARNING MEDIA

6 Candel (12/08)

The following trial balance relates to Candel at 30 September 20X8:

	$'000	$'000
Leasehold property – at valuation 1 October 20X7 (note (i))	50,000	
Plant and equipment – at cost (note (i))	76,600	
Plant and equipment – accumulated depreciation at 1 October 20X7		24,600
Capitalised development expenditure – at 1 October 20X7 (note (ii))	20,000	
Development expenditure – accumulated amortisation at 1 October 20X7		6,000
Closing inventory at 30 September 20X8	20,000	
Trade receivables	43,100	
Bank		1,300
Trade payables and provisions (note (iii))		23,800
Revenue (note (i))		300,000
Cost of sales	204,000	
Distribution costs	14,500	
Administrative expenses (note (iii))	22,200	
Preference dividend paid	800	
Interest on bank borrowings	200	
Equity dividend paid	6,000	
Research and development costs (note (ii))	8,600	
Equity shares of 25 cents each		50,000
8% redeemable preference shares of $1 each (note (iv))		20,000
Retained earnings at 1 October 20X7		24,500
Deferred tax (note (v))		5,800
Leasehold property revaluation reserve		10,000
	466,000	466,000

The following notes are relevant:

(i)   Non-current assets – tangible:

The leasehold property had a remaining life of 20 years at 1 October 20X7. The company's policy is to revalue its property at each year end and at 30 September 20X8 it was valued at $43 million. Ignore deferred tax on the revaluation.

On 1 October 20X7 an item of plant was disposed of for $2·5 million cash. The proceeds have been treated as sales revenue by Candel. The plant is still included in the above trial balance figures at its cost of $8 million and accumulated depreciation of $4 million (to the date of disposal).

All plant is depreciated at 20% per annum using the reducing balance method.

Depreciation and amortisation of all non-current assets is charged to cost of sales.

(ii) Non-current assets – intangible:

In addition to the capitalised development expenditure (of $20 million), further research and development costs were incurred on a new project which commenced on 1 October 20X7. The research stage of the new project lasted until 31 December 20X7 and incurred $1·4 million of costs. From that date the project incurred development costs of $800,000 per month. On 1 April 20X8 the directors became confident that the project would be successful and yield a profit well in excess of its costs. The project is still in development at 30 September 20X8.

Capitalised development expenditure is amortised at 20% per annum using the straight-line method. All expensed research and development is charged to cost of sales.

(iii) Candel is being sued by a customer for $2 million for breach of contract over a cancelled order. Candel has obtained legal opinion that there is a 20% chance that Candel will lose the case. Accordingly Candel has provided $400,000 ($2 million × 20%) included in administrative expenses in respect of the claim. The unrecoverable legal costs of defending the action are estimated at $100,000. These have not been provided for as the legal action will not go to court until next year.

(iv)   The preference shares were issued on 1 April 20X8 at par. They are redeemable at a large premium which gives them an effective finance cost of 12% per annum.

(v)   The directors have estimated the provision for income tax for the year ended 30 September 20X8 at $11·4 million. The required deferred tax provision at 30 September 20X8 is $6 million.

Required

(a)   Prepare the statement of profit or loss and other comprehensive income for the year ended 30 September 20X8.   **(12 marks)**

(b)   Prepare the statement of changes in equity for the year ended 30 September 20X8.   **(3 marks)**

(c)   Prepare the statement of financial position as at 30 September 20X8.   **(10 marks)**

Note: notes to the financial statements are not required.   **(Total = 25 marks)**

7 Pricewell (6/09)   45 mins

The following trial balance relates to Pricewell at 31 March 20X9:

	$'000	$'000
Leasehold property – at valuation 31 March 20X8 (note (i))	25,200	
Plant and equipment (owned) – at cost (note (i))	46,800	
Plant and equipment (leased) – at cost (note (i))	20,000	
Accumulated depreciation at 31 March 20X8		
Owned plant and equipment		12,800
Leased plant and equipment		5,000
Finance lease payment (paid on 31 March 20X9) (note (i))	6,000	
Obligations under finance lease at 1 April 20X8 (note (i))		15,600
Construction contract (note (ii))	14,300	
Inventory at 31 March 20X9	28,200	
Trade receivables	33,100	
Bank	5,500	
Trade payables		33,400
Revenue (note (iii))		310,000
Cost of sales (note (iii))	234,500	
Distribution costs	19,500	
Administrative expenses	27,500	
Preference dividend paid (note (iv))	2,400	
Equity dividend paid	8,000	
Equity shares of 50 cents each		40,000
6% redeemable preference shares at 31 March 20X8 (note (iv))		41,600
Retained earnings at 31 March 20X8		4,900
Current tax (note (v))	700	
Deferred tax (note (v))		
		8,400
	471,700	471,700

The following notes are relevant:

(i)   Non-current assets:

The 15 year leasehold property was acquired on 1 April 20X7 at cost $30 million. The company policy is to revalue the property at market value at each year end. The valuation in the trial balance of $25·2 million as at 31 March 20X8 led to an impairment charge of $2·8 million which was reported in profit or loss in the previous year (ie year ended 31 March 20X8). At 31 March 20X9 the property was valued at $24·9 million.

Owned plant is depreciated at 25% per annum using the reducing balance method.

The leased plant was acquired on 1 April 20X7. The rentals are $6 million per annum for four years payable in arrears on 31 March each year. The interest rate implicit in the lease is 8% per annum. Leased plant is depreciated at 25% per annum using the straight-line method.

BPP
LEARNING MEDIA

No depreciation has yet been charged on any non-current assets for the year ended 31 March 20X9. All depreciation is charged to cost of sales.

(ii) On 1 October 20X8 Pricewell entered into a contract to construct a bridge over a river. The agreed price of the bridge is $50 million and construction was expected to be completed on 30 September 20Y0. The $14·3 million in the trial balance is:

	$'000
Materials, labour and overheads	12,000
Specialist plant acquired 1 October 20X8	8,000
Payment from customer	(5,700)
	14,300

The sales value of the work done at 31 March 20X9 has been agreed at $22 million and the estimated cost to complete (excluding plant depreciation) is $10 million. The specialist plant will have no residual value at the end of the contract and should be depreciated on a monthly basis. Pricewell recognises profits on uncompleted contracts on the percentage of completion basis as determined by the agreed work to date compared to the total contract price.

(iii) Pricewell's revenue includes $8 million for goods it sold acting as an agent for Trilby. Pricewell earned a commission of 20% on these sales and remitted the difference of $6·4 million (included in cost of sales) to Trilby.

(iv) The 6% preference shares were issued on 1 April 20X7 at par for $40 million. They have an effective finance cost of 10% per annum due to a premium payable on their redemption.

(v) The directors have estimated the provision for income tax for the year ended 31 March 20X9 at $4·5 million. The required deferred tax provision at 31 March 20X9 is $5·6 million; all adjustments to deferred tax should be taken to profit or loss. The balance of current tax in the trial balance represents the under/over provision of the income tax liability for the year ended 31 March 20X8.

Required

(a) Prepare the statement of profit or loss for the year ended 31 March 20X9. **(12 marks)**
(b) Prepare the statement of financial position as at 31 March 20X9. **(13 marks)**

Note: a statement of changes in equity and notes to the financial statements are not required. **(Total = 25 marks)**

8 Sandown (12/09 amended)   45 mins

The following trial balance relates to Sandown at 30 September 20X9:

	$'000	$'000
Revenue (note (i))		380,000
Cost of sales	246,800	
Distribution costs	17,400	
Administrative expenses (note (ii))	50,500	
Loan interest paid (note (iii))	1,000	
Investment income		1,300
Profit on sale of investments (note (iv))		2,200
Current tax (note (v))	2,100	
Freehold property – at cost 1 October 20X0 (note (vi))	63,000	
Plant and equipment – at cost (note (vi))	42,200	
Brand – at cost 1 October 20X5 (note (vi))	30,000	
Accumulated depreciation – 1 October 20X8 – building		8,000
– plant and equipment		19,700
Accumulated amortisation – 1 October 20X8 – brand		9,000
Investments in equity instruments (note (iv))	26,500	
Inventory at 30 September 20X9	38,000	
Trade receivables	44,500	
Bank	8,000	
Trade payables		42,900
Equity shares of 20 cents each		50,000
Equity option		2,000
Other reserve (note (iv))		5,000
5% convertible loan note 20Y2 (note (iii))		18,440
Retained earnings at 1 October 20X8		26,060
Deferred tax (note (v))		5,400
	570,000	570,000

The following notes are relevant:

(i)   Sandown's revenue includes $16 million for goods sold to Pending on 1 October 20X8. The terms of the sale are that Sandown will incur ongoing service and support costs of $1·2 million per annum for three years after the sale. Sandown normally makes a gross profit of 40% on such servicing and support work. Ignore the time value of money.

(ii)   Administrative expenses include an equity dividend of 4·8 cents per share paid during the year.

(iii)   The 5% convertible loan note was issued for proceeds of $20 million on 1 October 20X7. It has an effective interest rate of 8% due to the value of its conversion option.

(iv)   During the year Sandown sold an equity investment for $11 million. At the date of sale it had a carrying amount of $8·8 million and had originally cost $7 million. Sandown has recorded the disposal of the investment. The remaining equity investments (the $26·5 million in the trial balance) have a fair value of $29 million at 30 September 20X9. The other reserve in the trial balance represents the net increase in the value of the equity investments as at 1 October 20X8. Sandown made an irrevocable election at initial recognition of these instruments to recognise all changes in fair value through other comprehensive income. Ignore deferred tax on these transactions.

(v)   The balance on current tax represents the under/over provision of the tax liability for the year ended 30 September 20X8. The directors have estimated the provision for income tax for the year ended 30 September 20X9 at $16·2 million. At 30 September 20X9 the carrying amounts of Sandown's net assets were $13 million in excess of their tax base. The income tax rate of Sandown is 30%.

BPP
LEARNING MEDIA

(vi)   Non-current assets:

The freehold property has a land element of $13 million. The building element is being depreciated on a straight-line basis.

Plant and equipment is depreciated at 40% per annum using the reducing balance method.

Sandown's brand in the trial balance relates to a product line that received bad publicity during the year which led to falling sales revenues. An impairment review was conducted on 1 April 20X9 which concluded that, based on estimated future sales, the brand had a value in use of $12 million and a remaining life of only three years. However, on the same date as the impairment review, Sandown received an offer to purchase the brand for $15 million. Prior to the impairment review, it was being depreciated using the straight-line method over a 10-year life.

No depreciation/amortisation has yet been charged on any non-current asset for the year ended 30 September 20X9. Depreciation, amortisation and impairment charges are all charged to cost of sales.

Required

(a)   Prepare the statement of profit or loss and other comprehensive income for Sandown for the year ended 30 September 20X9.   **(13 marks)**

(b)   Prepare the statement of financial position of Sandown as at 30 September 20X9.   **(12 marks)**

Notes to the financial statements are not required.

A statement of changes in equity is not required.   **(Total = 25 marks)**

9 Dune (6/10)   45 mins

The following trial balance relates to Dune at 31 March 20X1:

	$'000	$'000
Equity shares of $1 each		60,000
5% loan note (note (i))		20,000
Retained earnings at 1 April 20X0		38,400
Leasehold (15 years) property – at cost (note (ii))	45,000	
Plant and equipment – at cost (note (ii))	67,500	

	$'000	$'000
Accumulated depreciation – 1 April 20X0 – leasehold property		6,000
– plant and equipment		23,500
Investments at fair value through profit or loss (note (iii))	26,500	
Inventory at 31 March 20X1	48,000	
Trade receivables	40,700	
Bank		4,500
Deferred tax (note (v))		6,000
Trade payables		52,000
Revenue (note (iv))		400,000
Cost of sales	294,000	
Construction contract (note (vi))	20,000	
Distribution costs	26,400	
Administrative expenses (note (i))	34,200	
Dividend paid	10,000	
Loan note interest paid (six months)	500	
Bank interest	200	
Investment income		1,200
Current tax (note (v))		1,400
	613,000	613,000

BPP
LEARNING MEDIA

The following notes are relevant:

(i) The 5% loan note was issued on 1 April 20X0 at its nominal (face) value of $20 million. The direct costs of the issue were $500,000 and these have been charged to administrative expenses. The loan note will be redeemed on 31 March 20X3 at a substantial premium. The effective finance cost of the loan note is 10% per annum.

(ii) Non-current assets:

In order to fund a new project, on 1 October 20X0 the company decided to sell its leasehold property. From that date it commenced a short-term rental of an equivalent property. The leasehold property is being marketed by a property agent at a price of $40 million, which was considered a reasonably achievable price at that date. The expected costs to sell have been agreed at $500,000. Recent market transactions suggest that actual selling prices achieved for this type of property in the current market conditions are 15% less than the value at which they are marketed. At 31 March 20X1 the property had not been sold.

Plant and equipment is depreciated at 15% per annum using the reducing balance method.

No depreciation/amortisation has yet been charged on any non-current asset for the year ended 31 March 20X1. Depreciation, amortisation and impairment charges are all charged to cost of sales.

(iii) The investments at fair value through profit or loss had a fair value of $28 million on 31 March 20X1. There were no purchases or disposals of any of these investments during the year.

(iv) It has been discovered that goods with a cost of $6 million, which had been correctly included in the count of the inventory at 31 March 20X1, had been invoiced in April 20X1 to customers at a gross profit of 25% on sales, but included in the revenue (and receivables) of the year ended 31 March 20X1.

(v) A provision for income tax for the year ended 31 March 20X1 of $12 million is required. The balance on current tax represents the under/over provision of the tax liability for the year ended 31 March 20X0. At 31 March 20X1 the tax base of Dune's net assets was $14 million less than their carrying amounts. The income tax rate of Dune is 30%.

(vi) The details of the construction contract are:

	costs to 31 March 20X1	further costs to complete
	$'000	$'000
Materials	5,000	8,000
Labour and other direct costs	3,000	7,000
	8,000	15,000
Plant acquired at cost	12,000	
Per trial balance	20,000	

The contract commenced on 1 October 20X0 and is scheduled to take 18 months to complete. The agreed contract price is fixed at $40 million. Specialised plant was purchased at the start of the contract for $12 million. It is expected to have a residual value of $3 million at the end of the contract and should be depreciated using the straight-line method on a monthly basis. An independent surveyor has assessed that the contract is 30% complete at 31 March 20X1. The customer has not been invoiced for any progress payments. The outcome of the contract is deemed to be reasonably certain as at the year end.

Required

(a) Prepare the statement of profit or loss for Dune for the year ended 31 March 20X1. **(13 marks)**
(b) Prepare the statement of financial position for Dune as at 31 March 20X1. **(12 marks)**

Notes to the financial statements are not required.

A statement of changes in equity is not required.

(Total = 25 marks)

10 Cavern (12/10)

The following trial balance relates to Cavern as at 30 September 20X2:

	$'000	$'000
Equity shares of 20 cents each (note (i))		50,000
8% loan note (note (ii))		30,600
Retained earnings – 30 September 20X1		12,100
Other equity reserve		3,000
Revaluation surplus		7,000
Share premium		11,000
Land and buildings at valuation – 30 September 20X1:		
Land ($7 million) and building ($36 million) (note (iii))	43,000	
Plant and equipment at cost (note (iii))	67,400	
Accumulated depreciation plant and equipment – 30 September 20X1		13,400
Investments in equity instruments (note (iv))	15,800	
Inventory at 30 September 20X2	19,800	
Trade receivables	29,000	
Bank		4,600
Deferred tax (note (v))		4,000
Trade payables		21,700
Revenue		182,500
Cost of sales	128,500	
Administrative expenses (note (i))	25,000	
Distribution costs	8,500	
Loan note interest paid	2,400	
Bank interest	300	
Investment income		700
Current tax (note (v))	900	
	340,600	340,600

The following notes are relevant:

(i) Cavern has accounted for a fully subscribed rights issue of equity shares made on 1 April 20X2 of one new share for every four in issue at 42 cents each. The company paid ordinary dividends of 3 cents per share on 30 November 20X1 and 5 cents per share on 31 May 20X2. The dividend payments are included in administrative expenses in the trial balance.

(ii) The 8% loan note was issued on 1 October 20X0 at its nominal (face) value of $30 million. The loan note will be redeemed on 30 September 20X4 at a premium which gives the loan note an effective finance cost of 10% per annum.

(iii) Non-current assets:

Cavern revalues its land and building at the end of each accounting year. At 30 September 20X2 the relevant value to be incorporated into the financial statements is $41.8 million. The building's remaining life at the beginning of the current year (1 October 20X1) was 18 years. Cavern does not make an annual transfer from the revaluation reserve to retained earnings in respect of the realisation of the revaluation surplus. Ignore deferred tax on the revaluation surplus.

Plant and equipment includes an item of plant bought for $10 million on 1 October 20X1 that will have a 10-year life (using straight-line depreciation with no residual value). Production using this plant involves toxic chemicals which will cause decontamination costs to be incurred at the end of its life. The present value of these costs using a discount rate of 10% at 1 October 20X1 was $4 million. Cavern has not provided any amount for this future decontamination cost. All other plant and equipment is depreciated at 12.5% per annum using the reducing balance method.

No depreciation has yet been charged on any non-current asset for the year ended 30 September 20X2. All depreciation is charged to cost of sales.

(iv)   The investments in equity instruments held at 30 September 20X2 had a fair value of $13.5 million. There were no acquisitions or disposals of these investments during the year ended 30 September 20X2. Cavern made an irrevocable election at initial recognition of these instruments to recognise all changes in fair value through other comprehensive income.

(v)   A provision for income tax for the year ended 30 September 20X2 of $5.6 million is required. The balance on current tax represents the under/over provision of the tax liability for the year ended 30 September 20X1. At 30 September 20X2 the tax base of Cavern's net assets was $15 million less than their carrying amounts. The movement on deferred tax should be taken to profit or loss. The income tax rate of Cavern is 25%.

Required

(a)   Prepare the statement of profit or loss and other comprehensive income for Cavern for the year ended 30 September 20X2.   **(11 marks)**

(b)   Prepare the statement of changes in equity for Cavern for the year ended 30 September 20X2.   **(5 marks)**

(c)   Prepare the statement of financial position of Cavern as at 30 September 20X2.   **(9 marks)**

Notes to the financial statements are not required.

(Total = 25 marks)

11 Keystone (12/11)   45 mins

The following trial balance relates to Keystone at 30 September 20X1:

	$'000	$'000
Revenue (note (i))		380,000
Material purchases (note (ii))	64,000	
Production labour (note (ii))	124,000	
Factory overheads (note (ii))	80,000	
Distribution costs	14,200	
Administrative expenses (note (iii))	46,400	
Finance costs	350	
Investment income		800
Leased property – at cost (note (ii))	50,000	
Plant and equipment – at cost (note (ii))	44,500	
Accumulated amortisation/depreciation at 1 October 20X0		
– leased property		10,000
– plant and equipment		14,500
Financial asset: equity investments (note (v))	18,000	
Inventory at 1 October 20X0	46,700	
Trade receivables	33,550	
Trade payables		27,800
Bank		2,300
Equity shares of 20 cents each		50,000
Retained earnings at 1 October 20X0		33,600
Deferred tax (note (vi))		2,700
	521,700	521,700

The following notes are relevant:

(i)   Revenue includes goods sold and despatched in September 20X1 on a 30-day right of return basis. Their selling price was $2.4 million and they were sold at a gross profit margin of 25%. Keystone is uncertain as to whether any of these goods will be returned within the 30-day period.

BPP
LEARNING MEDIA

(ii)   Non-current assets:

During the year Keystone manufactured an item of plant for its own use. The direct materials and labour were $3 million and $4 million respectively. Production overheads are 75% of direct labour cost and Keystone determines the final selling price for goods by adding a mark-up on total cost of 40%. These manufacturing costs are included in the relevant expense items in the trial balance. The plant was completed and put into immediate use on 1 April 20X1.

All plant and equipment is depreciated at 20% per annum using the reducing balance method with time apportionment in the year of acquisition.

The directors decided to revalue the leased property in line with recent increases in market values. On 1 October 20X0 an independent surveyor valued the leased property at $48 million, which the directors have accepted. The leased property was being amortised over an original life of 20 years which has not changed. Keystone does not make a transfer to retained earnings in respect of excess amortisation. The revaluation gain will create a deferred tax liability (see note (vi)).

All depreciation and amortisation is charged to cost of sales. No depreciation or amortisation has yet been charged on any non-current asset for the year ended 30 September 20X1.

(iii)   On 15 August 20X1, Keystone's share price stood at $2·40 per share. On this date Keystone paid a dividend (included in administrative expenses) that was calculated to give a dividend yield of 4%.

(iv)   The inventory on Keystone's premises at 30 September 20X1 was counted and valued at cost of $54·8 million.

(v)   The equity investments had a fair value of $17·4 million on 30 September 20X1. There were no purchases or disposals of any of these investments during the year. Keystone has not made the election in accordance with IFRS 9 Financial Instruments. Keystone adopts this standard when accounting for its financial assets.

(vi)   A provision for income tax for the year ended 30 September 20X1 of $24·3 million is required. At 30 September 20X1, the tax base of Keystone's net assets was $15 million less than their carrying amounts. This excludes the effects of the revaluation of the leased property. The income tax rate of Keystone is 30%.

Required

(a)   Prepare the statement of comprehensive income for Keystone for the year ended 30 September 20X1.

(15 marks)

(b)   Prepare the statement of financial position for Keystone as at 30 September 20X1.   **(10 marks)**

Notes to the financial statements are not required.

A statement of changes in equity is not required.   **(Total = 25 marks)**

12 Fresco (6/12)

The following trial balance relates to Fresco at 31 March 20X2:

	$'000	$'000
Equity shares of 50 cents each (note (i))		45,000
Share premium (note (i))		5,000
Retained earnings at 1 April 20X1		5,100
Leased property (12 years) – at cost (note (ii))	48,000	
Plant and equipment – at cost (note (ii))	47,500	
Accumulated amortisation of leased property at 1 April 20X1		16,000
Accumulated depreciation of plant and equipment at 1 April 20X1		33,500
Inventory at 31 March 20X2	25,200	
Trade receivables (note (iii))	28,500	
Bank		1,400
Deferred tax (note (iv))		3,200
Trade payables		27,300
Revenue		350,000
Cost of sales	298,700	
Lease payments (note (ii))	8,000	
Distribution costs	16,100	
Administrative expenses	26,900	
Bank interest	300	
Current tax (note (iv))	800	
Suspense account (note (i))		13,500
	500,000	500,000

The following notes are relevant:

(i) The suspense account represents the corresponding credit for cash received for a fully subscribed rights issue of equity shares made on 1 January 20X2. The terms of the share issue were one new share for every five held at a price of 75 cents each. The price of the company's equity shares immediately before the issue was $1.20 each.

(ii) Non-current assets:

To reflect a marked increase in property prices, Fresco decided to revalue its leased property on 1 April 20X1. The Directors accepted the report of an independent surveyor who valued the leased property at $36 million on that date. Fresco has not yet recorded the revaluation. The remaining life of the leased property is eight years at the date of the revaluation. Fresco makes an annual transfer to retained profits to reflect the realisation of the revaluation surplus. In Fresco's tax jurisdiction the revaluation does not give rise to a deferred tax liability.

On 1 April 20X1, Fresco acquired an item of plant under a finance lease agreement that had an implicit finance cost of 10% per annum. The lease payments in the trial balance represent an initial deposit of $2 million paid on 1 April 20X1 and the first annual rental of $6 million paid on 31 March 20X2. The lease agreement requires further annual payments of $6 million on 31 March each year for the next four years. Had the plant not been leased it would have cost $25 million to purchase for cash.

Plant and equipment (other than the leased plant) is depreciated at 20% per annum using the reducing balance method.

No depreciation/amortisation has yet been charged on any non-current asset for the year ended 31 March 20X2. Depreciation and amortisation are charged to cost of sales.

(iii) In March 20X2, Fresco's internal audit department discovered a fraud committed by the company's credit controller who did not return from a foreign business trip. The outcome of the fraud is that $4 million of the company's trade receivables have been stolen by the credit controller and are not recoverable. Of this amount, $1 million relates to the year ended 31 March 20X1 and the remainder to the current year. Fresco is not insured against this fraud.

(iv) Fresco's income tax calculation for the year ended 31 March 20X2 shows a tax refund of $2·4 million. The balance on current tax in the trial balance represents the under/over provision of the tax liability for the year ended 31 March

BPP LEARNING MEDIA

20X1. At 31 March 20X2, Fresco had taxable temporary differences of $12 million (requiring a deferred tax liability). The income tax rate of Fresco is 25%.

Required:

(a) (i) Prepare the statement of comprehensive income for Fresco for the year ended 31 March 20X2. **(9 marks)**

   (ii) Prepare the statement of changes in equity for Fresco for the year ended 31 March 20X2. **(5 marks)**

   (iii) Prepare the statement of financial position of Fresco as at 31 March 20X2. **(8 marks)**

(b) Calculate the basic earnings per share for Fresco for the year ended 31 March 20X2. **(3 marks)**

Notes to the financial statements are not required.

(25 marks)

13 Preparation question: Plethora plc

The draft financial statements of Plethora plc for the year to 31 December 20X9 are being prepared and the accountant has requested your advice on dealing with the following issues:

(a) Plethora plc has an administration building which it no longer needs following a delayering exercise. On 1 July 20X9 Plethora plc entered into an agreement to let the building out to another company. The building cost $600,000 on 1 January 20X0 and is being depreciated over 50 years. Plethora plc applies the fair value model under IAS 40 and the fair value of the building was judged to be $800,000 on 1 July 20X9. This valuation had not changed at 31 December 20X9.

Another building has been let out for a number of years. It had a fair value of $550,000 at 31 December 20X8 and $740,000 at 31 December 20X9.

Required

Explain how these two buildings should be accounted for in the financial statements of Plethora plc for the year to 31 December 20X9 and quantify the amounts involved.

(b) Plethora plc owns a retail business which has suffered badly during the recession. Plethora plc treats this business as a separate cash generating unit.

The carrying amounts of the assets comprising the retail business are:

	$'000
Building	900
Plant and equipment	300
Inventory	70
Other current assets	130
Goodwill	40

An impairment review has been carried out as at 31 December 20X9 and the recoverable amount of the cash generating unit is estimated at $1.3m.

Required

Restate the carrying amounts of the assets of the retail business after accounting for the result of the impairment review.

14 Elite Leisure (2.5 12/05 part)

22 mins

Elite Leisure is a private limited liability company that operates a single cruise ship. The ship was acquired on 1 October 20W6 (ten years before 20X6). Details of the cost of the ship's components and their estimated useful lives are:

Component	Original cost ($ million)	Depreciation basis
Ship's fabric (hull, decks etc)	300	25 years straight–line
Cabins and entertainment area fittings	150	12 years straight–line
Propulsion system	100	Useful life of 40,000 hours

At 30 September 20X4 no further capital expenditure had been incurred on the ship.

In the year ended 30 September 20X4 the ship had experienced a high level of engine trouble which had cost the company considerable lost revenue and compensation costs. The measured expired life of the propulsion system at 30 September 20X4 was 30,000 hours. Due to the unreliability of the engines, a decision was taken in early October 20X4 to replace the whole of the propulsion system at a cost of $140 million. The expected life of the new propulsion system was 50,000 hours and in the year ended 30 September 20X5 the ship had used its engines for 5,000 hours.

At the same time as the propulsion system replacement, the company took the opportunity to do a limited upgrade to the cabin and entertainment facilities at a cost of $60 million and repaint the ship's fabric at a cost of $20 million. After the upgrade of the cabin and entertainment area fittings it was estimated that their remaining life was five years (from the date of the upgrade). For the purpose of calculating depreciation, all the work on the ship can be assumed to have been completed on 1 October 20X4. All residual values can be taken as nil.

Required

Calculate the carrying amount of Elite Leisure's cruise ship at 30 September 20X5 and its related expenditure in the statement of profit or lossfor the year ended 30 September 20X5. Your answer should explain the treatment of each item.

(12 marks)

15 Dearing (12/08)

18 mins

On 1 October 20X5 Dearing acquired a machine under the following terms:

	Hours	$
Manufacturer's base price		1,050,000
Trade discount (applying to base price only)		20%
Early settlement discount taken (on the payable amount of the base cost only)		5%
Freight charges		30,000
Electrical installation cost		28,000
Staff training in use of machine		40,000
Pre-production testing		22,000
Purchase of a three-year maintenance contract		60,000
Estimated residual value		20,000
Estimated life in machine hours	6,000	
Hours used – year ended 30 September 20X6	1,200	
– year ended 30 September 20X7	1,800	
– year ended 30 September 20X8 (see below)	850	

On 1 October 20X7 Dearing decided to upgrade the machine by adding new components at a cost of $200,000. This upgrade led to a reduction in the production time per unit of the goods being manufactured using the machine. The upgrade also increased the estimated remaining life of the machine at 1 October 20X7 to 4,500 machine hours and its estimated residual value was revised to $40,000.

Required

Prepare extracts from the statement of profit or loss and statement of financial position for the above machine for each of the three years to 30 September 20X8.

(10 marks)

BPP LEARNING MEDIA

16 Flightline (6/09)   18 mins

Flightline is an airline which treats its aircraft as complex non-current assets. The cost and other details of one of its aircraft are:

	$'000	Estimated life
Exterior structure – purchase date 1 April 20W5 *	120,000	20 years
Interior cabin fittings – replaced 1 April 20X5	25,000	5 years
Engines (2 at $9 million each) – replaced 1 April 20X5	18,000	36,000 flying hours

* 10 years before 20X5

No residual values are attributed to any of the component parts.

At 1 April 20X8 the aircraft log showed it had flown 10,800 hours since 1 April 20X5. In the year ended 31 March 20X9, the aircraft flew for 1,200 hours for the six months to 30 September 20X8 and a further 1,000 hours in the six months to 31 March 20X9.

On 1 October 20X8 the aircraft suffered a 'bird strike' accident which damaged one of the engines beyond repair. This was replaced by a new engine with a life of 36,000 hours at cost of $10·8 million. The other engine was also damaged, but was repaired at a cost of $3 million; however, its remaining estimated life was shortened to 15,000 hours. The accident also caused cosmetic damage to the exterior of the aircraft which required repainting at a cost of $2 million. As the aircraft was out of service for some weeks due to the accident, Flightline took the opportunity to upgrade its cabin facilities at a cost of $4·5 million. This did not increase the estimated remaining life of the cabin fittings, but the improved facilities enabled Flightline to substantially increase the air fares on this aircraft

Required

Calculate the charges to profit or loss in respect of the aircraft for the year ended 31 March 20X9 and its carrying amount in the statement of financial position as at that date.

Note: the post accident changes are deemed effective from 1 October 20X8.   **(10 marks)**

17 Apex (6/10)   18 mins

(a) Apex is a publicly listed supermarket chain. During the current year it started the building of a new store. The directors are aware that in accordance with IAS 23 *Borrowing costs* certain borrowing costs have to be capitalised.

Required

Explain the circumstances when, and the amount at which, borrowing costs should be capitalised in accordance with IAS 23.   **(5 marks)**

(b) Details relating to construction of Apex's new store:

Apex issued a $10 million unsecured loan with a coupon (nominal) interest rate of 6% on 1 April 20X8. The loan is redeemable at a premium which means the loan has an effective finance cost of 7·5% per annum. The loan was specifically issued to finance the building of the new store which meets the definition of a qualifying asset in IAS 23. Construction of the store commenced on 1 May 20X8 and it was completed and ready for use on 28 February 20X9, but did not open for trading until 1 April 20X9. During the year trading at Apex's other stores was below expectations so Apex suspended the construction of the new store for a two-month period during July and August 20X8. The proceeds of the loan were temporarily invested for the month of April 20X8 and earned interest of $40,000.

Required

Calculate the net borrowing cost that should be capitalised as part of the cost of the new store and the finance cost that should be reported in profit or loss for the year ended 31 March 20X9.

(5 marks)
(Total = 10 marks)

18 Derringdo II (2.5 6/03 part)

16 mins

Derringdo acquired an item of plant at a gross cost of $800,000 on 1 October 20X2. The plant has an estimated life of 10 years with a residual value equal to 15% of its gross cost. Derringdo uses straight-line depreciation on a time apportioned basis. The company received a government grant of 30% of its cost price at the time of its purchase. The terms of the grant are that if the company retains the asset for four years or more, then no repayment liability will be incurred. If the plant is sold within four years a repayment on a sliding scale would be applicable. The repayment is 75% if sold within the first year of purchase and this amount decreases by 25% per annum. Derringdo has no intention to sell the plant within the first four years. Derringdo's accounting policy for capital-based government grants is to treat them as deferred credits and release them to income over the life of the asset to which they relate.

Required

(a)   Discuss whether the company's policy for the treatment of government grants meets the definition of a liability in the IASB's Conceptual Framework; and **(3 marks)**

(b)   Prepare extracts of Derringdo's financial statements for the year to 31 March 20X3 in respect of the plant and the related grant:

–   applying the company's policy;

–   in compliance with the definition of a liability in the Framework. Your answer should consider whether the sliding scale repayment should be used in determining the deferred credit for the grant.

(6 marks)

(Total = 9 marks)

19 Emerald (12/07)

18 mins

Product development costs are a material cost for many companies. They are either written off as an expense or capitalised as an asset.

Required

(a)   Discuss the conceptual issues involved and the definition of an asset that may be applied in determining whether development expenditure should be treated as an expense or an asset. **(4 marks)**

(b)   Emerald has had a policy of writing off development expenditure to profit or loss as it was incurred. In preparing its financial statements for the year ended 30 September 20X7 it has become aware that, under IFRS rules, qualifying development expenditure should be treated as an intangible asset. Below is the qualifying development expenditure for Emerald:

	$'000
Year ended 30 September 20X4	300
Year ended 30 September 20X5	240
Year ended 30 September 20X6	800
Year ended 30 September 20X7	400

All capitalised development expenditure is deemed to have a four year life. Assume amortisation commences at the beginning of the accounting period following capitalisation. Emerald had no development expenditure before that for the year ended 30 September 20X4.

Required

Treating the above as the correction of an error in applying an accounting policy, calculate the amounts which should appear in the statement of profit or loss and statement of financial position (including comparative figures), and statement of changes in equity of Emerald in respect of the development expenditure for the year ended 30 September 20X7.

Note. Ignore taxation. **(6 marks)**

(Total = 10 marks)

20 Dexterity (2.5 6/04)

45 mins

(a) During the last decade it has not been unusual for the premium paid to acquire control of a business to be greater than the fair value of its tangible net assets. This increase in the relative proportions of intangible assets has made the accounting practices for them all the more important. During the same period many companies have spent a great deal of money internally developing new intangible assets such as software and brands. IAS 38 '*Intangible assets*' was issued in September 1998 and prescribes the accounting treatment for intangible assets.

Required

In accordance with IAS 38, discuss whether intangible assets should be recognised, and if so how they should be initially recorded and subsequently amortised in the following circumstances:

(i) When they are purchased separately from other assets

(ii) When they are obtained as part of acquiring the whole of a business

(iii) When they are developed internally.   **(10 marks)**

Note: Your answer should consider goodwill separately from other intangibles.

(b) Dexterity is a public listed company. It has been considering the accounting treatment of its intangible assets and has asked for your opinion on how the matters below should be treated in its financial statements for the year to 31 March 20X4.

(i) On 1 October 20X3 Dexterity acquired Temerity, a small company that specialises in pharmaceutical drug research and development. The purchase consideration was by way of a share exchange and valued at $35 million. The fair value of Temerity's net assets was $15 million (excluding any items referred to below). Temerity owns a patent for an established successful drug that has a remaining life of 8 years. A firm of specialist advisors, Leadbrand, has estimated the current value of this patent to be $10 million, however the company is awaiting the outcome of clinical trials where the drug has been tested to treat a different illness. If the trials are successful, the value of the drug is then estimated to be $15 million. Also included in the company's statement of financial position is $2 million for medical research that has been conducted on behalf of a client.   **(4 marks)**

(ii) Dexterity has developed and patented a new drug which has been approved for clinical use. The costs of developing the drug were $12 million. Based on early assessments of its sales success, Leadbrand have estimated its market value at $20 million.   **(3 marks)**

(iii) Dexterity's manufacturing facilities have recently received a favourable inspection by government medical scientists. As a result of this the company has been granted an exclusive five-year licence to manufacture and distribute a new vaccine. Although the licence had no direct cost to Dexterity, its directors feel its granting is a reflection of the company's standing and have asked Leadbrand to value the licence. Accordingly they have placed a value of $10 million on it.   **(3 marks)**

(iv) In the current accounting period, Dexterity has spent $3 million sending its staff on specialist training courses. Whilst these courses have been expensive, they have led to a marked improvement in production quality and staff now need less supervision. This in turn has led to an increase in revenue and cost reductions. The directors of Dexterity believe these benefits will continue for at least three years and wish to treat the training costs as an asset.   **(2 marks)**

(v) In December 20X3, Dexterity paid $5 million for a television advertising campaign for its products that will run for 6 months from 1 January 20X4 to 30 June 20X4. The directors believe that increased sales as a result of the publicity will continue for two years from the start of the advertisements.

(3 marks)

Required

Explain how the directors of Dexterity should treat the above items in the financial statements for the year to 31 March 20X4.   **(15 marks as indicated)**

Note: The values given by Leadbrand can be taken as being reliable measurements. You are not required to consider depreciation aspects.   **(Total = 25 marks)**

21 Darby (12/09)

27 mins

(a) An assistant of yours has been criticised over a piece of assessed work that he produced for his study course for giving the definition of a non-current asset as 'a physical asset of substantial cost, owned by the company, which will last longer than one year'.

Required

Provide an explanation to your assistant of the weaknesses in his definition of non-current assets when compared to the International Accounting Standards Board's (IASB) view of assets.   **(4 marks)**

(b) The same assistant has encountered the following matters during the preparation of the draft financial statements of Darby for the year ending 30 September 20X9. He has given an explanation of his treatment of them.

(i) Darby spent $200,000 sending its staff on training courses during the year. This has already led to an improvement in the company's efficiency and resulted in cost savings. The organiser of the course has stated that the benefits from the training should last for a minimum of four years. The assistant has therefore treated the cost of the training as an intangible asset and charged six months' amortisation based on the average date during the year on which the training courses were completed.   **(3 marks)**

(ii) During the year the company started research work with a view to the eventual development of a new processor chip. By 30 September 20X9 it had spent $1·6 million on this project. Darby has a past history of being particularly successful in bringing similar projects to a profitable conclusion. As a consequence the assistant has treated the expenditure to date on this project as an asset in the statement of financial position.

Darby was also commissioned by a customer to research and, if feasible, produce a computer system to install in motor vehicles that can automatically stop the vehicle if it is about to be involved in a collision. At 30 September 20X9, Darby had spent $2·4 million on this project, but at this date it was uncertain as to whether the project would be successful. As a consequence the assistant has treated the $2·4 million as an expense in the statement of profit or loss.   **(4 marks)**

(iii) Darby signed a contract (for an initial three years) in August 20X9 with a company called Media Today to install a satellite dish and cabling system to a newly built group of residential apartments. Media Today will provide telephone and television services to the residents of the apartments via the satellite system and pay Darby $50,000 per annum commencing in December 20X9. Work on the installation commenced on 1 September 20X9 and the expenditure to 30 September 20X9 was $58,000. The installation is expected to be completed by 31 October 20X9. Previous experience with similar contracts indicates that Darby will make a total profit of $40,000 over the three years on this initial contract. The assistant correctly recorded the costs to 30 September 20X9 of $58,000 as a non-current asset, but then wrote this amount down to $40,000 (the expected total profit) because he believed the asset to be impaired.

The contract is not a finance lease. Ignore discounting.   **(4 marks)**

Required

For each of the above items (i) to (iii) comment on the assistant's treatment of them in the financial statements for the year ended 30 September 20X9 and advise him how they should be treated under International Financial Reporting Standards.

Note: the mark allocation is shown against each of the three items above.   **(Total = 15 marks)**

BPP LEARNING MEDIA

22 Advent (2.5 12/04 amended)   23 mins

Advent is a publicly listed company.

Details of Advent's non-current assets at 1 October 20X8 were:

	Land and building $m	Plant $m	Telecommunications licence $m	Total $m
Cost/valuation	280	150	300	730
Accumulated depreciation/amortisation	(40)	(105)	(30)	(175)
Net book value	240	45	270	555

The following information is relevant:

(i)   The land and building were revalued on 1 October 20X3 with $80 million attributable to the land and $200 million to the building. At that date the estimated remaining life of the building was 25 years. A further revaluation was not needed until 1 October 20X8 when the land and building were valued at $85 million and $180 million respectively. The remaining estimated life of the building at this date was 20 years.

(ii)   Plant is depreciated at 20% per annum on cost with time apportionment where appropriate. On 1 April 20X9 new plant costing $45 million was acquired. In addition, this plant cost $5 million to install and commission. No plant is more than four years old.

(iii) The telecommunications licence was bought from the government on 1 October 20X7 and has a 10 year life. It is amortised on a straight line basis. In September 20X9, a review of the sales of the products related to the licence showed them to be very disappointing. As a result of this review the estimated recoverable amount of the licence at 30 September 20X9 was estimated at only $100 million.

There were no disposals of non-current assets during the year to 30 September 20X9.

Required

(a)   Prepare extracts from the statement of financial position relating to Advent's non-current assets as at 30 September 20X9 (including comparative figures), together with any disclosures (other than those of the accounting policies) under current International Financial Reporting Standards.   **(9 marks)**

(b)   Explain the usefulness of the above disclosures to the users of the financial statements.   **(4 marks)**

(Total = 13 marks)

23 Wilderness (2.5 12/05)   45 mins

(a)   IAS 36 *Impairment of assets* was issued in June 1998 and subsequently amended in March 2004. Its main objective is to prescribe the procedures that should ensure that an entity's assets are included in its statement of financial position at no more than their recoverable amounts. Where an asset is carried at an amount in excess of its recoverable amount, it is said to be impaired and IAS 36 requires an impairment loss to be recognised.

Required

(i)   Define an impairment loss explaining the relevance of fair value less costs to sell and value in use; and state how frequently assets should be tested for impairment;   **(6 marks)**

Note: your answer should NOT describe the possible indicators of an impairment.

(ii)   Explain how an impairment loss is accounted for after it has been calculated.   **(5 marks)**

(b)   The assistant financial controller of the Wilderness group, a public listed company, has identified the matters below which she believes may indicate an impairment to one or more assets:

(i)   Wilderness owns and operates an item of plant that cost $640,000 and had accumulated depreciation of $400,000 at 1 October 20X4. It is being depreciated at 12½% on cost. On 1 April 20X5 (exactly half way through the year) the plant was damaged when a factory vehicle collided into it. Due to the unavailability of replacement parts, it is not possible to repair the plant, but it still operates, albeit at a reduced capacity. Also it is expected that as a result of the damage the remaining life of the plant from the date of the damage will be only two years. Based on its reduced capacity, the estimated present value of the plant in use is $150,000. The plant has a current disposal value of $20,000 (which will be nil in two years' time), but Wilderness has been offered a trade–in value of $180,000 against a replacement machine which has a cost of $1 million (there would be no disposal costs for the replaced plant). Wilderness is reluctant to replace the plant as it is worried about the long–term demand for the produce produced by the plant. The trade–in value is only available if the plant is replaced.

Required

Prepare extracts from the statement of financial position and statement of profit or loss of Wilderness in respect of the plant for the year ended 30 September 20X5. Your answer should explain how you arrived at your figures. **(7 marks)**

(ii)   On 1 April 20X4 Wilderness acquired 100% of the share capital of Mossel, whose only activity is the extraction and sale of spa water. Mossel had been profitable since its acquisition, but bad publicity resulting from several consumers becoming ill due to a contamination of the spa water supply in April 20X5 has led to unexpected losses in the last six months. The carrying amounts of Mossel's assets at 30 September 20X5 are:

	$'000
Brand (Quencher – see below)	7,000
Land containing spa	12,000
Purifying and bottling plant	8,000
Inventories	5,000
	32,000

The source of the contamination was found and it has now ceased.

The company originally sold the bottled water under the brand name of 'Quencher', but because of the contamination it has rebranded its bottled water as 'Phoenix'. After a large advertising campaign, sales are now starting to recover and are approaching previous levels. The value of the brand in the statement of financial position is the depreciated amount of the original brand name of 'Quencher'.

The directors have acknowledged that $1.5 million will have to be spent in the first three months of the next accounting period to upgrade the purifying and bottling plant.

Inventories contain some old 'Quencher' bottled water at a cost of $2 million; the remaining inventories are labeled with the new brand 'Phoenix'. Samples of all the bottled water have been tested by the health authority and have been passed as fit to sell. The old bottled water will have to be relabelled at a cost of $250,000, but is then expected to be sold at the normal selling price of (normal) cost plus 50%.

Based on the estimated future cash flows, the directors have estimated that the value in use of Mossel at 30 September 20X5, calculated according to the guidance in IAS 36, is $20 million. There is no reliable estimate of the fair value less costs to sell of Mossel.

Required

Calculate the amounts at which the assets of Mossel should appear in the consolidated statement of financial position of Wilderness at 30 September 20X5. Your answer should explain how you arrive at your figures. **(7 marks)**

(Total = 25 marks)

BPP
LEARNING MEDIA

24 Telepath (6/12)

27 mins

(a) The objective of IAS 36 *Impairment of assets* is to prescribe the procedures that an entity applies to ensure that its assets are not impaired.

Required:

Explain what is meant by an impairment review. Your answer should include reference to assets that may form a cash generating unit.

Note: you are NOT required to describe the indicators of an impairment or how impairment losses are allocated against assets. **(4 marks)**

(b)(i) Telepath acquired an item of plant at a cost of $800,000 on 1 April 20X0 that is used to produce and package pharmaceutical pills. The plant had an estimated residual value of $50,000 and an estimated life of five years, neither of which has changed. Telepath uses straight-line depreciation. On 31 March 20X2, Telepath was informed by a major customer (who buys products produced by the plant) that it would no longer be placing orders with Telepath. Even before this information was known, Telepath had been having difficulty finding work for this plant. It now estimates that net cash inflows earned from the plant for the next three years will be:

	$'000
year ended: 31 March 20X3	220
31 March 20X4	180
31 March 20X5	170

On 31 March 20X5, the plant is still expected to be sold for its estimated realisable value.

Telepath has confirmed that there is no market in which to sell the plant at 31 March 20X2.

Telepath's cost of capital is 10% and the following values should be used:

value of $1 at:	$
end of year 1	0.91
end of year 2	0.83
end of year 3	0.75

(ii) Telepath owned a 100% subsidiary, Tilda, that is treated as a cash generating unit. On 31 March 20X2, there was an industrial accident (a gas explosion) that caused damage to some of Tilda's plant. The assets of Tilda immediately before the accident were:

	$'000
Goodwill	1,800
Patent	1,200
Factory building	4,000
Plant	3,500
Receivables and cash	1,500
	12,000

As a result of the accident, the recoverable amount of Tilda is $6.7 million.

The explosion destroyed (to the point of no further use) an item of plant that had a carrying amount of $500,000.

Tilda has an open offer from a competitor of $1 million for its patent. The receivables and cash are already stated at their fair values less costs to sell (net realisable values).

Required:

Calculate the carrying amounts of the assets in (i) and (ii) above at 31 March 20X2 after applying any impairment losses.

Calculations should be to the nearest $1,000.

The following mark allocation is provided as guidance for this requirement:

(i) **4 marks**

(ii) **7 marks** **(11 marks)**

(Total = 15 marks)

25 Tourmalet (2.5 12/03)

45 mins

The following extracted balances relate to Tourmalet at 30 September 20X4:

	$000	$000
Ordinary shares of 20 cents each		50,000
Retained earnings at 1 October 20X3		47,800
Revaluation surplus at 1 October 20X3		18,500
6% Redeemable preference shares 20X6		30,000
Trade accounts payable		35,300
Tax		2,100
Land and buildings – at valuation (note (iii))	150,000	
Plant and equipment – cost (note (v))	98,600	
Investment property – valuation at 1 October 20X3 (note (iv))	10,000	
Depreciation 1 October 20X3 – land and buildings		9,000
Depreciation 1 October 20X3 – plant and equipment		24,600
Trade accounts receivable	31,200	
Inventory – 1 October 20X3	26,550	
Bank	3,700	
Sales revenue (note (i))		313,000
Investment income (from properties)		1,200
Purchases	158,450	
Distribution expenses	26,400	
Administration expenses	23,200	
Interim preference dividend	900	
Ordinary dividend paid	2,500	
	531,500	531,500

The following notes are relevant:

(i)   Sales revenue includes $50 million for an item of plant sold on 1 June 20X4. The plant had a book value of $40 million at the date of its sale, which was charged to cost of sales. On the same date, Tourmalet entered into an agreement to lease back the plant for the next five years (being the estimated remaining life of the plant) at a cost of $14 million per annum payable annually in arrears. An arrangement of this type is deemed to have a financing cost of 12% per annum.

(ii)   The inventory at 30 September 20X4 was valued at cost of $28·5 million. This includes $4·5 million of slow moving goods. Tourmalet is trying to sell these to another retailer but has not been successful in obtaining a reasonable offer. The best price it has been offered is $2 million.

(iii)   On 1 October 20X0 Tourmalet had its land and buildings revalued by a firm of surveyors at $150 million, with $30 million of this attributed to the land. At that date the remaining life of the building was estimated to be 40 years. These figures were incorporated into the company's books. There has been no significant change in property values since the revaluation. $500,000 of the revaluation reserve will be realised in the current year as a result of the depreciation of the buildings and should be transferred to retained earnings.

(iv)   Details of the investment property are:

Value – 1 October 20X3	$10 million
Value – 30 September 20X4	$9.8 million

The company adopts the fair value method in IAS 40 'Investment Property' of valuing its investment property.

(v)   Plant and equipment (other than that referred to in note (i) above) is depreciated at 20% per annum on the reducing balance basis. All depreciation is to be charged to cost of sales.

(vi)   The above balances contain the results of Tourmalet's car retailing operations which ceased on 31 December 20X3 due to mounting losses. The results of the car retailing operation, which is to be treated as a discontinued operation, for the year to 30 September 20X4 are:

BPP
LEARNING MEDIA

	$'000
Sales	15,200
Cost of sales	16,000
Operating expenses (4,000 less 800 tax repayment due)	3,200

The operating expenses are included in administration expenses in the trial balance. Tourmalet is still paying rentals for the lease of its car showrooms. The rentals are included in operating expenses. Tourmalet is hoping to use the premises as an expansion of its administration offices. This is dependent on obtaining planning permission from the local authority for the change of use, however this is very difficult to obtain. Failing this, the best option would be early termination of the lease which will cost $1·5 million in penalties. This amount has not been provided for.

(vii) The balance on the taxation account in the trial balance is the result of the settlement of the previous year's tax charge. The directors have estimated the provision for income tax for the year to 30 September 20X4 at $9.2 million.

(viii) The preference shares will be redeemed at par. The finance cost is equivalent to the annual dividend.

Required

(a) Comment on the substance of the sale of the plant and the directors' treatment of it. **(5 marks)**

(b) Prepare the statement of profit or loss for the year ended 30 September 20X4. **(17 marks)**

(c) Prepare a statement of changes in equity for Tourmalet for the year to 30 September 20X4 in accordance with IFRS. **(3 marks)**

Note: A statement of financial position is NOT required. Disclosure notes are NOT required. **(Total = 25 marks)**

26 Partway (2.5 12/06)   45 mins

(a) (i) State the definition of both non-current assets held for sale and discontinued operations and explain the usefulness of information for discontinued operations. **(4 marks)**

Partway is in the process of preparing its financial statements for the year ended 31 October 20X6. The company's main activity is in the travel industry mainly selling package holidays (flights and accommodation) to the general public through the Internet and retail travel agencies. During the current year the number of holidays sold by travel agencies declined dramatically and the directors decided at a board meeting on 15 October 20X6 to cease marketing holidays through its chain of travel agents and sell off the related high-street premises. Immediately after the meeting the travel agencies' staff and suppliers were notified of the situation and an announcement was made in the press. The directors wish to show the travel agencies' results as a discontinued operation in the financial statements to 31 October 20X6. Due to the declining business of the travel agents, on 1 August 20X6 (three months before the year end) Partway expanded its Internet operations to offer car hire facilities to purchasers of its Internet holidays.

The following are Partway's summarised profit or loss results – years ended:

	31 October 20X6				31 October 20X5
	Internet	Travel agencies	Car hire	Total	Total
	$'000	$'000	$'000	$'000	$'000
Revenue	23,000	14,000	2,000	39,000	40,000
Cost of sales	(18,000)	(16,500)	(1,500)	(36,000)	(32,000)
Gross profit/(loss)	5,000	(2,500)	500	3,000	8,000
Operating expenses	(1,000)	(1,500)	(100)	(2,600)	(2,000)
Profit/(loss) before tax	4,000	(4,000)	400	400	6,000

The results for the travel agencies for the year ended 31 October 20X5 were: revenue $18 million, cost of sales $15 million and operating expenses of $1.5 million.

Required

(ii) Discuss whether the directors' wish to show the travel agencies' results as a discontinued operation is justifiable. **(4 marks)**

(iii) Assuming the closure of the travel agencies is a discontinued operation, prepare the (summarised) statement of of profit or loss of Partway for the year ended 31 October 20X6 together with its comparatives.

Note: Partway discloses the analysis of its discontinued operations on the face of its statement of profit or loss. **(6 marks)**

(b) (i) Describe the circumstances in which an entity may change its accounting policies and how a change should be applied. **(5 marks)**

The terms under which Partway sells its holidays are that a 10% deposit is required on booking and the balance of the holiday must be paid six weeks before the travel date. In previous years Partway has recognised revenue (and profit) from the sale of its holidays at the date the holiday is actually taken. From the beginning of November 20X5, Partway has made it a condition of booking that all customers must have holiday cancellation insurance and as a result it is unlikely that the outstanding balance of any holidays will be unpaid due to cancellation. In preparing its financial statements to 31 October 20X6, the directors are proposing to change to recognising revenue (and related estimated costs) at the date when a booking is made. The directors also feel that this change will help to negate the adverse effect of comparison with last year's results (year ended 31 October 20X5) which were better than the current year's.

Required

(ii) Comment on whether Partway's proposal to change the timing of its recognition of its revenue is acceptable and whether this would be a change of accounting policy. **(6 marks)**

(Total = 25 marks)

27 Tunshill (12/10)   27 mins

(a) IAS 8 *Accounting Policies, Changes in Accounting Estimates and Errors* contains guidance on the use of accounting policies and accounting estimates.

Required

Explain the basis on which the management of an entity must select its accounting policies and distinguish, with an example, between changes in accounting policies and changes in accounting estimates. **(5 marks)**

(b) The directors of Tunshill are disappointed by the draft profit for the year ended 30 September 20X3. The company's assistant accountant has suggested two areas where she believes the reported profit may be improved:

(i) A major item of plant that cost $20 million to purchase and install on 1 October 20X0 is being depreciated on a straight-line basis over a five-year period (assuming no residual value). The plant is wearing well and at the beginning of the current year (1 October 20X2) the production manager believed that the plant was likely to last eight years in total (ie from the date of its purchase). The assistant accountant has calculated that, based on an eight-year life (and no residual value) the accumulated depreciation of the plant at 30 September 20X3 would be $7.5 million ($20 million/8 years x 3). In the financial statements for the year ended 30 September 20X2, the accumulated depreciation was $8 million ($20 million/5 years x 2). Therefore, by adopting an eight-year life, Tunshill can avoid a depreciation charge in the current year and instead credit $0.5 million ($8 million – $7.5 million) to profit or loss in the current year to improve the reported profit. **(5 marks)**

(ii) Most of Tunshill's competitors value their inventory using the average cost (AVCO) basis, whereas Tunshill uses the first in first out (FIFO) basis. The value of Tunshill's inventory at 30 September 20X3 (on the FIFO basis) is $20 million, however on the AVCO basis it would be valued at $18 million. By adopting the same method (AVCO) as its competitors, the assistant accountant says the company would improve its profit for the year ended 30 September 20X3 by $2 million. Tunshill's inventory at 30 September 20X2 was reported as $15 million, however on the AVCO basis it would have been reported as $13.4 million. **(5 marks)**

BPP
LEARNING MEDIA

Required

Comment on the acceptability of the assistant accountant's suggestions and quantify how they would affect the financial statements if they were implemented under IFRS. Ignore taxation.

Note: the mark allocation is shown against each of the two items above. **(Total = 15 marks)**

28 Manco (12/10)   18 mins

Manco has been experiencing substantial losses at its furniture making operation which is treated as a separate operating segment. The company's year end is 30 September. At a meeting on 1 July 20X0 the directors decided to close down the furniture making operation on 31 January 20X1 and then dispose of its non-current assets on a piecemeal basis. Affected employees and customers were informed of the decision and a press announcement was made immediately after the meeting. The directors have obtained the following information in relation to the closure of the operation:

(i) On 1 July 20X0, the factory had a carrying amount of $3.6 million and is expected to be sold for net proceeds of $5 million. On the same date the plant had a carrying amount of $2.8 million, but it is anticipated that it will only realise net proceeds of $500,000.

(ii) Of the employees affected by the closure, the majority will be made redundant at cost of $750,000, the remainder will be retrained at a cost of $200,000 and given work in one of the company's other operations.

(iii) Trading losses from 1 July to 30 September 20X0 are expected to be $600,000 and from this date to the closure on 31 January 20X1 a further $1 million of trading losses are expected.

Required

Explain how the decision to close the furniture making operation should be treated in Manco's financial statements for the years ending 30 September 20X0 and 20X1. Your answer should quantify the amounts involved. **(10 marks)**

29 Preparation question: Group financial statements

(a) Set out the exemptions from the requirement to present consolidated financial statements which are available to a parent company.

(b) Explain why intra-group transactions and balances are eliminated on consolidation.

(c) IAS 24 is not examinable under the F7 syllabus, but you should know that group companies are related parties and the consequences of this.

In what ways could the relationship between group companies be exploited?

30 Preparation question with helping hands: Simple consolidation

Boo acquired 80% of Goose's equity for $300,000 on 1 January 20X8. At the date of acquisition Goose had retained earnings of $190,000. On 31 December 20X8 Boo despatched goods which cost $80,000 to Goose, at an invoiced cost of $100,000. Goose received the goods on 2 January 20X9 and recorded the transaction then. The two companies' draft financial statements as at 31 December 20X8 are shown below.

STATEMENTS OF PROFIT OR LOSS AND OTHER COMPREHENSIVE INCOME FOR THE YEAR ENDED 31 DECEMBER 20X8

	Boo	Goose
	$'000	$'000
Revenue	5,000	1,000
Cost of sales	2,900	600
Gross profit	2,100	400
Other expenses	1,700	320
Profit before tax	400	80
Income tax expense	130	25
Profit for the year	270	55
Other comprehensive income:		
Gain on revaluation of property	20	-
Total comprehensive income for the year	290	55

STATEMENTS OF FINANCIAL POSITION AT 31 DECEMBER 20X8

	$'000	$'000
Assets		
Non-current assets		
Property, plant and equipment	1,940	200
Investment in Goose	300	-
	2,240	200
Current assets		
Inventories	500	120
Trade receivables	650	40
Bank and cash	170	35
	1,320	195
Total assets	3,560	395
Equity and liabilities		
Equity		
Share capital	2,000	100
Retained earnings	500	240
Revaluation surplus	20	-
	2,520	340
Current liabilities		
Trade payables	910	30
Tax	130	25
	1,040	55
Total equity and liabilities	3,560	395

Required

Prepare a draft consolidated statement of profit or loss and other comprehensive income and statement of financial position. It is the group policy to value the non-controlling interest at acquisition at fair value. The fair value of the non-controlling interest in Goose at the date of acquisition was $60,000.

Helping hands

1   This is a very easy example to ease you into the technique of preparing consolidated accounts. There are a number of points to note.

2   Inventory in transit should be included in the statement of financial position and deducted from cost of sales at cost to the group.

3   Similarly, the intra-group receivable and sale should be eliminated as a consolidation adjustment.

4   Boo Co must have included its inter-company account in trade receivables as it is not specifically mentioned elsewhere in the accounts.

5   Remember that only the parent's issued share capital is shown in the group accounts.

BPP
LEARNING MEDIA

6   The non-controlling interest in the statement of profit or loss is easily calculated as 20% of post-tax profit for the year as shown in Goose's accounts. In the statement of financial position, the non-controlling interest will be the amount at acquisition plus 20% of Goose's post–tax profit for the year.

31 Preparation question: goodwill

At 1 January 20X9 Penguin plc paid $1.2m for an 80% share in Platypus Ltd. Platypus Ltd's net assets at the date of acquisition were as follows:

	$'000
Share capital	500
Retained earnings	850
Revaluation surplus	450

It is group policy is to measure non-controlling interests at acquisition at fair value. The fair value of the non-controlling interest at the date of acquisition was $400,000.

Statements of profit or loss for both companies for the year ended 31 December 20X9 were:

	Penguin	Platypus
	$'000	$'000
Revenue	12,500	2,600
Cost of sales	(7,400)	(1,090)
Gross profit	5,100	1,510
Distribution costs	(700)	(220)
Administrative expenses	(1,300)	(550)
Finance costs	(40)	-
Profit before tax	3,060	740
Income tax expense	(900)	(230)
Profit for the year	2,160	510

Required

Calculate the goodwill on acquisition and prepare the consolidated statement of profit or loss of the Penguin Group for the year ended 31 December 20X9.

32 Pedantic (12/08)   45 mins

On 1 April 20X8, Pedantic acquired 60% of the equity share capital of Sophistic in a share exchange of two shares in Pedantic for three shares in Sophistic. The issue of shares has not yet been recorded by Pedantic. At the date of acquisition shares in Pedantic had a market value of $6 each. Below are the summarised draft financial statements of both companies.

STATEMENTS OF PROFIT OR LOSS FOR THE YEAR ENDED 30 SEPTEMBER 20X8

	Pedantic	Sophistic
	$'000	$'000
Revenue	85,000	42,000
Cost of sales	(63,000)	(32,000)
Gross profit	22,000	10,000
Distribution costs	(2,000)	(2,000)
Administrative expenses	(6,000)	(3,200)
Finance costs	(300)	(400)
Profit before tax	13,700	4,400
Income tax expense	(4,700)	(1,400)
Profit for the year	9,000	3,000

STATEMENTS OF FINANCIAL POSITION AS AT 30 SEPTEMBER 20X8

	Pedantic $'000	Sophistic $'000
Assets		
Non-current assets		
Property, plant and equipment	40,600	12,600
Current assets	16,000	6,600
Total assets	56,600	19,200
Equity and liabilities		
Equity shares of $1 each	10,000	4,000
Retained earnings	35,400	6,500
	45,400	10,500
Non-current liabilities		
10% loan notes	3,000	4,000
Current liabilities	8,200	4,700
Total equity and liabilities	56,600	19,200

The following information is relevant:

(i)   At the date of acquisition, the fair values of Sophistic's assets were equal to their carrying amounts with the exception of an item of plant, which had a fair value of $2 million in excess of its carrying amount. It had a remaining life of five years at that date [straight-line depreciation is used]. Sophistic has not adjusted the carrying amount of its plant as a result of the fair value exercise.

(ii) Sales from Sophistic to Pedantic in the post acquisition period were $8 million. Sophistic made a mark up on cost of 40% on these sales. Pedantic had sold $5·2 million (at cost to Pedantic) of these goods by 30 September 20X8.

(iii) Other than where indicated, profit or loss items are deemed to accrue evenly on a time basis.

(iv) Sophistic's trade receivables at 30 September 20X8 include $600,000 due from Pedantic which did not agree with Pedantic's corresponding trade payable. This was due to cash in transit of $200,000 from Pedantic to Sophistic. Both companies have positive bank balances.

(v)   Pedantic has a policy of accounting for any non-controlling interest at full fair value. The fair value of the non-controlling interest in Sophistic at the date of acquisition was estimated to be $5.9m. Consolidated goodwill was not impaired at 30 September 20X8.

Required

(a)   Prepare the consolidated statement of profit or loss for Pedantic for the year ended 30 September 20X8.

(9 marks)

(b)   Prepare the consolidated statement of financial position for Pedantic as at 30 September 20X8.   **(16 marks)**

Note: a statement of changes in equity is not required.   **(Total = 25 marks)**

BPP
LEARNING MEDIA

33 Pyramid (6/12)

On 1 April 20X1, Pyramid acquired 80% of Square's equity shares by means of an immediate share exchange and a cash payment of 88 cents per acquired share, deferred until 1 April 20X2. Pyramid has recorded the share exchange, but not the cash consideration. Pyramid's cost of capital is 10% per annum.

The summarised statements of financial position of the two companies as at 31 March 20X2 are:

	Pyramid	Square
Assets	$'000	$'000
Non-current assets		
Property, plant and equipment	38,100	28,500
Investments –Square	24,000	
– Cube at cost (note (iv))	6,000	
– Loan notes (note (ii))	2,500	
– Other equity (note (v))	2,000	-
	72,600	28,500
Current assets		
Inventory (note (iii))	13,900	10,400
Trade receivables (note (iii))	11,400	5,500
Bank (note (iii))	900	600
Total assets	98,800	45,000
Equity and liabilities		
Equity		
Equity shares of $1 each	25,000	10,000
Share premium	17,600	
Retained earnings – at 1 April 20X1	16,200	18,000
– for year ended 31 March 20X2	14,000	8,000
	72,800	36,000
Non-current liabilities		
11% loan notes (note (ii))	12,000	4,000
Deferred tax	4,500	
Current liabilities (note (iii))	9,500	5,000
Total equity and liabilities	98,800	45,000

The following information is relevant:

(i)   At the date of acquisition, Pyramid conducted a fair value exercise on Square's net assets which were equal to their carrying amounts with the following exceptions:

– An item of plant had a fair value of $3 million above its carrying amount. At the date of acquisition it had a remaining life of five years. Ignore deferred tax relating to this fair value.

– Square had an unrecorded deferred tax liability of $1 million, which was unchanged as at 31 March 20X2.

Pyramid's policy is to value the non-controlling interest at fair value at the date of acquisition. For this purpose a share price for Square of $3·50 each is representative of the fair value of the shares held by the non-controlling interest.

(ii) Immediately after the acquisition, Square issued $4 million of 11% loan notes, $2·5 million of which were bought by Pyramid. All interest due on the loan notes as at 31 March 20X2 has been paid and received.

(iii) Pyramid sells goods to Square at cost plus 50%. Below is a summary of the recorded activities for the year ended 31 March 20X2 and balances as at 31 March 20X2:

	Pyramid	Square
	$'000	$'000
Sales to Square	16,000	
Purchases from Pyramid		14,500
Included in Pyramid's receivables	4,400	
Included in Square's payables		1,700

On 26 March 20X2, Pyramid sold and despatched goods to Square, which Square did not record until they were received on 2 April 20X2. Square's inventory was counted on 31 March 20X2 and does not include any goods purchased from Pyramid.

On 27 March 20X2, Square remitted to Pyramid a cash payment which was not received by Pyramid until 4 April 20X2. This payment accounted for the remaining difference on the current accounts.

(iv) Pyramid bought 1·5 million shares in Cube on 1 October 20X1; this represents a holding of 30% of Cube's equity. At 31 March 20X2, Cube's retained profits had increased by $2 million over their value at 1 October 20X1. Pyramid uses equity accounting in its consolidated financial statements for its investment in Cube.

(v) The other equity investments of Pyramid are carried at their fair values on 1 April 20X1. At 31 March 20X2, these had increased to $2·8 million.

(vi) There were no impairment losses within the group during the year ended 31 March 20X2.

Required :

Prepare the consolidated statement of financial position for Pyramid as at 31 March 20X2.   **(25 marks)**

34 Preparation question: Acquisition during the year

Port has many investments, but before 20X4 none of these investments met the criteria for consolidation as a subsidiary. One of these older investments was a $2.3m 12% loan to Alfred which was made fifteen years ago and is due to be repaid in twelve years time.

On 1st November 20X4 Port purchased 75% of the equity of Alfred for $650,000. The consideration was 35,000 $1 equity shares in Port with a fair value of $650,000.

Noted below are the draft statements of profit or loss and other comprehensive income for Port and its subsidiary Alfred for the year ending 31st December 20X4 along with the draft statements of financial position as at 31st December 20X4.

STATEMENTS OF PROFIT OR LOSS AND OTHER COMPREHENSIVE INCOME
FOR THE YEAR ENDING 31 DECEMBER 20X4

	Port $'000	Alfred $'000
Revenue	100	996
Cost of sales	(36)	(258)
Gross profit	64	738
Interest on loan to Alfred	276	–
Other investment income	158	–
Operating expenses	(56)	(330)
Finance costs	–	(276)
Profit before tax	442	132
Income tax expense	(112)	(36)
Profit for the year	330	96
Other comprehensive income:		
Gain on property revaluation	30	–
Total comprehensive income for the year	360	96

STATEMENTS OF FINANCIAL POSITION AS AT 31 DECEMBER 20X4

	Port $'000	Alfred $'000
Non-current assets		
Property, plant and equipment	130	3,000
Loan to Alfred	2,300	–
Other investments	600	–
	3,030	3,000
Current assets	800	139
Total assets	3,830	3,139

BPP
LEARNING MEDIA

	Port	Alfred
Equity and liabilities		
Equity		
$1 Equity shares	200	100
Share premium	500	85
Retained earnings	2,900	331
Revaluation surplus	30	-
	3,630	516
Non-current liabilities		
Loan from Port	–	2,300
Current liabilities		
Sundry	200	323
Total equity and liabilities	3,830	3,139

Notes

(a) Port has not accounted for the issue of its own shares or for the acquisition of the investment in Alfred.

(b) There has been no impairment in the value of the goodwill.

(c) It is the group policy to value the non-controlling interest at acquisition at fair value. The fair value of the non-controlling interest in Alfred at the date of acquisition was estimated to be $180,000.

Required

Prepare the consolidated statement of profit or loss and other comprehensive income for the Port Group for the year ending 31 December 20X4 and a consolidated statement of financial position as at that date.

Approaching the question

1 Establish the **group structure**, noting for how long Alfred was a subsidiary.

2 Adjust Port's statement of financial position for the issue of its own shares and the cost of the investment in Alfred.

3 Sketch out the **format** of the group statement of profit or loss and other comprehensive income and statement of financial position, and then fill in the amounts for each company directly from the question. (Note, sub-totals are not normally needed when you do this.)

4 **Time-apportion** the income, expenditure and taxation for the subsidiary acquired.

5 Calculate the **goodwill**.

6 Remember to time-apportion the non-controlling interest in Alfred.

35 Pandar (12/09)   45 mins

On 1 April 20X9 Pandar purchased 80% of the equity shares in Salva. The acquisition was through a share exchange of three shares in Pandar for every five shares in Salva. The market prices of Pandar's and Salva's shares at 1 April 20X9 were $6 per share and $3.20 respectively. On the same date Pandar acquired 40% of the equity shares in Ambra paying $2 per share.

The summarised statements of profit or loss for the three companies for the year ended 30 September 20X9 are:

	Pandar	Salva	Ambra
	$'000	$'000	$'000
Revenue	210,000	150,000	50,000
Cost of sales	(126,000)	(100,000)	(40,000)
Gross profit	84,000	50,000	10,000
Distribution costs	(11,200)	(7,000)	(5,000)
Administrative expenses	(18,300)	(9,000)	(11,000)
Investment income (interest and dividends)	9,500		
Finance costs	(1,800)	(3,000)	nil
Profit (loss) before tax	62,200	31,000	(6,000)
Income tax (expense) relief	(15,000)	(10,000)	1,000
Profit (loss) for the year	47,200	21,000	(5,000)

The following information for the equity of the companies at 30 September 20X9 is available:

Equity shares of $1 each	200,000	120,000	40,000
Share premium	300,000	nil	nil
Retained earnings 1 October 20X8	40,000	152,000	15,000
Profit (loss) for the year ended 30 September 20X9	47,200	21,000	(5,000)
Dividends paid (26 September 20X9)	nil	(8,000)	nil

The following information is relevant:

(i)   The fair values of the net assets of Salva at the date of acquisition were equal to their carrying amounts with the exception of an item of plant which had a carrying amount of $12 million and a fair value of $17 million. This plant had a remaining life of five years (straight-line depreciation) at the date of acquisition of Salva. All depreciation is charged to cost of sales.

In addition, Salva owns the registration of a popular internet domain name. The registration, which had a negligible cost, has a five year remaining life (at the date of acquisition); however, it is renewable indefinitely at a nominal cost. At the date of acquisition the domain name was valued by a specialist company at $20 million.

The fair values of the plant and the domain name have not been reflected in Salva's financial statements.

No fair value adjustments were required on the acquisition of the investment in Ambra.

(ii)   Immediately after its acquisition of Salva, Pandar invested $50 million in an 8% loan note from Salva. All interest accruing to 30 September 20X9 had been accounted for by both companies. Salva also has other loans in issue at 30 September 20X9.

(iii)   Pandar has credited the whole of the dividend it received from Salva to investment income.

(iv)   After the acquisition, Pandar sold goods to Salva for $15 million on which Pandar made a gross profit of 20%. Salva had one third of these goods still in its inventory at 30 September 20X9. There are no intra-group current account balances at 30 September 20X9.

(v)   The non-controlling interest in Salva is to be valued at its (full) fair value at the date of acquisition. For this purpose Salva's share price at that date can be taken to be indicative of the fair value of the shareholding of the non-controlling interest.

(vi)   The goodwill of Salva has not suffered any impairment; however, due to its losses, the value of Pandar's investment in Ambra has been impaired by $3 million at 30 September 20X9.

(vii)   All items in the above statements of profit or loss are deemed to accrue evenly over the year unless otherwise indicated.

Required

(a)   (i)   Calculate the goodwill arising on the acquisition of Salva at 1 April 20X9;   **(6 marks)**

        (ii)   Calculate the carrying amount of the investment in Ambra to be included within the consolidated statement of financial position as at 30 September 20X9.   **(3 marks)**

(b)   Prepare the consolidated statement of profit or loss for the Pandar Group for the year ended 30 September 20X9.   **(16 marks)**

(Total = 25 marks)

36 Premier (12/10)   45 mins

On 1 June 20X1, Premier acquired 80% of the equity share capital of Sanford. The consideration consisted of two elements: a share exchange of three shares in Premier for every five acquired shares in Sanford and the issue of a $100 6% loan note for every 500 shares acquired in Sanford. The share issue has not yet been recorded by Premier, but the issue of the loan notes has been recorded. At the date of acquisition shares in Premier had a market value of $5 each and the shares of Sanford had a stock market price of $3.50 each. Below are the summarised draft financial statements of both companies.

BPP
LEARNING MEDIA

STATEMENTS OF PROFIT OR LOSS AND OTHER COMPREHENSIVE INCOME YEAR ENDED 30 SEPTEMBER 20X1

	Premier	Sanford
	$'000	$'000
Revenue	92,500	45,000
Cost of sales	(70,500)	(36,000)
Gross profit	22,000	9,000
Distribution costs	(2,500)	(1,200)
Administrative expenses	(5,500)	(2,400)
Finance costs	(100)	nil
Profit before tax	13,900	5,400
Income tax expense	(3,900)	(1,500)
Profit for the year	10,000	3,900
Other comprehensive income:		
Gain on revaluation of land (note (i))	500	nil
Total comprehensive income	10,500	3,900

STATEMENTS OF FINANCIAL POSITION AS AT 30 SEPTEMBER 20X1

	Premier	Sanford
	$'000	$'000
Non-current assets		
Property, plant and equipment	25,500	13,900
Investments	1,800	nil
	27,300	13,900
Current assets	12,500	2,400
Total assets	39,800	16,300
Equity		
Equity shares of $1 each	12,000	5,000
Land revaluation reserve – 30 September 20X1 (note (i))	2,000	nil
Other equity reserve – 30 September 20X0 (note (iv))	500	nil
Retained earnings	12,300	4,500
	26,800	9,500
Non-current liabilities		
6% loan notes	3,000	nil
Current liabilities	10,000	6,800
Total equity and liabilities	39,800	16,300

The following information is relevant:

(i) At the date of acquisition, the fair values of Sanford's assets were equal to their carrying amounts with the exception of its property. This had a fair value of $1.2 million **below** its carrying amount. This would lead to a reduction of the depreciation charge (in cost of sales) of $50,000 in the post-acquisition period. Sanford has not incorporated this value change into its entity financial statements.

Premier's group policy is to revalue all properties to current value at each year end. On 30 September 20X1, the value of Sanford's property was unchanged from its value at acquisition, but the land element of Premier's property had increased in value by $500,000 as shown in other comprehensive income.

(ii) Sales from Sanford to Premier throughout the year ended 30 September 20X1 had consistently been $1 million per month. Sanford made a mark-up on cost of 25% on these sales. Premier had $2 million (at cost to Premier) of inventory that had been supplied in the post-acquisition period by Sanford as at 30 September 20X1.

(iii) Premier had a trade payable balance owing to Sanford of $350,000 as at 30 September 20X1. This agreed with the corresponding receivable in Sanford's books.

(iv) Premier's investments include some investments in equity instruments that have increased in value by $300,000 during the year. The other equity reserve relates to these investments and is based on their value as at 30 September 20X0. There were no acquisitions or disposals of any of these investments during the year ended 30 September 20X1. Premier made an irrevocable election at initial recognition of these instruments to recognise all changes in fair value through other comprehensive income.

(v)   Premier's policy is to value the non-controlling interest at fair value at the date of acquisition. For this purpose Sanford's share price at that date can be deemed to be representative of the fair value of the shares held by the non-controlling interest.

(vi)   There has been no impairment of consolidated goodwill.

Required

(a)   Prepare the consolidated statement of profit or loss and other comprehensive income for Premier for the year ended 30 September 20X1.   **(9 marks)**

(b)   Prepare the consolidated statement of financial position for Premier as at 30 September 20X1.   **(16 marks)**

                                                                                                              (Total = 25 marks)

37 Prodigal (6/11)   **45 mins**

On 1 October 20X0 Prodigal purchased 75% of the equity shares in Sentinel. The acquisition was through a share exchange of two shares in Prodigal for every three shares in Sentinel. The stock market price of Prodigal's shares at 1 October 20X0 was $4 per share.

The summarised statements of profit or loss and other comprehensive income for the two companies for the year ended 31 March 20X1 are:

	Prodigal	Sentinel
	$'000	$'000
Revenue	450,000	240,000
Cost of sales	(260,000)	(110,000)
Gross profit	190,000	130,000
Distribution costs	(23,600)	(12,000)
Administrative expenses	(27,000)	(23,000)
Finance costs	(1,500)	(1,200)
Profit before tax	137,900	93,800
Income tax expense	(48,000)	(27,800)
Profit for the year	89,900	66,000
Other comprehensive income		
Gain on revaluation of land (note(i))	2,500	1,000
Loss on fair value of equity financial asset investment	(700)	(400)
	1,800	600
Total comprehensive income for the year	91,700	66,600

The following information for the equity of the companies at 1 April 20X0 (i.e. before the share exchange took place) is available:

	$'000	$'000
Equity shares of $1 each	250,000	160,000
Share premium	100,000	nil
Revaluation reserve (land)	8,400	nil
Other equity reserve (re equity financial asset investment)	3,200	2,200
Retained earnings	90,000	125,000

The following information is relevant:

(i)   Prodigal's policy is to revalue the group's land to market value at the end of each accounting period. Prior to its acquisition Sentinel's land had been valued at historical cost. During the post acquisition period Sentinel's land had increased in value over its value at the date of acquisition by $1 million. Sentinel has recognised the revaluation within its own financial statements.

(ii)   Immediately after the acquisition of Sentinel on 1 October 20X0, Prodigal transferred an item of plant with a carrying amount of $4 million to Sentinel at an agreed value of $5 million. At this date the plant had a remaining life of two and half years. Prodigal had included the profit on this transfer as a reduction in its depreciation costs. All depreciation is charged to cost of sales.

(iii) After the acquisition Sentinel sold goods to Prodigal for $40 million. These goods had cost Sentinel $30 million. $12 million of the goods sold remained in Prodigal's closing inventory.

(iv) Prodigal's policy is to value the non-controlling interest of Sentinel at the date of acquisition at its fair value which the directors determined to be $100 million.

(v) The goodwill of Sentinel has not suffered any impairment.

(vi) All items in the above statements of profit or loss and other comprehensive income are deemed to accrue evenly over the year unless otherwise indicated.

Required

(a) (i) Prepare the consolidated statement of profit or loss and other comprehensive income of Prodigal for the year ended 31 March 20X1; **(14 marks)**

(ii) Prepare the equity section (including the non-controlling interest) of the consolidated statement of financial position of Prodigal as at 31 March 20X1. **(7 marks**

(b) IFRS 3 *Business combinations* permits a non-controlling interest at the date of acquisition to be valued by one of two methods:

(i) at its proportionate share of the subsidiary's identifiable net assets; or

(ii) at its fair value (usually determined by the directors of the parent company).

Required

Explain the difference that the accounting treatment of these alternative methods could have on the consolidated financial statements, including where consolidated goodwill may be impaired.

(4 marks)

(Total = 25 marks)

38 Preparation question: Laurel

CONSOLIDATED STATEMENT OF FINANCIAL POSITION

Laurel acquired 80% of the ordinary share capital of Hardy for $160m and 40% of the ordinary share capital of Comic for $70m on 1 January 20X7 when the retained earnings balances were $64m in Hardy and $24m in Comic. Laurel, Comic and Hardy are public limited companies.

The statements of financial position of the three companies at 31 December 20X9 are set out below:

	Laurel $'m	Hardy $'m	Comic $'m
Non-current assets			
Property, plant and equipment	220	160	78
Investments	230	-	-
	450	160	78
Current assets			
Inventories	384	234	122
Trade receivables	275	166	67
Cash at bank	42	10	34
	701	410	223
	1,151	570	301
Equity			
Share capital – $1 ordinary shares	400	96	80
Share premium	16	3	-
Retained earnings	278	128	97
	694	227	177
Current liabilities			
Trade payables	457	343	124
	1,151	570	301

You are also given the following information:

1   On 30 November 20X9 Laurel sold some goods to Hardy for cash for $32m. These goods had originally cost $22m and none had been sold by the year-end. On the same date Laurel also sold goods to Comic for cash for $22m. These goods originally cost $10m and Comic had sold half by the year end.

2   On 1 January 20X7 Hardy owned some items of equipment with a book value of $45m that had a fair value of $57m. These assets were originally purchased by Hardy on 1 January 20X5 and are being depreciated over 6 years.

3   Group policy is to measure non-controlling interests at acquisition at fair value. The fair value of the non-controlling interests in Hardy on 1 January 20X7 was calculated as $39m.

4   Cumulative impairment losses on recognised goodwill amounted to $15m at 31 December 20X9. No impairment losses have been necessary to date relating to the investment in the associate.

Required

Prepare a consolidated statement of financial position for Laurel and its subsidiary as at 31 December 20X9, incorporating its associate in accordance with IAS 28. Use the following pro-forma.

PROFORMA SOLUTION

Laurel Group – Consolidated statement of financial position as at 31 December 20X9

	$'m
Non-current assets	
Property, plant and equipment	
Goodwill	
Investment in associate	___
	___
Current assets	
Inventories	
Trade receivables	
Cash	___
	___
	═══
Equity attributable to owners of the parent	
Share capital – $1 ordinary shares	
Share premium	
Retained earnings	___
Non-controlling interests	___
	___
Current liabilities	
Trade payables	___
	═══

Workings

1   *Group structure*

BPP
LEARNING MEDIA

2   *Goodwill*

	$'m	$'m
Consideration transferred		
Non-controlling interests (at 'full' fair value)		
Fair value of net assets at acq'n:		
Share capital		
Share premium		
Retained earnings		
Fair value adjustment (W7)	___	
		___
Impairment losses		___
		___

3   *Investment in associate*

	$'m
Cost of associate	
Share of post acquisition retained reserves (W4)	
Unrealised profit (W6)	
Impairment losses	___
	___

4   *Consolidated retained earnings*

	Laurel $'m	Hardy $'m	Comic $'m
Per question			
Less: Provision for unrealised profit re Hardy (W6)			
Provision for unrealised profit re Comic (W6)			
Fair value adjustment movement (W7)			
Less: pre-acquisition retained earnings		___	___
		___	___
Group share of post acquisition retained earnings:			
Hardy			
Comic			
Less: group share of impairment losses	___		
	___		

5   *Non-controlling interests*

	$'m
Non-controlling interests at acquisition (W2)	
NCI share of post acquisition retained earnings:	
Hardy	
Less: NCI share of impairment losses	___
	___

6   *Unrealised profit*

Laurel's sales to Hardy:

    DR

    CR

Laurel's sales to Comic (associate):

    DR

    CR

7   *Fair value adjustments*

	At acquisition date $'m	Movement $'m	At year end $'m
Property, plant and equipment			
	↓	↓	↓
	Goodwill	Ret'd earnings	PPE

39 Preparation question: Tyson

CONSOLIDATED STATEMENT OF PROFIT OR LOSS AND OTHER COMPREHENSIVE INCOME

Below are the statements of profit or loss and other comprehensive income of Tyson, its subsidiary Douglas and associate Frank at 31 December 20X8. Tyson, Douglas and Frank are public limited companies.

	Tyson $'m	Douglas $'m	Frank $'m
Revenue	500	150	70
Cost of sales	(270)	(80)	(30)
Gross profit	230	70	40
Other expenses	(150)	(20)	(15)
Finance income	15	10	–
Finance costs	(20)	–	(10)
Profit before tax	75	60	15
Income tax expense	(25)	(15)	(5)
PROFIT FOR THE YEAR	50	45	10
Other comprehensive income:			
Gains on property revaluation, net of tax	20	10	5
TOTAL COMPREHENSIVE INCOME FOR THE YEAR	70	55	15

You are also given the following information:

1   Tyson acquired 80m shares in Douglas for $188m 3 years ago when Douglas had a credit balance on its reserves of $40m. Douglas has 100m $1 ordinary shares.

2   Tyson acquired 40m shares in Frank for $60m 2 years ago when that company had a credit balance on its reserves of $20m. Frank has 100m $1 ordinary shares.

3   During the year Douglas sold some goods to Tyson for $66m (cost $48m). None of the goods had been sold by the year end.

4   Group policy is to measure non-controlling interests at acquisition at fair value. The fair value of the non-controlling interests in Douglas at acquisition was $40m. An impairment test carried out at the year end resulted in $15m of the recognised goodwill relating to Douglas being written off and recognition of impairment losses of $2.4m relating to the investment in Frank.

Required

Prepare the consolidated statement of profit or loss and other comprehensive income for the year ended 31 December 20X8 for Tyson, incorporating its associate.

BPP LEARNING MEDIA

PROFORMA SOLUTION

Tyson Group - Consolidated statement of profit or loss and other comprehensive income for the year ended 31 December 20X8

	$'m
Revenue	
Cost of sales	_____
Gross profit	
Other expenses	
Finance income	
Finance costs	
Share of profit of associate	_____
Profit before tax	
Income tax expense	_____
PROFIT FOR THE YEAR	_____
Other comprehensive income:	
Gains on property revaluation, net of tax	
Share of other comprehensive income of associates	_____
Other comprehensive income for the year, net of tax	_____
TOTAL COMPREHENSIVE INCOME FOR THE YEAR	_____
Profit attributable to:	
Owners of the parent	
Non-controlling interests	_____
	_____
Total comprehensive income attributable to:	
Owners of the parent	
Non-controlling interests	_____
	_____

Workings

1   *Group structure*

2   *Non-controlling interests*

	PFY $'m	TCI $'m
PFY/TCI per question		
Unrealised profit (W3)		
Impairment loss	_____	_____
	_____	_____
× NCI share	_____	_____

3   *Unrealised profit*

	$'m
Selling price	
Cost	_____
Provision for unrealised profit	_____

40 Plateau (12/07)

On 1 October 20X6 Plateau acquired the following non-current investments:

– 3 million equity shares in Savannah by an exchange of one share in Plateau for every two shares in Savannah plus $1.25 per acquired Savannah share in cash. The market price of each Plateau share at the date of acquisition was $6 and the market price of each Savannah share at the date of acquisition was $3.25.

– 30% of the equity shares of Axle at a cost of $7.50 per share in cash.

Only the cash consideration of the above investments has been recorded by Plateau. In addition $500,000 of professional costs relating to the acquisition of Savannah are also included in the cost of the investment.

The summarised draft statements of financial position of the three companies at 30 September 20X7 are

	Plateau $'000	Savannah $'000	Axle $'000
Non-current assets			
Property, plant and equipment	18,400	10,400	18,000
Investments in Savannah and Axle	13,250	nil	nil
Investments in equity instruments	6,500	nil	Nil
	38,150	10,400	18,000
Current assets			
Inventory	6,900	6,200	3,600
Trade receivables	3,200	1,500	2,400
Total assets	48,250	18,100	24,000
Equity and liabilities			
Equity shares of $1 each	10,000	4,000	4,000
Retained earnings			
– at 30 September 20X6	16,000	6,000	11,000
– for year ended 30 September 20X7	9,250	2,900	5,000
	35,250	12,900	20,000
Non-current liabilities			
7% Loan notes	5,000	1,000	1,000
Current liabilities	8,000	4,200	3,000
Total equity and liabilities	48,250	18,100	24,000

The following information is relevant:

(i) At the date of acquisition Savannah had five years remaining of an agreement to supply goods to one of its major customers. Savannah believes it is highly likely that the agreement will be renewed when it expires. The directors of Plateau estimate that the value of this customer based contract has a fair value of £1 million and an indefinite life and has not suffered any impairment.

(ii) On 1 October 20X6, Plateau sold an item of plant to Savannah at its agreed fair value of $2.5 million. Its carrying amount prior to the sale was $2 million. The estimated remaining life of the plant at the date of sale was five years (straight-line depreciation).

(iii) During the year ended 30 September 20X7 Savannah sold goods to Plateau for $2.7 million. Savannah had marked up these goods by 50% on cost. Plateau had a third of the goods still in its inventory at 30 September 20X7. There were no intra-group payables/receivables at 30 September 20X7.

(iv) Impairment tests on 30 September 20X7 concluded that neither consolidated goodwill nor the value of the investment in Axle were impaired.

(v) The investments in equity instruments are included in Plateau's statement of financial position (above) at their fair value on 1 October 20X6, but they have a fair value of $9 million at 30 September 20X7.

(vi) No dividends were paid during the year by any of the companies.

(vii) It is the group policy to value non-controlling interest at acquisition at full (or fair) value. For this purpose the share price of Savannah at this date should be used.

Required

(a)   Prepare the consolidated statement of financial position for Plateau as at 30 September 20X7.   **(20 marks)**

(b)   A financial assistant has observed that the fair value exercise means that a subsidiary's net assets are included at acquisition at their fair (current) values in the consolidated statement of financial position. The assistant believes that it is inconsistent to aggregate the subsidiary's net assets with those of the parent because most of the parent's assets are carried at historical cost.

Comment on the assistant's observation and explain why the net assets of acquired subsidiaries are consolidated at acquisition at their fair values.   **(5 marks)**

(Total = 25 marks)

41 Patronic (6/08 amended)   45 mins

On 1 August 20X7 Patronic purchased 18 million of a total of 24 million equity shares in Sardonic. The acquisition was through a share exchange of two shares in Patronic for every three shares in Sardonic. Both companies have shares with a par value of $1 each. The market price of Patronic's shares at 1 August 20X7 was $5·75 per share. Patronic will also pay in cash on 31 July 20X9 (two years after acquisition) $2·42 per acquired share of Sardonic. Patronic's cost of capital is 10% per annum. The reserves of Sardonic on 1 April 20X7 were $69 million.

Patronic has held an investment of 30% of the equity shares in Acerbic for many years.

The summarised statements of profit or loss for the three companies for the year ended 31 March 20X8 are:

	Patronic	Sardonic	Acerbic
	$'000	$'000	$'000
Revenue	150,000	78,000	80,000
Cost of sales	(94,000)	(51,000)	(60,000)
Gross profit	56,000	27,000	20,000
Distribution costs	(7,400)	(3,000)	(3,500)
Administrative expenses	(12,500)	(6,000)	(6,500)
Finance costs (note (ii))	(2,000)	(900)	nil
Profit before tax	34,100	17,100	10,000
Income tax expense	(10,400)	(3,600)	(4,000)
Profit for the year	23,700	13,500	6,000

The following information is relevant:

(i)   The fair values of the net assets of Sardonic at the date of acquisition were equal to their carrying amounts with the exception of property and plant. Property and plant had fair values of $4.1 million and $2.4 million respectively in excess of their carrying amounts. The increase in the fair value of the property would create additional depreciation of $200,000 in the consolidated financial statements in the post acquisition period to 31 March 20X8 and the plant had a remaining life of four years (straight-line depreciation) at the date of acquisition of Sardonic. All depreciation is treated as part of cost of sales.

The fair values have not been reflected in Sardonic's financial statements. No fair value adjustments were required on the acquisition of Acerbic.

(ii)   The finance costs of Patronic do not include the finance cost on the deferred consideration.

(iii)   Prior to its acquisition, Sardonic had been a good customer of Patronic. In the year to 31 March 20X8, Patronic sold goods at a selling price of $1.25 million per month to Sardonic both before and after its acquisition. Patronic made a profit of 20% on the cost of these sales. At 31 March 20X8 Sardonic still held inventory of $3 million (at cost to Sardonic) of goods purchased in the post acquisition period from Patronic.

(iv)   An impairment test on the goodwill of Sardonic conducted on 31 March 20X8 concluded that it should be written down by $2 million. The value of the investment in Acerbic was not impaired.

(v)   All items in the above statements of profit or loss are deemed to accrue evenly over the year.

(vi)   Ignore deferred tax.

(vii)   It is the group policy to value the non-controlling interest at full fair value. At the date of acquisition the directors valued the non-controlling interest in Sardonic at $32m.

Required

(a)   Calculate the goodwill arising on the acquisition of Sardonic at 1 August 20X7.   **(6 marks)**

(b)   Prepare the consolidated statement of profit or loss for the Patronic Group for the year ended 31 March 20X8.
        Note. assume that the investment in Acerbic has been accounted for using the equity method since its acquisition.   **(15 marks)**

(c)   At 31 March 20X8 the other equity shares (70%) in Acerbic were owned by many separate investors. Shortly after this date Spekulate (a company unrelated to Patronic) accumulated a 60% interest in Acerbic by buying shares from the other shareholders. In May 20X8 a meeting of the board of directors of Acerbic was held at which Patronic lost its seat on Acerbic's board.

        Required
        Explain, with reasons, the accounting treatment Patronic should adopt for its investment in Acerbic when it prepares its financial statements for the year ending 31 March 20X9.   **(4 marks)**
               (Total = 25 marks)

42 Pacemaker (6/09)   **45 mins**

Below are the summarised statements of financial position for three companies as at 31 March 20X9:

	Pacemaker		Syclop		Vardine	
Assets	$ million	$ million	$ million	$ million	$ million	$ million
Non-current assets						
Property, plant and equipment		520		280		240
Investments		345		40		nil
		865		320		240
Current assets						
Inventory	142		160		120	
Trade receivables	95		88		50	
Cash and bank	8	245	22	270	10	180
Total assets		1,110		590		420
Equity and liabilities						
Equity shares of $1 each		500		145		100
Share premium	100		nil		nil	
Retained earnings	130	230	260	260	240	240
		730		405		340
Non-current liabilities						
10% loan notes		180		20		nil
Current liabilities		200		165		80
Total equity and liabilities		1,110		590		420

Notes

Pacemaker is a public listed company that acquired the following investments:

(i)   Investment in Syclop
        On 1 April 20X7 Pacemaker acquired 116 million shares in Syclop for an immediate cash payment of $210 million and issued at par one 10% $100 loan note for every 200 shares acquired. Syclop's retained earnings at the date of acquisition were $120 million.

(ii)   Investment in Vardine
        On 1 October 20X8 Pacemaker acquired 30 million shares in Vardine in exchange for 75 million of its own shares. The stock market value of Pacemaker's shares at the date of this share exchange was $1·60 each. Pacemaker has not yet recorded the investment in Vardine.

BPP
LEARNING MEDIA

(iii)   Pacemaker's other investments, and those of Syclop, are investments in equity instruments which are carried at their fair values as at 31 March 20X8. The fair value of these investments at 31 March 20X9 is $82 million and $37 million respectively.

Other relevant information:

(iv)   Pacemaker's policy is to value non-controlling interests at their fair values. The directors of Pacemaker assessed the fair value of the non-controlling interest in Syclop at the date of acquisition to be $65 million.

There has been no impairment to goodwill or the value of the investment in Vardine.

(v)   At the date of acquisition of Syclop owned a recently built property that was carried at its (depreciated) construction cost of $62 million. The fair value of this property at the date of acquisition was $82 million and it had an estimated remaining life of 20 years.

For many years Syclop has been selling some of its products under the brand name of 'Kyklop'. At the date of acquisition the directors of Pacemaker valued this brand at $25 million with a remaining life of 10 years. The brand is not included in Syclop's statement of financial position.

(vi)   The inventory of Syclop at 31 March 20X9 includes goods supplied by Pacemaker for $56 million (at selling price from Pacemaker). Pacemaker adds a mark-up of 40% on cost when selling goods to Syclop. There are no intra-group receivables or payables at 31 March 20X9.

(vii)   Vardine's profit is subject to seasonal variation. Its profit for the year ended 31 March 20X9 was $100 million. $20 million of this profit was made from 1 April 20X8 to 30 September 20X8.

(viii) None of the companies have paid any dividends for many years.

Required
Prepare the consolidated statement of financial position of Pacemaker as at 31 March 20X9.   **(25 marks)**

43 Picant (6/10)   **45 mins**

On 1 April 20X0 Picant acquired 75% of Sander's equity shares in a share exchange of three shares in Picant for every two shares in Sander. The market prices of Picant's and Sander's shares at the date of acquisition were $3.20 and $4.50 respectively.

In addition to this Picant agreed to pay a further amount on 1 April 20X1 that was contingent upon the post-acquisition performance of Sander. At the date of acquisition Picant assessed the fair value of this contingent consideration at $4·2 million, but by 31 March 20X1 it was clear that the actual amount to be paid would be only $2·7 million (ignore discounting). Picant has recorded the share exchange and provided for the initial estimate of $4·2 million for the contingent consideration.

On 1 October 20X0 Picant also acquired 40% of the equity shares of Adler paying $4 in cash per acquired share and issuing at par one $100 7% loan note for every 50 shares acquired in Adler. This consideration has also been recorded by Picant. Picant has no other investments.

The summarised statements of financial position of the three companies at 31 March 20X1 are:

	Picant	Sander	Alder
Assets	$'000	$'000	$'000
Non-current assets			
Property, plant and equipment	37,500	24,500	21,000
Investments	45,000	nil	nil
	82,500	24,500	21,000
Current assets			
Inventory	10,000	9,000	5,000
Trade receivables	6,500	1,500	3,000
Total assets	99,000	35,000	29,000

Equity and liabilities	Picant	Sander	Alder
Equity			
Equity shares of $1 each	25,000	8,000	5,000
Share premium	19,800	nil	nil
Retained earnings – at 1 April 20X0	16,200	16,500	15,000
– for the year ended 31 March 20X1	11,000	1,000	6,000
	72,000	25,500	26,000
Non-current liabilities			
7% loan notes	14,500	2,000	nil
Current liabilities			
Contingent consideration	4,200	nil	nil
Other current liabilities	8,300	7,500	3,000
Total equity and liabilities	99,000	35,000	29,000

The following information is relevant:

(i) At the date of acquisition the fair values of Sander's property, plant and equipment was equal to its carrying amount with the exception of Sander's factory which had a fair value of $2 million above its carrying amount. Sander has not adjusted the carrying amount of the factory as a result of the fair value exercise. This requires additional annual depreciation of $100,000 in the consolidated financial statements in the post-acquisition period.

Also at the date of acquisition, Sander had an intangible asset of $500,000 for software in its statement of financial position. Picant's directors believed the software to have no recoverable value at the date of acquisition and Sander wrote it off shortly after its acquisition.

(ii) At 31 March 20X1 Picant's current account with Sander was $3·4 million (debit). This did not agree with the equivalent balance in Sander's books due to some goods-in-transit invoiced at $1·8 million that were sent by Picant on 28 March 20X1, but had not been received by Sander until after the year end. Picant sold all these goods at cost plus 50%.

(iii) Picant's policy is to value the non-controlling interest at fair value at the date of acquisition. For this purpose Sander's share price at that date can be deemed to be representative of the fair value of the shares held by the non-controlling interest.

(iv) Impairment tests were carried out on 31 March 20X1 which concluded that the value of the investment in Adler was not impaired but, due to poor trading performance, consolidated goodwill was impaired by $3·8 million.

(v) Assume all profits accrue evenly through the year.

Required

(a) Prepare the consolidated statement of financial position for Picant as at 31 March 20X1. **(21 marks)**

(b) Picant has been approached by a potential new customer, Trilby, to supply it with a substantial quantity of goods on three months credit terms. Picant is concerned at the risk that such a large order represents in the current difficult economic climate, especially as Picant's normal credit terms are only one month's credit. To support its application for credit, Trilby has sent Picant a copy of Tradhat's most recent audited consolidated financial statements. Trilby is a wholly-owned subsidiary within the Tradhat group. Tradhat's consolidated financial statements show a strong statement of financial position including healthy liquidity ratios.

Required

Comment on the importance that Picant should attach to Tradhat's consolidated financial statements when deciding on whether to grant credit terms to Trilby. **(4 marks)**

(Total = 25 marks)

BPP
LEARNING MEDIA

44 Paladin (12/11)

45 mins

On 1 October 20X0, Paladin secured a majority equity shareholding in Saracen on the following terms:

An immediate payment of $4 per share on 1 October 20X0; and a further amount deferred until 1 October 20X1 of $5·4 million.

The immediate payment has been recorded in Paladin's financial statements, but the deferred payment has not been recorded. Paladin's cost of capital is 8% per annum.

On 1 February 20X1, Paladin also acquired 25% of the equity shares of Augusta paying $10 million in cash.

The summarised statements of financial position of the three companies at 30 September 20X1 are:

	Paladin	Saracen	Augusta
Assets	$'000	$'000	$'000
Non-current assets			
Property, plant and equipment	40,000	31,000	30,000
Intangible assets	7,500		
Investments – Saracen (8 million shares at $4 each)	32,000		
– Augusta	10,000	nil	nil
	89,500	31,000	30,000
Current assets			
Inventory	11,200	8,400	10,000
Trade receivables	7,400	5,300	5,000
Bank	3,400	nil	2,000
Total assets	111,500	44,700	47,000
Equity and liabilities			
Equity			
Equity shares of $1 each	50,000	10,000	10,000
Retained earnings – at 1 October 20X0	25,700	12,000	31,800
– for year ended 30 September 20X1	9,200	6,000	1,200
	84,900	28,000	43,000
Non-current liabilities			
Deferred tax	15,000	8,000	1,000
Current liabilities			
Bank	nil	2,500	nil
Trade payables	11,600	6,200	3,000
Total equity and liabilities	111,500	44,700	47,000

The following information is relevant:

(i)   Paladin's policy is to value the non-controlling interest at fair value at the date of acquisition. For this purpose the directors of Paladin considered a share price for Saracen of $3.50 per share to be appropriate.

(ii)   At the date of acquisition, the fair values of Saracen's property, plant and equipment was equal to its carrying amount with the exception of Saracen's plant which had a fair value of $4 million above its carrying amount. At that date the plant had a remaining life of four years. Saracen uses straight-line depreciation for plant assuming a nil residual value.

Also at the date of acquisition, Paladin valued Saracen's customer relationships as a customer base intangible asset at fair value of $3 million. Saracen has not accounted for this asset. Trading relationships with Saracen's customers last on average for six years.

(iii)   At 30 September 20X1, Saracen's inventory included goods bought from Paladin (at cost to Saracen) of $2.6 million. Paladin had marked up these goods by 30% on cost. Paladin's agreed current account balance owed by Saracen at 30 September 20X1 was $1.3 million.

(iv) Impairment tests were carried out on 30 September 20X1 which concluded that consolidated goodwill was not impaired, but, due to disappointing earnings, the value of the investment in Augusta was impaired by $2.5 million.

(v) Assume all profits accrue evenly through the year.

Required

Prepare the consolidated statement of financial position for Paladin as at 30 September 20X1. **(25 marks)**

45 Preparation question: Contract

The following details are as at the 31 December 20X5

	Contract 1	Contract 2	Contract 3	Contract 4
Contract value	$120,000	$72,000	$240,000	$500,000
Costs to date	$48,000	$8,000	$103,200	$299,600
Estimated costs to completion	$48,000	$54,000	$160,800	$120,400
Progress payments received and receivable	$50,400	–	$76,800	$345,200
Date started	1.3.20X5	15.10.20X5	1.7.20X5	1.6.20X4
Estimated completion date	30.6.20X6	15.9.20X6	30.11.20X6	30.7.20X6
% complete	45%	10%	35%	70%

You are to assume that profit accrues evenly over the contract.

The statement of profit or loss for the previous year showed revenue of $225,000 and expenses of $189,000 in relation to contract 4.

The company considers that the outcome of a contract cannot be estimated reliably until a contract is 25% complete. It is, however, probable that the customer will pay for costs incurred so far.

Required

Calculate the amounts to be included in the statement of profit or loss for the year ended 31 December 20X5 and the statement of financial position as at that date.

	Contract 1 $	Contract 2 $	Contract 3 $	Contract 4 $
Statement of profit or loss				
Revenue				
Expenses				
Expected loss				
Recognised profit/(loss)				
Statement of financial position				
Gross amount due from/to customers				
Recognised profits less recognised losses				
Less: progress billings to date				
Trade receivables				
Progress billings to date				
Less: cash received				

Workings

BPP
LEARNING MEDIA

46 Beetie (pilot paper)

18 mins

IAS 11 *Construction contracts* deals with accounting requirements for construction contracts whose durations usually span at least two accounting periods.

Required

(a) Describe the issues of revenue and profit recognition relating to construction contracts. **(4 marks)**

(b) Beetie is a construction company that prepares its financial statements to 31 March each year. During the year ended 31 March 20X6 the company commenced two construction contracts that are expected to take more than one year to complete. The position of each contract at 31 March 20X6 is as follows:

Contract	1	2
	$'000	$'000
Agreed contract price	5,500	1,200
Estimated total cost of contract at commencement	4,000	900
Estimated total cost at 31 March 20X6	4,000	1,250
Agreed value of work completed at 31 March 20X6	3,300	840
Progress billings invoiced and received at 31 March 20X6	3,000	880
Contract costs incurred to 31 March 20X6	3,900	720

The agreed value of the work completed at 31 March 20X6 is considered to be equal to the revenue earned in the year ended 31 March 20X6. The percentage of completion is calculated as the agreed value of work completed to the agreed contract price.

Required

Calculate the amounts which should appear in the statement of profit or loss and statement of financial position of Beetie at 31 March 20X6 in respect of the above contracts. **(6 marks)**

(Total = 10 marks)

47 Mocca (6/11)

18 mins

On 1 October 20X0 Mocca entered into a construction contract that was expected to take 27 months and therefore be completed on 31 December 20X2. Details of the contract are:

	$'000
Agreed contract price	12,500
Estimated total cost of contract (excluding plant)	5,500

Plant for use on the contract was purchased on 1 January 20X1 (three months into the contract as it was not required at the start) at a cost of $8 million. The plant has a four-year life and after two years, when the contract is complete, it will be transferred to another contract at its carrying amount. Annual depreciation is calculated using the straight-line method (assuming a nil residual value) and charged to the contract on a monthly basis at 1/12 of the annual charge.

The correctly reported profit or loss results for the contract for the year ended 31 March 20X1 were:

	$'000
Revenue recognised	3,500
Contract expenses recognised	(2,660)
Profit recognised	840

Details of the progress of the contract at 31 March 20X2 are:

	$'000
Contract costs incurred to date (excluding depreciation)	4,800
Agreed value of work completed and billed to date	8,125
Total cash received to date (payments on account)	7,725

The percentage of completion is calculated as the agreed value of work completed as a percentage of the agreed contract price.

Required

Calculate the amounts which would appear in the statement of profit or loss and statement of financial position of Mocca, including the disclosure note of amounts due to/from customers, for the year ended/as at 31 March 20X2 in respect of the above contract. **(10 marks)**

48 Bodyline (2.5 12/03)   45 mins

IAS 37 *Provisions, contingent liabilities and contingent assets* sets out the principles of accounting for these items and clarifies when provisions should and should not be made. Prior to its issue, the inappropriate use of provisions had been an area where companies had been accused of manipulating the financial statements and of creative accounting.

Required

(a) Describe the nature of provisions and the accounting requirements for them contained in IAS 37. **(6 marks)**

(b) Explain why there is a need for an accounting standard in this area. Illustrate your answer with three practical examples of how the standard addresses controversial issues. **(6 marks)**

(c) Bodyline sells sports goods and clothing through a chain of retail outlets. It offers customers a full refund facility for any goods returned within 28 days of their purchase provided they are unused and in their original packaging. In addition, all goods carry a warranty against manufacturing defects for 12 months from their date of purchase. For most goods the manufacturer underwrites this warranty such that Bodyline is credited with the cost of the goods that are returned as faulty. Goods purchased from one manufacturer, Header, are sold to Bodyline at a negotiated discount which is designed to compensate Bodyline for manufacturing defects. No refunds are given by Header, thus Bodyline has to bear the cost of any manufacturing faults of these goods.

Bodyline makes a uniform mark up on cost of 25% on all goods it sells, except for those supplied from Header on which it makes a mark up on cost of 40%. Sales of goods manufactured by Header consistently account for 20% of all Bodyline's sales.

Sales in the last 28 days of the trading year to 30 September 20X3 were $1,750,000. Past trends reliably indicate that 10% of all goods are returned under the 28-day return facility. These are not faulty goods. Of these 70% are later resold at the normal selling price and the remaining 30% are sold as 'sale' items at half the normal retail price.

In addition to the above expected returns, an estimated $160,000 (at selling price) of the goods sold during the year will have manufacturing defects and have yet to be returned by customers. Goods returned as faulty have no resale value.

Required

Describe the nature of the above warranty/return facilities and calculate the provision Bodyline is required to make at 30 September 20X3:

(i) For goods subject to the 28 day returns policy
(ii) For goods that are likely to be faulty **(8 marks)**

(d) Rockbuster has recently purchased an item of earth moving plant at a total cost of $24 million. The plant has an estimated life of 10 years with no residual value, however its engine will need replacing after every 5,000 hours of use at an estimated cost of $7.5 million. The directors of Rockbuster intend to depreciate the plant at $2.4 million ($24 million/10 years) per annum and make a provision of $1,500 ($7.5 million/5,000 hours) per hour of use for the replacement of the engine.

Required

Explain how the plant should be treated in accordance with International Financial Reporting Standards and comment on the Directors' proposed treatment. **(5 marks)**

(Total = 25 marks)

49 Promoil (12/08)   27 mins

(a)   The definition of a liability forms an important element of the IASB *Conceptual Framework for Financial Reporting* and is the basis for IAS 37 *Provisions, Contingent Liabilities and Contingent Assets*.

   Required

   Define a liability and describe the circumstances under which provisions should be recognised. Give two examples of how the definition of liabilities enhances the reliability of financial statements.   **(5 marks)**

(b)   On 1 October 20X7, Promoil acquired a newly constructed oil platform at a cost of $30 million together with the right to extract oil from an offshore oilfield under a government licence. The terms of the licence are that Promoil will have to remove the platform (which will then have no value) and restore the sea bed to an environmentally satisfactory condition in 10 years' time when the oil reserves have been exhausted. The estimated cost of this in 10 years time will be $15 million. The present value of $1 receivable in 10 years at the appropriate discount rate for Promoil of 8% is $0.46.

   Required

   (i)   Explain and quantify how the oil platform should be treated in the financial statements of Promoil for the year ended 30 September 20X8;   **(7 marks)**

   (ii)   Describe how your answer to (b)(i) would change if the government licence did not require an environmental clean up.   **(3 marks)**

                                                                   (Total = 15 marks)

50 Borough (12/11)   27 mins

(a)   IAS 37 *Provisions, contingent liabilities and contingent assets* prescribes the accounting and disclosure for those items named in its title.

   Required

   Define provisions and contingent liabilities and briefly explain how IAS 37 improves consistency in financial reporting.   **(6 marks)**

(b)   The following items have arisen during the preparation of Borough's draft financial statements for the year ended 30 September 20X1:

   (i)   On 1 October 20X0, Borough commenced the extraction of crude oil from a new well on the seabed. The cost of a 10-year licence to extract the oil was $50 million. At the end of the extraction, although not legally bound to do so, Borough intends to make good the damage the extraction has caused to the seabed environment. This intention has been communicated to parties external to Borough. The cost of this will be in two parts: a fixed amount of $20 million and a variable amount of 2 cents per barrel extracted. Both of these amounts are based on their present values as at 1 October 20X0 (discounted at 8%) of the estimated costs in 10 years' time. In the year to 30 September 20X1 Borough extracted 150 million barrels of oil.

                                                                              (5 marks)

   (ii)   Borough owns the whole of the equity share capital of its subsidiary Hamlet. Hamlet's statement of financial position includes a loan of $25 million that is repayable in five years' time. $15 million of this loan is secured on Hamlet's property and the remaining $10 million is guaranteed by Borough in the event of a default by Hamlet. The economy in which Hamlet operates is currently experiencing a deep recession, the effects of which are that the current value of its property is estimated at $12 million and there are concerns over whether Hamlet can survive the recession and therefore repay the loan.   **(4 marks)**

   Required

   Describe, and quantify where possible, how items (i) and (ii) above should be treated in Borough's statement of financial position for the year ended 30 September 20X1.

   In the case of item (ii) only, distinguish between Borough's entity and consolidated financial statements and refer to any disclosure notes. Your answer should only refer to the treatment of the loan and should not consider any impairment of Hamlet's property or Borough's investment in Hamlet.

   Note: the treatment in the income statement is NOT required for any of the items.   **(Total = 15 marks)**

51 Jedders

Your assistant at Jedders, a small listed company, has been preparing the financial statements for the year ended 31 December 20X0 and has raised the following queries.

(a) The company has three long leasehold properties in different parts of the region. The leases were acquired at different times, and the lease terms are all for fifty years. As at 1 January 20X0, their original cost, accumulated depreciation to date and carrying (book) values were as follows.

	Cost	Depreciation	Carrying value 1.1.20X0
	$'000	$'000	$'000
Property in North	3,000	1,800	1,200
Property in Central	6,000	1,200	4,800
Property in South	3,750	1,500	2,250

On 1 January an independent surveyor provided valuation information to suggest that the value of the South property was the same as book value, the North property had fallen against carrying value by 20% and the Central property had risen by 40% in value against the carrying value.

The directors of the company wish to include the revaluation of the Central property in the accounts to 31 December 20X0, whilst leaving the other properties at their depreciated historical cost.

The directors believe that this treatment of the North property is prudent and can be justified because property prices are expected to recover within the next few years so that this fall in value will be entirely reversed.

Required

(i)   Advise the directors whether their proposal is acceptable, assuming they are committed to the use of current value for the Central property. **(2 marks)**

(ii) Assuming that all of the properties are revalued, calculate the profit or loss charges and the non-current asset statement of financial position extracts for all the properties for the year ended 31 December 20X0. You should follow the requirements of IAS 16 *Property, plant and equipment*. **(3 marks)**

(b) On 1 October 20X0, Jedders signed a receivable factoring agreement with a company Fab Factors. Jedders' trade receivables are to be split into three groups, as follows.

- *Group A* receivables will not be factored or administered by Fab Factors under the agreement, but instead will be collected as usual by Jedders.

- *Group B* receivables are to be factored and collected by Fab Factors on a 'with recourse' basis. Fab Factors will charge a 1% per month finance charge on the balance outstanding at the beginning of the month. Jedders will reimburse in full any individual balance outstanding after three months.

- *Group C* receivables will be factored and collected by Fab Factors 'without recourse'; Fab Factors will pay Jedders 95% of the book value of the debtors.

Jedders has a policy of making a receivables allowance of 20% of a trade receivable balance when it becomes three months old.

The receivables groups have been analysed as follows.

	Balance @ 1 Oct 20X0	% of 1 October 20X0 balance collected in:		
		October	November	December
	$'000			
Group A	1,250	30%	30%	20%
Group B	1,500	40%	30%	20%
Group C	2,000	50%	25%	22%

Required

For the accounts of Jedders, calculate the finance costs and receivables allowance for each group of trade receivables for the period 1 October - 31 December 20X0 and show the financial position values for those trade receivables as at 31 December 20X0. **(5 marks)**

(c)   On 1 January 20X0, Jedders issued $15m of 7% convertible loan notes at par. The loan notes are convertible into equity shares in the company, at the option of the note holders, five years after the date of issue (31 December 20X4) on the basis of 25 shares for each $100 of loan stock. Alternatively, the loan notes will be redeemed at par.

Jedders has been advised by Fab Factors that, had the company issued similar loan notes without the conversion rights, then it would have had to pay interest of 10%; the rate is thus lower because the conversion rights are favourable.

Fab Factors also suggest that, as some of the loan note holders will choose to convert, the loan notes are, in substance, equity and should be treated as such on Jedders' statement of financial position. Thus, as well as a reduced finance cost being achieved to boost profitability, Jedders' gearing has been improved compared to a straight issue of debt.

The present value of $1 receivable at the end of each year, based on discount rates of 7% and 10% can be taken as:

End of year	7%	10%
1	0.93	0.91
2	0.87	0.83
3	0.82	0.75
4	0.76	0.68
5	0.71	0.62

Required

In relation to the 7% convertible loan notes, calculate the finance cost to be shown in the statement of profit or loss and the statement of financial position extracts for the year to 31 December 20X0 for Jedders and comment on the advice from Fab Factors.   **(5 marks)**

(Total = 15 marks)

52 Pingway (6/08)   18 mins

Pingway issued a $10 million 3% convertible loan note at par on 1 April 20X7 with interest payable annually in arrears. Three years later, on 31 March 20Y0, the loan note is convertible into equity shares on the basis of $100 of loan note for 25 equity shares or it may be redeemed at par in cash at the option of the loan note holder. One of the company's financial assistants observed that the use of a convertible loan note was preferable to a non-convertible loan note as the latter would have required an interest rate of 8% in order to make it attractive to investors. The assistant has also commented that the use of a convertible loan note will improve the profit as a result of lower interest costs and, as it is likely that the loan note holders will choose the equity option, the loan note can be classified as equity which will improve the company's high gearing position.

The present value of $1 receivable at the end of the year, based on discount rates of 3% and 8% can be taken as:

	3%	8%
	$	$
End of year 1	0.97	0.93
2	0.94	0.86
3	0.92	0.79

Required

Comment on the financial assistant's observations and show how the convertible loan note should be accounted for in Pingway's statement of profit or loss for the year ended 31 March 20X8 and statement of financial position as at that date.   **(10 marks)**

53 Bertrand (12/11)   18 mins

Bertrand issued $10 million convertible loan notes on 1 October 20X0 that carry a nominal interest (coupon) rate of 5% per annum. They are redeemable on 30 September 20X3 at par for cash or can be exchanged for equity shares in Bertrand on the basis of 20 shares for each $100 of loan. A similar loan note, without the conversion option, would have required Bertrand to pay an interest rate of 8%.

When preparing the draft financial statements for the year ended 30 September 20X1, the directors are proposing to show the loan note within equity in the statement of financial position, as they believe all the loan note holders will choose the equity option when the loan note is due for redemption. They further intend to charge a finance cost of $500,000 ($10 million x 5%) in the income statement for each year up to the date of redemption.

The present value of $1 receivable at the end of each year, based on discount rates of 5% and 8%, can be taken as:

		5%	8%
End of year	1	0.95	0.93
	2	0.91	0.86
	3	0.86	0.79

Required

(a) (i) Explain why the nominal interest rate on the convertible loan notes is 5%, but for non-convertible loan notes it would be 8%. **(2 marks)**

(ii) Briefly comment on the impact of the directors' proposed treatment of the loan notes on the financial statements and the acceptability of this treatment. **(3 marks)**

(b) Prepare extracts to show how the loan notes and the finance charge should be treated by Bertrand in its financial statements for the year ended 30 September 20X1. **(5 marks)**

(Total = 10 marks)

54 Triangle (2.5 6/05)   45 mins

Triangle, a public listed company, is in the process of preparing its draft financial statements for the year to 31 March 20X5. The following matters have been brought to your attention:

(i) On 1 April 20X4 the company brought into use a new processing plant that had cost $15 million to construct and had an estimated life of ten years. The plant uses hazardous chemicals which are put in containers and shipped abroad for safe disposal after processing. The chemicals have also contaminated the plant itself which occurred as soon as the plant was used. It is a legal requirement that the plant is decontaminated at the end of its life. The estimated present value of this decontamination, using a discount rate of 8% per annum, is $5 million. The financial statements have been charged with $1.5 million ($15 million/10 years) for plant depreciation and a provision of $500,000 ($5 million/10 years) has been made towards the cost of the decontamination. **(8 marks)**

(ii) On 15 May 20X5 the company's auditors discovered a fraud in the material requisitions department. A senior member of staff who took up employment with Triangle in August 20X4 had been authorising payments for goods that had never been received. The payments were made to a fictitious company that cannot be traced. The member of staff was immediately dismissed. Calculations show that the total amount of the fraud to the date of its discovery was $240,000 of which $210,000 related to the year to 31 March 20X5. (Assume the fraud is material). **(5 marks)**

(iii) The company has contacted its insurers in respect of the above fraud. Triangle is insured for theft, but the insurance company maintains that this is a commercial fraud and is not covered by the theft clause in the insurance policy. Triangle has not yet had an opinion from its lawyers. **(4 marks)**

(iv) On 1 April 20X4 Triangle sold maturing inventory that had a carrying value of $3 million (at cost) to Factorall, a finance house, for $5 million. Its estimated market value at this date was in excess of $5 million. The inventory will not be ready for sale until 31 March 20X8 and will remain on Triangle's premises until this date. The sale contract includes a clause allowing Triangle to repurchase the inventory at any time up to 31 March 20X8 at a price of $5 million plus interest at 10% per annum compounded from 1 April 20X4. The inventory will incur storage costs until maturity. The cost of storage for the current year of $300,000 has been included in trade receivables (in the name of Factorall). If Triangle chooses not to repurchase the inventory, Factorall will pay the accumulated storage costs on 31 March 20X8. The proceeds of the sale have been debited to the bank and the sale has been included in Triangle's sales revenue. **(8 marks)**

Required

Explain how the items in (i) to (iv) above should be treated in Triangle's financial statements for the year to 31 March 20X5 in accordance with current international accounting standards. Your answer should quantify the amounts where possible.

The mark allocation is shown against each of the four matters above. **(Total = 25 marks)**

BPP
LEARNING MEDIA

55 Angelino (2.5 12/06)

45 mins

(a) Recording the substance of transactions, rather than their legal form, is an important principle in financial accounting. Abuse of this principle can lead to profit manipulation, non-recognition of assets and substantial debt not being recorded in the statement of financial position.

Required

Describe how the use of off balance sheet financing can mislead users of financial statements.

Note: Your answer should refer to specific user groups and include examples where recording the legal form of transactions may mislead them. **(9 marks)**

(b) Angelino has entered into the following transactions during the year ended 30 September 20X6:

(i) In September 20X6 Angelino sold (factored) some of its trade receivables to Omar, a finance house. On selected account balances Omar paid Angelino 80% of their book value. The agreement was that Omar would administer the collection of the receivables and remit a residual amount to Angelino depending upon how quickly individual customers paid. Any balance uncollected by Omar after six months will be refunded to Omar by Angelino. **(5 marks)**

(ii) On 1 October 20X5 Angelino owned a freehold building that had a carrying amount of $7.5 million and had an estimated remaining life of 20 years. On this date it sold the building to Finaid for a price of $12 million and entered into an agreement with Finaid to rent back the building for an annual rental of $1.3 million for a period of five years. The auditors of Angelino have commented that in their opinion the building had a market value of only $10 million at the date of its sale and to rent an equivalent building under similar terms to the agreement between Angelino and Finaid would only cost $800,000 per annum. Assume any finance costs are 10% per annum. **(6 marks)**

(iii) Angelino is a motor car dealer selling vehicles to the public. Most of its new vehicles are supplied on consignment by two manufacturers, Monza and Capri, who trade on different terms.

Monza supplies cars on terms that allow Angelino to display the vehicles for a period of three months from the date of delivery or when Angelino sells the cars on to a retail customer if this is less than three months. Within this period Angelino can return the cars to Monza or can be asked by Monza to transfer the cars to another dealership (both at no cost to Angelino). Angelino pays the manufacturer's list price at the end of the three month period (or at the date of sale if sooner). In recent years Angelino has returned several cars to Monza that were not selling very well and has also been required to transfer cars to other dealerships at Monza's request.

Capri's terms of supply are that Angelino pays 10% of the manufacturer's price at the date of delivery and 1% of the outstanding balance per month as a display charge. After six months (or sooner if Angelino chooses), Angelino must pay the balance of the purchase price or return the cars to Capri. If the cars are returned to the manufacturer, Angelino has to pay for the transportation costs and forfeits the 10% deposit. Because of this Angelino has only returned vehicles to Capri once in the last three years. **(5 marks)**

Required

Describe how the above transactions and events should be treated in the financial statements of Angelino for the year ended 30 September 20X6. Your answer should explain, where relevant, the difference between the legal form of the transactions and their substance.

Note: the mark allocation is shown against each of the three transactions above. **(Total = 25 marks)**

56 Wardle (6/10 amended)

27 mins

(a) An important aspect of the International Accounting Standards Board's *Conceptual Framework for Financial Reporting* is that transactions should be faithfully represented. Implicit in this is the requirement that they should be recorded on the basis of their substance over their form.

Required

Explain why it is important that financial statements should reflect the substance of the underlying transactions and describe the features that may indicate that the substance of a transaction may be different from its legal form. **(5 marks)**

(b)   Wardle's activities include the production of maturing products which take a long time before they are ready to retail. Details of one such product are that on 1 April 20X0 it had a cost of $5 million and a fair value of $7 million. The product would not be ready for retail sale until 31 March 20X3.

On 1 April 20X0 Wardle entered into an agreement to sell the product to Easyfinance for $6 million. The agreement gave Wardle the right to repurchase the product at any time up to 31 March 20X3 at a fixed price of $7,986,000,at which date Wardle expected the product to retail for $10 million. The compound interest Wardle would have to pay on a three-year loan of $6 million would be:

	$
Year 1	600,000
Year 2	660,000
Year 3	726,000

This interest is equivalent to the return required by Easyfinance.

Required

Assuming the above figures prove to be accurate, prepare extracts from the statement of profit or loss of Wardle for the three years to 31 March 20X3 in respect of the above transaction:

(i)   Reflecting the legal form of the transaction   **(2 marks)**
(ii)   Reflecting the substance of the transaction   **(3 marks)**

Note: statement of financial position extracts are NOT required.

(c)   Comment on the effect the two treatments have on the statements of profit or loss and the statements of financial position and how this may affect an assessment of Wardle's performance.   **(5 marks)**

(Total = 15 marks)

57 Preparation question: Branch

Branch acquired an item of plant and equipment on a finance lease on 1 January 20X1. The terms of the agreement were as follows:

Deposit	:	$1,150 (non-refundable)
Instalments	:	$4,000 pa for seven years payable in arrears
Cash price	:	$20,000

The asset has useful life of four years and the interest rate implicit in the lease is 11%.

Required

Prepare extracts from the statement of profit or loss and statement of financial position for the year ending 31 December 20X1, using the following pro-forma.

Workings

STATEMENT OF PROFIT OR LOSS (EXTRACT) $
Depreciation
Finance costs

STATEMENT OF FINANCIAL POSITION (EXTRACT) $
Non-current assets
Property, plant and equipment – assets held under finance leases

Non-current liabilities
Finance lease liabilities

Current liabilities
Finance lease liabilities

BPP
LEARNING MEDIA

58 Evans

22 mins

On 1 October 20X3 Evans entered into a non-cancellable agreement whereby Evans would lease a new rocket booster. The terms of the agreement were that Evans would pay 26 rentals of $3,000 quarterly in advance commencing on 1 October 20X3, and that after this initial period Evans could continue, at its option, to use the rocket booster for a nominal rental which is not material. The cash price of this asset would have been $61,570 and the asset has a useful life of 10 years. Evans considers this lease to be a finance lease and charges a full year's depreciation in the year of purchase of an asset. The rate of interest implicit in the lease is 2% per quarter.

On 1 July 20X2 Evans entered into another non-cancellable agreement to lease a Zarkov rocket for a period of 10 years at a rental of $5,000 half-yearly to be paid in advance, commencing on 1 July 20X2. Evans considers this lease to be an operating lease.

Required

Show how these transactions would be reflected in the financial statements for the year ended 31 December 20X3.

(12 marks)

59 Fino (12/07 amended)

27 mins

(a)   An important requirement of the IASB's *Conceptual Framework for Financial Reporting* is that an entity's financial statements should represent faithfully the transactions and events that it has undertaken.

Required

Explain what is meant by faithful representation and how it makes financial information useful.   **(5 marks)**

(b)   On 1 April 20X7, Fino increased the operating capacity of its plant. Due to a lack of liquid funds it was unable to buy the required plant which had a cost of $350,000. On the recommendation of the finance director, Fino entered into an agreement to lease the plant from the manufacturer. The lease required four annual payments in advance of $100,000 each commencing on 1 April 20X7. The plant would have a useful life of four years and would be scrapped at the end of this period. The finance director, believing the lease to be an operating lease, commented that the agreement would improve the company's return on capital employed (compared to outright purchase of the plant).

Required

(i)   Discuss the validity of the finance director's comment and describe how IAS 17 *Leases* ensures that leases such as the above are faithfully represented in an entity's financial statements.   **(4 marks)**

(ii)   Prepare extracts of Fino's statement of profit or loss and statement of financial position for the year ended 30 September 20X7 in respect of the rental agreement assuming:

(1)   It is an operating lease   **(2 marks)**
(2)   It is a finance lease (use an implicit interest rate of 10% per annum).   **(4 marks)**

(Total = 15 marks)

60 Preparation question: Julian

Julian recognised a deferred tax liability for the year end 31 December 20X3 which related solely to accelerated tax depreciation on property, plant and equipment at a rate 30%. The net book value of the property, plant and equipment at that date was $310,000 and the tax written down value was $230,000.

The following data relates to the year ended 31 December 20X4:

(i)   At the end of the year the carrying value of property, plant and equipment was $460,000 and their tax written down value was $270,000. During the year some items were revalued by $90,000. No items had previously required revaluation. In the tax jurisdiction in which Julian operates revaluations of assets do not affect the tax base of an asset or taxable profit. Gains due to revaluations are taxable on sale.

(ii)   Julian began development of a new product during the year and capitalised $60,000 in accordance with IAS 38. The expenditure was deducted for tax purposes as it was incurred. None of the expenditure had been amortised by the year end.

(iii)   Julian's statement of profit or loss showed interest income receivable of $55,000, but only $45,000 of this had been received by the year end. Interest income is taxed on a receipts basis.

(iv)   During the year, Julian made a provision of $40,000 to cover an obligation to clean up some damage caused by an environmental accident. None of the provision had been used by the year end. The expenditure will be tax deductible when paid.

The corporate income tax rate recently enacted for the following year is 30% (unchanged from the previous year).

The current tax charge was calculated for the year as $45,000.

Current tax is settled on a net basis with the national tax authority.

Required

(a)   Prepare a table showing the carrying values, tax bases and temporary differences for each for the items above at 31 December 20X4.

(b)   Prepare the statement of profit or loss and statement of financial position notes to the financial statements relating to deferred tax for the year ended 31 December 20X4.

61 Deferred taxation   27 mins

(a)   Explain, with examples, the nature and purpose of deferred taxation.   **(10 marks)**

(b)   The information below relates to G for the year ended 31 March 20X3.

The balance on the provision for deferred taxation account at 1 April 20X2 was $35,000. This represented taxation at 35% on cumulative timing differences of $100,000 at 1 April 20X2. Capital allowances (tax depreciation) and depreciation for the year ending 31 March 20X3 are as follows.

	Capital allowances $'000	Depreciation $'000
20X3 (actual)	100	90

The income tax rate for 20X3 is 30% and is expected to remain at this level for the foreseeable future.

Required

State, with reasons, how to account for deferred tax in the year ended 31 March 20X3.   **(5 marks)**
                                                                         (Total = 15 marks)

62 Bowtock II (2.5 12/03 amended)   18 mins

(a)   IAS 12 *Income Taxes* was issued in 1996 and revised in 2000. It details the requirements relating to the accounting treatment of deferred taxes.

Required

Explain why it is considered necessary to provide for deferred tax and briefly outline the principles of accounting for deferred tax contained in IAS 12 *Income taxes*.   **(4 marks)**

(b)   Bowtock purchased an item of plant for $2,000,000 on 1 October 20X0. It had an estimated life of eight years and an estimated residual value of $400,000. The plant is depreciated on a straight-line basis. The tax authorities do not allow depreciation as a deductible expense. Instead a tax expense of 40% of the cost of this type of asset can be claimed against income tax in the year of purchase and 20% per annum (on a reducing balance basis) of its tax base thereafter. The rate of income tax can be taken as 25%.

Required

In respect of the above item of plant, calculate the deferred tax charge/credit in Bowtock's statement of profit or loss for the year to 30 September 20X3 and the deferred tax balance in the statement of financial position at that date.   **(6 marks)**

Note. Work to the nearest $'000.   **(Total = 10 marks)**

BPP
LEARNING MEDIA

63 Preparation question: Fenton

(a)   Fenton had 5,000,000 ordinary shares in issue on 1 January 20X1.

On 31 January 20X1, the company made a rights issue of 1 for 4 at $1.75. The cum rights price was $2 per share.

On 30 June 20X1, the company made an issue at full market price of 125,000 shares.

Finally, on 30 November 20X1, the company made a 1 for 10 bonus issue.

Profit for the year was $2,900,000.

The reported EPS for year ended 31 December 20X0 was 46.4c.

Required

What was the earnings per share figure for year ended 31 December 20X1 and the restated EPS for year ended 31 December 20X0?

(b)   Sinbad had the same 10 million ordinary shares in issue on both 1 January 20X1 and 31 December 20X1. On 1 January 20X1 the company issued 1,200,000 $1 units of 5% convertible loan stock. Each unit of stock is convertible into 4 ordinary shares on 1 January 20X9 at the option of the holder. The following is an extract from Sinbad's statement of profit or loss for the year ended 31 December 20X1:

	$'000
Profit before interest and tax	980
Interest payable on 5% convertible loan stock	(60)
Profit before tax	920
Income tax expense (at 30%)	(276)
Profit for the year	644

Required

What was the basic and diluted earnings per share for the year ended 31 December 20X1?

(c)   Talbot has in issue 5,000,000 50c ordinary shares throughout 20X3.

During 20X1 the company had given certain senior executives options over 400,000 shares exercisable at $1.10 at any time after 31 May 20X4. None were exercised during 20X3. The average market value of one ordinary share during the period was $1.60. Talbot had made a profit after tax of $540,000 in 20X3.

Required

What is the basic and diluted earnings per share for the year ended 31 December 20X3?

64 Barstead (12/09)   18 mins

(a)   The following figures have been calculated from the financial statements (including comparatives) of Barstead for the year ended 30 September 20X1:

Increase in profit after taxation	80%
Increase in (basic) earnings per share	5%
Increase in diluted earnings per share	2%

Required

Explain why the three measures of earnings (profit) growth for the same company over the same period can give apparently differing impressions.   **(4 marks)**

(b)   The profit after tax for Barstead for the year ended 30 September 20X1 was $15 million. At 1 October 20X0 the company had in issue 36 million equity shares and a $10 million 8% convertible loan note. The loan note will mature in 20X2 and will be redeemed at par or converted to equity shares on the basis of 25 shares for each $100 of loan note at the loan-note holders' option. On 1 January 20X1 Barstead made a fully subscribed rights issue of one new share for every four shares held at a price of $2·80 each. The market price of the equity shares of Barstead immediately before the issue was $3·80. The earnings per share (EPS) reported for the year ended 30 September 20X0 was 35 cents.

Barstead's income tax rate is 25%.

Required

Calculate the (basic) EPS figure for Barstead (including comparatives) and the diluted EPS (comparatives not required) that would be disclosed for the year ended 30 September 20X1. **(6 marks)**

(Total = 10 marks)

65 Rebound (6/11 amended)   27 mins

(a)   Your assistant has been reading the IASB's *Conceptual Framework for Financial Reporting* and as part of the qualitative characteristics of financial statements under the heading of 'relevance' he notes that the predictive value of information is considered important. He is aware that financial statements are prepared historically (i.e. after transactions have occurred) and offers the view that the predictive value of financial statements would be enhanced if forward-looking information (e.g. forecasts) were published rather than backward-looking historical statements.

Required:
By the use of specific examples, provide an explanation to your assistant of how IFRS presentation and disclosure requirements can assist the predictive role of historically prepared financial statements.

(6 marks)

(b)   The following summarised information is available in relation to Rebound, a publicly listed company:

Statement of profit or loss extracts years ended 31 March:

	20X2		20X1	
	Continuing	Discontinued	Continuing	Discontinued
	$'000	$'000	$'000	$'000
Profit after tax				
Existing operations	2,000	(750)	1,750	600
Operations acquired on 1 August 20X1	450		nil	

Analysts expect profits from the market sector in which Rebound's existing operations are based to increase by 6% in the year to 31 March 20X3 and by 8% in the sector of its newly acquired operations.

On 1 April 20X0 Rebound had in issue:
$3 million of 25 cents equity shares.
$5 million 8% convertible loan stock 20X7; the terms of conversion are 40 equity shares in exchange for each $100 of loan stock. Assume an income tax rate of 30%.

On 1 October 20X1 the directors of Rebound were granted options to buy 2 million shares in the company for $1 each. The average market price of Rebound's shares for the year ending 31 March 20X2 was $2.50 each.

Required :
(i)   Calculate Rebound's estimated profit after tax for the year ending 31 March 20X3 assuming the analysts' expectations prove correct;   **(3 marks)**
(ii)   Calculate the diluted earnings per share (EPS) on the continuing operations of Rebound for the year ended 31 March 20X2 and the comparatives for 20X1.   **(6 marks)**

(Total = 15 marks)

66 Victular (12/08)   45 mins

Victular is a public company that would like to acquire (100% of) a suitable private company. It has obtained the following draft financial statements for two companies, Grappa and Merlot. They operate in the same industry and their managements have indicated that they would be receptive to a takeover.

BPP
LEARNING MEDIA

STATEMENTS OF PROFIT OR LOSS FOR THE YEAR ENDED 30 SEPTEMBER 20X8

	Grappa $'000	Merlot $'000
Revenue	12,000	20,500
Cost of sales	(10,500)	(18,000)
Gross profit	1,500	2,500
Operating expenses	(240)	(500)
Finance costs – loan	(210)	(300)
– overdraft	nil	(10)
– lease	nil	(290)
Profit before tax	1,050	1,400
Income tax expense	(150)	(400)
Profit for the year	900	1,000
Note: dividends paid during the year	250	700

STATEMENTS OF FINANCIAL POSITION AS AT 30 SEPTEMBER 20X8

	Grappa $'000	Grappa $'000	$'000	Merlot $'000
Non-current assets				
Freehold factory (note (i))		4,400		nil
Owned plant (note (ii))		5,000		2,200
Leased plant (note (ii))		nil		5,300
		9,400		7,500
Current assets				
Inventory	2,000		3,600	
Trade receivables	2,400		3,700	
Bank	600		nil	
		5,000		7,300
Total assets		14,400		14,800
Equity and liabilities				
Equity shares of $1 each	2,000		2,000	
Property revaluation reserve	900		nil	
Retained earnings	2,600		800	
		5,500		2,800
Non-current liabilities				
Finance lease obligations (note (iii))	nil		3,200	
7% loan notes	3,000		nil	
10% loan notes	nil		3,000	
Deferred tax	600		100	
Government grants	1,200		nil	
		4,800		6,300
Current liabilities				
Bank overdraft	nil		1,200	
Trade payables	3,100		3,800	
Government grants	400		nil	
Finance lease obligations (note (iii))	nil		500	
Taxation	600		200	
		4,100		5,700
Total equity and liabilities		14,400		14,800

Notes

(i)   Both companies operate from similar premises.

(ii)   Additional details of the two companies' plant are:

	Grappa	Merlot
	$'000	$'000
Owned plant – cost	8,000	10,000
Leased plant – original fair value	nil	7,500

There were no disposals of plant during the year by either company.

(iii)   The interest rate implicit within Merlot's finance leases is 7·5% per annum. For the purpose of calculating ROCE and gearing, all finance lease obligations are treated as long-term interest bearing borrowings.

(iv)   The following ratios have been calculated for Grappa and can be taken to be correct:

Return on year end capital employed (ROCE)	14.8%
(capital employed taken as shareholders' funds plus long-term interest bearing borrowings – see note (iii) above)	
Pre-tax return on equity (ROE)	19.1%
Net asset (total assets less current liabilities) turnover	1.2 times
Gross profit margin	12.5%
Operating profit margin	10.5%
Current ratio	1.2:1
Closing inventory holding period	70 days
Trade receivables' collection period	73 days
Trade payables' payment period (using cost of sales)	108 days
Gearing (see note (iii) above)	35.3%
Interest cover	6 times
Dividend cover	3.6 times

Required

(a)   Calculate for Merlot the ratios equivalent to all those given for Grappa above.   **(8 marks)**

(b)   Assess the relative performance and financial position of Grappa and Merlot for the year ended 30 September 20X8 to inform the directors of Victular in their acquisition decision.   **(12 marks)**

(c)   Explain the limitations of ratio analysis and any further information that may be useful to the directors of Victular when making an acquisition decision.   **(5 marks)**

(Total = 25 marks)

67 Crosswire (12/09)

(a) The following information relates to Crosswire a publicly listed company.

Summarised statements of financial position as at:

	30 September 20X9		30 September 20X8	
	$'000	$'000	$'000	$'000
Assets				
Non-current assets				
Property, plant and equipment (note (i))		32,500		13,100
Development costs (note (ii))		1,000		2,500
		33,500		15,600
Current assets		8,200		6,800
Total assets		41,700		22,400
Equity and liabilities				
Equity				
Equity shares of $1 each		5,000		4,000
Share premium	6,000		2,000	
Other equity reserve	500		500	
Revaluation surplus	2,000		nil	
Retained earnings	5,700		3,200	
		14,200		5,700
		19,200		9,700
Non-current liabilities				
10% convertible loan notes (note (iii))	1,000		5,000	
Environmental provision	3,300		nil	
Finance lease obligations	5,040		nil	
Deferred tax	3,360		1,200	
		12,700		6,200
Current liabilities				
Finance lease obligations	1,760		nil	
Trade payables	8,040		6,500	
		9,800		6,500
Total equity and liabilities		41,700		22,400

Information from the statements of profit or loss for the year ended:

	30 September 20X9	30 September 20X8
	$'000	$'000
Revenue	52,000	42,000
Finance costs (note (iv))	1,050	500
Income tax expense	1,000	800
Profit for the year (after tax)	4,000	3,000

The following information is available:

(i) During the year to 30 September 20X9, Crosswire embarked on a replacement and expansion programme for its non-current assets. The details of this programme are:

On 1 October 20X8 Crosswire acquired a platinum mine at a cost of $5 million. A condition of mining the platinum is a requirement to landscape the mining site at the end of its estimated life of ten years. The present value of this cost at the date of the purchase was calculated at $3 million (in addition to the purchase price of the mine of $5 million).

Also on 1 October 20X8 Crosswire revalued its freehold land for the first time. The credit in the revaluation surplus is the net amount of the revaluation after a transfer to deferred tax on the gain. The tax rate applicable to Crosswire for deferred tax is 20% per annum.

On 1 April 20X9 Crosswire took out a finance lease for some new plant. The fair value of the plant was $10 million. The lease agreement provided for an initial payment on 1 April 20X9 of $2.4 million followed by eight six-monthly payments of $1.2 million commencing 30 September 20X9.

Plant disposed of during the year had a carrying amount of $500,000 and was sold for $1.2 million. The remaining movement on the property, plant and equipment, after charging depreciation of $3 million, was the cost of replacing plant.

(ii) From 1 October 20X8 to 31 March 20X9 a further $500,000 was spent completing the development project at which date marketing and production started. The sales of the new product proved disappointing and on 30 September 20X9 the development costs were written down to $1 million via an impairment charge.

(iii) During the year ended 30 September 20X9, $4 million of the 10% convertible loan notes matured. The loan note holders had the option of redemption at par in cash or to exchange them for equity shares on the basis of 20 new shares for each $100 of loan notes. 75% of the loan-note holders chose the equity option. Ignore any effect of this on the other equity reserve.

All the above items have been treated correctly according to International Financial Reporting Standards.

(iv) The finance costs are made up of:

For year ended:	30 September 20X9	30 September 20X8
	$'000	$'000
Finance lease charges	400	Nil
Unwinding of environmental provision	300	Nil
Loan-note interest	350	500
	1,050	500

Required

(i) Prepare a statement of the movements in the carrying amount of Crosswire's non-current assets for the year ended 30 September 20X9; **(9 marks)**

(ii) Calculate the amounts that would appear under the headings of 'cash flows from investing activities' and 'cash flows from financing activities' in the statement of cash flows for Crosswire for the year ended 30 September 20X9.

Note: Crosswire includes finance costs paid as a financing activity. **(8 marks)**

(b) A substantial shareholder has written to the directors of Crosswire expressing particular concern over the deterioration of the company's return on capital employed (ROCE).

Required

Calculate Crosswire's ROCE for the two years ended 30 September 20X8 and 20X9 and comment on the apparent cause of its deterioration.

Note: ROCE should be taken as profit before interest on long-term borrowings and tax as a percentage of equity plus loan notes and finance lease obligations (at the year end). **(8 marks)**

(Total = 25 marks)

68 Bengal (6/11) 45 mins

Bengal is a public company. Its most recent financial statements are shown below:

STATEMENTS OF PROFIT OR LOSS FOR THE YEAR ENDED 31 MARCH

	20X1	20X0
	$'000	$'000
Revenue	25,500	17,250
Cost of sales	(14,800)	(10,350)
Gross profit	10,700	6,900
Distribution costs	(2,700)	(1,850)
Administrative expenses	(2,100)	(1,450)
Finance costs	(650)	(100)
Profit before taxation	5,250	3,500
Income tax expense	(2,250)	(1,000)
Profit for the year	3,000	2,500

BPP LEARNING MEDIA

STATEMENTS OF FINANCIAL POSITION AS AT 31 MARCH

	20X1	20X1	20X0	20X0
	$'000	$'000	$'000	$'000
Non-current assets				
Property, plant and equipment		9,500		5,400
Intangibles		6,200		nil
		15,700		5,400
Current assets				
Inventory	3,600		1,800	
Trade receivables	2,400		1,400	
Bank	nil		4,000	
Non-current assets held for sale	2,000	8,000	nil	7,200
Total assets		23,700		12,600
Equity and liabilities				
Equity				
Equity shares of $1 each		5,000		5,000
Retained earnings		4,500		2,250
		9,500		7,250
Non-current liabilities				
5% loan notes		2,000		2,000
8% loan notes		7,000		nil
Current liabilities				
Bank overdraft	200		nil	
Trade payables	2,800		2,150	
Current tax payable	2,200	5,200	1,200	3,350
Total equity and liabilities		23,700		12,600

Notes:

(i) There were no disposals of non-current assets during the period; however Bengal does have some non-current assets classified as 'held for sale' at 31 March 20X1.

(ii) Depreciation of property, plant and equipment for the year ended 31 March 20X1 was $640,000.

A disappointed shareholder has observed that although revenue during the year has increased by 48% (8,250/17,250 x 100), profit for the year has only increased by 20% (500/2,500 x 100).

Required

(a) Prepare a statement of cash flows for Bengal for the year ended 31 March 20X1, in accordance with IAS 7 *Statement of cash flows*, using the indirect method. **(9 marks)**

(b) Using the information in the question and your answer to (a) above, comment on the performance (including addressing the shareholder's observation) and financial position of Bengal for the year ended 31 March 20X1.

Note: up to 5 marks are available for the calculation of appropriate ratios. **(16 marks)**

(Total = 25 marks)

69 Tangier (6/12)   45 mins

(a) Tangier is a public listed company. Its summarised financial statements for the years ended 31 March 20X2 and the comparative figures are shown below.

STATEMENTS OF COMPREHENSIVE INCOME FOR THE YEAR ENDED 31 MARCH:

	20X2	20X1
	$m	$m
Revenue	2,700	1,820
Cost of sales	(1,890)	(1,092)
Gross profit	810	728
Distribution costs	(230)	(130)
Administrative expenses	(345)	(200)
Finance costs	(40)	(5)
Profit before tax	195	393
Income tax expense	(60)	(113)
Profit for the year	135	280
Other comprehensive income	80	-
Total comprehensive income	215	280

STATEMENTS OF FINANCIAL POSITION AS AT 31 MARCH:

	20X2	20X1
	$m	$m
Assets		
Non-current assets		
Property, plant and equipment	680	410
Intangible asset: manufacturing licence	300	200
Investment at cost: shares in Raremetal	230	-
	1,210	610
Current assets		
Inventory	200	110
Trade receivables	195	75
Bank	-	120
Total assets	1,605	915
Equity and liabilities		
Equity		
Equity shares of $1 each	350	250
Revaluation surplus	80	-
Retained earnings	375	295
	805	545
Non-current liabilities		
5% loan notes	100	100
10% secured loan notes	300	-
Current liabilities		
Bank overdraft	110	-
Trade payables	210	160
Current tax payable	80	110
Total equity and liabilities	1,605	915

The following information is relevant:

Depreciation/amortisation charges for the year ended 31 March 20X2 were:

	$m
Property, plant and equipment	115
Intangible asset: manufacturing licence	25

BPP
LEARNING MEDIA

There were no sales of non-current assets during the year, although property has been revalued.

Required:

Prepare the statement of cash flows for the year ended 31 March 20X2 for Tangier in accordance with the indirect method in accordance with IAS 7 *Statement of cash flows*. **(11 marks)**

(b) The following additional information has been obtained in relation to the operations of Tangier for the year ended 31 March 20X2:

(i) On 1 June 20X1, Tangier won a tender for a new contract to supply Jetside with aircraft engines that Tangier manufactures under a recently-acquired licence. The bidding process was very competitive and Tangier had to increase its manufacturing capacity to fulfil the contract.

(ii) Tangier also decided to invest in Raremetal by acquiring 8% of its equity shares in order to secure supplies of specialised materials used in the manufacture of the engines. No dividends were received from Raremetal nor had the value of its shares changed since acquisition.

(iii) Tangier revalued its property during the year to facilitate the issue of the 10% loan notes.

On seeing the results for the first time, one of the company's non-executive directors is disappointed by the current year's performance.

Required:

Explain how the new contract and its related costs may have affected Tangier's operating performance, identifying any further information that may be useful to your answer.

Your answer may be supported by appropriate ratios (up to 4 marks available), but ratios and analysis of working capital are not required. **(14 marks)**

(Total = 25 marks)

70 Waxwork (6/09)   27 mins

(a)   The objective of IAS 10 *Events After the Reporting Period* is to prescribe the treatment of events that occur after an entity's reporting period has ended.

Required

Define the period to which IAS 10 relates and distinguish between adjusting and non-adjusting events.

(5 marks)

(b)   Waxwork's current year end is 31 March 20X9. Its financial statements were authorised for issue by its directors on 6 May 20X9 and the AGM (annual general meeting) will be held on 3 June 20X9. The following matters have been brought to your attention:

(i)   On 12 April 20X9 a fire completely destroyed the company's largest warehouse and the inventory it contained. The carrying amounts of the warehouse and the inventory were $10 million and $6 million respectively. It appears that the company has not updated the value of its insurance cover and only expects to be able to recover a maximum of $9 million from its insurers. Waxwork's trading operations have been severely disrupted since the fire and it expects large trading losses for some time to come. **(4 marks)**

(ii)   A single class of inventory held at another warehouse was valued at its cost of $460,000 at 31 March 20X9. In April 20X9 70% of this inventory was sold for $280,000 on which Waxworks' sales staff earned a commission of 15% of the selling price. **(3 marks)**

(iii)   On 18 May 20X9 the government announced tax changes which have the effect of increasing Waxwork's deferred tax liability by $650,000 as at 31 March 20X9. **(3 marks)**

Required

Explain the required treatment of the items (i) to (iii) by Waxwork in its financial statements for the year ended 31 March 20X9.

Note: assume all items are material and are independent of each other. **(10 marks as indicated)**

(Total =15 marks)

71 Hardy (12/10)   45 mins

Hardy is a public listed manufacturing company. Its summarised financial statements for the year ended 30 September 20X1 (and 20X0 comparatives) are:

STATEMENTS OF PROFIT OR LOSS FOR THE YEAR ENDED 30 SEPTEMBER:

	20X1	20X0
	$'000	$'000
Revenue	29,500	36,000
Cost of sales	(25,500)	(26,000)
Gross profit	4,000	10,000
Distribution costs	(1,050)	(800)
Administrative expenses	(4,900)	(3,900)
Investment income	50	200
Finance costs	(600)	(500)
Profit (loss) before taxation	(2,500)	5,000
Income tax (expense) relief	400	(1,500)
Profit (loss) for the year	(2,100)	3,500

STATEMENTS OF FINANCIAL POSITION AS AT 30 SEPTEMBER:

	20X1		20X0	
	$'000	$'000	$'000	$'000
Assets				
Non-current assets				
Property, plant and equipment		17,600		24,500
Investments at fair value through profit or loss		2,400		4,000
		20,000		28,500
Current assets				
Inventory and work-in-progress	2,200		1,900	
Trade receivables	2,200		2,800	
Tax asset	600		nil	
Bank	1,200	6,200	100	4,800
Total assets		26,200		33,300
Equity and liabilities				
Equity				
Equity shares of $1 each		13,000		12,000
Share premium		1,000		nil
Revaluation reserve		nil		4,500
Retained earnings		3,600		6,500
		17,600		23,000
Non-current liabilities				
Bank loan		4,000		5,000
Deferred tax		1,200		700
Current liabilities				
Trade payables	3,400		2,800	
Current tax payable	nil	3,400	1,800	4,600
Total equity and liabilities		26,200		33,300

The following information has been obtained from the Chairman's Statement and the notes to the financial statements:

'Market conditions during the year ended 30 September 20X1 proved very challenging due largely to difficulties in the global economy as a result of a sharp recession which has led to steep falls in share prices and property values. Hardy has not been immune from these effects and our properties have suffered impairment losses of $6 million in

BPP LEARNING MEDIA

the year. The excess of these losses over previous surpluses has led to a charge to cost of sales of $1.5 million in addition to the normal depreciation charge.

'Our portfolio of investments at fair value through profit or loss has been 'marked to market' (fair valued) resulting in a loss of $1.6 million (included in administrative expenses).'

There were no additions to or disposals of non-current assets during the year.

'In response to the downturn the company has unfortunately had to make a number of employees redundant incurring severance costs of $1.3 million (included in cost of sales) and undertaken cost savings in advertising and other administrative expenses.'

'The difficulty in the credit markets has meant that the finance cost of our variable rate bank loan has increased from 4.5% to 8%. In order to help cash flows, the company made a rights issue during the year and reduced the dividend per share by 50%.'

'Despite the above events and associated costs, the Board believes the company's underlying performance has been quite resilient in these difficult times.'

Required

Analyse and discuss the financial performance and position of Hardy as portrayed by the above financial statements and the additional information provided.

Your analysis should be supported by profitability, liquidity and gearing and other appropriate ratios (up to 10 marks available). **(25 marks)**

72 Preparation question: Dickson

Below are the statements of financial position of Dickson as at 31 March 20X8 and 31 March 20X7, together with the statement of profit or loss and other comprehensive income for the year ended 31 March 20X8.

	20X8 $'000	20X7 $'000
Non-current assets		
Property, plant and equipment	825	637
Goodwill	100	100
Development expenditure	290	160
	1,215	897
Current assets		
Inventories	360	227
Trade receivables	274	324
Investments	143	46
Cash	29	117
	806	714
	2,021	1,611

	20X8	20X7
Equity		
Share capital – $1 ordinary shares	500	400
Share premium	350	100
Revaluation surplus	152	60
Retained earnings	237	255
	1,239	815
Non-current liabilities		
6% debentures	150	100
Finance lease liabilities	100	80
Deferred tax	48	45
	298	225
Current liabilities		
Trade payables	274	352
Finance lease liabilities	17	12
Current tax	56	153
Debenture interest	5	–
Bank overdraft	132	54
	484	571
	2,021	1,611

STATEMENT OF PROFIT OR LOSS AND OTHER COMPREHENSIVE INCOME

	$'000
Revenue	1,476
Cost of sales	(962)
Gross profit	514
Other expenses	(157)
Finance costs	(15)
Profit before tax	342
Income tax expense	(162)
Profit for the year	180
Other comprehensive income:	
Gain on revaluation of property, plant and equipment	100
Total comprehensive income for the year	280

Notes

(1) Goodwill arose on the acquisition of unincorporated businesses. During 20X8 expenditure on development projects totalled $190,000.

(2) During 20X8 items of property, plant and equipment with a net book value of $103,000 were sold for $110,000. Depreciation charged in the year on property, plant and equipment totalled $57,000. Dickson transfers extra depreciation on revalued property, plant and equipment to retained earnings as allowed by IAS 16. Depreciation based on historical cost in 20X8 is $49,000. Dickson purchased $56,000 of property, plant and equipment by means of finance leases, payments being made in arrears on the last day of each accounting period.

(3) The current asset investments are government bonds and management has decided to class them as cash equivalents.

(4) The new debentures were issued on 1.4.X7. Finance cost includes debenture interest and finance lease finance charges only.

(5) During the year Dickson made a 1 for 8 bonus issue capitalising its retained earnings followed by a rights issue.

(6) Dividends totalling $156,000 were paid during the year.

Required

Using the pro-forma below:

(a) Prepare a statement of cash flows for Dickson in accordance with IAS 7 using the indirect method.

BPP
LEARNING MEDIA

(b) Prepare (additionally) net cash from operating activities using the direct method.

(a) DICKSON
STATEMENT OF CASH FLOWS FOR THE YEAR ENDED 31 MARCH 20X8

	$'000	$'000
Cash flows from operating activities		
Profit before taxation		
Adjustments for:		
Depreciation		
Amortisation		
Interest expense		
Profit on disposal of assets	_____	
Movement in trade receivables		
Movement in inventories		
Movement in trade payables	_____	
Cash generated from operations		
Interest paid		
Income taxes paid	_____	
Net cash from operating activities		
Cash flows from investing activities		
Development expenditure		
Purchase of property, plant & equipment		
Proceeds from sale of property, plant & equipment	_____	
Net cash used in investing activities		
Cash flows from financing activities		
Proceeds from issue of shares		
Proceeds from issue of debentures		
Payment of finance lease liabilities		
Dividends paid	_____	
Net cash from financing activities		_____
Net decrease in cash and cash equivalents		
Cash and cash equivalents at beginning of period		_____
Cash and cash equivalents at end of period		_____

Workings

(b)   CASH FLOWS FROM OPERATING ACTIVITIES (Direct method)

	$'000
Cash received from customers	
Cash paid to suppliers and employees	_____
Cash generated from operations	
Interest paid	
Income taxes paid	
Net cash from operating activities	======

Workings

BPP
LEARNING MEDIA

73 Pinto (6/08)

45 mins

Pinto is a publicly listed company. The following financial statements of Pinto are available:

STATEMENT OF PROFIT OR LOSS AND OTHER COMPREHENSIVE INCOME FOR YEAR ENDED 31 MARCH 20X8

	$'000
Revenue	5,740
Cost of sales	(4,840)
Gross profit	900
Income from and gains on investment property	60
Distribution costs	(120)
Administrative expenses (note (ii))	(350)
Finance costs	(50)
Profit before tax	440
Income tax expense	(160)
Profit for the year	280
Other comprehensive income	
Gains on property revaluation	100
Total comprehensive income	380

STATEMENTS OF FINANCIAL POSITION AS AT

	31 March 20X8		31 March 20X7	
	$'000	$'000	$'000	$'000
Assets				
Non-current assets (note (i))				
Property, plant and equipment		2,880		1,860
Investment property		420		400
		3,300		2,260
Current assets				
Inventory	1,210		810	
Trade receivables	480		540	
Income tax asset	nil		50	
Bank	10	1,700	nil	1,400
Total assets		5,000		3,660

Equity and liabilities

Equity shares of 20 cents each (note (iii))		1,000		600
Share premium	600		nil	
Revaluation reserve	150		50	
Retained earnings	1,440	2,190	1,310	1,360
		3,190		1,960
Non-current liabilities				
6% loan notes (note (ii))	nil		400	
Deferred tax	50	50	30	430
Current liabilities				
Trade payables	1,410		1,050	
Bank overdraft	nil		120	
Warranty provision (note (iv))	200		100	
Current tax payable	150	1,760	nil	1,270
Total equity and liabilities		5,000		3,660

The following supporting information is available:

(i)   An item of plant with a carrying amount of $240,000 was sold at a loss of $90,000 during the year. Depreciation of $280,000 was charged (to cost of sales) for property, plant and equipment in the year ended 31 March 20X8.

Pinto uses the fair value model in IAS 40 *Investment Property*. There were no purchases or sales of investment property during the year.

(ii)   The 6% loan notes were redeemed early incurring a penalty payment of $20,000 which has been charged as an administrative expense in the statement of profit or loss.

(iii)   There was an issue of shares for cash on 1 October 20X7. There were no bonus issues of shares during the year.

(iv)   Pinto gives a 12 month warranty on some of the products it sells. The amounts shown in current liabilities as warranty provision are an accurate assessment, based on past experience, of the amount of claims likely to be made in respect of warranties outstanding at each year end. Warranty costs are included in cost of sales.

(v)   A dividend of 3 cents per share was paid on 1 January 20X8.

Required

(a)   Prepare a statement of cash flows for Pinto for the year to 31 March 20X8 in accordance with IAS 7 *Statement of cash flows*.   **(15 marks)**

(b)   Comment on the cash flow management of Pinto as revealed by the statement of cash flows and the information provided by the above financial statements.

Note: ratio analysis is not required, and will not be awarded any marks.   **(10 marks)**

(Total = 25 marks)

74 Deltoid (6/10)   45 mins

(a)   The following information relates to the draft financial statements of Deltoid.

SUMMARISED STATEMENTS OF FINANCIAL POSITION AS AT:

	31 March 20X1		31 March 20X0	
	$'000	$'000	$'000	$'000
Assets				
Non-current assets				
Property, plant and equipment (note (i))		19,000		25,500
Current assets				
Inventory		12,500		4,600
Trade receivables		4,500		2,000
Tax refund due		500		nil
Bank		nil		1,500
Total assets		36,500		33,600

BPP
LEARNING MEDIA

Equity and liabilities		$'000		$'000
Equity				
Equity shares of $1 each (note (ii))		10,000		8,000
Share premium (note (ii))	3,200		4,000	
Retained earnings	4,500	7,700	6,300	10,300
		17,700		18,300
Non-current liabilities				
10% loan note (note (iii))	nil		5,000	
Finance lease obligations	4,800		2,000	
Deferred tax	1,200	6,000	800	7,800
Current liabilities				
10% loan note (note (iii))	5,000		nil	
Tax	nil		2,500	
Bank overdraft	1,400		nil	
Finance lease obligations	1,700		800	
Trade payables	4,700	12,800	4,200	7,500
Total equity and liabilities		36,500		33,600

SUMMARISED STATEMENTS OF PROFIT OR LOSS FOR THE YEARS ENDED:

	31 March 20X1	31 March 20X0
	$'000	$'000
Revenue	55,000	40,000
Cost of sales	(43,800)	(25,000)
Gross profit	11,200	15,000
Operating expenses	(12,000)	(6,000)
Finance costs (note (iv))	(1,000)	(600)
Profit (loss) before tax	(1,800)	8,400
Income tax relief (expense)	700	(2,800)
Profit (loss) for the year	(1,100)	5,600

The following additional information is available:

(i)   Property, plant and equipment is made up of:

As at:	31 March 20X1	31 March 20X0
	$'000	$'000
Leasehold property	nil	8,800
Owned plant	12,500	14,200
Leased plant	6,500	2,500
	19,000	25,500

During the year Deltoid sold its leasehold property for $8.5 million and entered into an arrangement to rent it back from the purchaser. There were no additions to or disposals of owned plant during the year. The depreciation charges (to cost of sales) for the year ended 31 March 20X1 were:

	$'000
Leasehold property	200
Owned plant	1,700
Leased plant	1,800
	3,700

(ii)   On 1 July 20X0 there was a bonus issue of shares from share premium of one new share for every 10 held. On 1 October 20X0 there was a fully subscribed cash issue of shares at par.

(iii)   The 10% loan note is due for repayment on 30 June 20X1. Deltoid is in negotiations with the loan provider to refinance the same amount for another five years.

The finance costs are made up of:
For year ended:

	31 March 20X1 $'000	31 March 20X0 $'000
Finance lease charges	300	100
Overdraft interest	200	nil
Loan note interest	500	500
	1,000	600

Required

(i) Prepare a statement of cash flows for Deltoid for the year ended 31 March 20X1 in accordance with IAS 7 Statement of cash flows, using the indirect method; **(12 marks)**

(ii) Based on the information available, advise the loan provider on the matters you would take into consideration when deciding whether to grant Deltoid a renewal of its maturing loan note. **(8 marks)**

(b) On a separate matter, you have been asked to advise on an application for a loan to build an extension to a sports club which is a not-for-profit organisation. You have been provided with the audited financial statements of the sports club for the last four years.

Required

Identify and explain the ratios that you would calculate to assist in determining whether you would advise that the loan should be granted. **(5 marks)**
(Total = 25 marks)

75 Mocha (12/11)   45 mins

(a) The following information relates to the draft financial statements of Mocha.

SUMMARISED STATEMENTS OF FINANCIAL POSITION AS AT 30 SEPTEMBER:

	20X1 $'000	20X0 $'000
Assets		
Non-current assets		
Property, plant and equipment (note (i))	32,600	24,100
Financial asset: equity investments (note (ii))	4,500	7,000
	37,100	31,100
Current assets		
Inventory	10,200	7,200
Trade receivables	3,500	3,700
Bank	nil	1,400
	13,700	12,300
Total assets	50,800	43,400

	20X1	20X0
Equity		
Equity shares of $1 each (note (iii))	14,000	8,000
Share premium (note (iii))	nil	2,000
Revaluation reserve (note (iii))	2,000	3,600
Retained earnings	13,000	10,100
	29,000	23,700
Non-current liabilities		
Finance lease obligations	7,000	6,900
Deferred tax	1,300	900
Current liabilities		
Tax	1,000	1,200
Bank overdraft	2,900	nil
Provision for product warranties (note (iv))	1,600	4,000
Finance lease obligations	4,800	2,100
Trade payables	3,200	4,600
Total equity and liabilities	50,800	43,400

SUMMARISED INCOME STATEMENTS FOR THE YEARS ENDED 30 SEPTEMBER:

	20X1	20X0
	$'000	$'000
Revenue	58,500	41,000
Cost of sales	(46,500)	(30,000)
Gross profit	12,000	11,000
Operating expenses	(8,700)	(4,500)
Investment income (note (ii))	1,100	700
Finance costs	(500)	(400)
Profit before tax	3,900	6,800
Income tax expense	(1,000)	(1,800)
Profit for the year	2,900	5,000

The following additional information is available:

(i) Property, plant and equipment:

	Cost	Accumulated depreciation	Carrying amount
	$'000	$'000	$'000
At 30 September 20X0	33,600	(9,500)	24,100
New finance lease additions	6,700		6,700
Purchase of new plant	8,300		8,300
Disposal of property	(5,000)	1,000	(4,000)
Depreciation for the year		(2,500)	(2,500)
At 30 September 20X1	43,600	(11,000)	32,600

The property disposed of was sold for $8.1 million.

(ii) Investments/investment income:

During the year an investment that had a carrying amount of $3 million was sold for $3.4 million. No investments were purchased during the year.

Investment income consists of:

Year to 30 September:	20X1	20X0
	$'000	$'000
Dividends received	200	250
Profit on sale of investment	400	nil
Increases in fair value	500	450
	1,100	700

BPP LEARNING MEDIA

(iii) On 1 April 20X1 there was a bonus issue of shares that was funded from the share premium and some of the revaluation reserve. This was followed on 30 April 20X1 by an issue of shares for cash at par.

(iv) The movement in the product warranty provision has been included in cost of sales.

Required

Prepare a statement of cash flows for Mocha for the year ended 30 September 20X1, in accordance with IAS 7 *Statement of cash flows*, using the indirect method. **(19 marks)**

(b) Shareholders can often be confused when trying to evaluate the information provided to them by a company's financial statements, particularly when comparing accruals-based information in the income statement and the statement of financial position with that in the statement of cash flows.

Required

In the two areas stated below, illustrate, by reference to the information in the question and your answer to (a), how information in a statement of cash flows may give a different perspective of events than that given by accruals-based financial statements:

(i) operating performance; and **(3 marks)**

(ii) investment in property, plant and equipment. **(3 marks)**

(Total = 25 marks)

76 Preparation question: Changing prices

The following information has been extracted from the accounts of Norwich prepared under the historical cost convention for 20X6.

STATEMENT OF PROFIT OR LOSS EXTRACTS 20X6

	$m
Revenue	200
Profit	15
Less finance costs	3
Profit for the year	12

SUMMARISED STATEMENT OF FINANCIAL POSITION AT 31 DECEMBER 20X6

Assets	$m	$m
Property, plant & equipment at cost less depreciation		60
Current assets		
Inventories	20	
Receivables	30	
Bank	2	
		52
Total assets		112
Equity and liabilities		
Equity		62
Non-current liabilities		20
Current liabilities		30
Total equity and liabilities		112

The company's accountant has prepared the following current cost data.

Current cost adjustments for 20X6	$m
Depreciation adjustment	3
Cost of sales adjustment	5
Replacement cost at 31 December 20X6	
Property, plant & equipment, net of depreciation	85
Inventories	21

Required

(a) Calculate the current cost operating profit of Norwich for 20X6 and the summarised current cost statement of financial position of the company at 31 December 20X6, so far as the information permits.

BPP LEARNING MEDIA

(b)   Calculate the following ratios from both the historical cost accounts and current cost accounts:

      (i)   Interest cover

      (ii)   Rate of return on shareholders' equity

      (iii)   Debt/equity ratio

(c)   Discuss the significance of the ratios calculated under (b) and of the reasons for differences between them.

Note. Ignore taxation.

Approaching the question

1   To save time in this question, the current cost adjustments are given to you. You should, of course, understand how they are calculated.

2   Part (b) is straightforward. Make sure you allow yourself time to give adequate weight to the discussion in part (c).

77 Update (2.5 6/03 part)   22 mins

Most companies prepare their financial statements under the historical cost convention. In times of rising prices it has been said that without modification such financial statements can be misleading.

Required

(a)   Explain the problems that can be encountered when users rely on financial statements prepared under the historical cost convention for their information needs.   **(6 marks)**

    Note. Your answer should consider problems with the statement of profit or loss and the statement of financial position.

(b)   Update has been considering the effect of alternative methods of preparing their financial statements. As an example they picked an item of plant that they acquired from Suppliers on 1 April 20X0 at a cost of $250,000.

    The following details have been obtained:

    –   the company policy is to depreciate plant at 20% per annum on the reducing balance basis.

    –   the movement in the retail price index has been:

1 April 20X0	180
1 April 20X1	202
1 April 20X2	206
31 March 20X3	216

    –   Suppliers' price catalogue at 31 March 20X3 shows an item of similar plant at a cost of $320,000. On reading the specification it appears that the new model can produce 480 units per hour whereas the model owned by Update can only produce 420 units per hour.

Required

Calculate for Update the depreciation charge for the plant for the year to 31 March 20X3 (based on year end values) and its carrying value in the statement of financial position on that date using:

    –   the historical cost basis;

    –   a current purchasing power basis; and

    –   a current cost basis.   **(6 marks)**

                                              (Total = 12 marks)

78 Appraisal (pilot paper part)   9 mins

Explain in what ways your approach to performance appraisal would differ if you were asked to assess the performance of a not-for-profit organisation.   **(5 marks)**

BPP
LEARNING MEDIA

Answers

BPP
LEARNING MEDIA

1 Porto

Text reference. Chapter 1.

Top tips. You should have had no trouble explaining the characteristics, but remember to state how they make financial information useful. Working out how the characteristics related to the scenarios took a bit more thought.

Easy marks. Part (a) was 9 easy marks.

Marking scheme

		Marks
(a)	3 marks each for relevance, faithful representation, comparability	9
(b)	2 marks for each transaction or event	4
	Total for question	13

(a) **Relevance**

The relevance of information must be considered in terms of the decision-making needs of users. It is relevant when it can influence their economic decisions or allow them to reassess past decisions and evaluations. Economic decisions often have a predictive quality – users may make financial decisions on the basis of what they expect to happen in the future. To some degree past performance gives information on expected future performance and this is enhanced by the provision of comparatives, so that users can see the direction in which the company is moving. The separate presentation of discontinued operations also shows how much profit or loss can be attributed to that part of the operation will be not be there in the future. This can also affect valuation of assets. One aspect of relevance is materiality. An item is material if its omission or misstatement could influence the economic decisions of users. Relevance would not be enhanced by the inclusion of immaterial items which may serve to obscure the important issues.

Faithful representation

Information can be considered to be a faithful representation when it is complete, neutral and free from bias. The statement of profit or loss must faithfully represent the results of the entity for the period in question and the statement of financial position must faithfully represent its financial position at the end of the period. Financial statements in which provision had not been made for known liabilities or in which asset values had not been correctly stated could not be considered reliable. This also brings in the issue of substance over form. Transactions should be represented in accordance with their economic substance, rather than their legal form. This principle governs the treatment of finance leases, sale and leaseback transactions and consignment inventory. If these types of transactions are not accounted for in accordance with their economic substance, then the financial statements are unreliable.

Comparability

Comparability operates in two ways. Users must be able to compare the financial statements of the entity with its own past performance and they must also be able to compare its results with those of other entities. This means that financial statements must be prepared on the same basis from one year to the next and that, where a change of accounting policy takes place, the results for the previous year must also be restated so that comparability is maintained. Comparability with other entities is made possible by use of appropriate accounting policies, disclosure of accounting policies and compliance with International Financial Reporting Standards. Revisions to standards have to a large degree eliminated alternative treatments, so this has greatly enhanced comparability.

(b)　(i)　The 'substance' of a finance lease is that the lessee has acquired an asset using a loan from the lessor. Porto should capitalise the asset and depreciate it over its useful life (which is the same as the lease term). A finance lease liability should be set up for the same amount. The liability will be reduced by the lease payments, less the notional finance charge on the loan, which will be charged to profit or loss. This presents the transaction in accordance with its substance.

(ii) This issue has to do with relevance. It could be said that the use of historical cost accounting does not adequately reflect the value of assets in this case. This can be remedied by revaluing the properties. If this is done, all properties in the category will have to be revalued. This will probably give rise to a higher depreciation charge, so it will not improve the operating loss in the statement of profit or loss, but the excess can be credited back to retained earnings in the statement of financial position.

2 Concepts

Marking scheme

		Marks
(a)	Explanations 1 mark each	5
(b)	Examples 2 marks each	10
	Total for question	15

(a) **Matching/accruals**
This dictates that the effects of transactions and other events are recognised in the financial statements in the period in which they occur, rather than in the period when cash is received or paid.

Going concern
This is the assumption that the entity has neither the intention nor the necessity to liquidate or curtail major operations. If this assumption did not apply, the financial statements would be prepared on a different basis.

Verifiability
This means that different, knowledgeable and independent observers could agree that a particular depiction of a transaction in the financial statements is a faithful representation.

Comparability
This requires consistent application of accounting policies and adequate disclosure in order that a) the financial statements of an entity can be compared with its financial statements for previous accounting periods and b) the financial statements of an entity can be compared with the financial statements of other entities.

Materiality
An item of information is material if omitting it or misstating it could influence the decisions that users make on the basis of the financial statements. An item can be material on account of its nature or on account of its magnitude.

(b) **Application to inventory**
Matching/accruals
Inventory is charged to profit or loss in the period in which it is used, not the period in which it is received or paid for. This is done by adjusting cost of sales for opening and closing inventory.

Going concern
As long as the going concern assumption applies, inventory valued at lower of cost and NRV will in most cases be valued at cost. If the business is subject to a forced sale, the NRV of inventory is likely to be below cost.

Verifiability
The cost element of inventory is easy to verify as it will be recorded in invoices. The calculation of NRV must also be based on verified information. The annual inventory count provides verifiability on quantities.

Comparability
Inventory should be valued in financial statements using FIFO or weighted average and this should be consistently applied from one period to the next. If a change is made to the method of valuation, it must be disclosed, so that the current and prior periods can still be compared.

Materiality

Inventory is counted at the end of each reporting period and the valuation is based on this physical count, because inventory is generally regarded as a material item. However, it could be decided that a small discrepancy in the count would not be investigated because the amounts involved were too small to affect the decisions of users and so were not material.

3 Baxen

Text references. Chapters 1 and 2.

Top tips. This is a written question on the *Conceptual Framework* and the advantages of IFRS. In a question like this, make sure that you are answering the question that has been set and that you are addressing the actual situation of Baxen.

Easy marks. This question did not require a lot of technical knowledge. You were bound to know something about principles-based systems such as IFRS and you could work out what the advantages of IFRS would be. Marks here were for valid points. If you made enough valid points you could score full marks.

Examiner's comments In section (a) some candidates were unable to properly distinguish between rules-based and principles-based systems and seemed not to know whether IFRS is rules-based or principles-based. But there were many good answers to part (b), mentioning issues such as simplifying consolidations, raising finance and improving comparability.

Examiner's answer. The examiner's answer to this question is at the end of this Kit.

Marking scheme

	Marks
(a) 1 mark per valid point	4
(b) 1 mark per valid point	6
Total for question	10

(a) A rules-based system of regulation is very prescriptive and seeks to set out specific requirements to cover every eventuality. In one sense this makes things straightforward for preparers of financial statements because they can easily demonstrate that they have prepared information in accordance with the rules. However, because it seeks to regulate for specific situations, a rules-based system will continue to expand as more situations arise. This is why US GAAP has about 250 accounting standards and new ones continually being drafted.

A principles-based system tends to be much less prescriptive and emphasises instead compliance with a set of concepts or principles. IFRS is a principles-based system.

While individual IFRSs do contain rules and requirements, they do not seek to regulate every type of transaction. IFRS is based on the *Conceptual Framework* and IFRSs are drafted to be in accordance with the concepts set out in the *Conceptual Framework*. This does mean that more judgement has to be used in applying IFRSs.

(b) The question does not tell us where Baxen is based but, if it is in the EU, it will be required to prepare its consolidated financial statements in accordance with IFRS when it acquires a subsidiary. It would therefore make sense for it to move to IFRS in anticipation of that.

There are also a number of advantages:

The influence of IFRS around the world continues to grow. IFRS financial statements are now accepted for listings in the EU, Hong Kong and Singapore and more recently in Japan. They will very soon be accepted in the US. Adopting IFRS will enhance Baxen's reputation at home and abroad.

If Baxen prepares its financial statements in accordance with IFRS, its shares will be accepted for listing in London and Tokyo and very few amendments to accord with US GAAP will be required before its shares are accepted for listing in New York. This gives Baxen access to foreign investor capital.

Baxen will be better able to appraise the financial statements of potential foreign trading partners who report under IFRS.

If it acquires a subsidiary that reports under IFRS, the consolidation process will be much easier and Baxen's own accounting staff will be much better able to judge the performance of the subsidiary.

4 Regulatory framework

Text reference. Chapter 2.

Top tips. A basic knowledge of the structure and processes of the IFRS Foundation would probably be enough to earn a pass mark, but parts of this question require a bit of thought. To earn a pass mark break each question down into its components and write a few lines on each. For example, in part (b) most people will sketch out the standard setting process, but make sure you also include a sentence or two on enforcing and on supplementing standards.

Easy marks. Part (a) is very straightforward and will earn you a maximum of ten easy marks. In part (b), five easy marks can be picked up by remembering the standard setting process.

Examiner's comments. Most answers were weak and very short. Enforcement issues were mostly ignored.

Marking scheme

		Marks
(a)	1 mark per relevant point to a maximum	10
(b)	1 mark per relevant point to a maximum	10
(c)	1 mark per relevant point to a maximum	5
	Maximum for question	25

(a)   **Structure and function of IFRSF**

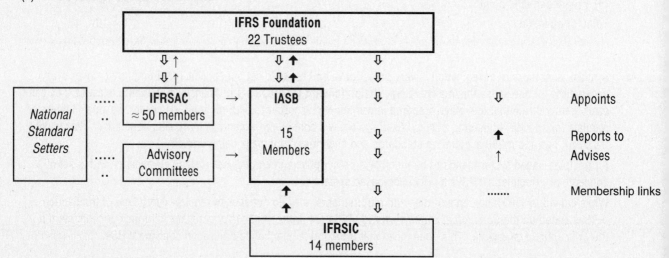

IFRSF (IFRS Foundation)

The Trustees of the IFRSF oversee the whole organisation. They arrange funding, appoint the IASB, IFRSIC and IFRSAC, and set the agenda for the IASB. The aims of the IFRSF are:

- to develop a single set of high quality global accounting standards,
- to promote the use of these standards, and
- to bring about convergence of national and international accounting standards.

IASB   International Accounting Standards Board

The IASB develops and issues International Financial Reporting Standards in its own right. It reports to the IFRSF. Members of the IASB are appointed for their technical competence and independence.

BPP
LEARNING MEDIA

IFRSIC (IFRS Interpretations Committee)

IFRSIC provides rapid guidance on accounting issues where divergent or unacceptable treatments are likely to arise. It reports to the IASB. Membership of IFRSIC is drawn from a diverse range of geographical and professional backgrounds.

IFRSAC (IFRS Advisory Council)

The IFRSAC provides a forum for organisations or individuals to take part in the standard setting process. It advises the IASB on agenda decisions, priorities, and its views on standard setting projects. Membership is drawn from a diverse range of geographical and professional backgrounds.

Advisory Committees

These are set up to advise the IASB on specific issues.

National Standard Setters

Although the IFRS Foundation is an independent organisation it works closely with national standard setters. The IASB, IFRSAC and advisory committees draw heavily on personnel from national bodies. In return, many national standard setters incorporate IFRS's into their own accounting standards.

(b) **Setting, enforcing and supplementing standards**

Setting standards

The IFRS Foundation sets the agenda for producing accounting standards, but the IASB produces and issues these standards. The process is as follows:

1   The IFRS Foundation, taking into account advice from the IFRSAC and others, identifies an issue requiring a financial reporting standard.

2   The IASB sets up an Advisory Committee to investigate the issue and report back to the IASB.

3   The IASB issues a Discussion Paper for public comment.

4   The IASB issues an Exposure Draft; comments must be received within ninety days.

5   The IASB issues an International Financial Reporting Standard on the internet. An IFRS must be approved by 8 of the 15 members of the IASB.

Public discussion is encouraged. The basis of conclusions for EDs and IFRSs are published, along with dissenting opinions. Most meetings of the IASB, IFRSIC and IFRSAC are open to the public, and they are exploring ways of using technology to make public access easier globally.

Enforcing standards

The IASB has no legal power to enforce adoption or compliance with standards, but enforcement of a sort is achieved (more or less successfully) in a number of ways:

- Quoted companies within the European Union must comply with IFRSs, but it is up to each member state to police compliance. Some countries have a formal process to review published financial statements and punish non-compliance (for example the Financial Reporting Review Panel in the UK), but this is not universal. To a certain extent the onus is on the auditors to police compliance, but auditing standards themselves are not globally consistent.

- Companies using IFRS to obtain cross-border listings are required to have their financial statements audited in accordance with International Auditing Standards. This will help to ensure that these companies are complying with IFRS.

- Many countries are bringing their own standards into line with IFRSs, but again policing of national standards is inconsistent.

Supplementing standards

The IFRSIC issues interpretations when divergent or unacceptable accounting treatments arise, whether through misinterpreting an existing standard or on an important issue not yet covered by a standard. Financial statements must comply with all of these interpretations if they claim to comply with International Financial Reporting Standards.

(c) **Has the move towards global accounting standards been successful?**

On a practical level the move towards global accounting standards has been one of the accounting successes of the last decade. The standards themselves have improved, with the elimination of contradictory alternatives and the creation of an open and independent standard setting organisation. This in turn has led to greater acceptance of these standards, culminating in 2005 with the adoption of IFRS for consolidated financial statements by all quoted companies in the European Union and in many other countries. The on-going project with the International Organisation of Securities Commissions will encourage the use of IFRS for cross-border listings, paving the way for acceptance of IFRS in the USA.

However, as mentioned earlier, there is no global system of enforcement, and so it is too early to say if IFRS are being adopted properly.

Some countries with their own highly developed accounting standards see the adoption of IFRS as a backward step, whereas other countries see IFRS as unnecessarily complicated.

There is also the assumption that the globalisation of accounting standards is a good thing. Recent developments in IFRS have focussed on quoted companies in the western world; they may not be suitable for all types and sizes of business organisation, or for all stages of economic development.

5 Preparation question: IFRS

(a) IFRS is not a rules-based system. It is a 'principles-based' system. International Financial Reporting Standards are formulated in accordance with the principles set out in the Conceptual Framework. For instance, the requirements for recognition of an asset or liability as stated in the Conceptual Framework must be complied with when a standard is being formulated.

This differs from a rules-based system where the regulation attempts to cover every eventuality. Obviously new eventualities will arise all the time, so regulation will be constantly expanding to cover them. In a system like this, accountants and auditors expect to be able to find specific rules to cover every situation, and to have rules specific to the industry with which they are involved.

IFRS only provides basic principles, so preparers of IFRS financial statements have to exercise judgement in dealing with transactions and in applying the principles to different industries. This puts more burden on preparers and some accountants and auditors in the US feel that it will afford them less protection from litigation.

(b) IFRS is currently mandatory for listed companies in the EU preparing consolidated financial statements, even if their individual company financial statements are prepared under local GAAP. Countries outside the EU which transition to IFRS may find that there are a number of advantages, and these advantages will increase as more countries adopt IFRS.

Multinational companies with subsidiaries which report under IFRS will have a set of group-wide accounting standards to follow. This will make group reporting easier and cheaper and make the accounting practices of their foreign subsidiaries more transparent, reducing the opportunities for fraud. They will also be able to transfer their accounting staff between group companies in different countries, without the need for them to deal with a new set of standards.

Companies can more easily compare their results with those of their competitors who report under IFRS. Similarly, investors can more easily compare the results of companies in different countries. Companies will be more able to appraise the position and results of foreign companies which are targets for takeovers or mergers and the accounting required to deal with takeovers and mergers will be less complex.

Cross-border listing will be more straightforward, making it easier for companies to raise capital abroad.

BPP
LEARNING MEDIA

6 Candel

Text references. Chapters 3 and 7

Top tips. There is quite a lot to do in this question, so it is important to tackle it in an organised manner. Get the formats down, put in any figures that do not require workings and then start the workings. Getting non-current assets done will enable you to fill in quite a few gaps.

Easy marks. The tricky parts of this question were the development costs and the legal provision. However, there were marks available in both the statement of profit or loss and other comprehensive income and the SFP for property, plant and equipment and even if your final figure for comprehensive income was incorrect, you could have obtained marks for presenting it correctly in the statement of changes in equity.

Examiner's comments. Most candidates were able to produce financial statements from a trial balance but some of the adjustments caused problems. Students had difficulties with:

- timing of the revaluation
- treatment of development costs
- reversal of the provision
- the deferred tax adjustment
- treatment of preference shares

Marking scheme

			Marks
(a)	*Statement of profit or loss and other comprehensive income:*		
	revenue	1	
	cost of sales	5	
	distribution costs	½	
	administrative expenses	1½	
	finance costs	1½	
	income tax	1½	
	other comprehensive income	1	12
(b)	*Statement of changes in equity:*		
	brought forward figures	1	
	dividends	1	
	comprehensive income	1	3
(c)	*Statement of financial position:*		
	property, plant and equipment	2	
	deferred development costs	2	
	inventory	½	
	trade receivables	½	
	deferred tax	1	
	preference shares	1	
	trade payables	1½	
	overdraft	½	
	current tax payable	1	10
Total for question			25

CANDEL
STATEMENT OF PROFIT OR LOSS AND OTHER COMPREHENSIVE INCOME FOR THE YEAR ENDED 30 SEPTEMBER 20X8

	$'000
Revenue (300,000 – 2,500 (plant disposal))	297,500
Cost of sales (W1)	(225,400)
Gross profit	72,100
Distribution costs	(14,500)
Administrative expenses (W1)	(21,900)
Finance costs (1,200 (W5) + 200)	(1,400)
Profit before tax	34,300
Income tax expense (W6)	(11,600)
Profit for the year	22,700
Other comprehensive income:	
Loss on property revaluation (W2)	(4,500)
Total comprehensive income for the year	18,200

CANDEL
STATEMENT OF CHANGES IN EQUITY FOR THE YEAR ENDED 30 SEPTEMBER 20X8

	Share capital $'000	Retained earnings $'000	Revaluation Surplus $'000	Total $'000
Balance at 1 October 20X7	50,000	24,500	10,000	84,500
Dividends paid	-	(6,000)	-	(6,000)
Total comprehensive income	-	22,700	(4,500)(W2)	18,200
Balance at 30 September 20X8	50,000	41,200	5,500	96,700

CANDEL
STATEMENT OF FINANCIAL POSITION AT 30 SEPTEMBER 20X8

	$'000	$'000
Assets		
Non-current assets		
Property, plant and equipment (W2)		81,400
Development expenditure (W3)		14,800
		96,200
Current assets		
Inventory	20,000	
Trade receivables	43,100	
		63,100
Total assets		159,300
Equity and liabilities		
Equity		
Share capital		50,000
Retained earnings		41,200
Revaluation surplus		5,500
		96,700
Non-current liabilities		
Redeemable preference shares (W5)		20,400
Deferred tax (5,800 + 200 (W6))		6,000
Current liabilities		
Trade payables	23,400	
Provision (W4)	100	
Tax payable	11,400	
Overdraft	1,300	
		36,200
Total equity and liabilities		159,300

BPP
LEARNING MEDIA

Workings

1   *Expenses*

	Cost of sales $'000	Distribution $'000	Admin $'000
Per question	204,000	14,500	22,200
Depreciation: Property	2,500	–	–
Plant and equipment	9,600	–	–
Loss on plant (4,000 – 2,500)	1,500	–	–
Research and development (W3)	3,800	–	–
Amortisation (W3)	4,000	–	–
Legal claim (W4)	–	–	(300)
	225,400	14,500	21,900

2   *Property, plant and equipment*

	Property $'000	P & E $'000	Total $'000
Cost/valuation b/d	50,000	76,600	
Acc depreciation b/d	-	(24,600)	
	50,000	52,000	102,000
Depn: Property (50,000/20)	(2,500)	–	(2,500)
P&E ((52,000 – 4,000) × 20%)	–	(9,600)	(9,600)
Disposal (8,000 – 4,000)	–	(4,000)	(4,000)
Revaluation (β)	(4,500)	–	(4,500)
	43,000	38,400	81,400

3   *Development expenditure*

	$'000
Cost b/d	20,000
Accumulated amortisation b/d	(6,000)
	14,000
Additional expenditure capitalised (800 × 6)	4,800
Amortisation (20,000 × 20%)	(4,000)
Balance c/d	14,800
Charged to cost of sales:	
Research	1,400
Development when criteria not met (800 × 3)	2,400
Amortisation	4,000
	7,800

4   *Legal claim*

	$'000	
Damages are not probable, therefore not accrued		
- Reverse in admin expenses	400	
Legal costs should be provided as results from past event (claim)	(100)	Provision
	300	Credit to Admin

5   Preference shares - Financial liability at amortised cost

	$'000
Financial liability b/d	20,000
Effective interest (× 12% × 6/12)	1,200
Coupon paid (per TB) (× 8% × 6/12)	(800)
Financial liability c/d	20,400
Adjustment required:	

	$'000
Dr Finance costs	400
Cr Financial liability	400

The $800k coupon paid in the TB is increased to effective cost of $1,200k.

BPP LEARNING MEDIA

6   *Taxes*

		$'000
Current tax:		
Dr	Income tax expense (profit or loss)	11,400
Cr	Current tax payable (SOFP)	11,400
Deferred tax:		
Dr	Income tax expense (6,000 – 5,800)	200
Cr	Deferred tax liability	200

7 Pricewell

Text references. Chapters 3 and 12

Top tips. This is a relatively straightforward accounts preparation question. Complications are the leasehold property, which could be mistaken for an investment property, and the construction contract. Remember that the preference shares are treated as debt.

Easy marks. There are easy marks here on property, plant and equipment, the lease and the sales commission, which would all have been worth some marks but were not complicated. The revenue and cost of sales on the construction contract were easy.

Examiner's comments. This question was less well answered than usual. Common errors were:

- not accounting for commission on the agency sales
- deducting closing inventory from cost of sales
- treating the revaluation as if it had taken place at the beginning of the year
- confusing the leasehold property with the leased plant

Marking scheme

		Marks
(a)	Statement of profit or loss	
	Revenue	2
	Cost of sales	5
	Distribution costs	½
	Administrative expenses	½
	Finance costs	2
	Income tax expense	2
		12
(b)	Statement of financial position	
	Property, plant and equipment	2½
	Inventory	½
	Due on construction contract	2
	Trade receivables	½
	Bank	½
	Equity shares	½
	Retained earnings (1 for dividend)	1½
	Deferred tax	1
	Finance lease – non-current liability	½
	Preferences shares	1
	Trade payables	½
	Finance lease – current liability	1
	Current tax payable	1
		13
		25

BPP
LEARNING MEDIA

PRICEWELL: STATEMENT OF PROFIT OR LOSS FOR THE YEAR ENDED 31 MARCH 20X9

	$'000
Revenue (310,000 + 22,000 (W4) – 6,400 (W5))	325,600
Cost of sales (W1)	(255,100)
Gross profit	70,500
Distribution costs	(19,500)
Administrative expenses	(27,500)
Finance costs (1,248 (W3) + 4,160 (W6))	(5,408)
Profit before tax	18,092
Income tax expense (W7)	(2,400)
Profit for the year	15,692

PRICEWELL: STATEMENT OF FINANCIAL POSITION AS AT 31 MARCH 20X9

	$'000	$'000
Assets		
Non-current assets		
Property, plant and equipment (W2)		66,400
Current assets		
Inventory	28,200	
Amount due from customer on contract (W4)	17,100	
Trade receivables	33,100	
Bank	5,500	
		83,900
Total assets		150,300
Equity and liabilities		
Equity shares of 50c each		40,000
Retained earnings (4,900 + 15,692 – 8,000)		12,592
		52,592
Non-current liabilities		
Deferred tax	5,600	
Obligation under finance lease (W3)	5,716	
Redeemable preference shares (W6)	43,360	
		54,676
Current liabilities		
Trade payables	33,400	
Obligation under finance lease (W3)	5,132	
Tax payable (W7)	4,500	
		43,032
Total equity and liabilities		150,300

Workings

1   *Expenses*

	Cost of sales $'000	Distribution costs $'000	Administrative expenses $'000
Per question	234,500	19,500	27,500
Depreciation (W2)	15,300		
Reversal of impairment (W2)	(1,500)		
Construction contract (W4)	13,200		
Agency sales (W5)	(6,400)		
	255,100		

2 Property, plant and equipment

	Leasehold property $'000	Owned plant $'000	Leased plant $'000	Total $'000
B/d per question	25,200	46,800	20,000	92,000
Depreciation b/d	–	(12,800)	(5,000)	(17,800)
	25,200	34,000	15,000	74,200
Depreciation L/hold (25,200/14 years)	(1,800)			
Depreciation (34,000 × 25%)		(8,500)		
Depreciation (20,000 × 25%)			(5,000)	(15,300)
Reversal of impairment loss (β)	1,500	–	–	1,500
	24,900	25,500	10,000	60,400
Construction contract plant (8,000 – 2,000 (W4))				6,000
				66,400

3 Finance lease

	$'000
Balance 1.4.X8 per question	15,600
Interest to 31.3.X9 at 8%	1,248
Payment 31.3.X9	(6,000)
Balance 31.3.X9	10,848
Interest to 31.3.Y0 at 8%	868
Payment due 31.3.Y0	(6,000)
Balance due – non current liability	5,716
Current liability (10,848 – 5,716)	5,132
	10,848

4 Construction contract

	$'000
Contract price	50,000
Materials to date	(12,000)
Plant	(8,000)
Further costs to complete	(10,000)
Profit on contract	20,000

Profit to date = 20 × 22/50 (44%) = 8,800

Revenue	22,000
Cost of sales (30 × 44%)	(13,200)
Profit	8,800

Amount due from customer:

Costs to date (12 + plant depreciation (8 × 6m/24m)	14,000
Profit to date	8,800
Progress billings	(5,700)
	17,100

5 Sales on commission

	DR	CR
Revenue	6,400	
Cost of sales		6,400

This leaves commission of $m 1.6 in revenue.

6 Preference shares

	$'000
Balance at 31.3.X8	41,600
Finance cost 10%	4,160
Dividend paid	(2,400)
Balance at 31.3.X9	43,360

BPP LEARNING MEDIA

7   *Income tax*

	$'000
Prior year underprovision	700
Current provision	4,500
Movement on deferred tax (8.4 – 5.6)	(2,800)
Charge for current year	2,400

8 Sandown

Text references. Chapters 3, 5 and 14

Top tips. This was a time-pressured question. It was important to deal with it efficiently and not get bogged down. The question requirement tells you that there will be some other comprehensive income, so this makes it possible to get down the correct proformas and then go straight through the workings.

Easy marks. The difficult issues here were the deferred revenue, the amortisation of the brand for the period after the impairment loss and accounting for the gains on the equity investment. Being given the equity element of the convertible loan note may also have confused some students. There were easy marks on PPE, on transferring back the dividend and on deferred tax.

Examiner's comments. A familiar accounts preparation question with a series of adjustments, some of which created difficulties. Few candidates correctly calculated the amount of revenue to be deferred. Many candidates applied the effective interest rate to the nominal amount of the convertible loan rather than its carrying amount and there were some errors in dealing with the investment and the deferred tax.

Marking scheme

		Marks
(a)	Statement of profit or loss and other comprehensive income	
	Revenue	1½
	Cost of sales	3
	Distribution costs	½
	Administrative expenses	1
	Investment income	½
	Finance costs	1
	Income tax expense	1½
	Other comprehensive income – gain on derecognition	2
	– revaluation of remaining investments	2
		13
(b)	Statement of financial position	
	Property, plant and equipment	2
	Brand	1
	Investments	1
	Inventory/trade receivables	½
	Bank	½
	Equity shares/equity option	½
	Other equity reserve	1
	Retained earnings (1 for dividend)	2
	Deferred tax	1
	Non-current deferred revenue	½
	5% loan note	1
	Current deferred revenue	½
	Trade payables/current tax payable	½
		12
	Total for question	25

SANDOWN

STATEMENT OF PROFIT OR LOSS AND OTHER COMPREHENSIVE INCOME FOR THE YEAR ENDED 30 SEPTEMBER 20X9

	$'000
Revenue (380,000 – 4,000 (W5))	376,000
Cost of sales (W1)	(265,300)
Gross profit	110,700
Distribution costs	(17,400)
Administrative expenses (W1)	(38,500)
Investment income	1,300
Finance costs (W7)	(1,475)
Profit before tax	54,625
Income tax expense (16,200 + 2,100 – 1,500 (W8))	(16,800)
Profit for the year	37,825
Other comprehensive income:	
Gain on investments in equity instruments((W2) 2,200 + 2,500)	4,700
Total comprehensive income for the year	42,525

SANDOWN

STATEMENT OF FINANCIAL POSITION AS AT 30 SEPTEMBER 20X9

	$'000	$'000
Non-current assets		
Property, plant and equipment (W3)		67,500
Intangible asset (W4)		12,500
Investments in equity instruments (W2(b))		29,000
		109,000
Current assets		
Inventory	38,000	
Receivables	44,500	
Bank	8,000	
		90,500
Total assets		199,500
Equity		
Share capital 20c		50,000
Equity option		2,000
Other reserve (W2)		5,700
Retained earnings (26,060 + 37,825 + 4,000 (W2(c)) – 12,000 (W6))		55,885
		113,585
Non-current liabilities		
Deferred tax (W8)	3,900	
Deferred revenue (W5)	2,000	
5% convertible loan note (W7)	18,915	
		24,815
Current liabilities		
Trade payables	42,900	
Deferred revenue (W5)	2,000	
Tax payable	16,200	
		61,100
Total equity and liabilities		199,500

BPP
LEARNING MEDIA

Workings

1   *Expenses*

	Cost of sales	Distribution costs	Administrative expenses
	$'000	$'000	$'000
Per question	246,800	17,400	50,500
Depreciation (W3)	10,000	–	–
Amortisation (1,500 + 2,500 (W4))	4,000	–	–
Impairment loss (W4)	4,500	–	–
Dividend transferred (W6)	–	–	(12,000)
	265,300	17,400	38,500

2   *Investments in equity instruments*

(a)   Investment disposed of:

	$'000
Proceeds	11,000
Carrying amount	(8,800)
Gain on disposal – other comprehensive income	2,200

(b)   *Remaining investments:*

	$'000
FV at end of reporting period	29,000
Carrying amount in TB	(26,500)
Gain in year – other comprehensive income	2,500

(c)   *Other reserve*

	$'000
Balance per TB	5,000
Gains in year (2,200 + 2,500)	4,700
Transfer of realised profit to retained earnings (1,800 + 2,200)	(4,000) *
	5,700

* Entities are permitted to make this transfer and can choose whether or not
to do so.

3   *Property, plant and equipment*

	Land	Buildings	Plant	Total
	$'000	$'000	$'000	$'000
Cost	13,000	50,000	42,200	105,200
Acc depreciation b/d	–	(8,000)	(19,700)	(27,700)
Carrying amount	13,000	42,000	22,500	77,500
Depreciation:				
Building (50,000/50 yrs*)	–	(1,000)	–	(1,000)
Plant (22,500 × 40%)	–	–	(9,000)	(9,000)
Carrying amount c/d	13,000	41,000	13,500	67,500

* $8m depreciation since 20X0 = 8 years. Therefore 50-year life.

4   *Intangible asset – brand*

	$'000
Cost	30,000
Accumulated amortisation b/d	(9,000)
	21,000
Amortisation to 1.4.X9 (30,000/10 × 6/12)	(1,500)
	19,500
Impairment loss	(4,500)
Recoverable amount (higher of FV less CTS and VIU)	15,000
Amortisation to 30.9.X9 (15,000/3 × 6/12)	(2,500)
Carrying amount at 30.9.X9	12,500

5   *Deferred revenue*

Per IAS 18 a proportion of the revenue from sales to Pending should be deferred to cover the ongoing service and support costs. The costs for the year to 30.9 X9 will already have been accounted for, but revenue must be deferred to cover the costs for the remaining two years.

The total amount deferred should include the 40% profit, so will be calculated as:

	$'000
$((1,200 \times 2) \times 100/60)$	4,000

This will be deducted from revenue and split 50:50 between current and non-current liabilities.

6   *Dividend*

Shares in issue ($50,000 of 20c shares)	250,000 ×
Dividend per share	4.8 cents = $12m

This is added back to administrative expenses and deducted from retained earnings.

7   *Convertible loan note*

	$'000
Balance per TB	18,440
Interest paid to 30.9.X9	(1,000)
Effective interest $(18,440 \times 8\%)$	1,475
Balance at 30.9.X9	18,915

Adjustment required: $(1,475 - 1,000) = 475$ Dr Finance costs/Cr Convertible loan note

8   *Deferred tax*

	$'000
Balance b/f	5,400
Balance to c/f $(13m \times 30\%)$	(3,900)
Adjustment	1,500

Dr Deferred tax (SOFP) / Cr Income tax expense

9 Dune

Text references. Chapters 3, 4, 12 and 14

Top tips. As always with these questions, get the formats down first and then work down the trial balance, taking all the numbers either to the financial statements or to workings. The complications in this question are a construction contract, a financial instrument and a non-current asset (leasehold property) held for sale. Do not confuse a leasehold property with a finance lease – a leasehold property is treated in the same way as any other owned asset.

Easy marks. 2½ marks were available for revenue. This just required working out how much revenue could be recognised on the construction contract and adjusting for the cut-off error. 3½ marks were available for the tax figures, which just required reading the information carefully and seeing that the deferred tax provision needed to be reduced. ½ marks were available for figures that just needed to be lifted from the TB. Make sure that your workings are very clear so that you get credit for whatever you have done correctly.

Examiner's comments. This was a familiar question of preparing financial statements from a trial balance with various adjustments required. These involved a sales 'cut-off' error, use of effective interest rate for a loan, a fair valued investment, a property held for sale, a construction contract and accounting for taxation. The most common errors were:

Errors in adjusting the cost to deal with the cut-off error

Incorrect treatment of the loan issue costs

Crediting the gain on the investment to equity

Failure to depreciate the leasehold property prior to calculating the impairment loss

The construction contract was often ignored, or workings were done but not then carried across.

Many errors in dealing with the current and deferred tax.

BPP
LEARNING MEDIA

		Marks
(a)	Statement of profit or loss	
	Revenue	2
	Cost of sales	4
	Distribution costs	½
	Administrative expenses	1
	Investment income	½
	Gain on investments	½
	Finance costs	1½
	Income tax expense	2
		12
(b)	Statement of financial position	
	Property, plant and equipment	1½
	Investments	½
	Inventory	½
	Construction contract	1½
	Trade receivables	1
	Non-current asset held for sale	1
	Equity shares	½
	Retained earnings (1 for dividend)	2
	Deferred tax	1
	5% loan note	1½
	Trade payables	½
	Accrued loan note interest	½
	Trade payables	½
	Current tax payable	½
		13
	Total for question	25

DUNE
STATEMENT OF PROFIT OR LOSS FOR THE YEAR ENDED 31 MARCH 20X1

	$'000
Revenue (400,000 + 12,000 (W2) – 8,000 (W3))	404,000
Cost of sales (W1)	(315,700)
Gross profit	88,300
Other income (W5)	2,700
Distribution costs	(26,400)
Administrative expenses (34,200 – 500 (W6))	(33,700)
Finance costs (200 + 1,950 (W6))	(2,150)
Profit before tax	28,750
Income tax expense (W7)	(8,800)
Profit for the year	19,950

DUNE
STATEMENT OF FINANCIAL POSITION AS AT 31 MARCH 20X1

	$'000
Assets	
Non-current assets	
Property, plant and equipment (W4)	46,400
Investments	28,000
	74,400
Current assets	
Inventory	48,000
Amount due from customer on construction contract (W2)	13,400
Trade receivables (40,700 – 8,000 (W3))	32,700
	94,100
Non-current asset held for sale (W4)	33,500
Total assets	202,000
Equity and liabilities	
Share capital – ordinary $1 shares	60,000
Retained earnings (38,400 + 19,950 – 10,000 dividend paid)	48,350
	108,350
Non-current liabilities	
Deferred tax (W7)	4,200
5% loan notes (W6)	20,450
	24,650
Current liabilities	
Trade payables	52,000
Bank overdraft	4,500
Tax payable	12,000
Accrual – loan note interest (W6)	500
	69,000
Total equity and liabilities	202,000

Workings

1   Expenses

	Cost of sales $'000	Distribution costs $'000	Admin exps $'000
Per question	294,000	26,400	34,200
Loan note direct costs			(500)
Construction contract (W1)	9,600		
Depreciation PPE (W4)	6,600		
Depreciation leasehold property (W4)	1,500		
Loss on reclassification of leasehold property (W4)	4,000	–	–
	315,700	26,400	33,700

Note: depreciation on the construction contract plant is already included in contract costs.

BPP
LEARNING MEDIA

2   *Construction contract*

	$'000	$'000
Contract price		40,000
Costs to date:		
Per question	(8,000)	
Plant depreciation ((12,000 − 3,000) × 6/18)	(3,000)	
		(11,000)
Costs to complete (15,000 + (12,000 − 3,000) × 12/18)		(21,000)
Total costs		(32,000)
Projected profit		8,000
Revenue to date (40,000 × 30%)		12,000
Costs (32,000 × 30%)		(9,600)
Profit to date		2,400
Costs to date		11,000
Profit to date		2,400
Gross amount due from customers		13,400

3   *Goods sold after year end*

	$'000	$'000
Dr Revenue ($6m × 100/75)	8'000	
Cr Receivables		8,000

4   *Property, plant and equipment*

	Plant and equipment $'000	Contract plant $'000	Leasehold property $'000	Total $'000
Cost	67,500		45,000	112,500
Additions	–	12,000	–	12,000
Balance at 31 March 20X1	67,500	12,000	45,000	124,500
Depreciation b/f	23,500		6,000	29,500
Charge for year:				
(67,500 − 23,500) × 15%	6,600			
(12,000 − 3,000) × 6/18		3,000		
(45,000 / 15) × 6/12			1,500	11,100
Loss on reclassification:				
(37,500 − ((40,000 × 85%) − 500)	–	–	4,000	4,000
	30,100	3,000	11,500	(44,600)
Transfer to held for sale	–	–	(33,500)	(33,500)
Carrying amount 31 March 20X1	37,400	9,000	–	46,400

5   *Other income*

	$'000
Investment income – per question	1,200
Gain on investments at fair value through profit or loss (28,000 − 26,500)	1,500
	2,700

BPP LEARNING MEDIA

6   *Loan notes*

	$'000
Nominal value	20,000
Direct costs	(500)
	19,500
Interest to 31.3.X1 at 10%	1,950
Interest paid/payable	(1,000)
Carrying amount	20,450

Interest charge (profit or loss)	1,950
Interest accrual (SFP) (1,000 – 500)	500

7   *Income tax*

	$'000
Current tax (12,000 – 1,400 overprovision)	10,600
Transfer from deferred tax (6,000 – 4,200 (14,000 x 30%))	(1,800)
	8,800

10 Cavern

Text references. Chapters 3, 13, 14 and 17

Top tips. As always with these questions, get the formats down first and then work down the trial balance, taking all the numbers either to the financial statements or to workings. The issues in this question are the dividend payments, a decontamination provision and a loan note at amortised cost. None of these were very difficult. What needed to be done in this question was to get all three statements done. To do this, you need to start with all three pro-formas and fill in as much straightforward information as possible before starting on the more complex workings.

Easy marks. A total of four marks were available for income tax. All of these marks could be derived from one fairly simple working. This just required reading the information carefully and seeing that the deferred tax provision needed to be reduced. ½ marks were available for figures that just needed to be lifted from the TB. Make sure that your workings are very clear so that you get credit for whatever you have done correctly.

Examiner's comments. Most candidates got the dividend calculation wrong, mainly because the first dividend was paid before the rights issue, so based on a smaller number of shares. A high number of candidates did not capitalise the future decontamination costs, which affected the depreciation and the provision. Some candidates treated the land and building revaluation as taking place at the beginning of the year rather than the end and some did not account for depreciation before calculating the revaluation gain. Many candidates failed to apply the effective (rather than the nominal) interest rate on the loan note.

Marking scheme

		Marks
(a)	Statement of profit or loss and other comprehensive income:	
	Revenue	½
	Cost of sales	3
	Distribution costs	½
	Administrative expenses	1
	Investment income	½
	Finance costs	2½
	Income tax expense	2
	Loss on investments in equity instruments	½
	Gain on revaluation of land and buildings	½
		11

BPP
LEARNING MEDIA

		Marks
(b)	Statement of changes in equity:	
	Balances b/f	1
	Rights issue	1
	Dividends	1
	Loss on investments in equity instruments	½
	Revaluation gain	½
	Profit for year	1
		5
(c)	Statement of financial position:	
	Property, plant and equipment	2½
	Investments in equity instruments	½
	Inventory	½
	Trade receivables	½
	Contamination provision	1
	8% loan note	1
	Deferred tax	1
	Trade payables	½
	Bank overdraft	½
	Current tax payable	1
		9
	Maximum for question	25

CAVERN – STATEMENT OF PROFIT OR LOSS AND OTHER COMPREHENSIVE INCOME FOR THE YEAR ENDED 30 SEPTEMBER 20X2

	$'000
Revenue	182,500
Cost of sales (W1)	137,400
Gross profit	45,100
Distribution costs (W1)	(8,500)
Administrative expenses (W1)	(6,500)
Investment income	700
Finance costs (W4)	(3,760)
Profit before tax	27,040
Income tax expense (W6)	(6,250)
Profit for the year	20,790
Other comprehensive income:	
Loss on investments in equity instruments (15,800 – 13,500)	(2,300)
Gain on revaluation of property (W2)	800
Total other comprehensive loss for the year	(1,500)
Total comprehensive income for the year	19,290

CAVERN – STATEMENT OF CHANGES IN EQUITY FOR THE YEAR ENDED 30 SEPTEMBER 20X2

	Share capital $'000	Share premium $'000	Retained earnings $'000	Revaluation surplus $'000	Other equity reserve $'000	Total $'000
Balance at 1 October 2009	40,000	–	12,100	7,000	3,000	62,100
Share issue (W7)	10,000	11,000				21,000
Dividends (W3)			(18,500)			(18,500)
Total comprehensive income	–	–	20,790	800	(2,300)	19,290
	50,000	11,000	14,390	7,800	700	83,890

CAVERN – STATEMENT OF FINANCIAL POSITION AT 30 SEPTEMBER 20X2

	$'000	$'000
Assets		
Non-current assets		
Property, plant and equipment (W2)		92,900
Investments in equity instruments		13,500
		106,400
Current assets		
Inventory	19,800	
Trade receivables	29,000	
		48,800
Total assets		155,200
Equity and liabilities		
Equity		
Share capital		50,000
Share premium		11,000
Revaluation surplus		7,800
Other equity reserve (3,000 – (15,800 – 13,500 (OCI))		700
Retained earnings		14,390
		83,890
Non-current liabilities		
8% loan note (W5)	31,260	
Decontamination provision (4,000 + 400 (W4))	4,400	
Deferred tax (W6)	3,750	
		39,410
Current liabilities		
Trade payables	21,700	
Bank overdraft	4,600	
Income tax payable	5,600	
		31,900
Total equity and liabilities		155,200

Workings

1 Expenses

	Cost of sales	Distribution costs	Administrative expenses
	$'000	$'000	$'000
Per question	128,500	8,500	25,000
Depreciation – buildings (W2)	2,000		
Plant (1,400 + 5,500 (W2))	6,900		
Dividends (W3)	–	–	(18,500)
	137,400	8,500	6,500

2 Property, plant and equipment

	Land and buildings	Plant and equipment	Total
	$'000	$'000	$'000
Cost/valuation b/d	43,000	67,400	110,400
Accumulated depreciation b/d		(13,400)	(13,400)
		54,000	97,000
Capitalisation of provision		4,000	4,000
		58,000	101,000
Depreciation – buildings (36,000/18 yrs)	(2,000)		(2,000)
new plant (10,000 + 4,000)/10		(1,400)	(1,400)
existing plant (58,000-14,000) × 12.5%		(5,500)	(5,500)
Revaluation	800	–	800
	41,800	51,100	92,900

BPP
LEARNING MEDIA

3   Dividends

		$'000
30 November 20X1	$40m × 5 (20c shares) × 3c	6,000
31 May 20X2	$50m × 5 × 5c	12,500
		18,500

4   Finance costs

	$'000
Per draft	300
Unwinding of discount on provision (4,000 × 10%)	400
Loan note interest (30,600 × 10%)	3,060
	3,760

5   Loan note

	$'000
Per draft	30,600
Interest (W4)	3,060
Less interest paid (per draft)	(2,400)
Balance at 30 September 20X2	31,260

6   Income tax

	$'000
Underprovided in prior year	900
Reduction in deferred tax	(250)
Charge for the year	5,600
Total to profit or loss	6,250
Deferred tax:	
Balance per draft	4,000
Balance at 30 September 20X2 ($15m × 25%)	(3,750)
Reduction in provision	(250)

7   Share issue

	Share capital $'000	Share premium $'000
Balance at 30 September 20X2 (250 shares)	50,000	11,000
Effect of rights issue (50,000 shares):		
Share capital (50,000 × 20c)	(10,000)	
Share premium (50,000 × 22c)	–	(11,000)
Balance at 1 October 20X1	40,000	–

11 Keystone

Text references. Chapters 3, 4, 7, 14, 17, 19.

Top tips. There were a number of complications in this question – self-constructed plant, goods on sale or return, deferred tax on a revaluation, a dividend to calculate back from the yield - and it was important not to get too bogged down in any of them. Make sure you get the proforma down and fill in any straightforward numbers first.

Easy marks. There were enough easy marks here. You could have scored on revenue, tax, inventory and receivables. Cost of sales was complex but a lot of marks were allocated to it, so you should have been able to get some of them.

Examiner's comments. This was a traditional accounts preparation question and generally well-answered. Most of the errors involved the calculation of cost of sales. Some candidates had trouble calculating a gross profit margin and some went on to apply the mark-up to the plant manufactured for own use, which had to be deducted and capitalised. This would have implied that the company was selling the plant to itself at a profit. Many candidates failed to include production, labour and factory overheads in cost of sales and some failed to adjust for opening and closing inventory. The property revaluation caused problems in accounting for deferred tax and some students failed to notice that the revaluation had taken place at the beginning, not the end, of the year.

	Marks
Statement of profit or loss	
Revenue	1
Cost of sales	7
Distribution costs	½
Administrative expenses	1½
Investment income	1
Loss on fair value of investment	1
Finance costs	½
Income tax expense	1½
Other comprehensive income	1
	15
Statement of financial position	
Property, plant and equipment	2
Equity investments	½
Inventory	½
Trade receivables	1
Equity shares	½
Revaluation surplus	1½
Retained earnings	1½
Deferred tax	1
Trade payables	½
Bank overdraft	½
Tax payable	½
	10
Total for question	25

STATEMENT OF PROFIT OR LOSS AND OTHER COMPREHENSIVE INCOME FOR THE YEAR ENDED 30 SEPTEMBER 20X1

	$'000
Revenue (380,000 – 2,400 (W3))	377,600
Cost of sales (W1)	(258,100)
Gross profit	119,500
Investment income	800
Loss on fair value of investments (18,000 – 17,400)	(600)
Distribution costs	(14,200)
Administrative expenses (46,400 – 24,000 (W1))	(22,400)
Finance costs	(350)
Profit before taxation	82,750
Income tax expense (24,300 + 1,800 (W4))	(26,100)
Profit for the year	56,650
Other comprehensive income:	
Revaluation gain on property	8,000
Less deferred tax (W4)	(2,400)
Total other comprehensive income	5,600
Total comprehensive income for the year	62,250

BPP
LEARNING MEDIA

STATEMENT OF FINANCIAL POSITION AS AT 30 SEPTEMBER 20X1

	$'000
Assets	
Non-current assets	
Property, plant and equipment (W2)	78,000
Investment in equity assets	17,400
	95,400
Current assets	
Inventory (54,800 + 1,800 (W3))	56,600
Receivables (33,550 – 2,400 (W3))	31,150
Total assets	183,150
Equity and liabilities	
Equity	
Share capital	50,000
Retained earnings (33,600 + 56,650 – 24,000 (W1))	66,250
Revaluation surplus (8,000 (W2) – 2,400 (W4))	5,600
	121,850
Non-current liabilities	
Deferred tax (2,700 + 1,800 + 2,400 (W4))	6,900
Current liabilities	
Trade payables	27,800
Tax payable	24,300
Bank overdraft	2,300
Total equity and liabilities	183,150

Workings

1 Expenses

	Cost of sales	Distribution costs	Administrative expenses
	$'000	$'000	$'000
Per trial balance		14,200	46,400
Opening inventory	46,700		
Material purchases	64,000		
Production labour	124,000		
Factory overheads	80,000		
Capitalised costs (W2)	(10,000)		
Depreciation (3,000 + 7,000 (W2))	10,000		
Closing inventories (54,800 + 1,800 (W3))	(56,600)		
Dividend paid ($2.4 x 4% x 250,000)			(24,000)
	258,100	14,200	22,400

2 Property, plant and equipment

	Leased property	Plant and equipment	Total
	$'000	$'000	$'000
Per trial balance:			
Cost	50,000	44,500	94,500
Accumulated depreciation b/d	(10,000)	(14,500)	(24,500)
	40,000	30,000	70,000
Own plant manufactured (3,000 + 4,000 + (4,000 × 75%))		10,000	10,000
Revaluation surplus	8,000		8,000
Revalued amount	48,000	40,000	88,000
Depreciation/amortisation			
Leased property (48,000 / (20 - 4 years*)	(3,000)		(3,000)
Plant and equipment ((30,000 × 20%) + (10,000 x 20% × 6/12))	-	(7,000)	(7,000)
	45,000	33,000	78,000

* At 1.10.20X0 leased property was (10/50 × 20) = 4 years old

BPP
LEARNING MEDIA

3 *Sale or return*

	$'000	$'000
Revenue:		
Dr Revenue	2,400	
Cr Receivables		2,400
Cost of sales:		
Dr Inventories	1,800	
Cr Cost of sales		1,800

4 *Deferred tax*

	$'000	$'000
Taxable difference (15,000 x 30%) less b/f 2,700)		
Dr Taxation expense (profit or loss)	1,800	
Cr Deferred tax		1,800
Deferred tax on revaluation: (8,000 x 30%)		
Dr Revaluation surplus	2,400	
Cr Deferred tax		2,400

12 Fresco

Text references. Chapters 3,4 and 16.

Top tips. There was a lot to get through in this question. Get the formats down quickly and then go through the question and transfer any figures that can go straight from the trial balance to the financial statements. You needed to do workings for PPE and for the leased plant but these were not complicated. Leave time for part (b).

Easy marks. The statement of changes in equity was all straightforward. If you had remembered the transfer to retained earnings it was possible to score full marks on this. The PPE working made it possible to score marks on both the statement of comprehensive income and the statement of financial position, so it was worth spending a bit of time on this. The lease working, on the other hand, carried very few marks and the EPS was quite time-consuming for 3 marks.

Examiner's comments Most candidates showed a sound knowledge of preparing financial statements. Most of the errors arose in the adjustments:

Some candidates deducted the loss on the fraud from revenue for the year rather adding it to expenses and treating it as a prior year adjustment, with the other entry being a deduction from receivables.

There were some difficulties with the finance lease, mainly involving the timing of the lease payments and the initial deposit.

Many candidates were confused with the tax, especially failing to realise that the tax for the year was a refund.

The EPS section was very poorly answered and many candidates did not even attempt it.

Examiner's answer. The examiner's answer to this question is at the end of this Kit.

Marking scheme

		Marks
Statement of comprehensive income:		
Revenue	½	
Cost of sales	3	
Distribution costs	½	
Administrative expenses	1	
Finance costs	1½	
Income tax	2	
Other comprehensive income	½	9

BPP
LEARNING MEDIA

Statement of changes in equity:

Balances b/f	1	
Prior year adjustment	1	
Rights issue	1	
Total comprehensive income	1	
Transfer to retained earnings	1	5

Statement of financial position:

Property, plant and equipment	2½	
Inventory	½	
Trade receivables	1	
Current tax	1	
Non-current lease obligation	½	
Deferred tax	1	
Trade payables	½	
Current lease obligation	½	
Bank overdraft	½	8

Basic EPS:

Loss for the year	½	
Theoretical ex-rights price	1	
Weighted average number of shares	1½	3
Total		25

(a) STATEMENT OF PROFIT OR LOSS AND OTHER COMPREHENSIVE INCOME FOR THE YEAR ENDED 31 MARCH 20X2

	$'000
Revenue	350,000
Cost of sales (W1)	(311,000)
Gross profit	39,000
Distribution costs (W1)	(16,100)
Administrative expenses (W1)	(29,900)
Finance costs (300 + 2,300 (W3))	(2,600)
Loss before tax	(9,600)
Income tax (W5)	1,800
Loss for the year	(7,800)
Other comprehensive income:	
Gain on revaluation of property (W2)	4,000
Total comprehensive loss for the year	(3,800)

STATEMENT OF CHANGES IN EQUITY FOR THE YEAR ENDED 31 MARCH 20X2

	Share capital	Share premium	Retained earnings	Revaluation surplus	Total
	$'000	$'000	$'000	$'000	$'000
Balance 31.3.X1	45,000	5,000	5,100	-	55,100
Prior year adj (W4)	-	-	(1,000)	-	(1,000)
Balance 1.4.X1	45,000	5,000	4,100	-	54,100
Share issue (W6)	9,000	4,500	-	-	13,500
Total comprehensive income	-	-	(7,800)	4,000	(3,800)
Transfer to retained earnings (W2)	-	-	500	(500)	-
Balance 31.3.X2	54,000	9,500	(3,200)	3,500	63,800

STATEMENT OF FINANCIAL POSITION AS AT 31 MARCH 20X2

	$'000
Assets	
Non-current assets	
Property, plant and equipment (W2)	62,700
Current assets	
Inventory	25,200
Receivables (28,500 – 4,000 (W4))	24,500
Tax asset (W5)	2,400
Total assets	114,800
Equity and liabilities	
Equity	
Share capital 50c shares	54,000
Share premium	9,500
Revaluation surplus	3,500
Retained earnings	(3,200)
	63,800
Non-current liabilities	
Deferred tax (W5)	3,000
Lease payable (W3)	15,230
Current liabilities	
Trade payables	27,300
Lease payable (19,300 – 15,230 (W3))	4,070
Bank overdraft	1,400
Total equity and liabilities	114,800

Workings

1 *Expenses*

	Cost of sales $'000	Distribution costs $'000	Administrative expenses $'000
Per trial balance	298,700	16,100	26,900
Depreciation (W2)	7,800	-	-
Amortisation (W2)	4,500	-	-
Fraud – current year cost (W4)	-	-	3,000
	311,000	16,100	29,900

2 *Property, plant and equipment*

	Leased property $'000	Plant and equipment $'000	Leased plant $'000	Total $'000
Cost	48,000	47,500		
Acc. amortisation/depreciation	(16,000)	(33,500)		
Balance 1 April 20X1	32,000	14,000	25,000	
Revaluation surplus	4,000			
Revised carrying amount	36,000			
Depreciation / amortisation:				
36,000 / 8	(4,500)			
14,000 x 20%		(2,800)		
25,000 / 5			(5,000)	
	31,500	11,200	20,000	62,700

BPP LEARNING MEDIA

3 Finance lease

	$'000
Cost	25,000
Deposit	(2,000)
Balance 1.4.X1	23,000
Interest 10%	2,300
Instalment 31.3.X2	(6,000)
Balance 31.3.X2	19,300
Interest 10%	1,930
Instalment 31.3.X3	(6,000)
Balance 31.3.X3	15,230

4 Fraud

	DEBIT	CREDIT
	$'000	$'000
Retained earnings - prior year	1,000	
Current year profit	3,000	
Receivables		4,000

5 Tax credit

	$'000
Underprovided in prior year	800
Tax refund due (asset in SFP)	(2,400)
Reduction in deferred tax provision (3,200 – (12,000 x 25%))	(200)
Current tax (credit to profit or loss)	(1,800)

6 Share issue

Shares issued = 13.5m / 0.75 = 18m

		$'000
Share capital	18m × 50c	9,000
Share premium	18m × 25c	4,500
		13,500

(b)   *Earnings per share*

Loss per statement of comprehensive income	$7.8m
Weighted average number of shares in issue (W)	99m

EPS = (7.8m) / 99m = Loss per share 7.9 cents

Working

Theoretical ex-rights price:

5 shares @ 1.20	6.00
1 share @ 0.75	0.75
	6.75 / 6 = 1.125

Weighted average number of shares:

1 April 20X1 to 31 December 20X1 ((90m × 1.20/1.125) × 9/12)	72m
1 January 20X2 to 31 March 20X2 ((90m + 18m) × 3/12)	27m
	99m

BPP
LEARNING MEDIA

13 Preparation question: Plethora plc

(a)   *Building transferred to investment property*

	$'000
Original cost	600
Depreciation 1.1.X0 to 1.7.X9 ((600/50) x 9.5)	(114)
Carrying amount at 1.7.X9	486
Revaluation surplus	314
Fair value	800

The amount of $314,000 will go to the revaluation surplus as per IAS 16 and the carrying amount of the building will be restated at $800,000. After this point the building will be accounted for under IAS 40 *Investment property*. If there had been any increase in value after 1.7.X9, this would have been credited to profit or loss.

Existing investment property

The increase in value in this case of $190,000 (740,000 – 550,000) will be credited to profit or loss in accordance with IAS 40.

(b)

	Prior to review	After review
	$'000	$'000
Building	900	825
Plant and equipment	300	275
Inventory	70	70
Other current assets	130	130
Goodwill	40	-
	1,440	1,300
Recoverable amount	(1,300)	
Impairment loss	140	

The impairment loss is allocated first against goodwill and then pro-rata against the tangible non-current assets. This means writing $75,000 off the carrying amount of the building and $25,000 off plant and equipment.

14 Elite Leisure

Elite Leisure's cruise ship

Although there is only one ship, the ship is a complex asset made up from a number of smaller assets with different costs and useful lives. Each of the component assets of the ship will be accounted for separately with its own cost, depreciation and profit or loss on disposal.

At 30 September 20X4 the ship is eight years old and its cost and carrying amount is as follows:

	Cost	Depreciation period	Accumulated depreciation	Carrying value
	$m		$m	$m
Ship's fabric	300	$\dfrac{8 \text{ years}}{25 \text{ years}}$	96	204
Cabins and entertainment areas	150	$\dfrac{8 \text{ years}}{12 \text{ years}}$	100	50
Propulsion system	100	$\dfrac{30,000 \text{ hours}}{40,000 \text{ hours}}$	75	25
	550		271	279

BPP
LEARNING MEDIA

Changes during Y/E 30 September 20X5

Replacing the propulsion system $140m

The old engines will be scrapped giving rise to a $25m loss on disposal.

The new engines will be capitalised and depreciated over their 50,000 hour working life. The charge for this year will be $140m $\times \dfrac{5,000 \text{ hours}}{50,000 \text{ hours}} = \$14m$.

Upgrading cabins and entertainment areas $60m

These costs can be capitalised because they are improvements and because they extend the useful life of the assets. The revised carrying value at 1 October 20X4 is $110m ($50m + $60m).

The depreciation charge for the year is $22m ($110 ÷ 5 years).

Repainting the ship's fabric $20m

This is a maintenance cost. It will be charged to profit or loss for the year. The depreciation for the ship itself will be $12m, based on its $300m cost and 25 year life.

Summary

STATEMENT OF FINANCIAL POSITION

	Ship's Fabric $m	Cabins etc $m	Propulsion $m	Total $m
Opening carrying value	204	50	25	279
Disposals	–	–	(25)	(25)
Additions	–	60	140	200
Depreciation	(12)	(22)	(14)	(48)
Closing carrying value	192	88	126	406

STATEMENT OF PROFIT OR LOSS

	$m
Depreciation	48
Loss on disposal	25
Repainting	20
Total charge	93

15 Dearing

Top tips. This question is quite complicated. Set out really clear workings so that you don't get lost.

Marking scheme

	Marks
Initial capitalised cost	2
Upgrade improves efficiency and life therefore capitalise	1
Revised carrying amount at 1 October 20X8	1
Annual depreciation (1 mark each year)	3
Maintenance costs charged at $20,000 each year	1
Discount received (profit or loss)	1
Staff training (not capitalised and charged to income)	1
Total for question	10

Year ended	30 Sept 20X6	30 Sept 20X7	30 Sept 20X8
Statement of profit or loss:	$	$	$
Depreciation (W3)	180,000	270,000	119,000
Maintenance (60,000/3)	20,000	20,000	20,000
Discount received (840,000 × 5%)	(42,000)	–	–
Staff training	40,000	–	–
	198,000	290,000	139,000

As at:	30 Sept 20X6	30 Sept 20X7	30 Sept 20X8
Statement of financial position	$	$	$
Property, plant and equipment:			
Cost/valuation (W1), (W2)	920,000	920,000	670,000
Accumulated depreciation	(180,000)	(450,000)	(119,000)
Carrying value	740,000	470,000	551,000

Workings

1   Cost price

	$
Base price	1,050,000
Trade discount (1,050,000 × 20%)	(210,000)
	840,000
Freight charges	30,000
Electrical installation cost	28,000
Pre-production testing	22,000
	920,000

2   Valuation after upgrade

	$
Original cost	920,000
Depreciation to 30 September 20X7 (W3)	(450,000)
Carrying amount	470,000
Upgrade	200,000
Valuation	670,000

3   Depreciation

	$
30 September 20X6:	
(920,000 – 20,000) × 1,200/6,000	180,000
30 September 20X7:	
(920,000 – 20,000) × 1,800/6,000	270,000
	450,000
30 September 20X8:	
(670,000 – 40,000) × 850/4,500	119,000

16 Flightline

Text reference. Chapter 4

Top tips. This was a very time pressured question with a lot of work to do for 10 marks. It is important in a question like this to provide really clear workings so that you get the marks for all the parts you do correctly.

Easy marks. The amounts for the exterior structure and the cabin fittings were relatively easy to calculate, so you should have done those before embarking on the engines.

Examiner's comments. A significant number of candidates did not start this question and many more appeared to run out of time. Many answers lacked a methodical approach and then got hopelessly lost in the detail, with the engines causing the most problems.

BPP LEARNING MEDIA

	Marks
Statement of profit or loss	
Depreciation – exterior	1
– cabin fittings	2
– engines	2
Loss on write off of engine	1
Repairs	1
Statement of financial position	
Carrying amount at 31 March 20X9	3
Total for question	10

STATEMENT OF PROFIT OR LOSS (EXTRACT) FOR THE YEAR ENDED 31 MARCH 20X9

	$'000
Depreciation:	
Exterior structure (W1)	6,000
Cabin fittings (W2)	6,500
Engines (W3)	1,300
	13,800
Loss on disposal of engine (W3)	6,000
Engine repairs	3,000
Exterior painting	2,000

STATEMENT OF FINANCIAL POSITION (EXTRACT) AT 31 MARCH 20X9

	$'000
Property, plant and equipment	
Aircraft – exterior (W1)	36,000
– cabin (W2)	8,000
– engines (W3)	16,100
	60,100

Workings

1   *Exterior structure*

	$'000
Cost	120,000
Accumulated depreciation to 31.3.X8 (120,000 × 13/20)	(78,000)
	42,000
Depreciation to 31.3.X9 (120,000/20)	(6,000)
Carrying value	36,000

2   *Cabin fittings*

	$'000
Cost	25,000
Accumulated depreciation to 31.3.X8 (25,000 × 3/5)	(15,000)
	10,000
Depreciation to 1.10.X8 (25,000 /5 × 6/12)	(2,500)
Upgrade	4,500
	12,000
Depreciation to 31.3.X9 (12,000 × 6/18)	(4,000)
Carrying value	8,000
Total depreciation for current year (2,500 + 4,000)	6,500

3   *Engines*

$'000

Replaced engine:
Cost   9,000
Depreciation to 31.3.X8 (9,000 × 10.8/36)   (2,700)
Carrying value at 1.4.X8   6,300
Depreciation to 1.10.X8 (9,000 × 1.2/36)   (300)
Written off at 1.10.X8   6,000

Replacement:
Cost   10,800
Depreciation to 31.3.X9 (10,800/36)   (300)
Carrying value   10,500

Damaged engine:
Carrying value at 1.4.X8   6,300
Depreciation to 1.10.X8   (300)
Carrying value at 1.10.X8   6,000
Depreciation to 31.3.X9 (6,000/15)   (400)
Carrying value at 31.3.X9   5,600

Total carrying value (10,500 + 5,600)   16,100
Total current year depreciation
(300 + 300 + 300 + 400)   1,300

17 Apex

Text reference. Chapter 4

Top tips. This was a question that was difficult to tackle if you had not revised the topic, but it was definitely worth making an attempt. Reading through part (b) would have given you some idea of what your answer to part (a) needed to cover. Similarly with part (b), if you put the information in order you could have arrived at all or most of the answer. You would know from leasing that the relevant interest rate is the effective interest rate, not the nominal rate.

Easy marks. If you knew this topic most of the marks were easy, especially those in part (a) where it was just a test of knowledge. Otherwise, you could still have scored marks in both parts of this question by reading it carefully and applying the principles that you are familiar with, as above.

Examiner's comments. Many candidates had not covered this topic in their revision and a considerable number did not attempt this question. Part (a) should have proved straightforward but many answers just guessed at the rules or wrote about other costs that could be capitalised during construction of a non-current asset. In part (b) the main errors were using the nominal rate of interest and not correctly calculating the period of capitalisation.

Marking scheme

		Marks
(a)	1 mark per valid point	5
(b)	Use of effective interest rate 7.5%	1
	Capitalise eight months	2
	Charge to P or L	1
	Interest received credited to P or L	1
	Total for question	10

(a) 'Qualifying' borrowing costs are borrowing costs incurred in the construction of qualifying assets. These are assets that necessarily take a substantial period of time to get ready for intended use or sale. Since the revision of IAS 23, qualifying borrowing costs now *must* be capitalised.

Where funds are borrowed specifically to finance the construction of a qualifying asset, the amount eligible for capitalisation will be the borrowing costs incurred at the effective rate of interest, less any investment income earned on the temporary investment of those borrowings.

Where funds are borrowed generally and the borrowings attributable to a particular asset cannot be readily identified, the amount eligible for capitalisation will have to be estimated by applying a weighted capitalisation rate to the funds used in constructing the asset.

Capitalisation commences when expenditure and necessary activities begin on the asset and borrowing costs are incurred. Capitalisation is suspended during any period in which activities on the asset are suspended and it ceases when substantially all activities necessary to prepare the asset for its intended use or sale are complete.

(b) The total finance costs for the year are $750,000 ($10m x 7.5%)

However, the finance costs can only be capitalised for those periods during which the activity was taking place, not before the development begins, while it is suspended or after it has ceased.

Finance costs to be capitalised are therefore

	$'000
May/June 20X8 ($10m $\times$ 7.5% $\times$ 2/12)	125
Sept X8 – Feb X9 ($10m $\times$ 7.5% $\times$ 6/12)	375
	500

$500,000 will be debited to PPE as part of the cost of the new store.

	$'000
Finance costs to be expensed (750 – 500)	250

These will be debited to profit or loss.

The period during which the funds were invested was before the development activity began, so during a period in which finance costs were not being capitalised. Therefore the interest received of $40,000 is not deducted from the capitalised finance costs, but is credited to profit or loss as investment income.

18 Derringdo

(a) *Liability*

There are two issues here:

1   Should a capital grant be treated as deferred income in the financial statements?
2   Should a liability be recognised for the potential repayment of the grant?

Derringdo has credited the $240,000 grant to a deferred income account which is shown as a liability in the statement of financial position. It is then released to profit or loss over the ten year life of the related asset. However, the *Conceptual Framework* states that a liability should only be recognised if there is a probable outflow of economic benefits. This is not true for a grant; under normal circumstances the grant will not have to be repaid and so a liability does not exist.

This example is complicated by the possibility of having to repay the grant if the asset is sold. At the end of the reporting period the asset has not been sold, and so there is no past event to give rise to a liability. Derringdo intends to keep the asset for its ten year useful life. Nor can it be classified as a contingent liability. Under IAS 37 the 'uncertain future event' that creates a contingent liability must be 'not wholly within the control of the entity'. In this case Derringdo will make the decision to keep or sell the asset.

Following on from the above, the *Conceptual Framework* would not permit the grant to be shown as a liability. Instead the grant would be claimed as income in the year that it was received (provided that there was no intention to sell the asset within the four year claw-back period). However, the treatment of the grant as deferred income is in accordance with IAS 20 *Accounting for government grants.*

(b) *Extracts* (Company policy complies with one of the two alternatives in IAS 20)

STATEMENT OF PROFIT OR LOSS

	$
Operating expenses	
Depreciation charge (W1)	34,000
Release of grant (W2)	(12,000)
	22,000

STATEMENT OF FINANCIAL POSITION

	$
Non-current assets	
Property, plant and equipment (W1)	766,000
Non-current liabilities	
Deferred income (W2)	204,000
Current liabilities	
Deferred income (W2)	24,000
	228,000

Workings

1	Property, plant, equipment	$
	Cost (gross, excluding grant)	800,000
	Depreciation (10 years straight line, 15% residual value for 6 months	
	800,000 × 85% × 10% × $^6/_{12}$)	(34,000)
	Carrying value	766,000

2	Deferred income	$
	Grant received ($800,000 × 30%)	240,000
	Release for this year ($240,000 × 10% × $^6/_{12}$)	(12,000)
	Total balance at year-end	228,000

	Presentation	
	Current liability ($240,000 × 10%)	24,000
	Non-current liability (balance)	204,000
		228,000

Theoretical approach under the Conceptual Framework

Because the 'deferred' element of the grant cannot be recognised as a liability, the grant will be claimed in full in the year that it is received. The repayment clause will not affect this policy because, at the end of the reporting period, Derringdo has not sold the asset and so no liability exists.

STATEMENT OF PROFIT OR LOSS

	$
Operating expenses	
Depreciation charge (as before)	34,000
Grant received and claimed	(240,000)
	(206,000)

STATEMENT OF FINANCIAL POSITION

	$'000
Non-current assets	
Property, plant and equipment	766,000

BPP
LEARNING MEDIA

19 Emerald

Text reference. Chapter 5

Top tips. There were two aspects to this question – the treatment of development costs and accounting for prior period adjustments. It was important to set out a proper working for the second part of the question so that you could see what you were doing.

Examiner's comments. Answers to this question were generally quite poor. Many candidates did not apply the definition of an asset to the development expenditure. In part (b) some candidates assumed that amortisation commenced in the year of capitalisation, rather than the following year. The prior period adjustment was rarely mentioned.

Marking scheme

		Marks
(a)	One mark per valid point to	4
(b)	Amortisation in profit or loss	1½
	Cost in statements of financial position	1
	Accumulated amortisation	1½
	Prior year adjustment in changes in equity	2
		6
Total for question		10

The IASB *Conceptual Framework* defines an asset as a resource controlled by the entity as a result of past events and from which future economic benefits are expected to flow to the entity. The recognition criteria also require that the asset has a cost or value that can be measured reliably.

In the case of development expenditure it is not always possible to determine whether or not economic benefits will result. IAS 38 deals with this issue by laying down the criteria for recognition of an intangible asset arising from development expenditure. An entity must be able to demonstrate that it is able to complete and use or sell the asset and has the intention to do so, that the asset will generate probable future economic benefits and that the expenditure attributable to the asset can be reliably measured. If these criteria are met, the asset is recognised and will be amortised from the date when it is available for use.

EMERALD	20X7	20X6
	$'000	$'000
Statement of profit or loss		
Amortisation of development expenditure (W)	335	135
Statement of financial position		
Intangible asset: development expenditure (W)	1,195	1,130
Statement of changes in equity		
Prior period adjustment		
Added to retained earnings balance at 1.10.X5 (W)		465

Working

	Expenditure	Amortisation	Carrying amount
	$'000	$'000	$'000
20X4	300		300
20X5	240	(75)*	165
Balance 20X5	540	(75)	465
20X6	800	(135)**	665
Balance 20X6	1,340	(210)	1,130
20X7	400	(335)***	65
	1,740	(545)	1,195

* 300 × 25%   ** 540 × 25%   *** 1,340 × 25%

20 Dexterity

Text reference. Chapter 5.

Top tips. Part (a) is a test of memory. Follow the structure given to you in the question; discuss three situations (purchase, business combination, internal generation) for two assets (goodwill and other intangibles). This gives you a minimum of six marks out of ten.

Part (b) requires you to apply theory. Explain both the correct treatment and why alternative treatments have been rejected. For example in (b)(ii) explain why $12m can be capitalised and why $20m can't be.

Easy marks. If you know the standards, then part (a) should be 10 easy marks,

Examiner's comments. Part (a) dealt with the treatment of goodwill and intangible assets. Part (b) included five scenarios to test the application of knowledge.

Candidates usually did very well in part (a) but performed really badly when it came to practical applications in part (b).

Marking scheme

			Marks
(a)		Discussion of goodwill	3
		Other intangibles – separate transactions	2
		– part of an acquisition	3
		– internally developed	3
		Available	11
		Maximum	10
(b)	(i)	One mark for each item in statement of financial position	4
	(ii)	Does it qualify as development expenditure	1
		The need for an active market	1
		Drugs are unique, not homogeneous	1
	(iii)	Neither an acquired asset nor internally generated	1
		Really recognition of goodwill	1
		Can recognise both the asset and the grant at fair value	1
		Or at cost – granted asset has zero cost	1
	(iv)	In reality a valuable asset, in accounting a pseudo-asset	1
		Cannot control workforce	1
		Does not meet recognition criteria	1
	(v)	Effective advertising really part of goodwill	1
		Cannot be recognised as a non-current asset	1
		Prepayment of $2.5 million	1
		Cannot spread over two years	1
		Available	18
		Maximum	15
		Maximum for question	25

(a) Recognition and amortisation

Goodwill

Only goodwill arising from a business combination is recognised. Under IFRS 3 goodwill is the excess of the cost of a business combination over the acquirer's interest in the net fair value of the assets, liabilities and contingent liabilities of the business acquired. Once recognised goodwill is held indefinitely, without amortisation but subject to impairment reviews.

One of the key aspects of goodwill is that it cannot be separated from the business that it belongs to. Therefore goodwill cannot be purchased separately from other assets. In addition, IAS 38 states that internally generated goodwill must not be capitalised.

Other intangible assets

Other intangibles can be recognised if they can be distinguished from goodwill; typically this means that they can be separated from the rest of the business, or that they arise from a legal or contractual right.

Intangibles acquired as part of a business combination are recognised at fair value provided that they can be valued separately from goodwill. The acquirer will recognise an intangible even if the asset had not been recognised previously. If an intangible cannot be valued, then it will be subsumed into goodwill.

Internally generated intangibles can be recognised if they are acquired as part of a business combination. For example, a brand name acquired in a business combination is capitalised whereas an internally generated brand isn't. Expenditure on research can not be capitalised. Development expenditure is capitalised if it meets the IAS 38 criteria. It is then amortised over the life-cycle of the product.

Goodwill and intangibles with an indefinite useful life are not amortised but tested annually for impairment.

(b) **Dexterity**

(i) *Temerity*

The following assets will be recognised on acquisition:

	$m
Fair value of sundry net assets	15
Patent at fair value	10
Research carried out for customer	2
Goodwill (balancing figure)	8
Total consideration	35

The patent is recognised at its fair value at the date of acquisition, even if it hadn't previously been recognised by Temerity. It will be amortised over the remaining 8 years of its useful life with an assumed nil residual value.

The higher value of $15m can't be used because it depends on the successful outcome of the clinical trials. The extra $5m is a contingent asset, and contingent assets are not recognised in a business combination. (Only assets, liabilities and contingent liabilities are recognised.)

Although research is not capitalised, this research has been carried out for a customer and should be recognised as work-in-progress in current assets. It will be valued at the lower of cost and net realisable value unless it meets the definition of a construction contract.

The goodwill is capitalised at cost. It is not amortised but it will be tested for impairment annually.

(ii) *New drug*

Under IAS 38 the $12m costs of *developing* this new drug are capitalised and then amortised over its commercial life. (The costs of *researching* a new drug are never capitalised.)

Although IAS 38 permits some intangibles to be held at valuation it specifically forbids revaluing patents, therefore the $20m valuation is irrelevant.

(iii) *Government licence*

IAS 38 states that assets acquired as a result of a government grant may be capitalised at fair value, along with a corresponding credit for the value of the grant.Therefore Dexterity may recognise an asset and grant of $10m which are then amortised/released over the five year life of the license. The net effect on profits and on shareholders funds will be nil.

(iv) *Training costs*

Although well trained staff adds value to a business IAS 38 prohibits the capitalisation of training costs. This is because an entity has 'insufficient control over the expected future economic benefits' arising from staff training; in other words trained staff are free to leave and work for someone else. Training is part of the general cost of developing a business as a whole.

(v) *Advertising costs*

IAS 38 Para 69 states that advertising and promotional costs should be recognised as an expense when incurred. This is because the expected future economic benefits are uncertain and they are beyond the control of the entity.

However, because the year-end is half way through the campaign there is a $2.5m prepayment to be recognised as a current asset.

21 Darby

Text references. Chapters 1, 5 and 6.
Top tips. It was important for this question to know the IASB definition. This made it possible to do a good answer to part (a) and know where you were going with part (b). It was important to spend time on all four parts of the question and read the scenarios carefully.
Easy marks. This was all quite easy until you got to (b) (iii), which was a slightly confusing scenario. The clue was in 'the assistant *correctly* recorded the costs..', which would have told you that the point at issue was the impairment write-down.

Marking scheme

		Marks
(a)	1 mark per valid point	4
(b)	(i) to (iii) – 1 mark per valid point as indicated	11
Total for question		15

(a) The IASB *Conceptual Framework* defines an asset as 'a resource controlled by the entity as a result of past events and from which future economic benefits are expected to flow to the entity'. IAS 1 sets out the defining features of a current asset (intended to be realised during the normal operating cycle or within 12 months of the year end, held for trading or classified as cash or a cash equivalent). All other assets are classified as non-current.

The assistant's definition diverges from this in a number of ways:

(i) A non-current asset does not have to be physical. The definition can include intangible assets such as investments or capitalised development costs.

(ii) A non-current asset does not have to be of substantial cost. An item of immaterial value is unlikely to be capitalised, but this is not part of the definition.

(iii) A non-current asset does not have to be legally owned. The accounting principle is based on 'substance over form' and relies on the ability of the entity to **control** the asset. This means for instance that an asset held under a finance lease is treated as an asset by the lessee, not the lessor.

(iv) It is generally the case that non-current assets will last longer than one year. IAS 16 specifies that property, plant and equipment 'are expected to be used during more than one period'. However, if a non-current asset failed to last longer than one year, it would **still be classified as a non-current asset during its life**.

(b) (i) IAS 38 makes the point that 'an entity usually has **insufficient control** over the expected future economic benefits arising from a team of skilled staff..' This is the case in this situation. Darby's trained staff may stay with the company for the next four years or they may decide to leave and take their skills with them. Darby has no control over that. For this reason, the expenditure on training **can not be treated as an asset** and must be charged to profit or loss.

(ii) The work on the new processor chip is research with the aim of eventually moving into development work. IAS 38 requires all research expenditure to be expensed as incurred. Even at the development stage, it **will not be possible to capitalise the development costs unless they satisfy the IAS 38 criteria**. When the criteria are satisfied and development costs can be capitalised, it will still not be possible to go back and capitalise the research costs. The company's past successful history makes no difference to this.

The research work on the braking system is a different case, because here the work has been commissioned by a customer and the customer will be paying, regardless of the outcome of the research. In this situation, as long as Darby has no reason to believe that the customer will not meet

BPP
LEARNING MEDIA

the costs in full, the costs should be treated as **work in progress**, rather than being charged to profit or loss.

(iii) If we agree that the assistant was correct to record $58,000 as a non-current asset, the only question is whether it should be regarded as impaired.

An impairment has occurred when the recoverable amount of an asset falls below its carrying amount.

The projected results for this contract are:

	$
Revenue (50,000 × 3)	150,000
Costs (bal)	(110,000)
Profit	40,000

If we ignore discounting, the future cash flows are $150,000, less remaining costs of $52,000 ($110,000 - $58,000), which amounts to $98,000. This is well in excess of the $58,000 carrying amount, so **no impairment has taken place** and the non-current asset should remain at $58,000.

22 Advent

(a) STATEMENT OF FINANCIAL POSITION EXTRACTS 30 SEPTEMBER 20X9

Assets	$m
Non-current assets	
Property, plant and equipment (Note 1)	316
Other intangible assets (Note 2)	100
	416

Note 1 *Property, plant and equipment*

	Land and buildings $m	Plant $m	Total $m
1 October 20X8			
Cost/ valuation	280	150	430
Accumulated depreciation	(40)	(105)	(145)
	240	45	285
30 September 20X9			
Cost/ valuation	265	200	465
Accumulated depreciation	(9)	(140)	(149)
	256	60	316
Carrying amount			
1 October 20X8	240	45	285
Additions		50	50
Revaluations	(15)	–	(15)
Depreciation:			
Charge for year	(9)	(35)	(44)
On revaluation	40	–	40
	256	60	316

Buildings are depreciated over 25 years and plant over 5 years.

On 1st October 20X8 the land and buildings were valued by XYZ, Chartered Surveyors, on an open market existing use basis.

Workings

1   *Plant*

Installation and commissioning costs are included in the cost of the asset.

Depreciation	$m
Opening cost of $150m (full year at 20%)	30
Additions of $50m (half year at 20%)	5
	35

2   *Property*

	Land	*Buildings: Value*	*Total Value*	*Building Dep'n*	*Carrying Value*
	$m	$m	$m	$m	$m
Opening	80	200	280	(40)	240
Revaluation	5	(20)	(15)	40	25
	85	180	265	–	265
Depreciation (20 years)	–	–	–	(9)	(9)
Closing	85	180	265	(9)	256

Note 2 *Intangible assets: Telecommunications license*

	$m
Cost	
Opening/closing	300
Depreciation	
Opening	30
Charge	30
Impairment loss	140
Closing	200
Carrying amount	
30. 9. 20X9	100
30. 9.20X8	270

The closing carrying amount must not exceed the impaired value of $100m; therefore the accumulated depreciation must be fixed at $200m. This in turn gives the impairment charge as a balancing figure of $140m.

The new carrying amount of $100m will be depreciated over the remaining 8 year life of the license.

(b)   *Usefulness of the disclosures*

The disclosures give the reader more information about the nature and value of the non-current assets.

Firstly, there is the split between tangible assets (property, plant and equipment) and intangible assets. Lenders are less willing to use intangibles as security for loans than tangibles, and in the event of a winding up intangibles are often worthless without the business to support them.

Within property, plant and equipment there is the split between land and buildings and the rest. Land and buildings are often seen as the best source of security by lenders.

Land and buildings can go up in value as well as down, and so the note indicates the effect of revaluations during the year. The revaluation reserve note elsewhere in the financial statements will show the total revaluation compared with original cost. Because valuations are subjective the identity and qualifications of the valuer are disclosed.

The rates of depreciation indicate how prudent (or otherwise) the depreciation policies are, and whether the reported profits are fairly stated. The ratio between carrying value and cost gives a rough idea of the age of the assets, and of how soon they will need replacing.

The disclosure of the impairment loss flags a bad investment; the shareholders will want more information about this at their annual general meeting.

BPP
LEARNING MEDIA

23 Wilderness

Text reference. Chapters 5 and 6.

Top tips. Part (a) is a straight forward description of impairment and how it is accounted for.

Part (b) applies the theory. In (b) (ii) remember that the impairment of the brand name should have been accounted for when it happened in April 20X5. This is before the impairment review of the whole cash generating unit in September.

Easy marks. There were no particular easy marks in this question. You needed to have a good knowledge of the principles of impairment and to understand all the terms.

Examiners comments. This question tested the principles of impairment of assets. It was not a popular question and candidates who attempted it scored on average less than half marks.

Answers to part (a) were generally correct but lacked important detail. The numerical examples in (b) were less well answered, showing an inability to apply principles. Part (b) (ii) answers were even worse. Many candidate did not realise that the Phoenix brand name was an internally – generated asset and could not be recognise. In some cases, no attempt was made to apportion the impairment loss over the relevant assets.

Marking scheme

				Marks
(a)	(i)	Impairment where carrying amounts higher than recoverable amounts		1
		Discussion of fair value		2
		Discussion of value in use		2
		Discussion of CGU		1
		Goodwill/ intangibles with in definite life tested annually		1
		Review for indicators of impairment		1
		Only test if there is an indication of impairment		1
			Available	9
			Maximum	6
	(ii)	Impairment loss – individual asset:		
		Impairment loss applied to carrying value of asset		1
		And changed to any previous revaluation surplus then income		2
		CGU:		
		Applied to goodwill		1
		Then pro rata to other assets		1
		Other assets not reduced below fair value/ value in use		1
			Available	6
			Maximum	5
(b)	(i)	Depreciation/ carrying value 1 April 20X5		2
		Fair value less costs to sell is disposal value of $20,000, not trade-in value		2
		Recoverable is therefore $150,000		1
		Impairment loss is $50,000		1
		Depreciation six months to 30 September 20X5		1
		Carrying value $112,500		1
			Available	8
			Maximum	7
	(ii)	Old brand written off, cannot recognise new brand		2
		Inventories correct at cost		2
		Improvement to plant not relevant		1
		Impairment loss is $5 million		1
		Land reduced to $9 million		1
		Plant reduced to $6 million		1
			Available	8
			Maximum	7
			Maximum for question	25

(a) (i) **Define an impairment loss**

An impairment occurs when the carrying value of an asset exceeds its recoverable amount. Recoverable amount represents the amount of cash that an asset will generate either through use (value in use) or through disposal (fair value less costs to sell).

The value in use is the present value of all future cash flows derived from an asset, including any disposal proceeds at the end of the asset's life. The present value of future cash flows will be affected by the timing, volatility and uncertainty of the cash flows. This can be reflected in the forecasted cash flows or the discount rate used.

Very few business assets generate their own cash flows, and so assets are often grouped together into cash generating units for impairment purposes. A cash generating is the smallest group of assets generating independent cash flows

Fair value less costs to sell is the amount obtainable for an asset in an arm's length transaction between knowledgeable, willing parties, less the cost of disposal. The fair value of used assets with no active market will have to be estimated. Valuations are based on willing parties, and so a 'forced sale' value would not normally be used.

Impairment reviews

- At each reporting date an entity shall assess whether there are any indications that an impairment has occurred; if there are such indications then the recoverable amount of the asset must be estimated.
- Intangible assets with indefinite lives (and those not ready for use) should be reviewed for impairment annually. The review should take place at the same time each year.
- Cash generating units that include goodwill should be reviewed for impairment annually.

(ii) **Accounting for an impairment loss**

Impairment losses should be recognised immediately. They will normally be charged to profit or loss alongside depreciation, but the impairment of a revalued asset should be taken directly to the revaluation surplus (until the balance on the revaluation surplus is reduced to zero). In the statement of financial position the impairment will normally be included within accumulated depreciation, although it could be disclosed separately if material. Future depreciation charges will be based on the impaired value and the remaining useful life at the date of the impairment.

Impairments of cash generating units must be apportioned to the individual assets within that unit. The impairment is firstly allocated to goodwill, and then it is apportioned to all other assets (both tangible and intangible) on a pro rata basis. However, individual assets are not impaired below their own realisable value; any unused impairment being re-apportioned to the other assets.

(b) (i)

STATEMENT OF PROFIT OR LOSS (EXTRACT)

		$
Depreciation	First six months	40,000
	Second six months	37,500
Impairment		50,000
		127,500

STATEMENT OF FINANCIAL POSITION AS AT 30 SEPTEMBER 20X5 (EXTRACT)

	$
Cost	640,000
Accumulated depreciation and impairment	
($400,000 + $40,000 + $50,000 + $37,500)	(527,500)
Carrying value	112,500

At 1 April 20X5 the asset should be restated at the lower of carrying value and recoverable amount. Recoverable amount is the higher of *value in use* and *fair value less costs to sell*.

BPP
LEARNING MEDIA

Carrying amount 1 April 20X5	$
Cost	640,000
Opening depreciation	(400,000)
Depreciation for 6 months ($640,000 × 12$\frac{1}{2}$% × $^6/_{12}$)	(40,000)
Carrying value 1 April 20X5	200,000

Recoverable amount	$
Value in use and recoverable amount	150,000
[Fair value less costs to sell*	20,000]

* Wilderness does not intend to replace the machine and so the trade-in value of $180,000 is irrelevant.

The asset is impaired and should be written down to the recoverable amount of $150,000, giving an impairment loss of $50,000. This new valuation will then be depreciated over the remaining useful life of the asset, which is two years from the date of the accident.

Carrying value 30 September 20X5		$
Impaired value 1 April 20X5		150,000
Depreciation for 6 months	$150,000 × $^6/_{24}$	(37,500)
Carrying value 1 April 20X5		112,500

(ii) **Mossel**

The question raises four issues:

- The value of the Quencher brand name,
- The $1.5m upgrade costs,
- The old bottles in inventories, and
- The overall impairment of the whole operation.

(1) *The value of the Quencher brand name*

The $7m Quencher brand name should have been written off in April as it is no longer used. The Phoenix brand name is internally generated and so it cannot be capitalised. This will reduce the carrying value of the net assets at 30 September to $25m.

(2) *The $1.5m upgrade costs*

These costs reflect the directors' intentions for the coming year. There is no obligation to incur these costs and so they cannot be recognised in the current year. However they may be disclosed in the notes.

(3) *The old bottles in inventories*

These should be stated at the lower of normal cost ($2m) and net realisable value ($2.75m), therefore they remain at their cost of $2m. The NRV is the normal sales price of $3m (normal cost of $2m plus 50%) less the $250,000 re-labelling costs.

(4) *The overall impairment of the whole operation at September 20X5*

The value in use and recoverable amount of the whole operation has been reduced to $20m. This is less than the carrying value of $25m and so an impairment has to be accounted for and apportioned to the assets within the cash generating unit. This is done as follows:

	Carrying value	Impairment	Impaired values
	$'000	$'000	$'000
Brand (already impaired)	–	–	–
Land	12,000	(3,000)	9,000
Plant	8,000	(2,000)	6,000
	20,000	(5,000)	15,000

Note. Inventory of $5m is not subject to impairment.

24 Telepath

Text reference: Chapter 6.

Top tips. This is a typical F7 question in which you are asked to write about the provisions of a standard and then apply them. In this case it was IAS 36. Part (a) is for 4 marks so it required more than two sentences, but it was important to leave time for part (b). Do not forget that the estimated residual value in (i) will be added to the year 3 cash flow. In (ii) the damaged plant must be written off before the remaining impairment is allocated.

Easy marks. This whole question was easy if you knew the basics of IAS 36. You should have been able to make some valid points in (a) and (b)(ii) had marks available for knowing what to write off, which was obvious with a bit of thought.

Examiner's comments In part (a) there were many irrelevant answers which discussed indicators of impairment or described scenarios, failing to even mention CGUs. A lot of mistakes were made in part (b), the most common of which was failing to include the residual amount as part of the cash flows. In the second example a lot of errors were made in allocating the impairment loss.

Examiner's answer. The examiner's answer to this question is at the end of this Kit.

Marking scheme

		Marks
(a) 1 mark per valid point		4
(b)(i)		
Carrying amount before impairment test	1	
Value in use	2	
Not impaired – leave at carrying amount	1	4
(b)(ii)		
Damaged plant written off	1	
Goodwill written off	1	
Patent at $1m	1	
Cash and receivables – no impairment	1	
Pro rata of remaining loss	1	
Apply to building and plant only	2	7
Total		15

(a) An impairment review as laid out in IAS 36 *Impairment of Assets* is carried out to determine whether the value of an asset may have fallen below its carrying amount in the statement of financial position. It is a requirement for goodwill carried in the statement of financial position that it should be tested annually for impairment.

An asset is considered to be impaired if its carrying amount exceeds its recoverable amount, defined as the higher of fair value less costs to sell and value in use. Value in use is the present value of the future cash flows which will be generated by the asset. It is often not possible to attribute cash flows to an individual asset, so in this case the impairment review is carried out at the level of the cash generating unit to which the asset belongs. A cash generating unit is a group of assets which together generate cash flows. For instance, a production unit in a factory could be treated as a cash generating unit and any impairment identified will be apportioned between the assets of the CGU.

(b)(i) Carrying amount of the plant at 31.3.X2

		$'000
1.4.X0	Cost	800,000
	Depreciation ((800,000 − 50,000) /5)	(150,000)
31.3.X1	Balance	650,000
	Depreciation	(150,000)
31.3.X2	Balance	500,000

BPP
LEARNING MEDIA

As there is currently no market in which to sell the plant, its recoverable amount will be its value in use, calculated as:

Year ended	Cash flow $'000	Discount factor 10%	Present value $'000
31 March 20X3	220	0.91	200
31 March 20X4	180	0.83	149
31 March 20X5	170 + 50	0.75	165
			514

As this is greater than the carrying amount, the plant is not impaired and will be left at its carrying amount of $500,000.

(ii) The impairment loss will be allocated as follows:

	$'000		$'000	$'000
Goodwill	1,800	Written off	(1,800)	-
Patent	1,200	W/D to realisable amount	(200)	1,000
Factory building	4,000	Working	(1,600)	2,400
Plant	3,500	Working	(1,700)	1,800
Receivables and cash	1,500	No impairment	-	1,500
	12,000		(5,300)	6,700

Working

The total amount of the impairment loss to be allocated is $5.3m.

		$'000
The initial write-offs are:	Damaged plant	500
	Goodwill	1,800
	Patent	200
		3,500

This leaves $2.8m impairment loss to be allocated between the factory building (4,000) and the remaining plant (3,000). The allocation will be:

Factory (2,800 x 4,000 / 7,000)	1,600
Plant (2,800 x 3,000 / 7,000)	1,200
	2,800

25 Tourmalet

Text reference. Chapters 7 and 15.

Top tips. As well as examining you on the format and content of the statement of profit or loss and statement of changes in equity, this question also tests your knowledge of seven specific situations.

One key point is to separate out the discontinued activities. Under IFRS 5 the profit or loss on these activities is reported after the profit after tax for continuing activities.

As always, be methodical and don't get bogged down in the detail.

Easy marks. Parts (a) and (c) are 8 easy marks. You should be able to answer these even if you get bogged down in the statement of profit or loss.

Examiner's comments. Part (a) covered the sale and leaseback of plant. Most candidates realised that this should be treated as a secured loan. However, some failed to recognise the correct treatment.

In part (b), candidates had to prepare a statement of profit or loss and this was generally well-answered. However some problems arose: discontinued operation, provision for slow moving inventory, and the treatment of interest on the loan from part (a).

Part (c) was generally ignored. Those who did attempt the statement of changes in equity failed to realise that the preference shares should be treated as debt and so the preference dividend should be treated as a finance cost.

			Marks
(a)	Should not be treated as sales/cost of sales		1
	Profit deferred and amortised		1
	The substance of the transaction is a secured loan		1
	Plant should be left on statement of financial position at new valuation		1
	'Sale' proceeds of $50 million shown as lease liability		1
	Rentals are partly interest and partly capital repayments		1
		Available	6
		Maximum	5
(b)	Statement of profit or loss		
	Discontinuing operations figures		3
	Sales		2
	Cost of sales		5
	Distribution expenses		1
	Administration expenses		2
	Finance costs (including 1 for preference dividends)		2
	Loss on investment properties		1
	Investment income		1
	Taxation		2
		Available	19
		Maximum	17
(c)	Changes in equity		
	Profit for period		1
	Dividends		1
	Transfer to realised profits		1
		Maximum	3
		Maximum for question	25

(a) Sale of plant

The substance of this transaction is a financing arrangement, not a sale.

- Tourmalet will continue to enjoy the risks and benefits of ownership for the remainder of the asset's life because of the leaseback deal.
- The lease appears to be a finance lease, so Tourmalet will continue to recognise the asset.
- Over the period of the lease Tourmalet will repay the sale proceeds in full, plus interest at 12%, indicating that this is a loan and not a sale.

Tourmalet should recognise the asset at its new carrying amount of $50m and depreciate over its remaining useful life. A corresponding lease liability should be set up for $50m and the $10m 'profit' is deferred and amortised over the remaining useful life of the asset.

Even if the sale was a genuine sale, it should not have been included within normal trading revenues and cost of sales.

BPP
LEARNING MEDIA

(b) TOURMALET
STATEMENT OF PROFIT OR LOSS FOR THE YEAR ENDED 30 SEPTEMBER 20X4

	$'000
Sales revenues (W1)	247,800
Cost of sales (W2)	(124,133)
Gross profit	123,667
Other income (W3)	1,867
Distribution costs (W4)	(26,400)
Administrative expenses (W5)	(20,000)
Other expenses (W6)	(200)
Finance costs (W7)	(3,800)
Profit before tax	75,134
Income tax expense (W8)	(7,100)
Profit for the year from continuing operations	68,034
Discontinued operations	
Loss for the year from discontinued operations (W9)	(5,500)
Profit for the year	62,534

Workings

Continuing operations	$'000
1 **Sales revenues**	
From TB	313,000
Disposal of plant	(50,000)
Discontinued activities	(15,200)
	247,800
2 **Cost of sales**	
Opening inventory	26,550
Purchases	158,450
Disposal of plant	(40,000)
Closing inventory: Cost 28,500	
less NRV allowance (4,500 – 2,000)	(26,000)
Depreciation	
Leased item $50m/5 years × 4/12	3,333
Others ($98.6m – $24.6m) × 20%	14,800
Buildings ($120m/40 years)	3,000
Discontinued activities	(16,000)
	124,133
3 **Other income**	
From the TB	1,200
Deferred income ($10m/5 years × 4/12)	667
	1,867
4 **Distribution costs**	
From the TB	26,400
5 **Administrative expenses**	
From the TB	23,200
Discontinued activities	(3,200)
	20,000
6 **Other expenses**	
Fall in value of investment property (10m – 9.8m)	200
7 **Finance costs**	
Interim preference dividend from the TB	900
Accrued final preference dividend ($30m × 6% × 6/12)	900
Finance cost of lease back ($50m × 12% × 4/12)	2,000
	3,800

8   *Income tax expense*

Over-provision from the trial balance	(2,100)
Charge for the year	9,200
	7,100

9   *Discontinued operations*

Revenue	15,200
Operating expenses (16,000 + 3,200 + 1,500 termination penalty)	(20,700)
Loss	(5,500)

(c)   TOURMALET
STATEMENT OF CHANGES IN EQUITY FOR THE YEAR TO 30 SEPTEMBER 20X4

	Share capital $'000	Revaluation surplus $'000	Retained earnings $'000	Total $'000
Opening	50,000	18,500	47,800	116,300
Transfer of depreciation on revaluation	–	(500)	500	–
Dividends	–	–	(2,500)	(2,500)
Total comprehensive income for the year	–	–	62,534	62,534
Closing	50,000	18,000	108,334	176,334

26 Partway

Text reference. Chapter 7.

Top tips. This question covers discontinued operations and changes of accounting policy. Not to be attempted unless you knew something about both of these. There are five separate parts to this question. Do something on each of them, do not get carried away with the statement of profit or loss.

Easy marks. (a) (i) and (ii) and (b) (i) were quite easy and you should have been able to do well on them. (a) (iii) was not difficult but you may have ended up spending too long on it and (b) (ii) was a bit tricky. However you were asked to comment, so a sensible comment supported by the evidence would have secured you a mark or two.

Examiner's comments. This question proved to be the least popular and, while answers were not good, they were better than for equivalent questions on recent papers. Candidates were able to define non-current assets held for sale and discontinued operations, but were less able to apply these definitions to the scenario. Most candidates were similarly able to define a change of accounting policy but few even attempted the scenario.

Marking scheme

				Marks
(a)	(i)	Definitions		2
		Usefulness of information		2
			Maximum	4
	(ii)	Discussion of whether a discontinued operation		3
		Conclusion		1
			Maximum	4
	(iii)	Revenue from continuing operations (20X5 and 20X6)		1
		Revenue from discontinued operations (20X5 and 20X6)		1
		Cost of sales from continuing operations (20X5 and 20X6)		1
		Cost of sales from discontinued operations (20X5 and 20X6)		1
		Profit from continuing operations (20X5 and 20X6)		1
		Profit from discontinued operations (20X5 and 20X6)		1
			Maximum	6

BPP
LEARNING MEDIA

(b)	(i)	1 mark per relevant point	Maximum	5
	(ii)	1 mark per relevant point	Maximum	6
			Maximum for question	25

(a) (i) IFRS 5 defines 'non-current assets held for sale' to be those non-current assets whose carrying amount will be recovered principally through a sale transaction rather than through continuing use'.

A discontinued operation is described in IFRS 5 as:

'a component of an entity that either has been disposed of, or is classified as held for sale, and:

(a) represents a separate major line of business or geographical area of operations

(b) is part of a single co-ordinated plan to dispose of a separate major line of business or geographical area of operations or

(c) is a subsidiary acquired exclusively with a view to resale.'

IFRS 5 states that *a component of an entity* comprises operations and cash flows that can be clearly distinguished, operationally and for financial reporting purposes, from the rest of the entity.

This very precise definition is needed to ensure that only operations which can properly be regarded as discontinued are classified as such. Users of accounts, particularly financial analysts, will be more interested in the results of continuing operations as a guide to the company's future profitability and it is not unacceptable for discontinued operations to show a loss. Companies could therefore be tempted to hide loss-making activities under the umbrella of discontinued operations, hence the requirement for the operations and cash flows of the discontinued operation to be clearly distinguishable from those of continuing operations. It is also conceivable that a company could seek to include the results of a profitable operation which has been sold under continuing operations.

IFRS 5 requires an entity to disclose a single amount on the face of the statement of profit or loss comprising the total of:

(i) the post tax profit or loss of discontinued operations and

(ii) the post-tax gain or loss recognised on the measurement to fair value less costs to sell or on the disposal of the assets constituting the discontinued operation

The separation of the results of continuing and discontinued operations on the face of the statement of profit or loss makes possible more meaningful year on year comparison. The inclusion of prior year information for discontinued operations means that it can be seen exactly how the continuing operations have performed, and it is possible to forecast more accurately how they can be expected to perform in the future.

(ii) This may be able to be classified as a discontinued operation provided certain criteria are met. The termination was decided on before the financial statements were approved and within two weeks of the year end date. The interested parties were notified at that time and an announcement was made in the press, making the decision irrevocable. Although the company will continue to sell holidays over the internet, the travel agency business represents a separate major line of business. The internet business will have quite different property and staffing requirements and a different customer base. The results of the travel agency business are clearly distinguished.

(iii) PARTWAY
STATEMENT OF PROFIT OR LOSS FOR THE YEAR ENDED

	31 October 20X6	31 October 20X5
Continuing operations	$'000	$'000
Revenue	25,000	22,000
Cost of sales	(19,500)	(17,000)
Gross profit	5,500	5,000
Operating expenses	(1,100)	(500)
Profit from continuing operations	4,400	4,500
Profit(loss) from discontinued operations	(4,000)	1,500
Profit for the year	400	6,000

Discontinued operations

Revenue	14,000	18,000
Cost of sales	(16,500)	(15,000)
Gross profit (loss)	(2,500)	3,000
Operating expenses	(1,500)	(1,500)
Profit(loss) from discontinued operations	(4,000)	1,500

(b) (i) Accounting policies can be described as the principles, conventions, rules and practices applied by an entity that prescribe how transactions and other events are to be reflected in its financial statements. This includes the recognition, presentation and measurement basis to be applied to assets, liabilities, gains, losses and changes to shareholders funds. Once these policies have been adopted, they are not expected to change frequently and comparability requires that ideally they do not change from year to year. However, IAS 8 does envisage situations where a change of accounting policy is required in the interests of fair presentation.

An entity may have to change an accounting policy in response to changes in a Standard or in applicable legislation. Or it may be an internal decision which can be justified on the basis of presenting a more reliable picture. An accounting policy adopted to deal with transactions or events which did not arise previously is not treated as a change of accounting policy.

Where a change of accounting policy has taken place it must be accounted for by retrospective restatement. This means that the comparative financial statements must be restated in the light of the new accounting policy. This makes it possible to compare results for these years as if the new accounting policy had always been in place. The financial statements must disclose the reason for the change of accounting policy and the effects of the change on the results for the previous year.

(ii) The directors' proposal here is that revenue recognition can be accelerated based on the imposition of compulsory holiday insurance. This is based on the presumption that the risk of not receiving the balance of the payment has now been covered. However, at the point when the deposit is received, Partway has not yet done anything to earn the revenue. Under IAS 18 *Revenue,* revenue from a service contract should be recognised by reference to the stage of completion of the transaction. Under this method, revenue is recognised in the accounting periods in which the services are rendered. In this case the service is rendered at the time when the holiday is taken. The existing policy is therefore correct and should not be changed.

27 Tunshill

Text references. Chapters 1, 4 and 12.

Top tips. Part (a) is for 5 marks, so you can work out that more than two sentences are required. Reading the rest of the question would have helped you to think about part (a) and so would considering the Conceptual Framework principles.

Easy marks. Part (b) was really quite easy, as long as you knew the difference between an accounting policy and an accounting estimate. Always work the numbers out carefully on paper, then if you make a mistake the marker can see what you were doing.

Examiner's comments. In part (a) many candidates wasted time explaining when an entity should change its accounting policy and the procedures to be followed. This was not what the question asked. Answers to part (b) were very mixed. In part (i) some candidates failed to calculate depreciation on the remaining useful life and some treated the example as an asset revaluation, which it was not. In part (ii) some candidates agreed with the assistant accountant that the change would improve profit by $2m.

Marking scheme

		Marks
(a)	1 mark per valid point	5

BPP
LEARNING MEDIA

(b)(i)	Recognise as a change in accounting estimate	1
	Appears an acceptable basis for change	1
	Correct method is to allocate carrying amount over new remaining life	1
	Depreciation for current year should be $2million	1
	Carrying amount at 30 September 20X3 is $10 million	1
		5

(ii)	Proposed change is probably not for a valid reason	1
	Change would cause decrease (not increase) in profit	1
	Changes in policy should be applied retrospectively	1
	Decrease in year to 30 September 20X3 is $400,000	1
	Retained earnings restated by $1.6 million	1
		5
		15

(a) IAS 8 *Accounting policies, changes in accounting estimates and errors* requires an entity to determine the accounting policy to apply to a transaction or event by reference to any IFRS specifically applying to that transaction or event. Where there is no specific IFRS applicable, management is expected to **use its judgement** in applying an accounting policy which will result in information which is relevant and reliable. In this they should consider the requirements and guidance in IFRSs dealing with similar and related issues and also the*Conceptual Framework* definitions, recognition criteria and measurement concepts for assets, liabilities, income and expenses.

Accounting policies are the specific principles, bases and rules applied in measuring and presenting financial information. **Changes of accounting policy are not very common**. One example would be a change from the FIFO method of valuing inventory to the weighted average method – this is a change in the basis of valuation.

A **change of accounting estimate** is a change in the way in which these principles and bases are applied which leads to an adjustment to any of the elements identified by the *Conceptual Framework* – assets, liabilities, income or expenses. One example would be a change from the straight line method of depreciation to the reducing balance method. In this case the accounting policy is that non-current assets are carried at cost less accumulated depreciation, the accounting estimate is how that depreciation is calculated.

(b) (i) As the plant is wearing well and the production manager now estimates its total life to be eight years, it is **reasonable to adjust its remaining life**. However, the adjustment proposed by the assistant accountant is incorrect. This is a **change in accounting estimate** and is **not applied retrospectively**. At 1 October 20X2 the remaining life of the plant will be six years – the new estimated life of eight year less the two years which have elapsed.

The correct adjustment will be calculated as follows:

	$m
Original cost 1 October 20X0	20
Two years depreciation ((20/5) × 2)	(8)
Carrying amount at 1 October 20X2	12
Depreciation to 30 September 20X3 (12/6)	(2)
Carrying amount at 30 September 20X3	10

There will be no credit to profit or loss for the year and depreciation will continue to be charged, but at a reduced rate.

(b) (ii) It looks here as if this change is being proposed simply in order to increase reported profit, rather than to make the financial information more relevant and reliable. However, if most of Tunshill's competitors are using AVCO this suggests that AVCO is the method generally used in the industry, so it may actually be a more appropriate method.

BPP LEARNING MEDIA

However the assistant accountant is mistaken to suppose that moving from closing inventory of $20m under FIFO to closing inventory of $18m under AVCO will increase profits by $2m. It will actually **reduce profits** by increasing cost of sales. In any case, this **cannot be done simply as an adjustment to the current year**. This is a change of accounting policy and has to be applied retrospectively.

The effect of the adjustment will be as follows:

	FIFO $m	AVCO $m	Current year profit $m	Retained earnings $m
Year to 30 September 20X2	15	13.4	(1.6)	(1.6)
B/f 1 October 20X2			1.6	1.6
Year to 30 September 20X3	20	18	(2.0)	(2.0)
At 30 September 20X3			(0.4)	(2.0)

The net effect at 30 September 20X3 of this proposal will be to reduce current year profits by $400,000 and to reduce retained earnings by $2m.

28 Manco

Text references. Chapters 7 and 13.

Top tips. This question required you to look at a situation in terms of both a restructuring and a discontinued operation. If you found it a bit off-putting it would be best to pick out the bits you knew how to deal with. For instance you could state that the press announcement made the decision to restructure irrevocable. You probably knew that the provision would cover the redundancy but not the retraining and you could allocate the trading losses to the correct years.

Easy marks. Any easy marks on this question would be the ones above, plus noting the impairment loss on the plant.

Examiner's comments. This was not generally a well-answered question. The information pointed to the closure being irrevocable and most candidates concluded that a provision was needed. What caused problems was which losses to provide for and in which period. It was disappointing that most candidates did not attempt to allocate the loss between the two reporting periods, despite the question specifically asking for this. Most of the marks were for reporting items in the right period.

Marking scheme

	Marks
Closure is a restructuring event under IAS 37	1
It is an obligating event in year ended 30 September 20X0	1
Provide for impairment of plant	1
Cannot recognise gain on property until sold	1
Provide for redundancy in year ended 30 September 20X0	1
Cannot provide for retraining costs in current year	1
Inclusion of trading losses in correct periods	2
Consider if and when should be treated as discontinued operation	2
	10

The actions taken by Manco have resulted in a **constructive obligation** to restructure as set out in IAS 37 *Provisions, contingent liabilities and contingent assets*. It has produced a formal plan and communicated it to those affected (employees and customers), thereby raising a valid expectation that the restructuring will be carried out. It will therefore be correct to make a provision in the financial statements for the year ended 30 September 20X0 for the costs of the restructuring.

BPP
LEARNING MEDIA

As a separate business segment is being closed down, this will be a **discontinued operation**. As they are due to be sold six months from the date of the closure announcement, the factory and plant could be classified as held for sale at 30 September 20X0. If Manco intends to continue using them and does not classify them as held for sale, they will continue to be depreciated up to 31 January 20X1. In this case the closure will not be treated as a discontinued operation at 30 September 20X0, but **will be reported as such in the year to 30 September 20X1 when the assets are sold**.

Year to 30 September 20X0

A **restructuring provision** should be recognised for $750,000, being the cost of redundancies.

The $600,000 trading losses will be included in profit or loss for the year.

The factory will be subject to the normal depreciation charge.

The plant should be written down to its recoverable amount, which will be $500,000.

Year to 30 September 20X1

The redundancies will take place and the costs will be offset against the provision.

The final $1m of trading losses will be treated as the results of a discontinued operation and shown in one figure on the statement of profit or loss combined with final profit/loss on disposal of the assets.

The retraining costs of $200,000 will be accounted for as part of continuing operations.

29 Preparation question: Group financial statements

(a)   A parent need not present consolidated financial statements if one of the following exemptions applies:

- It is itself a wholly or partly-owned subsidiary of another entity and its other owners do not object to it not preparing consolidated financial statements.

- Its shares or debt instruments are not traded on any stock exchange.

- Its financial statements are not being filed with any regulatory organisation for the purpose of issuing any debt or equity instruments on any stock exchange.

- Its own or ultimate parent produces publicly-available financial statements that comply with IFRS.

(b)   IFRS 10 requires intragroup balances, transactions, income and expenses to be eliminated in full. The purpose of consolidated financial statements is to present the financial position of the parent and subsidiaries as that of a **single entity**, the group. This means that, in the consolidated statement of profit or loss, the only profits recognised should be those earned by the group in trading with entities outside the group. Similarly, inventory should be valued at cost to the group.

When a company sells goods to another company in the same group it will recognise revenue and profit in its individual financial statements. However, from the point of view of the group, no sale has taken place, because the goods are still held by the group. The sale must therefore be eliminated from revenue and the unrealised profit must be eliminated from group inventory.

Where one group company owes money to another group company or one company holds loan stock of another company, the asset and liability balances will be eliminated on consolidation. As far as the group is concerned, they do not represent amounts due to or from third parties.

(c)   The parent-subsidiary relationship is one between related parties and can be used to manipulate trading results and balances.

If the purpose is to improve the financial statements of the parent, a number of options are possible. Transfer prices can be fixed so that the subsidiary sells cheaply to the parent and/or the parent sells to the subsidiary at an inflated price. Intercompany loans can be similarly fixed so that the subsidiary lends to the parent at a low interest rate and borrows from the parent at a high interest rate. Assets being transferred between the parent and the subsidiary can be priced in the same way.

The parent company shareholders, including the directors, are paid dividends on the basis of the parent company's individual financial statements, so there may be a temptation to boost the parent company's results at the expense of those of the subsidiary. However, the situation may also arise where the parent is planning to sell the subsidiary and so wants it to present favourable results. In this case, the transactions above could be reversed.

This is an issue that must be kept in mind when analysing group financial statements – that transactions between group companies may not represent an 'orderly transaction between market participants'.

30 Preparation question: Simple consolidation

BOO GROUP – CONSOLIDATED STATEMENT OF PROFIT OR LOSS AND OTHER COMPREHENSIVE INCOME FOR THE YEAR ENDED 31 DECEMBER 20X8

	$'000
Revenue (5,000 + 1,000 – 100 (W5))	5,900
Cost of sales (2,900 + 600 – 100 + 20 (W5))	(3,420)
Gross profit	2,480
Other expenses (1,700 + 320)	(2,020)
Profit before tax	460
Tax (130 + 25)	(155)
Profit for the year	305
Other comprehensive income	
Gain on property revaluation	20
Total comprehensive income for the year	325
Profit attributable to	
Owners of the parent	294
Non-controlling interest (20% × 55)	11
	305
Total comprehensive income attributable to	
Owners of the parent (ß)	314
Non-controlling interest	11
	325

CONSOLIDATED STATEMENT OF FINANCIAL POSITION AS AT 31 DECEMBER 20X8

	$'000	$'000
Assets		
Non-current assets (1,940 + 200)		2,140
Goodwill (W2)		70
Current assets		
Inventory (500 + 120 + 80)	700	
Trade receivables (650 – 100 (W5) + 40)	590	
Bank and cash (170 + 35)	205	
		1,495
Total assets		3,705
Equity and liabilities		
Equity attributable to owners of the parent		
Share capital (Boo only)		2,000
Retained earnings (W3)		520
Revaluation surplus		20
		2,540
Non-controlling interest (W4)		70
Total equity		2,610
Current liabilities		
Trade payables (910 + 30)	940	
Tax (130 + 25)	155	
		1,095
Total equity and liabilities		3,705

BPP LEARNING MEDIA

Workings

1   *Group structure*

Boo

| 80%

↓

Goose

2   *Goodwill*

	$'000	$'000
Consideration transferred		300
Fair value of non-controlling interest		60
		360
Fair value of net assets:		
Share capital	100	
Retained earnings	190	(290)
Goodwill		70

3   *Retained earnings*

	Boo	Goose
	$'000	$'000
Per question	500	240
Unrealised profit (W5)	(20)	
	480	
Less pre acquisition		(190)
		50
Goose: 80% × 50	40	
Group total	520	

4   *Non-controlling interest*

	$'000
NCI at acquisition	60
NCI share of post acquisition retained earnings (50 × 20%)	10
	70

5   *Inter company issues*

Step 1: Record Goose's purchase

DEBIT Cost of sales	$100,000	
CREDIT Payables		$100,000
DEBIT Closing inventory (SFP)	$100,000	
CREDIT Cost of sales		$100,000

These transactions can be simplified to:

DEBIT Inventory	$100,000	
CREDIT Payables		$100,000

Step 2: Cancel unrealised profit

DEBIT COS (and retained earnings) in Boo	$20,000	
CREDIT Inventory (SFP)		$20,000

Step 3: Cancel intragroup transaction

DEBIT Revenue	$100,000	
CREDIT Cost of sales		$100,000

Step 4: Cancel intragroup balances

DEBIT Payables	$100,000	
CREDIT Receivables		$100,000

31 Preparation question: Goodwill

Goodwill on acquisition

	$'000	$'000
Consideration transferred		1,200
Fair value of non-controlling interest		400
Net assets at acquisition:		
Share capital	500	
Retained earnings	850	
Revaluation surplus	450	
		(1,800)
Negative goodwill *		(200)

* *Note.* Negative goodwill is known as 'gain on a bargain purchase' (IFRS 3 *Business combinations*).

CONSOLIDATED STATEMENT OF PROFIT OR LOSS FOR THE YEAR ENDED 31 DECEMBER 20X9

	$'000
Revenue (12,500 + 2,600)	15,100
Cost of sales (7,400 + 1,090)	(8,490)
Gross profit	6,610
Distribution costs (700 + 220)	(920)
Administrative expenses (1,300 + 550 – 200*)	(1,650)
Finance costs	(40)
Profit before tax	4,000
Income tax expense (900 + 230)	(1,130)
Profit for the year	2,870
Profit attributable to:	
Owners of Penguin (ß)	2,768
Non controlling interest (510 × 20%)	102
	2,870

* *Note.* Penguin plc should double-check the valuation of Platypus Ltd's assets and liabilities and reassess the valuation of the consideration paid. If it is satisfied that it has indeed secured a 'bargain purchase' then $200,000 should be credited to profit or loss. Note that IFRS 3 requires this gain to be attributed to the acquirer; none of it is attributed to the non-controlling interest.

32 Pedantic

Text references. Chapters 9 and 10

Top tips. The first point to note here is that the subsidiary was acquired mid-year. Remember this when it comes to preparing the statement of profit or loss and working out the depreciation on the fair value adjustment. This question had lots to do but no real problems. Get the formats down, note the adjustments on the question paper and then start working through.

Easy marks. There were lots of easy marks here. The statement of profit or loss needed no real working out apart from cost of sales and non-controlling interest. There were lots of marks available in the statement of financial position even if you did not get the goodwill quite right. Correctly calculating the figures from the share exchange would have gained you marks on goodwill, share capital and share premium.

Examiner's comments. This question was generally well answered by most candidates. The two areas of serious errors were:

- Failure to time apportion the results of the subsidiary
- Proportional consolidation of 60% of the subsidiary's figures.

BPP LEARNING MEDIA

			Marks
(a)	Statement of profit or loss:		
	revenue	1½	
	cost of sales	3	
	distribution costs	½	
	administrative expenses	1	
	finance costs	½	
	income tax	½	
	non-controlling interest	2	9
(b)	Statement of financial position:		
	property, plant and equipment	2	
	goodwill	5	
	current assets	1½	
	equity shares	1	
	share premium	1	
	retained earnings	2	
	non-controlling interest	2	
	10% loan notes	½	
	current liabilities	1	16
Total for question			25

PEDANTIC
CONSOLIDATED STATEMENT OF PROFIT OR LOSS FOR THE YEAR ENDED 30 SEPTEMBER 20X8

	$'000
Revenue (85,000 + (42,000 × 6/12) – 8,000 (W7))	98,000
Cost of sales (W8)	(72,000)
Gross profit	26,000
Distribution costs (2,000 + (2,000 × 6/12))	(3,000)
Administrative expenses (6,000 + (3,200 × 6/12))	(7,600)
Finance costs (300 + (400 × 6/12))	(500)
Profit before tax	14,900
Income tax expense (4,700 + (1,400 × 6/12)	(5,400)
Profit for the year	9,500
Profit attributable to:	
Owners of the parent	9,300
Non-controlling interests (W4)	200
	9,500

PEDANTIC
CONSOLIDATED STATEMENT OF FINANCIAL POSITION AT 30 SEPTEMBER 20X8

	$'000
Non-current assets	
Property, plant and equipment (40,600 + 12,600 + 1,800 (W6))	55,000
Goodwill (W2)	4,500
	59,500
Current assets (W9)	21,400
Total assets	80,900

Equity attributable to owners of the parent

Share capital (10,000 +1,600 (W5))	11,600
Share premium (W5)	8,000
Retained earnings (W3)	35,700
	55,300
Non-controlling interests (W4)	6,100
	61,400

Non-current liabilities

10% loan notes (3,000 + 4,000)	7,000
Current liabilities (8,200 + 4,700 – 400 (W10))	12,500
	80,900

Workings

1   *Group structure*

Pedantic

1.4.X8   ↓   60%   Mid-year acquisition, 6 months before year end.

Sophistic

2   *Goodwill*

	$'000	$'000
Consideration transferred (W5)		9,600
Fair value of non-controlling interests		5,900
Less: Fair value of net assets at acquisition:		
Share capital	4,000	
Retained earnings (6,500 – (3,000 × 6/12))	5,000	
Fair value adjustment (W6)	2,000	
		(11,000)
Goodwill		4,500

3   *Retained earnings*

	Pedantic $'000	Sophistic $'000
Per question	35,400	6,500
Movement on FV adjustment (W6)		(200)
PUP (W7)		(800)
Pre- acquisition (W2)		(5,000)
		500
Group share (500 × 60%)	300	
	35,700	

4   *Non-controlling interests*

Statement of profit or loss

	$'000
Post acquisition profit of Sophistic (3,000 × 6/12)	1,500
PUP (W7)	(800)
Movement on FVA (W6)	(200)
	500
× 40%	200

Statement of financial position

	$'000
NCI at acquisition (W2)	5,900
NCI share of post acquisition retained earnings ((W3) 500 × 40%)	200
	6,100

BPP
LEARNING MEDIA

5   Share exchange

	DR $'000	CR $'000
Consideration transferred (4,000 × 60% × 2/3 = 1,600 × $6)	9,600	
Share capital of Pedantic (1,600 × $1)		1,600
Share premium of Pedantic (1,600 × $5)		8,000

6   Fair value adjustments

	$,000 Acq'n 1.4.X8	$'000 Mov't 6/12	$'000 Year end 30.9.X8
Plant (*$2m/5 × 6/12)	2,000	(200)*	1,800

7   Intragroup trading

	DEBIT	CREDIT
Cancel intragroup sales/purchases:		
Sales	8,000	
Purchases		8,000
Eliminate unrealised profit:		
Cost of sales/retained earnings ((8,000 – 5,200) × 40/140)	800	
Inventories (SOFP)		800

8   Cost of sales

	$,000
Pedantic	63,000
Sophistic (32,000 × 6/12)	16,000
Movement on FV adjustment (W6)	200
Intragroup purchases (W7)	(8,000)
Unrealised profit (W7)	800
	72,000

9   Current assets

	$'000
Pedantic	16,000
Sophistic	6,600
Unrealised profit in inventory (W7)	(800)
Intercompany receivables (per question)	(600)
Cash in transit (W10)	200
	21,400

10   Cash in transit

	DR	CR
Receivables		600
Payables	400	
Group cash	200	

BPP LEARNING MEDIA

33 Pyramid

Text references. Chapters 9 and 11.

Top tips. This is a standard consolidated statement of financial position with which students should be very familiar. It was very important to begin by reading the whole of the question carefully as it was not until note iv that you learned that there was an associate to deal with.

Easy marks. The only complex bits in this question were the deferred consideration and the intragroup trading. Other than that, there were plenty of easy marks. You should have been able to reconcile the intragroup balances with a bit of care, and you then had to remember to cancel them out.

Examiner's comments The majority of candidates scored well on this question. Errors occurred in the more complex aspects. Some candidates failed to correctly discount the deferred consideration or to show it as a liability. Some either ignored the unrecorded deferred tax liability or treated it as an addition to, rather than a deduction from, net assets at acquisition. Some treated the $2m earned since acquisition as the annual profits of the subsidiary and time apportioned it. There were a lot of errors in group trading and URP. Some candidates adjusted for the share issue despite being told that it had already been recorded.

Examiner's answer. The examiner's answer to this question is at the end of this Kit.

Marking scheme

	Marks
Property, plant and equipment	2
Goodwill	4½
Investment in associate	1
Other investments	1
Inventory	2
Receivables	1½
Bank	1
Equity shares	½
Share premium	½
Retained earnings	4½
Non-controlling interest	1½
11% loan notes	1½
Deferred tax	1
Deferred consideration	1
Other current liabilities	1½
Total for question	25

CONSOLIDATED STATEMENT OF FINANCIAL POSITION AS AT 31 MARCH 20X2

ASSETS	$'000
Non-current assets	
Property, plant and equipment (38,100 + 28,500 + 2,400 (W6))	69,000
Goodwill (W2)	7,400
Investment in associate (W3)	6,600
Investment in equity instruments (per Qn)	2,800
	85,800
Current assets	
Inventory (13,900 + 10,400 + 1,500 (W7) – 500 (W7))	25,300
Receivables (11,400 + 5,500 – 1,200 (W7) – 3,200 (W7))	12,500
Cash and cash equivalents (900 + 600 + 1,200 (W7))	2,700
	40,500
Total assets	126,300

BPP
LEARNING MEDIA

	$'000
EQUITY AND LIABILITIES	
Equity attributable to owners of Pyramid	
Equity shares $1	25,000
Share premium	17,600
Retained earnings (W4)	36,380
	78,980
Non-controlling interests (W5)	8,480
	87,460
Non-current liabilities	
11% loan notes (12,000 + 4,000 – 2,500)	13,500
Deferred tax (4,500 + 1,000)	5,500
	19,000
Current liabilities (9,500 + 5,000 + 1,500 (W7) – 3,200 (W7))	12,800
Deferred consideration (W8)	7,040
	19,840
Total equity and liabilities	126,300

Workings

1 *Group structure*

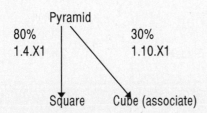

Pyramid

80% 1.4.X1

30% 1.10.X1

Square   Cube (associate)

2 *Goodwill*

	$'000	$'000
Consideration transferred:		
Share exchange (per investments SFP)	24,000	
Deferred consideration ((8,000 × 0.88) × 1/1.1)	6,400	
		30,400
Non-controlling interest at fair value (2,000 × 3.5)		7,000
		37,400
Fair value of net assets:		
Shares	(10,000)	
Retained earnings	(18,000)	
Fair value adjustment on plant	(3,000)	
Deferred tax liability	1,000	
		(30,000)
Goodwill		7,400

3 *Investment in associate*

	$'000
Consideration transferred (SFP)	6,000
Share of post-acquisition retained earnings (2,000(W4) × 30%)	600
	6,600

BPP LEARNING MEDIA

4 Retained earnings

	Pyramid $'000	Square $'000	Cube $'000
Per question	30,200	8,000	2,000
Unwinding of discount on deferred consideration (W8)	(640)		
PURP (W7)	(500)		
Depreciation on FV adjustment (W6)		(600)	
Gain on equity investments ($2.8m – $2m)	800		
		7,400	2,000
Group share of Square (80%)	5,920		
Group share of Cube (30%)	600		
	36,380		

5 Non-controlling interests

	$'000
FV of NCI at acquisition (W2)	7,000
Share of post-acquisition retained earnings (7,400 × 20%)	1,480
	8,480

6 Fair value adjustment

	Acquisition $'000	Movement $'000		Year end $'000
Plant	3,000	(600)	(3,000 / 5)	2,400

7 Intragroup trading

	DEBIT $'000	CREDIT $'000
Group inventory	1,500	
Payables		1'500
Being goods in transit		
Receivables		1,200
Cash	1,200	
Being cash in transit		
Receivables		3,200
Payables	3,200	
Being intragroup receivables / payables cancelled		
Retained earnings	500	
Inventory		500
Being PURP (1,500 x 50/150)		

8 Deferred consideration

	$'000
Fair value at acquisition (8,000 × 0.88) × 1/1.1	6,400
Discount unwound	640
Fair value at 31.3.X2 (8,000 × 0.88)	7,040

BPP
LEARNING MEDIA

34 Preparation question: Acquisition during the year

CONSOLIDATED STATEMENTOF PROFIT OR LOSS AND OTHER COMPREHENSIVE INCOME FOR THE YEAR
ENDING 31 DECEMBER 20X4

	Port	Alfred 2/12	Adjustment	Group
	$'000	$'000		$'000
Revenue	100	166		266
Cost of sales	(36)	(43)		(79)
Gross profit				187
Interest on loan to Alfred	276	–	(46)	230
Other investment income	158	–		158
Operating expenses	(56)	(55)		(111)
Finance costs	–	(46)	46	–
Profit before tax				464
Taxation	(112)	(6)		(118)
Profit for the year				346
Other comprehensive income:				
Gain on property revaluation	30			30
Total comprehensive income for the year				376
Profit attributable to:				
Owners of the parent				342
Non-controlling interest (W5)				4
				346
Total comprehensive income attributable to:				
Owners of the parent				372
Non-controlling interest				4
				376

PORT GROUP STATEMENT OF FINANCIAL POSITION AS AT 31 DECEMBER 20X4

		Adjustments	Group
Assets			$'000
Non-current assets			
Goodwill		(W2)	330
Property, plant and equipment	130 + 3,000		3,130
Investments			
Loan to Alfred	2,300 + 0	(2,300)	–
Other investments	600 + 0		600
			4,060
Current assets	800 + 139		939
Total assets			4,999
Equity and liabilities			
Equity attributable to owners of the parent			
$1 equity shares		(W3)	235
Share premium		(W3)	1,115
Retained earnings		(W4)	2,912
Revaluation surplus			30
			4,292
Non-controlling interest		(W5)	184
Total equity			4,476
Non-current liabilities			
Loan from Port	0 + 2,300	(2,300)	–
Current liabilities	200 + 323		523
Total equity and liabilities			4,999

Workings

1   *Group structure*

Port	
	75% Subsidiary
	Two months only
Alfred	

2   *Goodwill*

	$'000	$'000	$'000
Consideration transferred (shares)			650
Non-controlling interests at acquisition			180
Net assets at date of acquisition (Note)			
Share capital		100	
Share premium		85	
Retained earnings:			
Opening (331 – 96)	235		
Add: accrued profit for the year: $96,000 × 10/12	80		
Pre-acquisition retained earnings		315	
			(500)
Goodwill			330

Note. The net assets at the date of acquisition are also calculated by time-apportioning profits. The share capital and retained earnings brought forward obviously all arose before acquisition. The profit for the year is assumed to have arisen evenly over time.

3   *Issue of shares*

	Draft $'000	New issue $'000	Revised $'000
Share capital	200	35	235
Share premium	500	615	1,115
Fair value of proceeds		650	

4   *Group retained earnings*

	Port $'000	Alfred $'000
Per question	2,900	331
Less pre acquisition (W2)		(315)
		16
Share of Alfred: (16 × 75%)	12	
	2,912	

5   *Non-controlling interests*

Statement of profit or loss

The rule here is to time apportion the non-controlling interest in the subsidiary acquired during the year. After all, you can only take out in respect of the non-controlling interest what was put in the first place. So, if two months were consolidated then two months of non-controlling interest will be deducted.

$96,000 × 2/12 × 25% = $4,000.

Statement of financial position

	$'000
NCI at acquisition	180
NCI share of post-acquisition retained earnings ((W4) 16 × 25%)	4
	184

BPP
LEARNING MEDIA

35 Pandar

Text references. Chapters 9 and 10

Top tips. This question involves calculation of goodwill and then a consolidated statement of profit or loss with NCI at FV. This is a mid-year acquisition, so the subsidiary's results need to be apportioned. The other point to note is that the subsidiary's interest payable needs to be fully attributed to the post-acquisition period.

Easy marks. There were easy marks to be earned on the goodwill calculation even if you failed to get the reserves right and the investment in associate was quite straightforward. Easy marks could also have been earned on the unrealised profit and the line items of the statement of profit or loss.

Examiner's comments. This was generally well answered. Main areas where errors were made were: in part (a) not charging the interest on the 8% loan entirely to the post-acquisition period, not calculating NCI at FV and not time-apportioning the losses of the associate; in part (b) there were some problems with depreciation and amortisation.

Marking scheme

				Marks
(a)	(i)	Goodwill of Salva:		
		Consideration		2
		Net assets acquired calculated as:		
		Equity shares		1
		Pre-acquisition reserves		2
		Fair value adjustments		$\dfrac{1}{6}$
	(ii)	Carrying value of Ambra		
		Cost		1
		Share of post-acquisition losses		1
		Impairment charge		$\dfrac{1}{3}$
(b)		Statement of profit or loss:		
		Revenue		2
		Cost of sales		4
		Distribution costs and administrative expenses		1
		Investment income		2½
		Finance costs		1½
		Share of associate's losses and impairment charge		1
		Income tax		1
		Non-controlling interests		2
		Domain name not amortised		$\dfrac{1}{16}$
		Total for question		$\underline{\underline{25}}$

(a) (i) *Goodwill*

	$'000	$'000
Consideration transferred (120m × 80% × 3/5 × $6)		345,600
Non-controlling interest (120m × 20% × $3.20)		76,800
FV of identifiable net assets acquired:		
Share capital	120,000	
Reserves (152,000 + ((21,000 + (W4) 2,000*) × 6/12))	163,500	
FV adjustments (W3)	25,000	
		(308,500)
		113,900

* Note that the interest on the loan note is a post-acquisition cost for Salva, so it is added back for the purpose of calculating pre-acquisition reserves.

(ii) *Investment in Ambra*

	$'000
Cost (40m × 40% × $2)	32,000
Share of post-acquisition loss (5,000 × 40% × 6/12)	(1,000)
Impairment loss	(3,000)
	28,000

(b) PANDAR GROUP
CONSOLIDATED STATEMENT OF PROFIT OR LOSS FOR THE YEAR ENDED 30 SEPTEMBER 20X9

	$'000
Revenue (210,000 + (150,000 × 6/12) – (W5) 15,000)	270,000
Cost of sales (126,000+(100,000 × 6/12) + (W3) 500 - (W5)15,000 + (W5) 1,000)	(162,500)
Gross profit	107,500
Distribution costs (11,200 + (7,000 × 6/12)	(14,700)
Administrative expenses (18,300 + (9,000 × 6/12)	(22,800)
Investment income (9,500 – (W4) 2,000 – (8,000 × 80%))	1,100
Finance costs (1,800 + (3,000 x 6/12) –((W4) 2,000 × 6/12) + (W4) 2,000- (W4) 2,000)	(2,300)
Share of loss of associate ((5,000 × 40% × 6/12)+(3,000) impairment)	(4,000)
Profit before tax	64,800
Income tax expense (15,000 + (10,000 × 6/12))	(20,000)
Profit for the year	44,800
Profit attributable to:	
Owners of the parent	43,000
Non-controlling interest (W2)	1,800
	44,800

Workings

1   Timeline

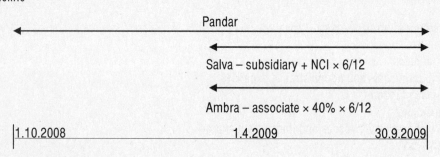

2   *Non-controlling interest*

	$'000
Salva's post acquisition profit ((21,000 × 6/12) + ((W4)2,000 × 6/12) – (W4)2,000)*	9,500
Depreciation on FVA (W3)	(500)
	9,000
× 20%	1,800

3   *Fair value adjustments*

	Acquisition 1.4.X9		Movement	Year end 30.9.X9
	$'000		$'000	$'000
Plant (17,000 – 12,000)	5,000	5000/5 × 6/12	(500)	4,500
Domain name	20,000		–	20,000
	25,000			24,500

4   *Intragroup interest*

Interest   50,000 × 8% × 6/12 = $2,000
Dr Finance income/Cr Finance costs

BPP
LEARNING MEDIA

5   *Intragroup trading*

Cancel intragroup sales/purchases:
Dr Revenue 15,000/Cr Cost of sales 15,000

Unrealised profit 15,000 × 1/3 × 20%:
Dr Cost of sales 1,000/Cr Inventories (SOFP) 1,000

[The following supplementary workings are included for additional explanation. Note that in the exam you will not have time to prepare these workings and you should do them as shown above, on the face of the statement of profit or loss.]

Cost of sales

	$'000
Pandar	126,000
Salva (100,000 × 6/12)	50,000
Intragroup (W5)	(15,000)
Depreciation on FVA (W3)	500
Unrealised profit (W5)	1,000
	162,500

Investment income

	$'000
Pandar	9,500
Intragroup interest (W4)	(2,000)
Intragroup dividend (8,000 × 80%)	(6,400)
	1,100

Finance costs

	$'000
Pandar	1,800
Salva ((3,000 − 2,000) × 6/12) + 2,000)*	2,500
Intragroup (W4)	(2,000)
	2,300

* Note that the finance costs associated with the loan note are separated out and charged in full to the post-acquisition period. Of the 3,000 ($'000) finance costs in Salva's statement of profit or loss, 2,000 is intragroup and relates only to the *post-acquisition period*. The remaining 1,000 is correctly 6/12. The 2,000 intragroup is then cancelled on consolidation, leaving a balance in group finance costs of 1,800 + (1,000 × 6/12) = 2,300.

36 Premier

Text references. Chapters 9 and 10.

Top tips. This is a consolidated statement of profit or loss and other comprehensive income and statement of financial position with just a parent and subsidiary. It is always important to note dates. In this case the subsidiary was acquired during the year. There is a negative fair value adjustment to deal with, but otherwise just the usual adjustments. What is challenging in this question is having to prepare two statements in the time. This requires being very well organised, getting the formats down quickly and filling in the numbers as you go through the workings.

Easy marks. There were plenty of marks here for the standard workings – goodwill, property, plant and equipment, non-controlling interest. There were two easy marks for adjusting correctly for the share issue.

Examiner's comments. Most candidates have a good working knowledge of consolidation techniques, but errors occurred in the more complex aspects:

-Intra-group sales should only have been eliminated for the post-acquisition period (4 months) and unrealised profit should have been calculated as a mark up on *cost*.

-Some candidates omitted unrealised profit and the depreciation adjustment from the NCI calculation.

-Some candidates treated the fair value reduction of the property value as an increase.

-Many failed to correctly account for the share exchange.

		Marks
(a)	Statement of profit or loss and other comprehensive income:	
	Revenue	1½
	Cost of sales	3
	Distribution costs	½
	Administrative expenses	½
	Finance costs	½
	Income tax	½
	Other comprehensive income – gain on investments	½
	Other comprehensive income – gain on property	½
	Non-controlling interest – profit for year	1
	Split of total comprehensive income	½
		9
(b)	Statement of financial position:	
	Property, plant and equipment	2
	Goodwill	3½
	Investments in equity instruments	1
	Current assets	1½
	Equity shares	1
	Share premium	1
	Revaluation surplus	½
	Other equity reserve	1
	Retained earnings	1½
	Non-controlling interests	1½
	6% loan notes	½
	Current liabilities	1
	Maximum	16
	Maximum for question	25

CONSOLIDATED STATEMENT OF PROFIT OR LOSS AND OTHER COMPREHENSIVE INCOME FOR THE YEAR ENDED 30 SEPTEMBER 20X1

	$'000
Revenue (92,500 + (45,000 × 4/12) – 4,000 (W8))	103,500
Cost of sales (70,500 + (36,000 × 4/12) – 50(W7) – 4,000(W8) + 400 (W8))	(78,850)
Gross profit	24,650
Distribution costs (2,500 + (1,200 × 4/12))	(2,900)
Administrative expenses (5,500 + (2,400 × 4/12)	(6,300)
Finance costs	(100)
Profit before tax	15,350
Income tax expense (3,900 + (1,500 × 4/12))	(4,400)
Profit for the year	10,950
Other comprehensive income	
Investments in equity instruments (W9)	300
Gain on property revaluation	500
Other comprehensive income for the year	800
Total comprehensive income for the year	11,750
Profit attributable to:	
Owners of the parent	10,760
Non-controlling interests (W2)	190
	10,950

BPP LEARNING MEDIA

Total comprehensive income attributable to:	$'000
Owners of the parent	11,560
Non-controlling interests (W2)	190
	11,750

CONSOLIDATED STATEMENT OF FINANCIAL POSITION AT 30 SEPTEMBER 20X1

	$'000
Assets	
Non-current assets	
Property, plant and equipment (25,500 + 13,900 – 1,150 (W7))	38,250
Goodwill (W3)	9,300
Investments in equity instruments (1,800 – 800 (W6) + 300 (W9))	1,300
	48,850
Current assets (12,500 + 2,400 – 400 (W8) – 350 (W8))	14,150
Total assets	63,000
Equity and liabilities	
Equity attributable to owners of the parent	
Share capital (12,000 + 2,400 (W6))	14,400
Share premium (W6)	9,600
Retained earnings (W4)	13,060
Revaluation surplus	2,000
Other components of equity (500 + 300 (W9))	800
	39,860
Non-controlling interests (W5)	3,690
Total equity	43,550
Non-current liabilities	
6% loan notes	3,000
Current liabilities (10,000 + 6,800 – 350 (W8))	16,450
Total liabilities	19,450
Total equity and liabilities	63,000

Workings

1   Group structure

```
                    Premier
   1.6.X1              |
(4m before year end)   |
                       ↓
                    Sanford
                     80%
```

2   Non-controlling interests (SOCI)

	Profit for year	Total comprehensive income
	$'000	$'000
Per question (3,900 × 4/12)	1,300	1,300
FV movement (W7)	50	50
Provision for unrealised profit (W8)	(400)	(400)
	950	950
NCI × 20%	190	190

BPP
LEARNING MEDIA

3 Goodwill

	$'000	$'000
Consideration transferred (W6)		12,800
FV of non-controlling interests (5m × 20% x $3.50)		3,500
Less FV of net assets at acquisition:		
Share capital	5,000	
Retained earnings (4,500 − (3,900 × 4/12))	3,200	
Fair value adjustments (W7)	(1,200)	
		(7,000)
		9,300

4 Retained earnings

	Premier $'000	Sanford $'000
Per question	12,300	4,500
FV movement (W7)		50
Provision for unrealised profit (W8)		(400)
Pre-acquisition (W3)		(3,200)
		950
Group share (950 × 80%)	760	
	13,060	

5 Non-controlling interests (SOFP)

	$'000
NCI at acquisition (W3)	3,500
NCI share of post-acquisition retained earnings (950 (W4) × 20%)	190
	3,690

6 Purchase of Sanford

				$'000
1.6.20X1	Dr	Cost of Sanford	(balancing figure)	12,800
Not recorded	Cr	Share capital	(5m x 80% × 3/5 × $1)	2,400
Not recorded	Cr	Share premium	(5m x 80% × 3/5 × $4)	9,600
Recorded	Cr	Loan notes	(5m x 80% /500 × $100)	800

7 Fair value adjustment

	Acquisition 1.6.20X1 $'000	Movement (4 months) $'000	Year end 30.9.20X1 $'000
Property	(1,200)	50	(1,150)

8 Intragroup trading

	$'000	$'000
(1) Cancel intragroup sales/purchases		
DEBIT Group revenue (1,000 × 4)	4,000	
CREDIT Group cost of sales		4,000
(2) Eliminate unrealised profit		
DEBIT Cost of sales/retained earnings (2,000 × 25/125)	400	
CREDIT Group inventories		400

(3) Cancel intragroup balances	$'000	$'000
DEBIT Group payables	350	
CREDIT Group receivables		350

BPP LEARNING MEDIA

9   *Investments in equity instruments (revaluation)*

	$'000	$'000
DEBIT Investments in equity instruments	300	
CREDIT Other comprehensive income		300

37 Prodigal

Text reference. Chapter 10.

Top tips. The first point to note is that Sentinel was acquired mid-year. Always pay close attention to dates. Although you do not need to calculate goodwill for this question, you will need to account for the acquisition of Sentinel in order to show the correct equity balances in (a) (ii).

Easy marks. Revenue is relatively straightforward for 2 marks and for all of the expense categories apart from cost of sales it was only necessary to take Prodigal's balance plus 6/12 Sentinel. The other comprehensive income was also easy, and you should have been able to score well on part (b).

Examiner's comments. There were many good scores here. Two problem areas were dealing with the elimination of intra-group sales and the additional depreciation on the asset transfer. Some candidates failed to calculate NCI in the total comprehensive income. Very few candidates correctly calculated 'other equity reserve' and many calculated goodwill, which was not required. The written section of part (b) was often ignored and a lot of answers did not answer the question ie did not explain the **effect** of the two treatments.

Marking scheme

				Marks
(a)	(i)	Statement of profit or loss and other comprehensive income		
		Revenue	2	
		Cost of sales	4	
		Distribution costs and administrative expenses	1	
		Finance costs	1	
		Income tax expense	1	
		Non-controlling interest in profit for the year	1½	
		Other comprehensive income	2	
		Non-controlling interest in other comprehensive income	1½	
				14
(a)	(ii)	Consolidated equity		
		Share capital	1	
		Share premium	1	
		Revaluation surplus (land)	1	
		Other equity reserve	1	
		Retained earnings	1½	
		Non-controlling interest	1½	
				7
(b)		1 mark per valid point		4
				25

(a)(i) CONSOLIDATED STATEMENT OF PROFIT OR LOSS AND OTHER COMPREHENSIVE INCOME FOR THE YEAR ENDED 31 MARCH 20X1

	$'000
Revenue (450,00 + (240,000 × 6/12) – (W4) 40,000)	530,000
Cost of sales (260,000 + (110,000 × 6/12) + (W3) 800 – (W4) 40,000 + 3,000)	(278,800)
Gross profit	251,200
Distribution costs (23,600 + (12,000 × 6/12))	(29,600)
Administrative expenses (27,000 + (23,000 × 6/12))	(38,500)
Finance costs (1,500 + (1,200 × 6/12))	(2,100)
Profit before tax	181,000
Income tax expense (48,000 + (27,800 × 6/12))	(61,900)
Profit for the year	119,100
Other comprehensive income:	
Gain on land revaluation (2,500 + 1,000) *	3,500
Investments in equity instruments ** (700 + (400 × 6/12))	(900)
Other comprehensive income, net of tax	2,600
Total comprehensive income for the year	121,700
Profit attributable to:	
Owners of the parent (bal)	111,600
Non-controlling interests (W2)	7,500
	119,100
Total comprehensive income attributable to:	
Owners of the parent (bal)	114,000
Non-controlling interests (W2)	7,700
	121,700

> * all post- acquisition
> ** could also be described as equity financial asset investments

(ii)

	$'000
Equity attributable to owners of the parent:	
Share capital (250,000 + (W7) 80,000)	330,000
Share premium (100,000 + (W7) 240,000)	340,000
Retained earnings (W5)	201,600
Revaluation surplus (8,400 + 2,500 + (1,000 × 75%))	11,650
Other equity reserve (3,200 – 700 – (400 × 6/12 × 75%))	2,350
	885,600
Non-controlling interests (W6)	107,700
	993,300

(b) The argument behind allowing the non-controlling interest to be valued at fair value is that the traditional method (valued at proportionate share of subsidiary's net assets) does not take account of goodwill attributable to the non-controlling interest. Goodwill is based upon the amount the parent paid for shares in the subsidiary. The non-controlling interest were also holding shares which would have had the same market value at the acquisition date, so their holding also includes an element of goodwill. The fair value option takes account of this.

The fair value of the non-controlling interest can be based on share price or on a valuation by the parent company. Use of the fair value option means that the goodwill amount in the consolidated statement of financial position will normally be higher than where share of net assets is used, and the non-controlling interest will also be higher. Also, when goodwill is impaired, the impairment will be allocated between the group and the non-controlling interest, based on their relative shareholdings.

BPP LEARNING MEDIA

Workings

1 *Group structure and timeline*

Prodigal

$\downarrow$

Sentinel 1.10.20X0 75%

1.4.20X0	1.10.20X0	31.3.20X1

Prodigal   >

Sentinal x 6/12

2 *Non-controlling interests*

	Profit for year	Total comprehensive income
	$'000	$'000
Per question (66,000 × 6/12) ((66,000–400) × 6/12 + 1,000))	33,000	33,800
PUP (W4)	(3,000)	(3,000)
	30,000	30,800
x	25%	25%
	7,500	7,700

3 *Transfer of plant*

	$'000
1.10.20X0 Profit on transfer (5,000 – 4,000)	1,000
Proportion depreciated (½ / 2½)	(200)
Unrealised profit	800
Required adjustment:	
Dr Cost of sales (and retained earnings)	800
Cr Plant	800

4 *Intragroup trading*

Cancel intragroup sales/purchases:

	$'000	$'000
Dr Group revenue	40,000	
Cr Group cost of sales		40,000
((40,000 – 30,000) × 12,000/40,000) = 3,000		
DR Cost of sales (Sentinel) (NCI)	3,000	
CR Group inventories		3,000

5 *Retained earnings*

	Prodigal	Sentinel
	$'000	$'000
Per question: (90,000 + 89,900) (125,000 + 66,000)	179,900	191,000
PUP on transfer of plant (W3)	(800)	
PUP on transfer of inventories (W4)		(3,000)
Pre-acq retained earnings (125,000 + (66,000 × 6/12))		(158,000)
		30,000
Group share (30,000 × 75%)	22,500	
	201,600	

BPP
LEARNING MEDIA

6   Non-controlling interests

	$'000
NCI at acquisition	100,000
NCI share of post-acquisition:	
- retained earnings ((W5) 30,000 × 25%)	7,500
- revaluation surplus (1,000 × 25%)	250
- investment in equity instruments ((400 × 6/12) × 25%)	(50)
	107,700

7   Share for share exchange

	$'000	$'000
Dr Cost of investment in S	320,000	
Cr Share capital (160,000 × 75% × 2/3 × $1)		80,000
Cr Share premium (160,000 × 75% × 2/3 × $3)		240,000

38 Preparation question: Laurel

LAUREL GROUP - STATEMENT OF FINANCIAL POSITION AS AT 31 DECEMBER 20X9

	$m
Non-current assets	
Property, plant and equipment (220 + 160 + (W7) 3)	383
Goodwill (W2)	9
Investment in associate (W3)	96.8
	488.8
Current assets	
Inventories (384 + 234 – (W6) 10)	608
Trade receivables (275 + 166)	441
Cash (42 + 10)	52
	1,101
	1,589.8
Equity attributable to owners of the parent	
Share capital – $1 ordinary shares	400
Share premium	16
Retained earnings (W4)	326.8
	742.8
Non-controlling interests (W5)	47
	789.8
Current liabilities	
Trade payables (457 + 343)	800.0
	1,589.8

Workings

1   Group structure

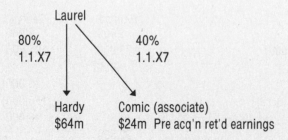

```
                    Laurel
        80%         │        40%
        1.1.X7      │        1.1.X7
                    │
                    ▼
                  Hardy      Comic (associate)
                  $64m       $24m  Pre acq'n ret'd earnings
```

BPP
LEARNING MEDIA

2   *Goodwill*

	$'m	$'m
Consideration transferred		160
Non-controlling interests (at fair value)		39
Fair value of net assets at acq'n:		
Share capital	96	
Share premium	3	
Retained earnings	64	
Fair value adjustment (W7)	12	
		(175)
		24
Impairment losses		(15)
		9

3   *Investment in associate*

	$'m
Cost of associate	70
Share of post acquisition retained reserves (W4)	29.2
Unrealised profit (W6)	(2.4)
Impairment losses	(0)
	96.8

4   *Consolidated retained earnings*

	Laurel	*Hardy*	*Comic*
	$'m	$'m	$'m
Per question	278	128	97
Less: PUP re Hardy (W6)	(10)		
PUP re Comic (W6)	(2.4)		
Fair value adjustment movement (W7)		(9)	
Less: pre-acquisition retained earnings		(64)	(24)
		55	73
Group share of post acquisition retained earnings:			
Hardy (55 × 80%)	44		
Comic (73 × 40%)	29.2		
Less: group share of impairment losses (15 × 80%)	(12.0)		
	326.8		

5   *Non-controlling interests*

	$'m
Non-controlling interests at acquisition (W2)	39
NCI share of post acquisition retained earnings:	
Hardy (55 × 20%)	11
Less: NCI share of impairment losses (15 × 20%)	(3)
	47

6   *Unrealised profit*

Laurel's sales to Hardy: $32m – $22m = $10m

DR Retained earnings (Laurel)	$10m
CR Group inventories	$10m

Laurel's sales to Comic (associate) ($22m – $10m) × ½ × 40% share = $2.4m.

DR Retained earnings (Laurel)	$2.4m
CR Investment in associate	$2.4m

BPP
LEARNING MEDIA

7   *Fair value adjustments*

	At acquisition date $'m	Movement $'m	At year end $'m
PPE (57 – 45)	+12	(9)*	+3

*Extra depreciation $12m × ¾

+12 → Goodwill
(9)* → Ret'd earnings
+3 → PPE

39 Preparation question: Tyson

STATEMENT OF PROFIT OR LOSS AND OTHER COMPREHENSIVE INCOME FOR THE YEAR ENDED 31 DECEMBER 20X8

	$'m
Revenue (500 + 150 – 66)	584
Cost of sales (270 + 80 – 66 + (W3) 18)	(302)
Gross profit	282
Other expenses (150 + 20 + 15)	(185)
Finance income (15 + 10)	25
Finance costs	(20)
Share of profit of associate [(10 × 40%) – 2.4*]	1.6
Profit before tax	103.6
Income tax expense (25 + 15)	(40)
PROFIT FOR THE YEAR	63.6
Other comprehensive income:	
Gains on property revaluation, net of tax (20 + 10)	30
Share of other comprehensive income of associate (5 × 40%)	2
Other comprehensive income for the year, net of tax	32.0
TOTAL COMPREHENSIVE INCOME FOR THE YEAR	95.6
Profit attributable to:	
Owners of the parent (63.6 – 2.4)	61.2
Non-controlling interests (W2)	2.4
	63.6
Total comprehensive income attributable to:	
Owners of the parent (95.6 – 4.4)	91.2
Non-controlling interests (W2)	4.4
	95.6

*   Impairment losses could either be included in expenses or deducted from the share of profit of associates figure. IAS 28 is not prescriptive.

Workings

1   *Group structure*

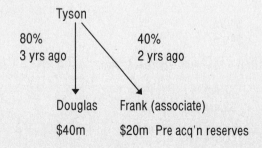

Tyson

80%
3 yrs ago

40%
2 yrs ago

Douglas

Frank (associate)

$40m

$20m Pre acq'n reserves

BPP
LEARNING MEDIA

2   Non-controlling interests

	PFY $'m	TCI $'m
PFY/TCI per question	45	55
Unrealised profit (W3)	(18)	(18)
Impairment loss	(15)	(15)
	12	22
× NCI share (20%)	2.4	4.4

3   Unrealised profit

	$'m
Selling price	66
Cost	(48)
PUP	18

40 Plateau

Text references. Chapters 10 and 11.

Top tips. This is a standard consolidation question, with a subsidiary and associate. You have to record the share issues. Note that the gain on the investment goes through profit or loss.

Easy marks. Apart from the fair value adjustment and the NCI at fair value there were no other particular complications and easy marks were available on investments, current assets and liabilities. Do not neglect part (b) which is 5 easy marks.

Examiner's comments. The consolidated statement of financial position was well answered but few candidates got to grips with the written section and many did not attempt it at all. The main areas where candidates went wrong were:

- deducting fall in fair value of land from PPE, when it had already been written down
- failing to adjust for additional depreciation
- not using equity accounting for the associate
- failing to adjust share capital and premium for the share issue on acquisition.

Marking scheme

		Marks
(a)	Statement of financial position	
	Property, plant and equipment	2
	Goodwill	4
	Investments	3
	Current assets	2
	Equity shares	1
	Share premium	1
	Retained earnings	4
	Non-controlling interest	1
	7% loan notes	1
	Current liabilities	1
		20
(b)	One mark per relevant point	5
	Total for question	25

(a) PLATEAU – CONSOLIDATED STATEMENT OF FINANCIAL POSITION AS AT 30 SEPTEMBER 20X7

	$'000
Non-current assets	
Property, plant and equipment (18,400 + 10,400 – (W7) 400)	28,400
Goodwill (W3)	5,000
Intangible asset – customer contract	1,000
Investment in associate (W4)	10,500
Investment in equity instruments (note v to question)	9,000
	53,900
Current assets	
Inventories (6,900 + 6,200 – (W7) 300)	12,800
Trade receivables (3,200 + 1,500)	4,700
	17,500
Total assets	71,400
Equity and liabilities	
Equity attributable to owners of the parent	
Share capital (10,000 + (W2) 1,500)	11,500
Share premium (W2)	7,500
Retained earnings (W5)	30,300
	49,300
Non-controlling interest (W6)	3,900
	53,200
Non-current liabilities	
7% loan notes (5,000 + 1,000)	6,000
Current liabilities (8,000 + 4,200)	12,200
Total equity and liabilities	71,400

Workings

1 Group structure

Plateau

1.10.X6   1.10.X6

75%   30%

Savannah   Axle

2 Purchase of Savannah

DEBIT Cost of Savannah (3m/2 × $6) + (3m × $1.25)	12.75m
CREDIT Share capital (3m/2 × $1)	1.5m
CREDIT Share premium (3m/2 × $5)	7.5m
CREDIT Cash	3.75m

3 Goodwill– Savannah

	$'000	$'000
Consideration transferred		12,750
Non-controlling interests at acquisition (1,000 shares @ $3,25)		3,250
Less: Net fair value of assets and liabilities at acquisition:		
Share capital	4,000	
Retained earnings	6,000	
Fair value adjustment (W8)	1,000	
		(11,000)
		5,000

4 Investment in Axle

	$'000
Cost : (4,000 × 30% × $7.50)	9,000
Share of post-acquisition retained earnings (W5)	1,500
	10,500

BPP LEARNING MEDIA

5   *Group retained earnings*

	Plateau	Savannah	Axle
	$'000	$'000	$'000
Per statement of financial position	25,250	2,900	5,000
Unrealised profit (W7)	(400)	(300)	–
	24,850	2,600	5,000
Group share: 2,600 × 75%	1,950		
5,000 × 30%	1,500		
Gain on investment			
(9,000 – 6,500)	2,500		
Professional costs of acquisition	(500)		
Group retained earnings	30,300		

6   *Non-controlling interests – Savannah*

	$'000
NCI at acquisition (W3)	3,250
NCI share of post acquisition retained earnings ((W5) 2,600 × 25%)	650
	3,900

7   *Intragroup trading*

Unrealised profit on sale of inventories:

$2.7m × 50/150 × 1/3 $0.3m

DR Cost of sales/CR Inventories in books of Savannah (affects NCI)

Unrealised profit on transfer of plant:

Unrealised profit ($2.5m – $2m)	0.5m
Less realised by use (depreciation) 1/5	(0.1m)
	0.4m

DEBIT Retained earnings/CREDIT Property, plant and equipment in books of Plateau

8   *Fair value adjustment – customer contract*

Acquisition date		*End of reporting period*
1.10.X6	Movement	30.9.X7
1,000	–	1,000

9   *Investments in equity instruments*

	$'000
Fair value at 1 October 20X6	6,500
Fair value at 30 September 20X7	9,000
Increase in fair value	2,500

DEBIT Investments in equity instruments/CREDIT Retained earnings

(b)   IFRS 3 requires the consideration for a business combination to be allocated to the fair values of the assets, liabilities and contingent liabilities acquired.

Although this is usually not the same as the original cost of the asset when acquired by the subsidiary, it is taken to be the cost of the asset to the group. If assets are not valued at fair value, this leads to an incorrect goodwill valuation and incorrect depreciation and goodwill impairment charges in subsequent years.

The financial assistant is confusing two different issues. The assets of the subsidiary are assumed to be acquired at their fair value at the date of acquisition by the parent. After acquisition they will be carried at depreciated amount, rather than subjected to regular revaluations. So they will be treated in the same way as other assets owned by the parent. The parent may decide to revalue all the assets of a class, including those acquired as part of a business combination, in which case they would all be carried at revalued amount.

41 Patronic

Text references. Chapters 10 and 11.

Top tips. The most important thing to notice here is that Patronic acquired its interest in Sardonic eight months before the year end. Always pay attention to dates. This also affects the intragroup sales which need to be cancelled.

Easy marks. Part (a) was 6 easy marks if you could deal with the deferred consideration. Note that it only required goodwill on acquisition, not at the year end.

Examiner's comments. Most candidates failed to discount the deferred consideration correctly and a surprising number did not time apportion the subsidiary's results for eight months in the statement of profit or loss. Answers to part (c) were disappointing with many candidates not attempting it at all.

Marking scheme

			Marks
(a)	Goodwill of Sardonic:		
	Consideration	2	
	Net assets acquired calculated as:		
	- equity shares	1	
	- pre-acquisition reserves	2	
	- fair value adjustments	1	
			6
	Statement of profit or loss:		
	Revenue	2	
	Cost of sales	5	
	Distribution costs and administrative expenses	1	
	Finance costs	2	
	Impairment of goodwill	1	
	Share of associate's profit	1	
	Income tax	1	
	Non-controlling interest	2	15
(b)	One mark per relevant point		4
	Total for question		25

(a)	Goodwill	$'000	$'000
	Consideration transferred:		
	Shares (12m × $5.75)		69,000
	Deferred consideration (18m × $2.42 × 1/1.21(10% over 2 years))		36,000
			105,000
	Fair value of NCI at acquisition:		32,000
	Fair value of identifiable net assets acquired:		
	Share capital	24,000	
	Reserves b/f	69,000	
	Current year to date (13,500 × 4/12)	4,500	
	Fair value adjustments (W3)	6,500	
			(104,000)
	Goodwill		33,000

(b) CONSOLIDATED STATEMENT OF PROFIT OR LOSS FOR THE YEAR ENDED 31 MARCH 20X8

	$'000
Revenue (W4)	192,000
Cost of sales (W5)	(119,100)
Gross profit	72,900
Distribution costs (7,400 + (3,000 × 8/12))	(9,400)
Administrative expenses (12,500 + (6,000 × 8/12))	(16,500)
Finance costs (W6)	(5,000)
Impairment of goodwill	(2,000)
Share of profit of associate (6,000 × 30%)	1,800
Profit before tax	41,800
Income tax expense (10,400 + (3,600 × 8/12)	(12,800)
Profit for the year	29,000
Profit attributable to:	
Owners of the parent	27,400
Non-controlling interest (W2)	1,600
	29,000

Workings

1   *Group structure*

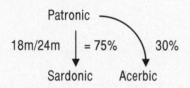

Patronic

18m/24m = 75%   30%

Sardonic   Acerbic

2	*Non-controlling interest*	$'000
	Profit after tax (13,500 × 8/12)	9,000
	Additional depreciation (W3)	(600)
		8,400
	Non-controlling share 25%	2,100
	Less goodwill impairment (2,000 × 25%)	(500)
		1,600

3   *Fair value adjustments*

	Acquisition 1.8.X7 $'000	Movement 8/12 $'000	Year end 31.3.X8 $'000
Property	4,100	(200)*	3,900
Plant	2,400	(400)**	2,000
	6,500	(600)	5,900

* given in the question
** 2,400/4 × 8/12

4   *Revenue* $'000

Patronic	150,000
Sardonic (78,000 × 8/12)	52,000
Intra-group (1,250 × 8)	(10,000)
	192,000

BPP
LEARNING MEDIA

	5	*Cost of sales*	
		Patronic	94,000
		Sardonic (51,000 × 8/12)	34,000
		Intragroup (W3)	(10,000)
		URP in inventory (3,000 × 20/120)	500
		Additional depreciation on FVA:	
		Property	200
		Plant (2.4m/4 × 8/12)	400
			119,100
	6	*Finance costs*	
		Patronic	2,000
		Sardonic (900 × 8/12)	600
		Unwinding of discount (36,000 × 10% × 8/12)	2,400
			5,000

(c)   At 31 March 20X8 Patronic could be presumed to have 'significant influence' over Acerbic arising from its 30% shareholding. Acerbic was therefore treated as an associate and its results were brought into Patronic's financial statements using the equity method.

Spekulate's purchase of 60% changes Patronic's position. Spekulate now has control, so Patronic can no longer be regarded as having significant influence. This is illustrated by the fact that Patronic has lost its seat on the board. Patronic's investment in Acerbic should be treated in 20X9 under IFRS 9, carried at fair value, with any gains or losses taken to profit or loss.

42 Pacemaker

Text references. Chapters 9 and 11.

Top tips. This is a relatively straightforward consolidated statement of financial position including an associate. Complications are NCI at fair value, and sorting out the investments. Pay attention to which items are already included in the individual financial statements and which are not.

Easy marks. There are easy marks here on property, plant and equipment and inventory – both required just one adjustment. The investment in associate was also straightforward and would have been worth a few marks.

Examiner's comments. This was the best answered question. Areas where candidates went wrong were:

- Failing to account for the loan note and the non-controlling element in the goodwill calculation
- Treating the post-acquisition period as one year, rather than two
- URP in inventory ignored or incorrectly calculated
- Non-controlling interest not calculated as per revised standard

Marking scheme

	Marks
Property, plant and equipment	2
Brand	1
Goodwill	4½
Investment in associate	2
Other investments	1
Inventories	2
Trade receivables, cash and bank	1
Equity shares	1
Share premium	1
Retained earnings	6½
Non-controlling interest	2
Loan notes	½
Current liabilities	½
Total for question	25

BPP
LEARNING MEDIA

PACEMAKER – CONSOLIDATED STATEMENT OF FINANCIAL POSITION AS AT 31.3.20X9

	$m
Non-current assets	
Property, plant and equipment (520 + 280 + 18 (W7))	818
Goodwill (W2)	23
Other intangible assets (W7)	20
Investment in associate (W3)	144
Investments in equity instruments (W9)	119
	1,124
Current assets	
Inventories (142 + 160 – 16 (W8)	286
Trade receivables (95 + 88)	183
Cash and cash equivalents (8 + 22)	30
	499
	1,623
Equity attributable to owners of the parent	
Share capital (500 + 75 (W6))	575
Share premium (100 + 45 (W6))	145
Retained earnings (W4)	247
	967
Non-controlling interest (W5)	91
	1,058
Non-current liabilities	
10% loan notes (180 + 20)	200
Current liabilities (200 + 165)	365
	1,623

Workings

1   *Group structure*

	Pacemaker	
1.4.X7		1.10.X8
116/145 = 80%		30/100 = 30%
Pre-acq reserves		Pre-acq =
= 120m		240 – 100 + 20=160m
Syclop		Vardine

2   *Goodwill*

	$m	$m
Consideration transferred (W6)		268
NCI at fair value		65
Fair value of net assets at acquisition		
Share capital	145	
Retained earnings	120	
Fair value adjustments (W7)	45	
		(310)
		23

3   *Investment in associate*

	$m
Cost (W6)	120
Share of post-acquisition retained earnings (W4)	24
	144

BPP
LEARNING MEDIA

4   *Retained earnings*

	Pacemaker $m	Syclop $m	Vardine $m
Per question	130	260	240
Fair value movement (W7)		(7)	
PUP (W8)	(16)		
Gain on investments (82 – (345 – 268))	5		
Loss on investments (37 – 40)		(3)	
Pre-acquisition earnings (W1)		(120)	(160)
		130	80
Group share of Syclop 80%	104		
Group share of Vardine 30%	24		
	247		

5   *Non-controlling interest*

	$m
At acquisition per question	65
Share of post-acquisition retained earnings (130 (W4) × 20%)	26
	91

6   *Investments in subsidiary/associate*

	$m	$m	
DR Cost of investment in Syclop	268		
CR Cash		210	Already
CR Loan notes		58	recorded
DR Cost of investment in Vardine (75 × 1.60)	120		
CR Share capital (75 × 1)		75	Not
CR Share premium (75 × 0.60)		45	recorded

7   *Fair value adjustments*

	Acquisition 1.4.20X7 $m	Movement (2 years) $m	Year end 31.3.20X9 $m
Property (82 – 62)	20	(2)	18
Brand	25	(5)	20
	45	(7)	38

8   *Intragroup trading*

Unrealised profit: PUP = 56 × 40/140 = 16

DR Cost of sales (retained earnings)	16	
CR Inventories		16

9   *Investments in equity instruments*

	$m	$m
Pacemaker (345 – 268)	77	
Gain (W4)	5	
		82
Syclop	40	
Loss (W4)	(3)	
		37
		119

BPP LEARNING MEDIA

43 Picant

Text references. Chapters 9 and 11.

Top tips. This is a consolidated statement of financial position with a subsidiary and associate. It is always important to note dates. In this case the associate was acquired mid-year. Note that the software was written off on acquisition and then written off by the subsidiary, so it now has to be written back to retained earnings as a consolidation adjustment. The post-acquisition movement in contingent consideration does not affect the goodwill working, it is just added to retained earnings.

Easy marks. There were plenty of marks here for the standard workings – goodwill, investment in associate, NCI. The goods in transit and group inventory were also straightforward. Part (b) required a bit of thought but it should have been easy to pick up 3-4 marks.

Examiner's comments. The preparation of the consolidated statement of financial position was generally well answered but answers to part (b) were very mixed. The main errors in the consolidation were:
- Adjusting the goodwill for the contingent consideration
- Incorrectly dealing with the adjustment to the software
- Errors in intragroup adjustments
- Not using equity accounting for the associate

Marking scheme

	Marks
Statement of financial position	
Property, plant and equipment	2
Goodwill	5
Investment in associate	1½
Inventory	1½
Trade receivables	1
Equity shares	½
Share premium	½
Retained earnings	4½
Non-controlling interest	2
Loan notes	½
Contingent consideration	1
Current liabilities	1
	21
(b) 1 mark per relevant point	4
	25

(a)   PICANT GROUP - CONSOLIDATED STATEMENT OF FINANCIAL POSITION AS AT 31.3.20X1

	$'000
Assets	
Non-current assets	
Property, plant and equipment (37,500 + 24,500 + 1,900 (W6))	63,900
Goodwill (W2)	12,200
Investment in associate (W3)	13,200
	89,300
Current assets	
Inventories (10,000 + 9,000 + 1,800 (W7) – 600 (W7))	20,200
Trade receivables (6,500 + 1,500 – 3,400 (W7))	4,600
	24,800
Total assets	114,100

Equity and liabilities		$'000
Equity attributable to owners of the parent		
Share capital		25,000
Share premium		19,800
Retained earnings (W4)		27,500
		72,300
Non-controlling interests (W5)		8,400
Total equity		80,700
Non-current liabilities		
7% loan notes (14,500 + 2,000)		16,500
Current liabilities		
Contingent consideration (4,200 − 1,500 (W4))		2,700
Other current liabilities (8,300 + 7,500 + 1,800 − 3,400 (W7))		14,200
		16,900
Total equity and liabilities		114,100

Workings

1   *Group structure*

	1.4.20X0	1.10.20X0
	75%	40%
	Sander	Adler
Retained earnings at acquisition:	16,500	15,000 + (6,000 × 6/12) = 18,000

2   *Goodwill*

	$'000	$'000
Consideration transferred		
- shares (8,000 × 75% × 3/2 × $3.20)		28,800
- contingent consideration		4,200
		33,000
FV of non-controlling interests (8,000 × 25% × $4.50)		9,000
Fair value of net assets at acquisition:		
Share capital	8,000	
Retained earnings	16,500	
Fair value adjustments	1,500	
		(26,000)
Impairment loss		(3,800)
Goodwill at year end		12,200

3   *Investment in associate*

	$'000
Cash payment (5,000 × 40% × $4)	8,000
Loan notes (5,000 × 40%/50 × $100)	4,000
	12,000
Share of post-acquisition retained earnings (W4)	1,200
	13,200

BPP LEARNING MEDIA

4 *Retained earnings*

	Picant $'000	Sander $'000	Adler $'000
Per question – at 1/4/20X0	16,200	16,500	15,000
year to 31/3/20X1	11,000	1,000	6,000
	27,200	17,500	21,000
Fair value movement (W6)		400	
Unrealised profit (W7)	(600)		
Contingent consideration (4,200 – 2,700)	1,500		
Pre-acquisition retained earnings (W1)		(16,500)	(18,000)
		1,400	3,000
Group share – Sander (1,400 × 75%)	1,050		
Adler (3,000 × 40%)	1,200		
Impairment losses (3,800 × 75%)	(2,850)		
	27,500		

5 *Non-controlling interests*

	$'000
NCI at acquisition (W2)	9,000
NCI share of post-acquisition retained earnings (1,400 (W4) × 25%)	350
NCI share of impairment losses (3,800 (W4) × 25%)	(950)
	8,400

6 *Fair value adjustments*

	Acquisition 1.4.20X0 $'000	Movement $'000	Year end 31.3.20X1 $'000
Factory	2,000	(100)	1,900
Software	(500)	500	-
	1,500	400	1,900

7 *Intragroup trading*

Consolidation adjustments:

			$'000	$'000
Goods in transit	Dr	Inventories	1,800	
	Cr	Payables (Sander)		1,800
Cancel current accounts	Dr	Payables	3,400	
	Cr	Receivables		3,400
PURP ($1.8m × 50/150)	Dr	Retained earnings	600	
	Cr	Group inventory		600

(b) Picant cannot take assurance from the Tradhat group financial statements that Trilby would be able to meet its liability in respect of the goods. The group financial statements will have aggregated the assets and liabilities of all the group companies and it will not be possible to use them to calculate liquidity ratios for any one company.

This is important, because Picant's contract would not be with the Tradhat group, it would be with Trilby. If Trilby defaulted on its obligations, the Tradhat group would be under no legal obligation to step in, so that the fact that the group has a strong financial position is not really relevant. It would only become relevant if Tradhat were willing to offer a parent company guarantee.

In the absence of a parent company guarantee, Picant must base its decision on the financial position of Trilby as shown in its individual company financial statements. It should also obtain references from other suppliers of Trilby, specifically those who supply it with large orders on 90-day credit terms.

44 Paladin

Text references. Chapters 5 and 9.

Top tips. This is a pretty straightforward consolidated statement of financial position. Set out the proformas and then work methodically through the numbers. There are quite a few adjustments to retained earnings, so make sure your retained earnings working is very clear.

Easy marks. There are a lot of easy marks in this question. The complications are dealing with the deferred payment and the unwinding of the discount, capitalising and amortising the intangible asset and remembering to deduct the intercompany balance from receivables and payables. Most of the rest of it is quite easy, the PURP is only in the parent and two marks are available for investment in associate, which is not a complicated working.

Examiner's comments. The parts of this question that related to basic consolidation adjustments were well dealt with by most candidates. Errors occurred in the more complex aspects. Some candidates failed to discount the deferred consideration and some did not treat the customer relationship as an intangible asset. Others deducted the post-acquisition additional depreciation from the goodwill. Some students only deducted 25% of the impairment loss on the investment in associate, when the loss applied to the whole of the investment. A common error was to offset the subsidiary's overdraft against the parent's bank balance. No such right of offset exists.

Marking scheme

	Marks
Property, plant and equipment	2½
Goodwill	5
Other intangibles	2½
Investment in associate	2
Inventory	1
Receivables	1
Bank	½
Equity shares	½
Retained earnings	5
Non-controlling interest	2
Deferred tax	½
Bank overdraft	½
Deferred consideration	1
Trade payables	1
Total for question	25

CONSOLIDATED STATEMENT OF FINANCIAL POSITION AS AT 30 SEPTEMBER 20X1

	$'000
Assets	
Non-current assets	
Property, plant and equipment (40,000 + 31,000 + 3,000 (W6))	74,000
Goodwill (W2)	15,000
Intangible assets (7,500 + 2,500 (W6))	10,000
Investment in associate (W3)	7,700
	106,700
Current assets	
Inventories (11,200 + 8,400 − 600 (W7))	19,000
Trade receivables (7,400 + 5,300 − 1,300 (W7))	11,400
Bank	3,400
	33,800
Total assets	140,500

Equity and liabilities	$'000
Equity attributable to owners of Paladin	
Share capital	50,000
Retained earnings (W4)	35,200
	85,200
Non-controlling interests (W5)	7,900
	93,100
Non-current liabilities	
Deferred tax (15,000 + 8,000)	23,000
Current liabilities	
Overdraft	2,500
Payables (11,600 + 6,200 – 1,300 (W7))	16,500
Deferred consideration (5,000 + 400 (W2))	5,400
	24,400
Total equity and liabilities	140,500

Workings

1 *Group structure*

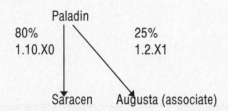

2 *Goodwill*

	$'000	$'000
Consideration transferred:		
Cash		32,000
Deferred consideration (5,400 x 1/1.08)		5,000
		37,000
Non-controlling interest (2,000 x $3.50)		7,000
		44,000
Fair value of net assets:		
Share capital	10,000	
Retained earnings	12,000	
Fair value adjustment on plant	4,000	
Intangible asset	3,000	
		(29,000)
Goodwill		15,000

3 *Investment in associate*

	$'000
Cost of investment	10,000
Share of post-acquisition retained earnings (800 (W4) x 25%)	200
Impairment	(2,500)
	7,700

BPP LEARNING MEDIA

4 Retained earnings

	Paladin $'000	Saracen $'000	Augusta $'000
Per question - 1.10.20X0	25,700	12,000	31,800
- year to 30/9/20X1	9,200	6,000	1,200
		18,000	33,000
PURP (W7)	(600)		
Depreciation on fair value adjustments (W6)		(1,500)	
Unwinding of discount (5,400 – 5,000 (W2))	(400)		
Less pre-acquisition retained earnings to 1.10.20X0		(12,000)	(31,800)
Less pre-acquisition to 1.2.X1 (1,200 × 4/12)		-	(400)
		4,500	800
Impairment of investment in associate (W3)	(2,500)		
Saracen (4,500 × 80%)	3,600		
Augusta (800 × 25%)	200		
	35,200		

5 Non-controlling interests

	$'000
NCI at acquisition (W2)	7,000
Share of post-acquisition retained earnings (4,500 (W4) × 20%)	900
	7,900

6 Fair value adjustments

	Acquisition $'000		Movement $'000	Year end $'000
Plant	4,000	1/4	(1,000)	3,000
Intangible asset (customer relationships)	3,000	1/6	(500)	2,500
	7,000		(1,500)	5,500

7 Intragroup trading
Unrealised profit:

	$'000	$'000
Dr Cost of sales/retained earnings (2,600 × 30/130)	600	
Cr Inventories		600
Current account:		
Dr Group trade payables	1,300	
Cr Group trade receivables		1,300

45 Preparation question: Contract

	Contract 1 $	Contract 2 $	Contract 3 $	Contract 4 $
Statement of profit or loss				
	(W1)	(W2)	(W3)	(W4)
Revenue	54,000	8,000	84,000	125,000
Expenses	(43,200)	(8,000)	(92,400)	(105,000)
Expected loss	–	–	(15,600)	–
Recognised profit/(loss)	10,800	–	(24,000)	20,000

BPP LEARNING MEDIA

	Contract 1 $	Contract 2 $	Contract 3 $	Contract 4 $
Gross amounts due from/to customers				
Contract costs incurred	48,000	8,000	103,200	299,600
Recognised profits less recognised losses	10,800	–	(24,000)	56,000
	58,800	8,000	79,200	355,600
Less: progress billings to date	(50,400)	–	(76,800)	(345,200)
	8,400	8,000	2,400	10,400
Trade receivables				
Progress billings to date	50,400	–	76,800	345,200
Less: cash received	(50,400)	–	(76,800)	(345,200)
	–	–	–	–

Workings

1   *Contract 1* $

   Revenue   45% ×120,000 =   54,000
   Expenses 45% × (48,000 + 48,000) =   43,200

2   *Contract 2*

   Expenses All costs to date charged as expense ∴ 8,000
   Revenue   Probable that all costs incurred will be recovered ∴ 8,000

3   *Contract 3* $

   Revenue   35% × 240,000 =   84,000
   Expenses 35% × (103,200 + 160,800) =   (92,400)
   Loss   (8,400)
   ∴ Expected loss   (15,600)
   Total loss 240,000 – (103,200 + 160,800) =   (24,000)

4   *Contract 4* $

   Revenue   (70% × 500,000) – 225,000 =   125,000
   Expenses (70% × 420,000) – 189,000 =   105,000

46 Beetie

Text references. Chapters 12 and 15.

Top tips. Construction contracts feature regularly in F7. Make sure you know how to calculate the amounts for the statement of financial position. Note that one contract is loss-making.

Easy marks. Part (a) was 4 easy marks and you could get another two easy marks for getting the profit or loss amounts correct.

Marking scheme

			Marks
(a)	One mark per valid point to	Maximum	4
(b)	Revenue (½ mark for each contract)		1
	Profit/loss (½ mark for each contract)		1
	Amounts due from customers (contract 1)		2
	Amounts due to customers (contract 2)		2
		Maximum	6
		Total for question	10

(a) Revenue recognition is an important issue in financial reporting and it is generally accepted that revenue is earned when goods have been accepted by the customer or services have been delivered. At that stage revenue is said to have been realised. However, if this were applied to construction contracts, the effect would not necessarily be to give a faithful representation.

As a construction contract can span several accounting periods, if no revenue were recognised until the end of the contract, this would certainly be prudent but would not be in accordance with the accruals concept. The financial statements would show all of the profit in the final period, when in fact some of it had been earned in prior periods. This is remedied by recognising attributable profit as the contract progresses, as long as ultimate profitability is expected. Any foreseeable loss is recognised immediately.

(b) STATEMENT OF PROFIT OR LOSS

	Contract 1	Contract 2	Total
	$'000	$'000	$'000
Contract revenue	3,300	840	4,140
Contract expenses: (Contract 1: 4,000 × 60%)	(2,400)	(720)	(3,120)
Expected loss recognised (Contract 2)	–	(170)	(170)
Attributable profit/(loss)	900	(50)	850

STATEMENT OF FINANCIAL POSITION

	$'000
Current assets	
Gross amount due from customers	1,800
Current liabilities	
Gross amounts due to customers	210

Workings

Contract 1

	$'000
Contract price	5,500
Costs to date	(3,900)
Costs to complete (4,000 – 3,900)	(100)
Estimated total profit	1,500
	$'000
Profit to date: 1,500 × 3,300/5,500 =	900

Gross amount due from customers

Costs to date	3,900
Profit to date	900
Less progress billings	(3,000)
	1,800

Contract 2

	$'000
Contract price	1,200
Costs to date	(720)
Costs to complete (1,250 – 720)	(530)
Expected total loss	(50)

Gross amount due to customers

Costs to date	720
Loss to date	(50)
Less progress billings	(880)
	(210)

BPP LEARNING MEDIA

47 Mocca

Text reference. Chapter 12

Top tips. Start by working out the total profit on the contract and you can then deduct the amounts that were accounted for in the previous year. Note that the contract should only be charged with half of the useful life of the plant as it will be kept in use after the contract.

Easy marks. This is quite an easy question and should have been no problem for those who had revised IAS 11. Even if you were not familiar with it, a careful reading of the question and the application of general accounting principles would have secured some marks on the profit or loss extracts.

Examiner's comments. Candidates that gave this question serious attention scored quite well. Most calculated the profit and percentage of completion correctly but failed to deduct the results of the previous year. In amounts due from customers candidates often deducted progress payments received rather progress billings.

Marking scheme

	Marks
Revenue	3
Profit	1½
Plant in statement of financial position	1½
Amounts due from customers	1
Trade receivables	1
Disclosure note	2
	10

Profit or loss amounts

	$'000
Revenue (8,125 – 3,500)	4,625
Cost of sales ((9,500 (W1) x 65%) – 2,660)	(3,515)
Profit (1,950 (W2) – 840)	1,110

Statement of financial position amounts

	$'000
Current assets	
Trade receivables (8,125 – 7,725)	400
Amounts due from customers (Note)	1,125

Note	
Costs to date (4,800 + 2,500)	7,300
Profit to date (W2)	1,950
Less progress billings	(8,125)
Amounts due from customers	1,125

Workings

1. Total contract profit

	$'000	$'000
Contract price		12,500
Costs to date	4,800	
Further costs to complete (5,500 – 4,800)	700	
Depreciation to date (8,000 x 15/48)	2,500	
Remaining depreciation (8,000 x 9/48)	1,500	
Total expected costs		(9,500)
Total expected profit on contract		3,000

2. Profit to date

% work completed = 8,125/12,500 = 65%

Profit to date = 3,000 x 65% = 1,950

48 Bodyline

Text reference. Chapter 13.

Top tips. Parts (a) and (b) require you to rehearse the standard discussion about the nature of provisions and the need for IAS 37. The well-prepared candidate should score highly.

The calculations in Part (c) can be tricky, but if you lay out your workings in a methodical manner then you should score good marks even if you don't get the answer perfectly right.

Part (d) requires you to criticise the directors' proposed treatment and then to outline and explain the correct accounting treatment.

Easy marks. The discussion parts (a) and (b) represent 12 easy marks.

Examiner's comments. This question dealt with the nature and treatment of provisions. Parts (a) and (b) were discursive; while (c) and (d) were practical examples of the application.

Generally candidates answered parts (a) and (b) well, but failed to deal with the practical applications in part (c) and (d).

Marking scheme

		Marks
(a)	One mark per valid point to max	6
(b)	The need for the Standard and examples to a max of 2 each	6
(c)	28 day refund policy – constructive obligation	1
	Calculation of provision for unrealised profits where goods resold at full price	1
	Calculation of provision for loss on goods sold at half normal price	1
	The product warranties are treated collectively	1
	Warranty cost can be estimated reliably therefore a liability, not a contingency	1
	Faulty goods other than from Header – not a loss, but	1
	Must remove profit made on them – quantified	1
	Return of faulty goods manufactured by Header creates a loss	1
	Quantification of loss	1
	Available	9
	Maximum	8
(d)	Director's treatment is incorrect	1
	This is an example of a complex asset	1
	Depreciation is $1.65m per annum plus $1,500 per machine hour	2
	Replacement does not meet the definition of a liability	1
		5
	Total for question	25

(a)   **Provisions and IAS 37**

Provisions are liabilities of uncertain timing or amount. Because they are liabilities they must meet the recognition criteria for liabilities - that is there must be:

- A *present* obligation arising from *past* transactions or events
- The *transfer* of economic benefits to settle the obligation must be *probable*
- A *reliable estimate* can be made of the amount of the obligation

The obligation giving rise to a provision can be legal or constructive. A constructive obligation can arise when the actions or statements made by an entity create an expectation that they will meet certain

obligations, even if there is no legal requirement for them to do so; for example they may have a well- known policy of replacing goods beyond the normal warranty period.

Provisions are recognised in full as soon as an entity is aware of them, but long term provisions are recognised at present value. As time goes by the discount unwinds, increasing the provision. The increase in the provision is charged to profit or loss as a finance cost.

If an obligation depends upon a future event, then it is a contingent liability, not a provision. Also, if the amount of an obligation cannot be measured reliably, then it is a contingent liability. Contingent liabilities are not recognised in the financial statements, although they need to be disclosed unless the possibility of an outflow of economic benefits is remote.

(In the past the term provision has been used to describe the reduction in the carrying value of an asset; for example the provision for depreciation. This use of the word provision does not meet the criteria of IAS 37, and so the term allowance is used instead; for example the allowance for receivables.)

(b) **The need for a standard**

Although provisions have been a key area of financial reporting for many years, IAS 37 was the first standard to address this issue. Before IAS 37 there were no rules governing the

- Definition
- Recognition
- Measurement
- Use, and
- Presentation

of provisions.

IAS 37 definition of a provision as a liability of uncertain timing or amount means that provisions must meet the recognition for liabilities. This means that provisions cannot be created to suit management needs. In the past provisions were often created and released in order to smooth profits, rather than to provide for a specific liability. These were sometimes called 'big bath provisions' because they could be used for any and every purpose.

A specific example of this was the creation of provisions for reorganisation or restructuring. The charge to set these provisions up could be explained away by management to their investors as one-off exceptional items, but the release of the provision in the future would boost profits. Under IAS 37 provisions for restructuring can only be recognised if the restructuring has begun or if the restructuring has been announced publicly.

The measurement rules have standardised practice in an area where there were genuine differences of opinion. For example there are at least three ways in which the cost of cleaning up an industrial site after it is closed down (restoration costs) can be accounted for:

- ignore the costs until the site is abandoned,
- accrue the costs evenly over the productive life of the site, or
- provide for the costs in full immediately.

IAS 37 states that these costs should be provided for in full immediately, but at their present value.

Under IAS 37 provisions can only be used for the purpose that they were created for; if a provision is no longer needed it must be released. In the past provisions were sometimes created for one purpose and then used to cover the costs of another.

IAS 37 includes detailed disclosure requirements, including the movement on provisions during the year and an explanation of what each provision has been created for. This ensures that the rules set out above have been complied with.

(c) **Bodyline**

This provision can be reliably measured on the basis of past experience. Although Bodyline does not know which items will be returned or develop faults, it can make an estimate of the total value of returns and faults that there will probably be.

The question does not make it clear whether the 28 day refund is part of the sales contract (in which case it is a legal obligation) or whether it is just a well-known and established part of Bodyline's trading practices (in which case it is a constructive obligation). Either way, an obligation exists that needs to be provided for.

The provision itself can be reliably measured on the basis of past experience. Although Bodyline does not know which items will be returned or develop faults, it can make an estimate of the total value of returns and faults that there will probably be.

The returns provision is $52,850, calculated as follows:

- Of the 10% of sales that are returned under this policy, 70% are resold at the full price. Therefore only the profit element is provided against on these items.

- A further 30% are sold at half the normal sales price, so the provision required will be half of the sale proceeds.

		$
70% resold at full price		
Goods from Header	$1.75m × 20% × 10% × 70% × 40/140	7,000
Other goods	$1.75m × 80% × 10% × 70% × 25/125	19,600
		26,600
30% resold at half price	$1.75m × 10% × 30% × ½	26,250
		52,850

The faulty goods provision is $57,600, calculated as follows:

- 20% of the goods returned will have been supplied by Header; Bodyline will suffer the loss in full on these items.

- Bodyline reclaims the cost of the other 80% returned. Only the profit element is provided for.

		$
Goods from Header	$160,000 × 20%	32,000
Other goods	$160,000 × 80% × 25/125	25,600
		57,600

(d) **Rockbuster**

No obligation exists to replace the engine and so it is wrong to create a provision for its replacement. Rockbuster may decide to trade in the earthmover rather than replace the engine. Also, the $2.4m depreciation charge includes an element in respect of the engine, so to make a provision as well is double-counting.

Instead IAS 16 states that the earth-mover should be treated as an asset with two separate components (the engine and the rest) with different useful lives. The engine (cost $7.5m) will be depreciated on a machine hours basis over 5,000 hours, while the rest of the machine (cost $16.5m) will be depreciated over ten years.

	Cost	Depreciation charge
	$'000	
Engine	7,500	Depreciated on a machine hours basis over 5,000 hours. The charge is $1,500 per hour
The rest	16,500	Depreciated on a straight line basis over its ten year useful life. The charge is $1,650,000 per annum.
Total	24,000	

When the engine is replaced the cost and accumulated depreciation on the existing engine will be retired and the cost of the new engine will be capitalised and depreciated over its working life.

49 Promoil

			Marks
(a)		1 mark per relevant point	5
(b)	(i)	Explanation of treatment	2
		Depreciation	1
		Finance cost	1
		Non-current asset	2
		Provision	1
			7
	(ii)	Figures for asset and depreciation if not a constructive obligation	1
		What may cause a constructive obligation	1
		Subsequent treatment if it is a constructive obligation	1
			3
			15

(a) The *Conceptual Framework* defines a liability as a present obligation of an entity arising from past events, the settlement of which is expected to result in an outflow from the entity of resources embodying economic benefits. The obligation can be legal or constructive.

A provision is a liability of uncertain timing or amount. It can be recognised when the outflow of resources is probable and when the amount concerned can be reliably estimated. Because it is regarded as a liability, a provision must meet the definition of a liability. This regulates when a provision should, or should not, be made. For instance, entities are not allowed to provide for future operating losses, which used to be a means of 'profit smoothing', because the losses are in the future, rather than arising from past events. At the same time, an entity which has a future environmental liability because of past polluting activities, is required to make a provision as soon as the liability becomes apparent.

(b) (i) Promoil must provide for dismantling and restoration costs at 30 September 20X8, as the liability came into existence with the granting of the licence and the cost has been reliably estimated.

The provision at 30 September 20X8 will be for the future cost discounted over 10 years. This will be added to the carrying amount of the oil platform and depreciated over 10 years. The discount will be 'unwound' each year and charged to finance costs. The credit entry will increase the provision until at the end of 10 years it will stand at $15m.

At 30 September 20X8:

STATEMENT OF PROFIT OR LOSS

	$'000
Depreciation (see SFP)	3,690
Finance costs (6,900 (see SFP) × 8%)	552

STATEMENT OF FINANCIAL POSITION

		$'000
Non-current assets:		
Oil platform	30,000	
Dismantling (15m × .46)	6,900	
		36,900
Depreciation (36,900/10)		(3,690)
Carrying value		33,210
Non-current liabilities:		
Environmental provision at 1 October 20X7		6,900
Discount unwound (6,900 × 8%)		552
		7,452

(ii)   If the government licence did not require an environmental clean up, Promoil would have no legal obligation. It would then be necessary to determine whether or not Promoil had a constructive obligation. This would apply if on past performance it had established a practice of carrying out an environmental clean up where required, which would give rise to the expectation that it would do so in this case. If a constructive obligation existed, the accounting would be as per the above.

If no obligation were established, there would be no liability. No provision would be made for the clean-up. The platform would be capitalised at $30m and depreciated over 10 years. There would be no finance costs.

50 Borough

Text references. Chapters 8, 13.

Top tips. Note that 6 marks are available for part (a), so a proper answer to this part of the question is required, not just a couple of sentences. (b) (ii) looks more complex than it is, looking at the entity and consolidated financial statements will help you sort it out.

Easy marks. Part (a) was easy and (b)(i) was straightforward, although you may have wondered about the variable amount.

Examiner's comments. Most candidates had learned the definitions from IAS 37 but had more trouble explaining the consistency aspects. Part (b) tested application to environmental costs and a contingent liability. Many candidates did not know how to deal with the variable element of the environmental costs and few were able to deal with the loan guarantee or determine in which financial statements it should be disclosed.

Marking scheme

			Marks
(a)		Definition of provisions	2
		Definition of contingent liabilities	2
		How IAS 37 improves comparability	2
			6
(b)	(i)	Constructive obligation	1
		Explanation of treatment	1
		Non-current asset and amortisation	1½
		Environmental provision and unwinding of discount	1½
	(ii)	Entity financial statements – contingent liability	1
		No obligation for secured $15m	1
		Consolidated statements - $25m liability	1
		If not going concern – current liability in entity statements	1
			9
		Total for question	15

(a)   A provision is a liability of uncertain timing or amount. A provision should be recognised when an entity has a present obligation, it is probable that it will result in an outflow of economic benefits and a reliable estimate can be made of the amount.

A contingent liability is a possible obligation relying on the occurrence or non-occurrence of a future event which the entity cannot control, or an obligation regarding which the outflow of economic resources is not probable or cannot be reliably estimated.

IAS 37 was introduced to regulate the use of provisions. A provision cannot be made unless it satisfies the criteria above. This prevents companies from making excessive provisions in profitable years and the writing these amounts back to boost profits in less profitable years. Companies cannot make provisions for expected future losses or for restructuring to which they are not irrevocably committed. This makes financial statements more transparent and improves consistency from year to year and between entities.

IAS 37 also requires companies to provide for a liability if it meets the criteria. For instance, deferred environmental obligations must be provided for in full at the outset rather than being accrued for over the period of the obligation.

(b) (i) Borough has a constructive obligation to deal with these environmental costs, so a provision must be set up.

The fixed cost of making good the damage must be added to the cost of the licence and set up as a provision. The provision will be increased each year according to the number of barrels extracted.

At 30 September 20X1 the statement of financial position will show:

	$'000
Non-current assets	
Intangible asset – extraction licence ((50m + 20m) x 9/10)	63,000
Non-current liabilities	
Environmental provision (20m + (150m x 0.02)) x 1.08	24,840

(ii) Legally, Borough and Hamlet are separate companies and in its individual financial statements Borough will simply show its investment in Hamlet as an asset. The guarantee of $10m will be disclosed as a contingent liability. Borough will not need to reflect the $15m which is secured on Hamlet's property. If at some point it is decided that Hamlet is not a going concern, then Borough's loan guarantee will need to be provided for.

In its group financial statements Borough will consolidate the whole of the $25m loan.

51 Jedders

Top tips. This is a type of question which is likely to arise in this paper, covering various standards. In this case, you need to know about IASs 16 and 32.

(a) (i) IAS 16 *Property, plant and equipment* does not allow **selective revaluations** of non-current tangible assets: if one asset is revalued, all in that class must be revalued, thus avoiding 'cherry picking' of asset gains where others in the class may have fallen in value. In addition, non-recording of a fall in value of an asset cannot be justified on the basis that a recovery in market prices is expected in the future.

(ii) STATEMENT OF PROFIT OR LOSS (EXTRACTS)

	$'000
Depreciation charge	
North (($1.2m × 80%)/20 years)	48
Central (($4.8m × 140%)/40 years)	168
South ($2.25m/30 years)	75
	291
Loss on revaluation	
(20% × $1.2m)	240

STATEMENT OF FINANCIAL POSITION (EXTRACTS)

	Cost/revaluation	Depreciation	NBV
	$'000	$'000	$'000
North	960	48	912
Central	6,720	168	6,552
South	2,250	75	2,175
	9,930	291	9,639

At 1 January 20X0 the accumulated depreciation of the Central property is $1.2m, which represents 10 years' worth of depreciation, leaving 40 years remaining life. For the South and North properties, the respective lives on these calculations are 30 and 20 years. If there is no previous revaluation

surplus on the North property, then the loss in the current year is classed as an impairment and must be taken to profit or loss.

(b) A statement of how the trade receivables should be treated:

Group A. These are normal non-factor receivables and the allowance should be calculated as usual.

Group B. Although these receivables have been factored, the risks of late collection and irrecoverable debts remain with Jedders. Thus, the outstanding balance less the receivables allowance should still appear in Jedders' statement of financial position, with a liability recorded for the amount received from Fab Factors. In addition, an interest charge would be made for the 1% charge for the monies advanced.

Group C. In a non-recourse situation such as this, Jedders has effectively sold its receivables for 95% of their value. The receivables would therefore be taken off Jedders' statement of financial position, leaving cash and a residual finance charge.

Applying these treatments to the figures given:

STATEMENT OF PROFIT OR LOSS

	$
Receivables allowance	
Group A (20% × (1,250 × 20%))	50,000
Group B (20% × (1,500 × 10%))	30,000
Group C	nil
	80,000
Finance charge	
Group A	nil
Group B (1% × 1,500) + (1% × 900) + (1% × 450)	28,500
Group C (5% × 2,000)	100,000
	128,500

STATEMENT OF FINANCIAL POSITION (EXTRACTS)

Trade receivables		Less allowance	Net balance
			$
Group A	(1,250 × 20%)	20%	200,000
Group B	(1,500 × 10%)	20%	120,000
Group C		nil	nil
			320,000

(c) IAS 32 *Financial instruments: presentation* requires the issuer of a **hybrid or compound instrument** of this nature – containing elements that are characteristic of both debt and equity – to separate out the components of the instrument and classify them separately. Fab Factors are thus wrong in their advice that such instruments should be recorded and shown as debt.

The proceeds of issue should be split between the amounts attributable to the conversion rights, which are classed as **equity**, and the remainder which must be classed as a **liability**. Although there are several methods that might be used, the question only gives sufficient information to allow the amounts of debt liability to be calculated, leaving the equity element as the residual.

Year	Cash flows	Factor at 10%	Present value
	$'000		$'000
1 Interest ($15m × 7%)	1,050	0.91	955.5
2	1,050	0.83	871.5
3	1,050	0.75	787.5
4	1,050	0.68	714.0
5 Interest + capital	16,050	0.62	9,951.0
Total debt component			13,279.5
Proceeds of issue			15,000.0
Equity component (residual)			1,720.5

BPP LEARNING MEDIA

STATEMENT OF PROFIT OR LOSS (EXTRACTS)

	$'000
Interest paid ((7% × $15m) + 278 (W1))	1,328

Working

((10% × $13.2795m) − $1.05m) (rounded)	278

STATEMENT OF FINANCIAL POSITION (EXTRACTS)

	$'000
Non-current liabilities	
7% convertible loan notes (13,279.5 + 278)	13,557.5
Equity	
Option to convert to equity	1,720.5

52 Pingway

> **Top tips.** This question was doable if you had revised financial instruments. If you had recognised that the loan was a compound instrument and made some sensible comments there would have been marks for that even if the calculations were incorrect.
>
> **Examiner's comments.** The majority of answers to this question were poor. The proceeds of the loan had to be split between debt and equity by discounting the future cash flows at 8% to give the debt element, with the balance being the equity element. Common mistakes were to project the cash flows with an interest rate of 8% (rather than 3%), to discount them at 3% (rather than 8%) and to calculate the interest charge as 3% of $10m (rather than 8% of the debt element).

Marking scheme

	Marks
1 mark per valid comment up to	4
use of 8%	1
initial carrying amount of debt and equity	2
finance cost	2
carrying amount of debt at 31 March 20X8	1
Total for question	10

This convertible loan note is a compound financial instrument. It contains both a liability and an equity component and IAS 32 *Financial Instruments: Presentation* requires these components to be separately recognised. Interest costs on the liability element will be based on the non-convertible rate of 8%, so the charge to profit or loss will not be significantly lower than if a non-convertible instrument were issued. The liability element will also add to gearing. So the financial assistant's observations are incorrect.

FINANCIAL STATEMENT EXTRACTS

	$
STATEMENT OF PROFIT OR LOSS	
Finance costs (8,674,000 × 8%)	693,920
STATEMENT OF FINANCIAL POSITION	
Equity – option to convert (W1)	1,326,000
Non-current liabilities	
3% convertible loan note (W2)	9,067,920

Workings

1   *Equity and liability elements*

	$
Proceeds of loan note	10,000,000
3 years interest (10,000 × 3% × (0.93 + 0.86 + 0.79))	(774,000)
Redemption (10,000 × 0.79)	(7,900,000)
Equity element of loan note	1,326,000
Liability element (10,000 − 1,326)	8,674,000

2   *Loan note balance*

	$
Liability element	8,674,000
Interest at 8%	693,920
Less interest paid	(300,000)
Carrying value at 31 March 20X8	9,067,920

53 Bertrand

Text reference. Chapter 14

Top tips. This was a quite easy question on convertible loan notes – easy if you had revised this and knew what to do with them. Remember that the interest charge must use the effective interest rate, not the nominal rate.

Easy marks. Even if you got mixed up with the calculations, you should have been able to do part (a), which was worth half the marks.

Examiner's comments. Some candidates were able to explain how the convertible loan should be treated in part (a) but were then unable to apply it in practice in part (b). Candidates who had studied this topic were able to score full marks, those who had not scored very few.

Marking scheme

			Marks
(a)	(i)	1 mark per valid point	2
	(ii)	1 mark per valid point	3
(b)		Finance cost	2
		Value of equity option	1
		Value of debt at 30 September 20X1	2
		Total for question	10

(a)   (i)   The convertible loan notes carry a lower rate of interest because holders are considered to have foregone 3% interest in order to have the conversion option. Without the conversion option, Bertrand would have to offer 8% in order to attract investors.

        (ii)   The directors' proposed treatment will classify an amount that should be shown as a non-current liability as equity, which will make the financial statements misleading. A finance cost of 5% on the whole amount is not correct and will understate the cost of the loan to the company.

(b)

	$'000
Interest payable ($10m × 5% × 2.58*)	1,290
Capital repayable ($10m × 0.79)	7,900
Debt element	9,190
Equity element	810
	10,000

* (0.93 + 0.86 + 0.79)

BPP
LEARNING MEDIA

The debt element of $9,190,000 will appear under non-current liabilities, the equity element should appear under equity.

At 30 September 20X1 the following entries will be made:

	DR $'000	CR $'000
Profit or loss	735	
Loan notes		735

Being finance charge (9,190 x 8%)

Loan notes	500	
Cash		500

Being interest paid (10,000 x 5%)

So the balance on the loan notes at 30 September 20X1 will be (9,190 + 735 – 500) = $9,425,000.

54 Triangle

Text references. Chapters 13 and 15.

Top tips. This question had four short sections dealing with various matters: environmental costs, events after the reporting period, contingent assets and substance over form.

The way to deal with such questions is to identify the issue and so the accounting standard needed. After that, it is simply a matter of applying the provision of the relevant standard. This does require good knowledge of the standards.

Examiner's comments. This question was not popular and very poorly answered. Candidates still show a lack of understanding in applying standards to practical situations. Even those who understood the areas examined did not go into sufficient depth in their answers.

Marking scheme

			Marks
(i)	Explanation of treatment of provision		2
	Cost of plant at $20 million		1
	Revised depreciation		1
	Provision initially at $5 million		1
	Increase by finance cost		1
	Profit or loss charges 1 mark each		2
		Maximum	8
(ii)	An example of an adjusting event		1
	No overall effect on profit, but presentation incorrect		1
	Remove from cost of sales and show as an expense		1
	$30,000 is a non-adjusting event if material		1
	Disclose as a note to the financial statements		1
		Maximum	5
(iii)	Due to the dispute this is an example of a contingent asset		1
	Describe the treatment of contingent assets		1
	Not probable therefore ignore, financial statements unchanged		2
		Maximum	4

BPP LEARNING MEDIA

(iv)	Identify it as a sale and repurchase agreement (or financing arrangement)	1
	Substance is not likely to be a sale	1
	Will repurchase if value is more than $7,320,500 plus storage costs	2
	Business of Factorall is financing therefore terms likely to favour repurchase	1
	Adjustments to – sales/loan; cost of sales/inventory;	2
	– trade receivables/inventory (re storage costs); accrued finance costs/loan	2
	Available	9
	Maximum	8
	Maximum for question	25

(i) *Contamination*

There are two errors in the current accounting treatment.

Firstly, the obligation to clean up the contamination existed in full from the day that the plant was brought into use. Therefore the provision should be recognised in full immediately at present value; it should not be accrued incrementally over the life of the plant. Over the next ten years the present value will increase as the discount unwinds. This will be reported by increasing the provision and charging the increase to profit or loss as a finance cost.

Secondly, on initial recognition, the cost of the plant should include the present value of the decontamination.

The plant and the provision should be reported as follows:

	$'000
Plant (a non-current asset)	
1 April 20X4: cost ($15m + $5m)	20,000
Depreciation ($20m/10 years)	(2,000)
31 March 20X5: carrying value	18,000
Provision (a non-current liability)	
1 April 20X4	5,000
Finance cost @ 8%	400
31 March 20X5	5,400

(ii) *Fraud*

The fraud means that the draft financial statements for the year-ended 31 March 20X5 are incorrect. This probably won't affect the net profit for the year, but it will affect the amounts shown for cost of sales and gross profit.

The discovery of this fraud provides new evidence about conditions existing at the end of the reporting period, and so it is classified as an adjusting event. The $210,000 fraud that occurred during the year will be charged to profit or loss as an operating expense and disclosed.

The $30,000 fraud occurring after the year-end does not affect conditions existing at the end of the reporting period and so it will not be adjusted for. However it will be disclosed if it is considered to be material in its own right.

(iii) *Insurance claim*

The insurance claim gives rise to a contingent asset for $240,000. However, under IAS 37 contingent assets are not recognised unless the realisation of income is virtually certain, and this is not the case here because the insurers are disputing the claim.

A contingent asset is disclosed when an inflow of economic benefits is probable, but without legal opinion it is not possible to regard the success of the claim as probable.

Following on from the above, the insurance claim should be ignored altogether in the financial statements for the year-ending 31 March 20X5.

BPP LEARNING MEDIA

(iv)   *Factorall*

The $5m proceeds from Factorall cannot be claimed as income because the substance of the transaction appears to be a $5m loan secured on the maturing inventory.

This is because Triangle still retains the cost and benefits of ownership through its option to repurchase the inventory before 31 March 20X8. Although legally Triangle could refuse to repurchase the inventory, there is evidence of a constructive obligation to do so as noted below:

- The initial sale was below market price, and so there is an opportunity cost arising from not repurchasing.
- The repurchase price is based on the sales price plus interest rather than on its true market value at the date of repurchase. The market price will probably be higher, suggesting an additional opportunity cost from not repurchasing.
- Factorall, as a finance house, will not have the expertise to bring the product to market, and so it will be expecting Triangle to repurchase. If Triangle refuses to repurchase then it is unlikely that Factorall (or any similar company) will be willing to enter into such an agreement with Triangle again.

Because there is a constructive obligation to repurchase the inventory Triangle should recognise this as a liability (at present value) and continue to recognise the inventory at cost (including the storage costs).

For Factorall the benefit of this arrangement is the 10% compound interest receivable, not the purchase of the product.

The correct accounting treatment for this transaction in Triangle's books is as follows:

STATEMENT OF PROFIT OR LOSS

Finance costs ($5m @ 10%) $500,000

STATEMENT OF FINANCIAL POSITION
Current assets
Inventory ($3m + $300,000 holding costs) $3,300,000
Non-current liabilities
Secured loan ($5m + 10%) $5,500,000

The journal to correct the old treatment is as follows:

			Debit $'000	Credit $'000
DEBIT	P/L	Sales (Proceeds)	5,000	
CREDIT	F/P	Secured loan (Proceeds)		5,000
DEBIT	F/P	Inventory (Cost of inventory)	3,000	
CREDIT	P/L	Cost of sales (Cost of inventory)		3,000
DEBIT	F/P	Inventory (Holding costs)	300	
CREDIT	F/P	Receivables (Holding costs)		300
DEBIT	P/L	Finance costs (10% interest)	500	
CREDIT	F/P	Secured loan (10% interest)		500

(F/P = Statement of financial position / P/L = Statement of profit or loss)

55 Angelino

Text reference. Chapter 15.

Top tips. This was not a question to attempt unless you knew something about the various issues involved in off-balance sheet finance. (a) may look like something you can waffle your way through, but that is not the case. In scenarios like (b) it is always worth taking the time to read the information twice, then you will understand the situation before you try to evaluate it.

Easy marks. (a) may have looked like easy marks, but only if you knew something about the issues. If you did know enough to answer (a), then (b) was easy marks. These were all classic off-balance sheet situations and you should have had no trouble dealing with them.

Examiner's comments. This question was more popular than equivalent questions on recent papers and attracted comparatively higher marks. Part (a) was generally well answered, with good answers linking examples of off-balance sheet finance, users and the possible detrimental effect on those users. In part (b) poor answers merely repeated the details in the scenarios without concluding what the substance of the arrangements were or their required accounting treatments.

Marking scheme

				Marks
(a)		1 mark per relevant point to a	Maximum	9
(b)	(i)	1 mark per relevant point to a	Maximum	5
	(ii)	sale price not at fair value raises substance issues		1
		leaseback is not a finance lease		1
		treat building as sold (derecognise) at a profit of $2.5m		1
		rental treated as: $800,000 rental cost		1
		$200,000 finance cost		1
		$300,000 loan repayment		1
			Maximum	6
	(iii)	general discussion of risks and rewards re consignment goods		2
		Issues and accounting treatment relating to supplies from Monza		2
		Issues and accounting treatment relating to supplies from Capri		2
			Available	6
			Maximum	5
			Maximum for question	25

(a) Off balance sheet finance is a form of creative accounting which seeks to obscure financial transactions. It has been described as 'the funding or refinancing of a company's operations in such a way that, under legal requirements and existing accounting conventions, some or all of the finance may not be shown on its balance sheet.' (Note that the IASB now refers to the 'balance sheet' as the 'statement of financial position'. However, the term 'off-balance sheet finance' is still in use.)

In practice, most off-balance sheet finance transactions are intended to keep debt off the statement of financial position. In order to achieve this, the related asset is also kept off the statement of financial position. An example of this is where an asset is actually acquired under a finance lease. Rather than show the asset and the related loan, the acquirer may decide that the asset is not to be capitalised and the lease is accounted for as an operating lease. Or inventory may be purchased on consignment, under a legal agreement which allows the purchaser to not record the current asset or the related trade payable. Potential suppliers doing a credit reference check on the company will not discover the true value of its existing trade payables or be able to accurately assess its payment record. Another example can be where an asset is 'sold' and 'repurchased' under an arrangement which is in substance a loan secured on the asset. The asset disappears from the statement of financial position and the loan is represented as sale proceeds.

Obviously, this conflicts with the requirement for 'faithful representation' in financial statements and the IASB has sought to deal with the off balance sheet problem by means of the definitions and recognition criteria for assets and liabilities in the *Conceptual Framework*. In a situation such as that above the reporting of a sale would not represent faithfully the transaction entered into.

Why do companies want to keep debt out of the statement of financial position? Mainly to improve the appearance of the statement of financial position and avoid any impact on gearing. They want to satisfy the expectations of analysts. An increase in borrowing brings an increase in interest payments, which reduces the amount left to distribute to shareholders. An increase in borrowing above a certain limit can therefore be negatively perceived by investors, leading to a possible fall in the share price. A fall in the share price can leave the company vulnerable to takeover.

BPP
LEARNING MEDIA

A company which is short of funds and needs to raise further loans also needs to convince lenders that it is a good risk. If it already has large loans outstanding, lenders will be less willing to make further loans, or will require a higher rate of interest to compensate for the increased risk of default. The company may therefore seek to move some of its borrowing off balance sheet (perhaps by paying off one loan with another disguised as a sale and repurchase) and thereby reduce its gearing to a more acceptable level.

Off balance sheet finance is to some degree a dynamic issue; new forms of it will continue to arise and it will continue to be a problem for standard setters, auditors, lenders and investors. A number of the high-profile collapses of recent years have revealed substantial amounts of borrowing off balance sheet.

(b)   (i)   In this situation the trade receivables have been factored 'with recourse'. Angelino still bears the risks of slow payment (they receive a residual amount depending upon how quickly customers pay) and non-payment (they refund to Omar any balances uncollected after six months). The substance of the transaction is therefore that Omar is providing a loan to Angelino on the security of the trade receivables.

The receivables have therefore not been sold and should not be derecognised. The payment from Omar should be accounted for as a loan. When a customer pays, the amount lent in respect of his balance should be debited to the loan and credited to his account and the amount needed to clear his balance should be charged to loan interest/ debt collection expenses.

(ii)   This is a sale and leaseback transaction in which the sale price has been inflated to include a loan and the lease payments have been inflated to include interest and loan repayments.

Taking the transaction at its face value, Angelino could record the sale at $12m, showing a profit on disposal of $4.5m. The lease payments of $1.3m per annum would be charged to profit or loss as rent.

However, representing the substance of the transaction, the sale should be recorded at market value of $10m, giving a profit on disposal of $2.5m and the additional $2m should be recorded as a loan. The $0.5m per annum above market value in the lease payments should be treated as loan repayments.

The loan will be accounted for as follows:

	$'000
Initial balance	2,000
Finance cost 10%	200
Instalment paid	(500)
Balance 30.9.X6	1,700
Finance cost 10%	170
Instalment paid	(500)
Balance 30.9.X7	1,370
Current liability (1,700 – 1,370)	330
Non-current liability	1,370

(iii)   Angelino's contract with Monza is a typical consignment agreement. The cars remain the property of Monza and Angelino bears none of the risks of ownership. When Angelino sells a car or decides to keep it at the end of three months, it purchases it at that point from Monza, at the list price in force at that date. This is therefore the point at which the risks and rewards pass to Angelino. Up to that point there is no sale and the cars should not appear in inventory.

The agreement with Capri is of the nature of purchase under a credit agreement. Angelino pays a 10% deposit and obtains ownership of the vehicles at that point. If it fails to pay the balance, it forfeits its deposit and has to return the cars at its own expense, so it has taken on the risks of ownership, principally the risk of not being able to sell the vehicle. In this case Angelino should show the cars in inventory and set up a trade payable for the list price, less the deposit paid. The 1% display charge should be accounted for as interest.

56 Wardle

Text references. Chapters 15 and 16

Top tips. Part (a) was straightforward as long as you remembered to answer the question. It asked for why the principle of substance over form is important and for features that indicate that substance is different from legal form. If you stick to those two issues you are far more likely to get the marks than if you just put down everything you know and hope there's something relevant in there. Part (b) required an understanding of what a sale and repurchase transaction is. It's important to remember that all the information you are give has a purpose. In this case, the interest information told you that the substance of the transaction was a secured loan. Setting out a sensible format for the statement of profit or loss extract was vital for this part, and it gave you the information you needed to answer part (c).

Easy marks. It was not hard to pick up at least a few marks in part (a). Part (b) was easy once you knew what you were doing and part (c) was simple if you had managed to deal with part (b).

Examiner's comments. Most answers to part (a) started well referring to matters such as relevance, reliability and faithful representation. However the discussion of finance leases dominated many answers (to the exclusion of other issues) and few attempted to describe the features that indicate that substance may differ from form. It was clear that very few understood the issues in part (b), which was a sale and repurchase of maturing inventory. Many candidates got confused between the substance of the transaction and its legal form and many showed statement of financial position extracts when only profit or loss extracts were required. Those who got the numbers correct in part (b) tended to do well in part (c).

Marking scheme

		Marks
(a)	1 mark per valid point	5
(b)	(i) and (ii) 1 mark per reported profit figure	5
(c)	1 mark per valid point	5
		15

(a) It is important that financial statements should reflect the economic substance of a transaction, where this differs from legal form, because this provides users with a 'faithful representation' of the transaction.

For instance, if an asset held under a finance lease were treated according to its legal form it would not appear under non-current assets and the related lease liability would not be shown. This would make the entity's gearing look lower than it actually was and probably inflate its ROCE. This treatment is not allowed under IFRS.

Sale and leaseback or sale and repurchase arrangements can be used to disguise the substance of loan transactions by taking them 'off balance sheet'. In this case the legal position is that the asset has been sold, but the substance of the transaction is that the seller still retains the benefits of ownership.

Features which suggest that the substance of a transaction may differ from its legal form are:

- The seller of an asset retains the ability to use the asset
- The seller remains exposed to the risks of ownership eg. maintenance
- An asset which has been sold is one that can reasonably only be used by the seller
- A 'sold' asset remains on the sellers premises
- An asset has been transferred at a price substantially above or below its fair value
- An asset has been 'sold' under terms which make it very unlikely that it will not be repurchased
- A number of linked transactions have taken place

All of these features suggest that 'control' has been separated from legal ownership and that the substance of the transaction may not have been correctly represented.

(b)	(i)	Legal form	31 March: 20X1	20X2	20X3	Total
			$'000	$'000	$'000	$'000
		Revenue	6,000	–	10,000	16,000
		Cost of sales	(5,000)	–	(7,986)	(12,986)
		Gross profit	1,000	–	2,014	3,014
		Finance costs	–	–	–	–
		Net profit	1,000	–	2,014	3,014

	(ii)	Substance	31 March: 20X1	20X2	20X3	Total
			$'000	$'000	$'000	$'000
		Revenue	–	–	10,000	10,000
		Cost of sales	–	–	(5,000)	(5,000)
		Gross profit	–	–	5,000	5,000
		Finance costs	(600)	(660)	(726)	(1,986)
		Net profit	(600)	(660)	4,274	3,014

(c)   While net profit at the end of the three-year period is the same under both treatments, we can see that under the legal form revenue is much greater, because of the assumption that Wardle has 'sold' the asset twice. This leads to profit being split between two of the three years rather than shown wholly in year 3, so there is some 'smoothing' effect. Reporting under the legal form of the transaction removes the finance cost, which will have a favourable effect on interest cover, and will also have removed the loan from the statement of financial position, thus making gearing appear lower. Similarly, under the legal form, the asset will not appear in the statement of financial position, which will make ROCE appear higher than it would otherwise have been.

57 Preparation question: Branch

STATEMENT OF PROFIT OR LOSS (EXTRACT)

	$
Depreciation (W1)	5,000
Finance costs (W2)	2,074

STATEMENT OF FINANCIAL POSITION (EXTRACT)	$
Non-current assets	
Property, plant and equipment	
Assets held under finance leases (20,000 – (20,000/4))	15,000
Non-current liabilities	
Finance lease liabilities (W2)	14,786
Current liabilities	
Finance lease liabilities (W2) (16,924 – 14,786)	2,138

Workings

1   *Depreciation*

$$\frac{20,000}{4} = \$5,000 \text{ pa}$$

2   *Finance leases liabilities*

		$
Year ended 31 December 20X1		
1.1.X1	Liability b/d	20,000
1.1.X1	Deposit	(1,150)
		18,850
1.1.X1 – 31.12.X1	Interest at 11%	2,074
31.12.X1	Instalment	(4,000)
31.12.X1	Liability c/d	16,924
Year ended 31 December 20X2		
1.1.X2 – 31.12.X2	Interest at 11%	1,862
31.12.X2	Instalment	(4,000)
31.12.X2	Liability c/d	14,786

58 Evans

STATEMENT OF PROFIT OR LOSS (extract)

	$
Depreciation ($61,570/10)*	6,157
Operating lease rentals (2 × 5,000)	10,000
Finance costs (W)	1,171

STATEMENT OF FINANCIAL POSITION (extract)

	$
Non-current assets	
Property, plant and equipment ($61,570 – $6,157)	55,413
Non-current liabilities	
Finance lease liabilities (W)	51,033
Current liabilities	
Finance lease liabilities (59,741 – 51,033 (W))	8,708

Working

Interest on finance lease

	$
Cash price	61,570
Instalment 1 October 20X3	(3,000)
	58,570
Interest October - December 20X3 (2%)	1,171
Balance 31 December 20X3	59,741
Instalment 1 January 20X4	(3,000)
	56,741
Interest January - March 20X4 (2%)	1,135
Balance 31 March 20X4	57,876
Instalment 1 April 20X4	(3,000)
	54,876
Interest April - June 20X4 (2%)	1,098
Balance 30 June 20X4	55,974
Instalment 1 July 20X4	(3,000)
	52,974
Interest July - September 20X4 (2%)	1,059
Balance 30 September 20X4	54,033
Instalment 1 October 20X4	(3,000)
	51,033

*As there is a secondary lease period for which only a nominal rental is payable we can assume that Evans will keep the rocket booster for the full 10 years of its useful life. If this were not the case it would be depreciated over the 6.5 years of the lease term.

BPP LEARNING MEDIA

59 Fino

Text references: Chapter 16.
Top tips: Only 5 marks were available for calculations here. Intelligent comment on faithful representation and its application to leasing would have earned the greater part of the marks.
Examiner's comments. Answers to this question were very mixed. Weaker answers did not pinpoint the importance of the commercial substance of transactions in part (a) or identify effect on ROCE in part (b). In the last part some candidates failed to treat the payments under the finance lease as being in advance and so based the finance costs on $350,000 rather than $250,000.

Marking scheme

	Marks
(a) 1 mark per valid point to	5
(b) (i) 1 mark per valid point to	4
(b) (ii)(1) operating lease – charge to profit or loss	1
- prepayment	1
(b) (ii) (2) finance lease – depreciation and finance costs	1
Asset, current and non-current liability	3
	15

(a)   The concept of faithful representation requires that the financial statements give a true picture of the nature and effect of financial transactions. If users can be confident that this is the case, then the financial statements can be relied upon.

This means that assets and liabilities as shown in the statement of financial position exist, are assets or liabilities of the entity and are shown at the correct amount, in accordance with the stated accounting policies of the entity. For instance, it may seem that a property shown at original cost when its market value is twice that amount is not faithfully represented, but if the disclosed accounting policy of the entity is not to revalue its properties, users will know what they are looking at and can adjust accordingly.

The most obvious examples of faithful representation not being adhered to involve off-balance-sheet finance transactions, such as sale and leaseback, where secured loans are disguised as the sale of assets. This keeps borrowing out of the statement of financial position and avoids any consequent impact on gearing. The accounting scandals of the past decade revealed numerous off-balance-sheet schemes and underlined the importance of faithful representation.

(b)   (i)   The finance director is correct in that, if the plant is regarded as being held under an operating lease, it will not be capitalised. In this case the cost of the plant will not be included in capital employed and so will not have an adverse effect on ROCE.

However, the finance director's comments betray an ignorance of IAS 17. Under IAS 17 leases are classified according to the *substance* of the transaction, on the basis of whether or not the risks and rewards of ownership have been transferred. The standard gives examples of situations where a lease would normally be classified as a finance lease, including:

- where the lease transfers ownership to the lessee at the end of the lease term
- where an option to purchase exists on terms which make it reasonably certain that the option will be exercised
- where the lease term is for the major part of the asset's economic life
- where the present value of the minimum lease payments amounts to at least substantially all of the fair value of the asset

In this case the lease term is for the whole of the asset's economic life and the present value of the minimum lease payments (four payments of $100,000 over three years) amounts to substantially all of the fair value of the plant. This must therefore be regarded as a finance lease and consequently will impact the ROCE.

(ii) 1 *Operating lease*

		$
Statement of profit or loss		
Payment under operating lease (100,000 × 6/12)		50,000
Statement of financial position		
Current assets		
Prepayment (100,000 × 6/12)		50,000

2 *Finance lease*

	$
Statement of profit or loss	
Depreciation (350,000/4 × 6/12)	43,750
Finance costs (W)	12,500
Non-current assets	
Leased plant (350,000 – 43,750)	306,250
Non-current liabilities	
Amount due under finance lease (W)	175,000
Current liabilities	
Amount due under finance lease	
(262,500 – 175,000)	87,500

Working

	$
Cost 1.4.X7	350,000
1.4.X7 deposit	(100,000)
Balance 1.4.X7	250,000
Interest to 30.9.X7 (250,000 × 10% × 6/12)	12,500
Balance 30.9.X7	262,500
Interest to 1.4.X8 (250,000 × 10% × 6/12)	12,500
1.4.X8 payment	(100,000)
Capital balance due 30.9.X8	175,000

60 Preparation question: Julian

(a)

	Carrying amount $'000	Tax base $'000	Temporary difference $'000
Property, plant and equipment	460	270	190
Development expenditure	60		60
Interest receivable (55 – 45)	10		10
Provision	(40)		(40)
			220

(b) **Notes to the statement of financial position**

Deferred tax liability

	$'000
Accelerated depreciation for tax purposes [(190 – 90) × 30%]	30
Product development costs deducted from taxable profit (60 × 30%)	18
Interest income taxable when received (10 × 30%)	3
Provision for environmental costs deductible when paid (40 × 30%)	(12)
Revaluations (90 × 30%)	27
	66

BPP LEARNING MEDIA

	$'000
At 1 January 20X4 [(310 – 230) × 30%]	24
Amount charged to profit or loss (balancing figure)	15
Amount charged to equity (90 × 30%)	27
At 31 December 20X4 (220 × 30%)	66

Note to the statement of profit or loss

Income tax expense

	$'000
Current tax	45
Deferred tax	15
	60

61 Deferred taxation

(a)   IAS 12 *Income taxes* prescribes the accounting treatment for income taxes including the recognition of deferred tax assets and liabilities. These assets and liabilities arise due to **temporary differences** between the tax base of an asset or liability and its carrying amount in the statement of financial position. The tax base of an asset or liability is the amount attributed to that asset or liability for tax purposes. Temporary differences may be either taxable or deductible.

Taxable temporary differences will result in taxable amounts in determining taxable profit (loss) of future periods when the carrying amount of the asset or liability is recovered or settled.

Deductible temporary differences will result in amounts that are deductible in determining taxable profit (tax loss) of future periods when the carrying amount of the asset is recovered or settled.   (IAS12)

IAS 12 identifies the main categories in which temporary differences can occur, which include the following:

(i)   **Interest revenue** is included in accounting profit on a time proportion basis but may, in some jurisdictions, be included in taxable profit when cash is collected. The tax base of any receivable recognised in the statement of financial position with respect to such revenues is nil because the revenues do not affect taxable profit until cash is collected;

(ii)   **Depreciation** used in determining taxable profit (tax loss) may differ from that used in determining accounting profit. The temporary difference is the difference between the carrying amount of the asset and its tax base which is the original cost of the asset less all deductions in respect of that asset permitted by the taxation authorities in determining taxable profit of the current and prior periods. A taxable temporary difference arises, and results in a deferred tax liability, when tax depreciation is accelerated (if tax depreciation is less rapid than accounting depreciation, a deductible temporary difference arises, and results in a deferred tax asset);

(iii)   **Development costs** may be capitalised and amortised over future periods in determining accounting profit but deducted in determining taxable profit in the period in which they are incurred. Such development costs have a tax base of nil as they have already been deducted from taxable profit. The temporary difference is the difference between the carrying amount of the development costs and their tax base of nil.

(iv)   **Research costs** are recognised as an expense in determining accounting profit in the period in which they are incurred but may not be permitted as a deduction in determining taxable profit (tax loss) until a later period. The difference between the tax base of the research costs, being the amount the taxation authorities will permit as a deduction in future periods, and the carrying amount of nil is a deductible temporary difference that results in a deferred tax asset;

(iv)   Certain assets may be carried at **fair value**, or may be revalued, without an equivalent adjustment being made for tax purposes. A deductible temporary difference arises if the tax base of the asset exceeds its carrying amount.

(b)   **G Co**

Temporary difference at 31 March 20X3:

	$
Temporary differences b/f at 1 April 20X2	100
Arising in year (100 – 90)	10
	110

Deferred tax liability will be 110 × 30% = $33,000

This figure will be included in the statement of financial position.

The decrease in the provision of ($35,000 – $33,000) = $2,000 will reduce the tax charge for the year.

62 Bowtock

(a)   **Principles of deferred tax**

In many countries different rules are used for calculating accounting profit (as used by investors) and taxable profit. This can give rise to **temporary differences**.

Temporary differences arise when income or expenditure is recognised in the financial statements in one year, but is charged or allowed for tax in another. Deferred tax needs to be provided for on these items.

The most important temporary difference is that between depreciation charged in the financial statements and capital allowances in the tax computation. In practice capital allowances tend to be higher than depreciation charges, resulting in accounting profits being higher than taxable profits. This means that the actual tax charge (known as *current tax*) is too low in comparison with accounting profits. However, these differences even out over the life of an asset, and so at some point in the future the accounting profits will be lower than the taxable profits, resulting in a relatively high current tax charge.

These differences are misleading for investors who value companies on the basis of their post tax profits (by using EPS for example). Deferred tax adjusts the reported tax expense for these differences. As a result the reported tax expense (the current tax for the period plus the deferred tax) will be comparable to the reported profits, and in the statement of financial position a provision is built up for the expected increase in the tax charge in the future.

There are many ways that deferred tax could be calculated. IAS 12 states that the *liability method* should be used. This provides for the tax on the difference between the carrying value of an asset (or liability) and its tax base. The tax base is the value given to an asset (or liability) for tax purposes. The deferred tax charge (or credit) in profit or loss is the increase (or decrease) in the provision reported in the statement of financial position.

(b)   *Bowtock*

The provision for deferred tax in Bowtock's statement of financial position at 30 September 20X3 will be the potential tax on the difference between the accounting carrying value of $1,400,000 and the tax base of $768,000. The difference is $632,000 and the tax on the difference is $158,000.

The charge (or credit) for deferred tax in profit or loss is the increase (or decrease) in the provision during the year. The closing provision of $158,000 is less than the opening provision of $160,000, so there is a credit for $2,000 in respect of this year.

Movement in the provision for deferred tax for the year-ending 30 September 20X3

	$
Opening provision	160,000
Credit released to profit or loss	(2,000)
Closing provision	158,000

BPP
LEARNING MEDIA

Workings

		Accounting Carrying value		Tax base	Difference	Tax @ 25%
Y/E 09/X1		$		$	$	$
Purchase		2,000,000		2,000,000	–	–
Depreciation	W1	(200,000)	W2	(800,000)		
Balance		1,800,000		1,200,000	600,000	150,000
Y/E 09/X2						
Depreciation		(200,000)	W3	(240,000)		
Balance		1,600,000		960,000	640,000	160,000
Y/E 09/X3						
Depreciation		(200,000)	W4	(192,000)		
Balance		1,400,000		768,000	632,000	158,000

(W1) $2,000,000 cost - $400,000 residual value over 8 years.
(W2) $2,000,000 × 40%
(W3) $1,200,000 × 20%
(W3) $960,000 × 20%

63 Preparation question: Fenton

(a)

Date	Narrative	Shares	Time	Bonus fraction	Weighted average
1.1.X1	b/d	5,000,000	$\times \frac{1}{12}$	$\times \frac{2.00}{1.95} \times \frac{11}{10}$	470,085
31.1.X1	Rights issue	+ 1,250,000			
		6,250,000	$\times \frac{5}{12}$	$\times \frac{11}{10}$	2,864,583
30.6.X1	FMP	+ 125,000			
		6,375,000	$\times \frac{5}{12}$	$\times \frac{11}{10}$	2,921,875
30.11.X1	Bonus issue	+ 637,500			
		7,012,500	$\times \frac{1}{12}$		584,375
					6,840,918

TERP	4 @ 2	=	8.00
	1 @ 1.75	=	1.75
	5		9.75
	∴ 1.95		

$$\text{EPS for y/e } 31.12.X1 = \frac{\$2,900,000}{6,840,918} = 42.4c$$

$$\text{Restated EPS for y/e } 31.12.X0 = 46.4c \times \frac{1.95}{2.00} \times \frac{10}{11} = 41.1c$$

(b) **Sinbad**

$$\text{Basic EPS} = \frac{\$644,000}{10,000,000} = 6.44$$

Earnings	
Profit for the year	644,000
Interest saving (1,200,000 @ 5% × 70%)	42,000
	686,000
Number of shares	
Basic	10,000,000
On conversion	4,800,000
	14,800,000

$$\text{Diluted EPS} = \frac{\$686,000}{14,800,000} = 4.64c$$

BPP LEARNING MEDIA

(c) **Talbot**

Basic EPS = $\dfrac{540,000}{5,000,000}$ = 10.8c

Diluted EPS:

Consideration on exercise
400,000 × $1.10 = $440,000

Shares acquired at FV
$440,000/$1.60 = 275,000

∴ shares issued for no consideration
(400,000 − 275,000) = 125,000

EPS = $\dfrac{540,000}{5,000,000 + 125,000}$ = 10.5c

64 Barstead

Text references. Chapter 18.

Top tips. The answer to part(a) may have seemed fairly obvious, but the question asked you to *explain* and allowed four marks for it, so clearly more than three sentences were required. It was worth spending a few moments thinking about this and writing a proper answer.

Easy marks. Part (a) was easy with a bit of thought and (b) was easy for students who had revised EPS and knew what they were doing. Otherwise it would have been difficult to score much at all on (b).

Examiner's comments. Part (a) seemed to baffle most candidates. Few candidates could relate the differentials to new shares being issued. Part (b) was answered better, although some candidates thought the dilution was caused by the rights issue rather than the convertible loan stock.

Marking scheme

		Marks
(a)	1 mark per valid point	4
(b)	Basic EPS for 20X1	3
	Restated EPS for 20X0	1
	Diluted EPS for 20X1	2
		6
Total for question		10

(a) An increase in profit after tax of 80% **will not translate into a comparable increase in EPS** unless the number of shares in issue has remained constant. The disparity between the increase in profit and the increase in EPS shows that Barstead has obtained the resources it needed in order to generate higher profit through share issue(s). This may have been done as part of an acquisition drive, obtaining a controlling interest in other entities through share exchange. In this way, EPS is a more reliable indicator of performance than pure profit because **it matches any additional profit with the resources used to earn it**.

Diluted EPS takes into account the existence **of potential ordinary shares**, arising from financial instruments such as options, warrants and convertible debt. Diluted EPS shows what EPS would be if all of these potential shares came into existence in the current year. In the case of Barstead, the diluted EPS has increased by less than the basic EPS. This shows that some of the profit increase has been financed by the issue of financial instruments carrying future entitlement to ordinary shares. These instruments will carry a lower finance cost than non-convertible debt, which helps to boost current profits. But this means that the finance costs saved when these instruments are converted will probably be insufficient to offset the adverse effect of the additional shares, leading to dilution. This is an advance warning signal to investors.

(b)   Theoretical ex-rights price will be:

4 shares at $3.80 –   15.2
1 share at $2.80 –   2.8
                             18.0 / 5 = $3.60

Weighted average calculation:

Date	Narrative	No. shares (m)	Time period	Bonus fraction	Weighted average (m)
1.10.20X0	b/d	36	× 3/12	× $3.80/$3.60	9.5
1.1.20X1	Rights issue	9			
		45	× 9/12		33.75
					43.25

Basic EPS for the year ended 30 September 20X1 is therefore:

$15m/43.25m = 34.7c

Comparative EPS = 35c × 3.6/3.8 = 33.2c

Diluted EPS:

The additional earnings will be $800,000 ($10m × 8%) less 25% tax = $600,000
The additional shares will be (10m/100) × 25 = 2.5m
The net effect is therefore $600,000/2.5m = 24c. This is below basic EPS and therefore dilutive.

Earnings = $15.6m
Shares = 43.25 + 2.5 = 45.75
Diluted EPS = 34.1c

65 Rebound

Text references. Chapters 7 and 18.

Top tips. Part (a) took a bit of thought. You just had to look at what information in published financial statements deals with expected future events, and IFRS 5 is an obvious example. In (b) it is important to note that the new operation in 20X1 was acquired 8 months before the year end, so its results need to be grossed up to allow for 12 months.

Easy marks. You should have been able to get some marks on (a) and (b) (i) was easy. (b) (ii) had a few issues to deal with, like adding back the loan stock interest and deducting the notional number of fully-paid shares under the option.

Examiner's comments. Most candidates did not attempt part (a), but part (b) (i) was generally well answered, the main mistake being failing to adjust the results of the new operation for 12 months. In (ii) some candidates used projected 20X3 figures to calculate the 20X2 EPS and the treatment of the share options was not well understood.

Marking scheme

				Marks
(a)		1 mark per valid point/example		6
(b)	(i)	Profit from continuing operations	1	
		Profit from newly acquired operations	2	
				3
	(ii)	EPS for 20X1 and 20X2 at 3 marks each		6
				15

(a)

Historically-prepared financial statements of limited companies are used by analysts and stockbrokers to value the company's shares. The valuation placed on a company's shares is an indication of how it is expected to perform in the future. So financial statements are relied upon for their predictive value and this is one reason why it is so important that they faithfully represent financial information.

The difference between historical financial statements and forecasts is that historical financial statements record financial transactions which have already taken place, so they are highly reliable. Forecasts have a much lower degree of reliability because they are based on estimates, which are subjective.

IFRS presentation and disclosure requirements are intended to enhance the quality of information provided to users. For instance, entities are required to present separately the results of discontinued operations and to disclose a breakdown of these results between gains or losses on disposal or reclassification of assets and trading results. They are also required to show separately the details of non-current assets held for sale and to disclose details of the discontinued operation. This give important predictive information to shareholders because they know that this operation will not be running during the next accounting period and that the assets in question are expected to be sold within 12 months.

Another area where financial statements supply predictive information concerns provisions. A provision can be made in the current year for an event expected to arise in a later accounting period. Details of the amount of the provision and why it is being made have to be disclosed, users are aware of the nature and extent of the liability. Entities also disclose contingent liabilities, so users are aware of possible future liabilities of which either the probability or the amount is not certain.

Diluted EPS provides another piece of predictive information. Although it does not represent specific future EPS, it does alert shareholders to the degree of dilution inherent in the entity's financial instruments and users will be able to see from the notes the relevant dates of exercise of options. The notes will also disclose proposed dividends, so shareholders can see how much cash will be paid out and how much they can expect to receive.

(b)

(i) Profit after tax for year to 31.3.20X3

	$'000
Existing operations (2,000 × 1.06)	2,120
New operation (450 × 12/8 months × 1.08)	729
	2,849

(ii) Diluted EPS

Earnings	20X2	20X1
	$'000	$'000
Continuing operations	2,450	1,750
Saving on loan stock interest, less tax ($5m × 8% × 70%)	280	280
	2,730	2,030

Shares	20X2	20X1
	'000	'000
Existing ($3m × 4)	12,000	12,000
Loan stock (5m × 40/100)	2,000	2,000
Options ((W) × 6 months)	600	–
	14,600	14,000

Diluted EPS (cents)	20X2	20X1
(2,730,000 / 14,600,000) × 100	18.7	
(2,030,000 / 14,000,000) × 100		14.5

Working

	'000
Shares issued under options	2,000
Shares fully paid (2m/2.5)	(800)
Dilutive shares	1,200

BPP
LEARNING MEDIA

66 Victular

Text references. Chapters 19 and 20

Top tips. Note that only 8 marks are available for calculating the ratios. If you had trouble remembering how to calculate any of them, you could work back the ratios given for Grappa. The major part of the answer is the analysis and it's best to organise this under headings.

Easy marks. The ratios were easy marks and so was part (c). The analysis was slightly challenging because it was not a clear-cut picture, but you should have found enough useful points to make.

Examiner's comments. Many candidates were able to calculate the ratios but analysing and interpreting them was a different matter. Much of the information in the scenario was ignored and many candidates failed to attempt part (c), thereby throwing away 5 marks.

Marking scheme

		Marks
(a)	Merlot's ratios	8
(b)	1 mark per valid comment up to	12
(c)	1 mark per relevant point	5
Total for question		25

(a)

ROCE	$(2,500 - 500 - 10) / (2,800 + 3,200 + 3,000 + 500)$ %	= 20.9%
Pre-tax ROE	$(1,400/2,800)$%	= 50%
Net asset turnover	$20,500/(14,800 - 5,700)$	= 2.3 times
Gross profit margin	$(2,500/20,500)$%	= 12.2%
Operating profit margin	$(2,000/20,500)$%	= 9.8%
Current ratio	$7,300/5,700$	= 1.3 : 1
Closing inventory holding period	$(3,600/18,000) \times 365$	= 73 days
Trade receivables collection period	$(3,700 / 20,500) \times 365$	= 66 days
Trade payables payment period	$(3,800 / 18,000) \times 365$	= 77 days
Gearing	$(3,200 + 500 + 3,000) / 9,500$%	= 71%
Interest cover	$2,000 / 600$	= 3.3 times
Dividend cover	$1,000 / 700$	= 1.4 times

(b) **Assessment of relative position and performance of Grappa and Merlot**

Profitability

At first sight it appears that Victular would see a much greater return on its investment if it acquired Merlot rather than Grappa. A closer analysis of the figures suggests that this may not be the case.

Merlot has an ROCE over 40% higher than Grappa's and an ROE more than double Grappa's ROE. However, the difference is due more to the lower level of equity in Merlot than to the superiority of its profit. Merlot's equity (2,800) is only half that of Grappa (5,500). This reduces the denominator for ROCE and doubles the ROE. A closer look at the profits of both companies shows that the operating profit margin of Grappa is 10.5% and that of Merlot is 9.75%.

The net asset turnover of Merlot (2.3 times) suggests that it is running the more efficient operation. Merlot has certainly achieved a much greater turnover than Grappa and with a lower level of net assets. The problem is that, on a much higher level of turnover, its net profit is not much higher than Grappa's.

Further analysis of net assets shows that Grappa owns its factory, while Merlot's factory must be rented, partly accounting for the higher level of operating expenses. Grappa's factory is carried at current value, as shown by the property revaluation reserve, which increases the negative impact on Grappa's ROCE.

Gearing

Merlot has double the gearing of Grappa, due to its finance lease obligations. At 7.5% Merlot is paying less on the finance lease than on its loan notes, but this still amounts to a doubling of its interest payments. Its interest cover is 3.4 times compared to 6 times for Grappa, making its level of risk higher. In a bad year Merlot could have trouble servicing its debts and have nothing left to pay to shareholders. However, the fact that Merlot has chosen to operate with a higher level of gearing rather than raise funds from a share issue also increases the potential return to shareholders.

Liquidity

Grappa and Merlot have broadly similar current ratios, but showing a slightly higher level of risk in the case of Merlot. Merlot is also running an overdraft while Grappa has $1.2m in the bank. Grappa is pursuing its receivables slightly less aggressively than Merlot, but taking significantly longer to pay its suppliers. As this does not appear to be due to shortage of cash, it must be due to Grappa being able to negotiate more favourable terms than Merlot.

Summary

Merlot has a higher turnover than Grappa and a policy of paying out most of its earnings to shareholders. This makes it an attractive proposition from a shareholder viewpoint. However, if its turnover were to fall, there would be little left to distribute. This is the risk and return of a highly geared company. Merlot is already running an overdraft and so has no cash to invest in any more plant and equipment. In the light of this, its dividend policy is not particularly wise. Grappa has a lower turnover and a much more conservative dividend policy but may be a better long-term investment. Victular's decision will probably depend upon its attitude to risk and the relative purchase prices of Grappa and Merlot

(c) While ratio analysis is a useful tool, it has a number of limitations, particularly when comparing ratios for different companies.

Some ratios can be calculated in different ways. For instance, gearing can be expressed using debt as a proportion of debt and equity or simply debt as a proportion of equity. Ratios can be distorted by inflation, especially where non-current assets are carried at original cost.

Ratios are based upon financial statements which may themselves not be comparable due to the adoption of different accounting policies and different estimation techniques. For instance, whether non-current assets are carried at original cost or current value will affect ROCE, as will the use of different depreciation rates. In addition, financial statements are often prepared with the key ratios in mind, so may have been subject to creative accounting. The year end values also may not be representative of values during the year, due to seasonal trading.

Victular will find further information useful in making a decision regarding this acquisition. Victular should look at the composition of the Board of each company and the expertise it may be acquiring. It will also want to see the audited final statements and any available management information, such as management accounts, budgets and cash flow forecasts.

BPP
LEARNING MEDIA

67 Crosswire

Text references Chapters 4, 19 and 21

Top tips This was a mixed question, comprising calculation of movement on non-current assets, calculation of two elements of the statement of cash flows and calculation of and comment on ROCE. The only part that may have given some trouble was analysing the share issue to see how much cash was actually received. It is important in a question like this to allocate an equal amount of time to each part and note that the requirement in (a)(i) also includes intangible assets.

Easy marks There were plenty of easy marks in this question. Students should have had no trouble with the movement on non-current assets in part (a) or with 'cash flows from investing activities'. A careful re-reading of the question would have provided some sensible comments to make about the ROCE.

Examiner's comments. In part (a) many candidates made a good attempt at the movement in non-current assets, including the increase in cost due to the environmental provision. In the cash flow section, very few accurately accounted for the cash flow aspects of a partial loan to equity conversion. In part (b) very few correct answers were given for the ROCE calculation and few attempted to identify the components of ROCE in order to identify the cause of its deterioration.

Marking scheme

			Marks
(a)	(i)	Property, plant and equipment	
		Mine	1½
		Land revaluation	1½
		Leased plant	1
		Plant disposal	1
		Depreciation	1
		Replacement plant	1
			7
		Development expenditure	2
			9
	(ii)	Investing activities:	
		Purchase of property, plant and equipment	2
		Disposal proceeds of plant	½
		Development expenditure	1
		Financing activities:	
		Issue of equity shares	1½
		Redemption of convertible loan notes	1
		Lease obligations	1
		Loan interest	1
			8
(b)		Calculation of ROCE	2
		Supporting components ratios	2
		Explanatory comments – up to	4
			8
Total for question			25

(a)　(i)　*Property, plant and equipment*

	$'000
Balance at 30 September 20X8	13,100
Addition – mine (5m + 3m restoration)	8,000
Plant obtained under finance lease	10,000
Revaluation surplus on land (2,000 × 100/80)	2,500
Plant disposal	(500)
Depreciation	(3,000)
Plant replacement (balance)	2,400
Balance at 30 September 20X9	32,500

Intangible asset – development costs

	$'000
Balance at 30 September 20X8	2,500
Additions	500
Impairment charge (balance)	(2,000)
Balance at 30 September 20X9	1,000

　　(ii)　*Cash flows from investing activities*

	$'000	$'000
Purchase of PPE:		
Mine	5,000	
Plant	2,400	
		(7,400)
Development costs		(500)
Proceeds from sale of plant		1,200
Net cash used in investing activities		(6,700)

Cash flows from financing activities

	$'000
Proceeds of share issue (400 + 1,600 (W))	2,000
Loan notes redeemed (W)	(1,000)
Capital payments under finance lease (10,000 – (5,040 + 1,760))	(3,200)
Finance lease interest paid	(400)
Loan note interest	(350)
Net cash used in financing activities	(2,950)

Working:

	Share capital $'000	Share premium $'000
At 30 September 20X8	4,000	2,000
Issued on conversion:		
$4m × 20/100 × 75%	600	
Premium – ((100/20 x 600) – 600)		2,400
Issued for cash (balance)	400	1,600
At 30 September 20X9	5,000	6,000

(b)　Loan notes redeemed for cash are therefore $4m × 25% = $1m

ROCE		20X8	20X9
$\dfrac{4,300}{14,700}$	$\dfrac{(3,000+800+500)}{(9,700+5,000)}$	29.3%	
$\dfrac{5,750}{27,000}$	$\dfrac{(4,000+1,000+400+350)}{(19,200+1,000+5,040+1,760)}$		21.3%

We can see that profit before interest and tax has increased between 20X8 and 20X9 both in real terms and as a percentage:

20X8 – (4,300/42,000) × 100 = 10.2%
20X9 – (5,750/52,000%) × 100 = 11%

BPP LEARNING MEDIA

The decline is therefore due to changes in asset turnover:

20X8 – 42,000/14,700 = 2.8 times
20X9 – 52,000/27,000 = 1.9 times

This points to **capital being utilised less efficiently** in the year to 30 September 20X9. This can be analysed further by looking at the nature of the additional capital.

During the year Crosswire spent $5m on a platinum mine which has an expected life of 10 years. It is possible that the mine was not running at full capacity for the first year.

$6.8m is owed on a finance lease for plant. The lease was not taken out until April 20X9, so this equipment has only had 6 months to show a return.

$2m arises from a revaluation of freehold land. This will not give rise to any increase in return.

We are told that during 20X9 Crosswire embarked on a **replacement and expansion programme** for its non-current assets. It is to be expected that such a programme would have a **temporarily adverse effect** on its ROCE. In future years it can expect to reap the benefit of this expenditure and see an improved ROCE.

68 Bengal

> **Text references**. Chapters 19, 20 and 21.
>
> **Top tips**. Start with the proforma for the statement of cash flows, fill in the easy numbers and then do the standard workings for tax, PPE and retained earnings. Leave plenty of time for part (b) which is worth a lot more marks. In part (b), note that only 5 marks are available for ratios – the rest is for your analysis, so it needs to make sense. Review the information you have in the context of profitability, gearing and liquidity. This will tell you which ratios need to be included.
>
> **Easy marks**. The statement of cash flows was very easy and you could get full marks on it. Then you just have to pick up as many marks as possible in (b). This is done by reviewing all the information and making as many useful points as you can, not just calculating loads of ratios. Try to bear in mind the shareholder's comments and arrive at a conclusion.
>
> **Examiner's comments**. The statement of cash flows was well answered by most candidates, although some failed to take into account the asset held-for-sale and the dividend. In the interpretation most did well on the ratios but not so well on the performance analysis, often failing to see that the decline in profit was due to the finance costs and the tax charge.

Marking scheme

		Marks
(a)	Statement of cash flows	
	Profit before tax	½
	Depreciation of non-current assets	½
	Finance costs added back	½
	Working capital items	1½
	Finance costs paid	½
	Income tax paid	1
	Purchase of property, plant and equipment	1½
	Purchase of intangibles	½
	8% loan note	½
	Equity dividends paid	1
	Cash and cash equivalents at beginning of period	½
	Cash and cash equivalents at end of period	½
		9
(b)	1 mark per valid point (including up to 5 points for ratios)	16
		25

BENGAL - STATEMENT OF CASH FLOWS FOR THE YEAR ENDED 31 MARCH 20X1

	$'000	$'000
Cash flows from operating activities		
Profit before tax	5,250	
Depreciation	640	
Finance costs	650	
Increase in inventories (3,600 – 1,800)	(1,800)	
Increase in receivables (2,400 – 1,400)	(1,000)	
Increase in payables (2,800 – 2,150)	650	
Cash generated from operations	4,390	
Interest paid	(650)	
Income taxes paid (W1)	(1,250)	
Net cash from operating activities		2,490
Purchase of property, plant and equipment (W2)	(6,740)	
Purchase of intangibles	(6,200)	
Net cash used in investing activities		(12,940)
Cash flows from financing activities		
Issue of 8% loan notes	7,000	
Dividend paid (W3)	(750)	
Net cash from financing activities		6,250
Net decrease in cash and cash equivalents		(4,200)
Cash and cash equivalents at beginning of period		4,000
Cash and cash equivalents at end of period		(200)

Workings

1   *Income tax paid*

TAX PAYABLE

	$'000		$'000
Tax paid (β)	1,250	Balance 31.3.20X0	1,200
Balance 31.3.20X1	2,200	Profit or loss	2,250
	3,450		3,450

2   *Purchase of PPE*

PROPERTY, PLANT AND EQUIPMENT

	$'000		$'000
Balance 31.3.20X0	5,400	Depreciation	640
		Transfer to held for sale	2,000
Purchase of PPE (β)	6,740	Balance 31.3.20X1	9,500
	12,140		12,140

3   *Dividend paid*

RETAINED EARNINGS

	$'000		$'000
Dividend paid (β)	750	Retained earnings 31.3.20X0	2,250
Retained earnings 31.3.20X1	4,500	Profit to 31.3.20X1	3,000
	5,250		5,250

(b)

It is correct that revenue has increased by 48% while profit for the year has only increased by 20%. However, on closer inspection, we can see that this is to a large degree attributable to the tax charge for the year. The tax charge was 28.6% of the profit before tax in the year ended 31.3.20X0 and 42.8% of the profit before tax in the year ended 31.3.20X1. We do not have a breakdown of the tax charge but it could include underpayments in previous years, which distorts the trading results.

A better comparison between the two years is the profit before tax % and the gross profit %. Both of these are higher in 20X1 than in 20X0. The shareholders will also be interested in the ROCE. There has been a significant increase in capital employed during the year ended 31.3. 20X1. Bengal has acquired nearly $13m in tangible and

BPP
LEARNING MEDIA

intangible assets, financed from cash reserves and a new issue of 8% loan notes. An additional $2m non-current assets have been reclassified as held for sale. This suggests that Bengal has taken over the trade of another business and is disposing of the surplus assets. This is a long-term project which may take time to show a return and the ROCE does show a significant drop in 20X1. However, if we disregard the loan capital and look at the ROE we can see a considerable increase in 20X1.

The increase in loan capital does have significance for shareholders. The interest charge has increased from $100,000 to $650,000, which reduces the amount available for dividend. Gearing has increased significantly. The rate that Bengal has to offer to loan note holders has already increased from 5% to 8%. If it required further borrowing, with this high gearing, it would have to pay substantially more. Shares in Bengal have become a riskier investment. One indicator of this is the interest cover, which has fallen from 36 times to 9 times. The acquisition could presumably have been financed from a share issue or share exchange, rather than loan capital. However, this would have diluted the return available to shareholders.

The area in which there is most cause for concern is liquidity. As we can see from the statement of cash flows, cash and cash equivalents have fallen by $4.2m and the company is now running an overdraft. It has tax to pay of $2.2m and this will incur penalties if it is not paid on time. The current ratio has declined from 2.1:1 to 1.5:1 and this is including the non-current assets held for sale as part of non-current assets. The quick ratio, excluding inventory and non-current assets held for sale, indicates the immediate cash situation and this shows a fall from 1.6:1 to 0.46:1. Bengal needs to remedy this by disposing of the non-current assets held for sale as soon as possible and selling off surplus inventory, which may have been acquired as part of the acquisition.

Overall, the shareholder should be reassured that Bengal is profitable and expanding. The company has perhaps overstretched itself and significantly raised its gearing, but it is to be hoped that the investment will bring in future returns. This is no doubt the picture the company wants to give to shareholders, which is why it has paid a dividend in spite of having very little cash with which to do so.

Appendix: Ratios

		20X1	20X0
Net profit %	(3,000 / 25,500) / (2,500 / 17,250)	11.8%	14.5%
Net profit % (pre-tax)	(5,250 / 25,500) / (3,500 / 17,250)	20.6%	20.3%
Gross profit %	(10,700 / 25,500) / (6,900 / 17,250)	42%	40%
ROCE	(5,900 / 18,500) / (3,600 / 9,250)	31.9%	38.9%
ROE	(5,250 / 9,500) / (3,500 / 7,250)	55.3%	48.3%
Gearing	(9,000 / 9,500) / (2,000 / 7,250)	94.7%	27.6%
Interest cover	(5,900 / 650) / (3,600 / 100)	9 times	36 times
Current ratio	(8,000 / 5,200) / (7,200 / 3,350)	1.5:1	2.1:1
Quick ratio	(2,400 / 5,200) / (5,400 / 3,350)	0.5:1	1.6:1

69 Tangier

Text references. Chapters 19 and 21.

Top tips. Note how the marks are allocated here. The statement of cash flows is only 11 marks so you should not spend more than 20 minutes on it. Always remember to check the retained earnings to see what dividends have been paid. There are 14 marks for part (b) but only 4 are for ratios. Most of the marks are for your analysis, so read the information carefully and make sure you are answering the question.

Easy marks. The statement of cash flows had no real complications, so plenty of marks were available there. Only four marks were available for ratios, so it was important to decide which were the important ratios. The question helped by ruling out working capital ratios.

Examiner's comments The cash flow section of this question was well answered with many candidates scoring full marks. The analysis part of the question was much weaker with many candidates calculating lots of unnecessary ratios, despite being told that only four marks were available for them. These more 'general' answers failed to focus on the effect of the new contract on Tangiers operating performance, which was what the question required.

Examiner's answer. The examiner's answer to this question is at the end of this Kit.

Marks

(a)

Profit before tax	½
Depreciation/amortisation	1
Finance cost adjustment	½
Working capital items	1½
Interest paid	½
Income tax paid	1
Purchase of PPE	1½
Purchase of intangibles	1
Purchase of investment	½
Share issue	½
10% loan note issue	½
Equity dividends paid	1
Cash b/f	½
Cash c/f	½
	11

(b)

1 mark per valid point (up to 4 for ratios)	<u>14</u>
Total	<u>25</u>

(a) STATEMENT OF CASH FLOWS FOR THE YEAR ENDED 31 MARCH 20X2

	$m	$m
Net cash from operating activities (see below)		85
Cash flows from investing activities		
Purchase of property, plant and equipment (W2)	(305)	
Addition to licence (W3)	(125)	
Purchase of shares in Raremetal	<u>(230)</u>	
Net cash used in investing activities		(660)
Cash flows from financing activities		
Share issue	100	
10% loan notes issued	300	
Equity dividend paid (W4)	<u>(55)</u>	
Net cash from financing activities		<u>345</u>
Net decrease in cash and cash equivalents		(230)
Cash and cash equivalents at 1 April 20X1		<u>120</u>
Cash and cash equivalents at 31 March 20X2		<u>(110)</u>

Reconciliation of profit before tax to net cash from operating activities

	$m
Profit before tax	195
Depreciation/amortisation	140
Finance costs	40
Increase in inventory (200 – 110)	(90)
Increase in receivables (195 – 75)	(120)
Increase in payables (210 – 160)	<u>50</u>
Cash generated from operations	215
Interest paid	(40)
Tax paid (W1)	<u>(90)</u>
Net cash from operating activities	<u>85</u>

BPP
LEARNING MEDIA

Workings

1   *Tax paid*

INCOME TAX

	$m		$m
Paid (ß)	90	B/f 1.4.X1	110
C/f 31.3.X2	80	Charge for the year	60
	170		170

2   *Purchase of property, plant and equipment*

PROPERTY, PLANT AND EQUIPMENT – CARRYING AMOUNT

	$m		$m
B/f 1.4.X1	410	Depreciation	115
Revaluation	80		
Purchases (ß)	305	C/f 31.3.X2	680
	795		795

3   *Addition to intangible asset*

INTANGIBLE ASSET – CARRYING AMOUNT

	$m		$m
B/f 1.4.X1	200	Amortisation	25
Addition (ß)	125	C/f 31.3.X2	300
	325		325

4   *Dividends paid*

RETAINED EARNINGS

	$m		$m
Dividends paid (ß)	55	B/f 1.4.X1	295
C/f 31.3.X2	375	Profit for the year	135
	430		430

(b) It is not difficult to see why the non-executive director of Tangier is disappointed at the results for the year to 31 March 20X2. Revenue has increased by $880m but has only generated an additional $82m gross profit and an increase in expenses has left profit before tax at less than half of the 20X1 profit. Profit appears to have been sacrificed to revenue and, if the executive directors are being paid bonuses on the basis of revenue, this is something that the non-executive directors will want to investigate.

The first thing we notice is that the gross profit % has fallen from 40% to 30%. This is because the increase in revenue has been accompanied by an increase of $798m in cost of sales. As the bidding process for the contract was very competitive, Tangier has probably gone in at a very low price in order to secure the contract and is now making a loss on it.

In order to fulfil the contract Tangier has had to pay $125m for a manufacturing licence and invest $230m in shares of Raremetal. This was in order to secure material supplies, but the low profit margin on this contract implies that the investment did not result in any agreement to deliver materials at a competitive price. Perhaps, as its name suggests, Raremetal has no competitors. The shareholding in Raremetal has also performed very poorly as an investment, yielding neither dividend nor capital growth.

ROCE for the year ended 31 March 20X2 has fallen from 61.7% to 19.5%. This reflects both the fall in net profit % from 21.86% to 8.7% and the fall in asset turnover from 2.82 to 2.24. Capital employed has increased from $645m to $1,205m, reflecting the debt and equity issued to fund the increase in non-current assets, but this has not generated additional profits.

BPP
LEARNING MEDIA

The debt issued has increased finance costs by $35m and Tangier has sought to keep gearing under control by revaluing its property. Even so, gearing has more than doubled, from 15% to 33% - an increase from 18.3% to 49.7% if we measure it as debt/equity. Tangier's new loan is at twice the interest rate of the existing loan and is secured, presumably on its property. This suggests that the markets are worried about the company's level of debt. Tangier is now running an overdraft of $110m.

It would be useful to know when production actually commenced on the Jetside contract and what the duration of the contract is. It could be that productivity and profit on the contract will improve over the next financial year. It would also be useful to have a breakdown of distribution and administrative expenses, which also seem to have been adversely affected by this contract. There could be one-off expenses included, perhaps relating to the negotiation of the contract, which will not recur.

Ratios

		20X2	20X1
Gross profit %		30%	40%
ROCE		19.5%	61.7%
Net profit %	(Before interest and tax)	8.7%	21.86%
Asset turnover		2.23	2.98
Gearing	(Debt / debt + equity)	33%	15%
Debt / equity %		49.7%	18.3%

70 Waxwork

Text reference. Chapter 20.

Top tips. Note that part (a) carries five marks. This means that the examiner is expecting more than two sentences. If you really think about this and answer it properly it will help you with part (b).

Easy marks. This was quite an easy question as long as you were clear about the period dealt with by IAS 10 and the distinction between adjusting and non-adjusting events. You may have been uncertain whether or not the commission earned should have been deducted to arrive at NRV in (b) (ii), but this would only have lost you a mark.

Examiner's comments. Performance was particularly disappointing on this question. There was confusion over the period covered by the Standard and over the definition of an adjusting event, and candidates who were unable to correctly answer part (a) did not gain many marks in part (b).

Marking scheme

		Marks
(a)	Definition	1
	Discussion of adjusting events	2
	Reference to going concern	1
	Discussion of non-adjusting events	1
		5
(b)	(i) to (iii) 1 mark per valid point as indicated	10
		15

(a) IAS 10 relates to events taking place between the last day of the reporting period (the year end date) and the date on which the financial statements are approved and signed by the directors. This period is usually several months.

Adjusting events are events taking place after the reporting period which provide further evidence of conditions existing at the end of the reporting period or which call into question the going concern status of

BPP
LEARNING MEDIA

the entity. For this reason, adjusting events require adjustment to be made to the financial statements. If going concern is no longer applicable, the financial statements must be prepared on a break-up basis.

Non-adjusting events provide evidence of conditions arising **after** the end of the reporting period. If material, these should be disclosed by note, but they do not require that the financial statements be adjusted.

(b)   (i)   This is a non-adjusting event as it does not affect the valuation of property or inventory at the year end. However, it would be treated as adjusting if the scale of losses were judged to threaten the going concern status of Waxwork. It will certainly need to be disclosed in the notes to the financial statements, disclosing separately the $16m loss and the expected insurance recovery of $9m.

        (ii)   The sale in April 20X9 gives further evidence regarding the realisable value of inventory at the year end and so an adjustment will be required. If 70% of the inventory was sold for $280,000 less commission of $42,000, it had a net realisable value of $238,000. On this basis, the total cost of $460,000 should be restated at NRV of $340,000. So inventory at the end of the reporting period should be written down by $120,000.

        (iii)   This change has occurred outside the period specified by IAS 10, so it is not treated as an event after the reporting period. Had it occurred prior to 6 May 20X9, it would have been treated as a non-adjusting event requiring disclosure in the notes. The increase in the deferred tax liability will be accounted for in the 20Y0 financial statements.

77 Hardy

Text references. Chapters 19 and 20.

Top tips. The question tells you that up to 10 marks are available for the ratios, so you can spend up to 18 minutes calculating them – but no more. Put the ratios in a separate section and then they are easy to refer to and compare. The remaining 15 marks are available for analysis – which means getting behind the ratios, to see why they have gone up or down. You have been specifically told about the one-off costs, so you must look at the significance of these and consider the effect they will have had on the ratios. If these were discounted, how would the underlying trading position look? The question asks for profitability, liquidity and gearing ratios, so it is a good idea to structure your analysis under these headings.

Easy marks. The question allows 10 marks for ratios and the remaining 15 allocated as one mark per valid point. You should have been able to get most of the marks for the ratios, as long as you adjusted them, where appropriate, for the exceptional costs. This leaves the other 15 marks. Go through the ratios under each heading and look at the financial statements. You should be able to make enough valid points to pass this question

Examiner's comments. This question required candidates to assess the performance of a company against the background of a global recession and additional issues – falling property prices, decline in value of investments and redundancy costs. A good answer would have looked at the underlying performance ie adjusting for these one-off costs, but most candidates did not attempt this analysis. However, most candidates scored well on the calculation of ratios and many made intelligent comments about changes in the ratios.

Marking scheme

	Marks
Comments – 1 mark per valid point up to	15
A good answer must consider the effects of the one-off costs	
Ratios – up to	<u>10</u>
	<u>25</u>

Hardy's **revenue has declined by 18% and its gross profit by 60%**. This alone paints the picture of a very challenging trading environment. The results are worsened by the $1.6m charged to administrative expenses for loss on investments, which contributes to a net loss of $2.1m, down from a net profit of $3.5m in 20X0.

However, it is important to note that cost of sales in 20X1 has had to bear $1.5m for impairment losses and $1.3m for restructuring expenses. These are **exceptional costs** and, like the loss on investments, **serve to obscure the picture given by the trading results**.

If we were to adjust for these amounts the gross profit for 20X1 would be $6.8m (4 + 1.5 + 1.3) and the net profit would be $2.3m ((2.1) + 1.5 + 1.3 + 1.6). These results would be more comparable to the 2009 results and would therefore reflect profits lost due to the trading downturn.

Profitability

Hardy's gross profit percentage is 13.5%, compared to 27.7% in 20X0. However, if we were to take the adjusted profit of $6.8m the gross profit percentage would be 23%. The same effect can be seen on the net profit percentage. The net loss of $2.1 gives a net profit percentage of -7.1%, set against 9.7% for 20X0. The adjusted net profit gives a net profit of 7.8%. So it is clear that **profit is down, but actual trading profit has not fallen as far as may at first appear**. The one-off losses which have reduced Hardy's net profit have also reduced equity, thereby favourably affecting the ROE. Although the ROE based on reported figures is negative, ROE based on the underlying profits is only 2% below the figure for 20X0.

Working capital

Hardy's **receivables days have not changed significantly**, but payables days (calculated using cost of sales as we can not calculate purchases for 20X0) have **increased** from 39 to 49 days. If we adjust cost of sales for property losses and severance costs the underlying payables days show up as 55 days. This would appear to be a **deliberate policy** rather than an inability to pay, as Hardy has cash available. There may be trouble in the future with suppliers if this is not addressed. The inventory holding period has risen by 4 days, 8 days based on underlying costs of sales. This could be due to raw materials price rises, which would partly account for the 'real terms' fall of nearly 5% in the gross profit percentage.

Liquidity

Despite the downturn in trading, Hardy's **liquidity position has improved**. Both the current and quick ratios have improved. This is partly due to the tax repayment situation and partly due to an improvement in cash balances. The actual cash in the bank has increased by $1.1m, attributable to the $2m proceeds of the rights issue, which has also allowed the company to repay part of the bank loan. As the interest rate has climbed so steeply, it is important to reduce the loan as much as possible. The losses on property and investments in 20X1 have not had cash consequences, which is fortunate for Hardy, bearing in mind that liquidity problems lead to more company failures than lack of profitability. Looking at the retained earnings we can see that the company paid a dividend of $800,000. According to the Chairman's statement this is 50% of the dividend per share paid the previous year, but since the rights issue Hardy has 1m more shares on which the dividend has to be paid. The directors may have decided that it was important to continue to pay the dividend, even at a reduced rate, in order to maintain shareholder confidence.

Gearing

Gearing has increased in 20X1, but only by 1%. This outcome has been achieved by paying off $1m of the loan and by the rights issue. **Keeping gearing under control** will make it more possible for Hardy to obtain further loan finance in the future, although given the movement on interest rates it will probably prefer to avoid this.

Conclusion

Hardy's results are **not as bad as they appear at first glance**. A more detailed analysis generally bears out the Chairman's comments. They have been affected by the global economic downturn, but they are still trading profitably and liquidity is being maintained.

Appendix

		20X1	20X1 adjusted	20X0
Gross profit %	4,000/29,500 ; 10,000/36,000	13.5%		27.7%
	6,800/29,500		23%	
Net profit %	(2,100)/29,500 ; 3,500/36,000	(7.1)%		9.7%
	2,300/29,500		7.8%	
ROE	(2,100)/17,600 ; 3,500/23,000	(11.9)%		15.2%
	2,300/17,600		13.1%	
Asset turnover	29,500 /17,600 ; 36,000/23,000	1.67 times		1.6 times

BPP
LEARNING MEDIA

Current ratio	6,200/3,400 ; 4,800/4,600	1.8:1		1.04:1
Quick ratio	4,000/3,400 ; 2,900/4,600	1.2:1		0.6:1
Gearing ratio	4,000/17,600 ; 5,000/23,000	22.7%		21.7%
Receivables days	2,200/29,500 × 365	27 days		28 days
Payables days	3,400/25,500 × 365	49 days		39 days
	3,400/22,700 × 365		55 days	
Inventory days	2,200/25,500 × 365	31 days		27 days
	2,200/22,700 × 365		35 days	

72 Preparation question: Dickson

(a)   DICKSON
STATEMENT OF CASH FLOWS FOR YEAR ENDED 31 MARCH 20X8

	$'000	$'000
Cash flows from operating activities		
Profit before taxation	342	
Adjustments for:		
Depreciation	57	
Amortisation (W2)	60	
Interest expense	15	
Profit on disposal of assets	(7)	
	467	
Decrease in trade receivables (274 – 324)	50	
Increase in inventories (360 – 227)	(133)	
Decrease in trade payables (274 – 352)	(78)	
Cash generated from operations	306	
Interest paid (W5)	(10)	
Income taxes paid (W4)	(256)	
Net cash from operating activities		40
Cash flows from investing activities		
Development expenditure	(190)	
Purchase of property, plant & equipment (W1)	(192)	
Proceeds from sale of property, plant & equipment	110	
Net cash used in investing activities		(272)
Cash flows from financing activities		
Proceeds from issue of shares [850 – 500 – (400 ×1/8)]	300	
Proceeds from issue of debentures	50	
Payment of finance lease liabilities (W3)	(31)	
Dividends paid	(156)	
Net cash from financing activities		163
Net decrease in cash and cash equivalents		(69)
Cash and cash equivalents at beginning of period		109
Cash and cash equivalent at end of period		40

Notes to the statement of cash flows

Note 1: Property, plant and equipment

During the period, the company acquired property, plant and equipment with an aggregate cost of $248,000 of which $56,000 was purchased by means of finance leases. Cash payments of $192,000 were made to acquire property, plant and equipment.

Workings

1   *Additions to property, plant and equipment*

PROPERTY, PLANT AND EQUIPMENT

	$'000		$'000
Bal b/d	637	Depreciation	57
Revaluations (152 – 60 + 8)	100	Disposals	103
Finance leases	56		
∴ Additions	192		
		Bal c/d	825
	985		985

2   *Development expenditure amortisation*

DEVELOPMENT EXPENDITURE

	$'000		$'000
Bal b/d	160		
Expenditure	190	∴ Amortisation	60
		Bal c/d	290
	350		350

3   *Finance lease payments*

FINANCE LEASE LIABILITY

	$'000		$'000
		Bal b/d – > 1 year	80
		– < 1 year	12
∴ Paid	31	New finance leases	56
Bal c/d – > 1 year	100		
– > 1 year	17		
	148		148

4   *Income taxes paid*

INCOME TAX PAYABLE

	$'000		$'000
		Bal b/d – current	153
		– deferred	45
∴ Paid	256	Profit or loss	162
Bal c/d – current	56		
– deferred	48		
	360		360

BPP LEARNING MEDIA

5   *Interest paid*

INTEREST PAYABLE

	$'000		$'000
		Bal b/d	-
∴ Paid	10	Profit or loss	15
Bal c/d	5		
	15		15

(b)   CASH FLOWS FROM OPERATING ACTIVITIES (Direct method)

	$'000
Cash received from customers (W1)	1,526
Cash paid to suppliers and employees (W2)	(1,220)
Cash generated from operations	306
Interest paid	(10)
Income taxes paid	(256)
Net cash from operating activities	40

Workings

1

RECEIVABLES

	$'000		$'000
Bal b/d	324	Cash received (bal)	1,526
Sales revenue	1,476	Bal c/d	274
	1,800		1,800

2

PAYABLES

	$'000		$'000
Payments (bal)	1,220	Bal b/d	352
		Purchases (W3)	1,095
Bal c/d	274	Other expenses (W4)	47
	1,494		1,494

3

INVENTORY

	$'000		$'000
Bal b/d	227	To cost of sales	962
Purchases (bal)	1,095	Bal c/d	360
	1,322		1,322

4   *Other expenses*

	$'000
Balance per statement of profit or loss	157
Depreciation	(57)
Amortisation	(60)
Profit on disposal	7
	47

73 Pinto

Text references. Chapters 19,20,21.

Top tips. There are only 15 marks for the statement of cash flows here and the other 10 are for comment, so it is important to make time for both. Don't get bogged down in the statement of cash flows – get the format down and push on with the workings.

Easy marks. The statement of cash flows was easy apart from the tax working. Even if you got that wrong, there were plenty of marks available for the rest of the cash flow and for useful comment.

Examiner's comments. Cash flows are generally popular and many candidates scored well on this one. A number had trouble with the tax cash flow being a refund and there were mistakes in calculating the dividend by those who had not realised that the shares were 20c. The interpretative part of the question often lacked depth and some candidates calculated ratios despite specific instructions not to do so. Some candidates discussed issues such as ROCE and profit margins which are not part of cash management while not mentioning issues such as the investment in non-current assets and the tax cash flow.

Marking scheme

		Marks
(a)	Operating activities	
	Profit before tax	½
	Depreciation/loss on sale	1
	Warranty adjustment	½
	Adjustments for investment income/finance costs	½
	Adjustment for redemption penalty	1
	Working capital items	1½
	Finance costs	1
	Income tax received	2
	Investing activities (including 1 for investment income)	3
	Financing activities	1
	Issue of equity shares	1
	Redemption of 6% loan note	1
	Dividend paid	1
	Cash and cash equivalents b/f and c/f	15
(b)	1 mark per relevant point	10
	Total for question	25

BPP
LEARNING MEDIA

(a) PINTO – STATEMENT OF CASH FLOWS FOR THE YEAR TO 31 MARCH 20X8

	$'000	$'000
Cash flows from operating activities		
Profit before tax		440
Loss on sale of plant		90
Depreciation		280
Early redemption penalty		20
Finance costs		50
Investment income		(60)
Increase in warranty provision (200 – 100)		100
		920
Increase in inventory (1,210 – 810)		(400)
Decrease in receivables (480 − 540)		60
Increase in trade payables (1,410 – 1,050)		360
Cash generated from operations		940
Interest paid		(50)
Tax refund received (W1)		60
Net cash from operating activities		950
Cash flows from investing activities		
Proceeds of sale of plant (240 – 90)	150	
Purchase of plant (W2)	(1,440)	
Income from investment property (60 – 20)	40	
Net cash used in investing activities		(1,250)
Cash flows from financing activities		
Share issue ((1,000 – 600) + 600)	1,000	
Loan notes repaid	(400)	
Early redemption penalty	(20)	
Dividend paid (1,000 × 5 × 0.03)	(150)	
Net cash from financing activities		430
Net increase in cash and cash equivalents		130
Cash and cash equivalents at beginning of period		(120)
Cash and cash equivalents at end of period		10

Workings

1

INCOME TAX PAYABLE

	$'000		$'000
Bal b/d (current tax)	50	Bal b/d (deferred tax)	30
Bal c/d (current tax)	150	Profit or loss charge	160
Bal c/d (current tax)	50	Cash received (balancing figure)	60
	250		250

2

PROPERTY, PLANT AND EQUIPMENT

	$'000		$'000
Bal b/d	1,860	Disposal	240
Revaluation (150 – 50)	100	Depreciation	280
Additions (balancing figure)	1,440	Bal c/d	2,880
	3,400		3,4000

(b) **Comments on cash flow management**

Pinto provides a good illustration of why a statement of cash flows often provides more insight than a statement of profit or loss. The most noticeable feature of the statement of profit or loss is that $5.7m revenue has produced only $280,000 net profit and it can be seen from the statement of financial position that only $130,000 has been added to retained earnings at the end of the year. However, it is apparent from the statement of cash flows that Pinto's financial position is quite healthy.

Pinto has invested heavily in property, plant and equipment during the year, which has led to a high depreciation charge. Adjusting for this and for the increase in warranty costs and loss on sale of plant gives cash generated from operations of $940,000. The doubling of the warranty provision together with the fact that Pinto has $150,000 tax to pay this year, against a refund of $50,000 for the previous year, means that both turnover and profit must have increased substantially this year. Inventory and payables have both increased, inventory by 50%. This suggests an increased level of production, which ties in with the investment in new plant. At the same time, receivables have fallen, suggesting tighter credit control.

Pinto made a share issue during the year which contributed towards the increased investment in non-current assets and the repayment of the $400,000 loan notes. This has reduced its gearing to nil, but it should be noted that these additional shares increased the cost of the dividend by $60,000 – substantially more than the finance cost on the loan notes.

Overall, the cash management of Pinto presents a positive picture. During the year substantial investment has been made in productive capacity, gearing has been reduced to nil and an overdraft of $120,000 has been converted to a cash balance of $10,000.

74 Deltoid

Text references. Chapters 19, 20 and 21

Top tips. It is important to note that less than half of the marks in this question are available for the statement of cash flows, so time spent on it must be strictly monitored. The finance lease and the tax required workings as they often do when dealing with cash flows and these are best tackled as T accounts. Always check the opening and closing retained earnings. This will tell you whether a dividend has been paid. Part (a) (ii) was worth 8 marks so it required a proper answer. This meant looking at a few key ratios and analysing all of the rest of the available information in order to answer the question – rather than calculating every ratio you can think of and saying whether they went up or down. Part (c) did not require any real knowledge of the accounting records kept by not-for-profit organisations, but it did require some thought about their sources of income and the types of expense they will incur.

Easy marks. Plenty of easy marks were available for the statement of cash flows. Many of the marks were for items that did not even require a written working, so just working methodically through this should have been enough to secure a pass. The tax calculation was tricky and would not have been worth spending too long over. The written parts of the question were the areas that students tend not to score well on, but keeping to the point of the question and concentrating on what movements in the ratios *mean* should have enabled most students to gain reasonable marks.

Examiner's comments. Cash flows remain popular with candidates and those that had practised past questions generally scored well. Tricky areas were non-current assets, the finance lease liability and the taxation cash flow. A significant number of candidates showed a lack of understanding, including poor format knowledge. Many candidates answered Part (a) (ii) as if it were a general interpretation of financial performance, giving little regard to addressing the issue of whether they would advise that the loan renewal be granted. The answer should have concentrated on the expectations of a lender – does the company have good liquidity, interest cover, acceptable gearing and securitisable assets. In Part (b) many candidates did recognise and state that a not-for-profit organisation does not have profits, but then went on to describe profit-related ratios. What was required was a recognition that the granting of the loan was a commercial activity and should be decided based on similar principles to that of a commercial organisation.

		Marks
(a)(i)	Operating activities	
	Loss before tax	½
	Add back interest charge	½
	Depreciation charge	1
	Loss on sale of leasehold	1
	Working capital items	1½
	Interest paid	½
	Income tax paid	1½
	Sale proceeds of leasehold	1
	Repayment of lease obligations	1½
	Issue of equity shares	1
	Dividend paid	1
	Cash and cash equivalents b/f and c/f	1
		12
(ii)	1 mark per valid point	8
(b)	1 mark per valid point	5
		25

(a)   (i)   DELTOID – STATEMENT OF CASH FLOWS FOR THE YEAR ENDED 31.3.20X1

	$'000	$'000
Cash flows from operating activities		
Loss before tax	(1,800)	
Depreciation (W1)	3,700	
Interest expense	1,000	
Loss on disposal of leasehold property(8,500 – (8,800 – 200))	100	
Increase in inventories (12,500 – 4,600)	(7,900)	
Increase in receivables (4,500 – 2,000)	(2,500)	
Increase in payables (4,700 – 4,200)	500	
Cash used in operations	(6,900)	
Interest paid	(1,000)	
Tax paid (W2)	(1,900)	
Net cash used in operating activities		(9,800)
Cash flows from investing activities		
Cash from sale of leasehold property	8,500	
Net cash from investing activities		8,500
Cash flows from financing activities		
Dividends paid (6,300 – 4,500 – 1,100)	(700)	
Payments made under finance leases (W3)	(2,100)	
Share issue (10,000 + 3,200) – (8,000 + 4,000)	1,200	
Net cash used in financing activities		(1,600)
Net decrease in cash and cash equivalents		(2,900)
Cash and cash equivalents at 31.3.20X0		1,500
Cash and cash equivalents at 31.3.20X1		(1,400)

Workings

1   PPE – CARRYING AMOUNT

	$'000		$'000
B/d	25,500	Disposal (8,800 – 200)	8,600
Lease plant additions		Depreciation (β)	3,700
(6,500 – 2,500 + 1,800)	5,800	C/d	19,000
	31,300		31,300

2   INCOME TAX

	$'000		$'000
Profit or loss	700	31.3.X0 – Current tax	2,500
31.3.X1 - Deferred tax	1,200	31.3.X0 – Deferred tax	800
Tax paid β	1,900	Refund due	500
	3,800		3,800

3   FINANCE LEASE LIABILITY

	$'000		$'000
Payments made β	2,100	Balance b/f (2,000 + 800)	2,800
		Additions (W1)	5,800
Balance c/f (4,800 + 1,700)	6,500		–
	8,600		8,600

(ii)   Deltoid's statement of cash flows does not afford a lot of reassurance to a loan provider. In 12 months it has turned a cash balance of $1.5m into an overdraft of $1.4m. Looking at the statement of financial position, Deltoid has been paying its loan interest on time, but it may be less able to do so in the future as it now also has to pay overdraft interest. There has also been a large increase in finance lease obligations. During the year to 31 March 20X0 Deltoid had interest cover of 15 times (9,000/600). That interest cover is now negative.

Similarly, gearing has increased from 43% ((5,000 + 2,000 + 800) / 18,300) to 65% ((4,800 + 5,000 + 1,700) / 17,700). Any lender would see this as a warning sign.

The cash used in operations of $6.9m is in itself a cause for concern and seems to originate in serious profitability problems. A gross profit percentage of 37.5% in 20X0 has been reduced to 20% in 20X1 and this has been compounded by a doubling of operating expenses to bring it down to a loss. The company has tripled year end inventory – it could be that orders have failed to materialise or that it is carrying obsolete or unsaleable inventory. A loan provider would be justified in requiring a set of management accounts, to get some idea of where all the money went.

The management of Deltoid have been doing what they can to raise or conserve cash. They have sold their property and leased it back, obtained additional plant under finance leases rather than for cash and made an issue of new shares. But there are issues involved in all of these transactions. The property is no longer available to act as security for any loan, the finance leases give rise to increased interest payments, while the plant acquired thereby does not legally belong to Deltoid and so equally cannot act as loan security. The share issue raised a small amount of money and had a small favourable impact on Deltoid's gearing, but the fact that it had to be issued at par shows that the markets do not consider Deltoid a desirable investment.

All of these issues suggest that renewal of the loan for another five years may not be wise.

(b)   Although the sports club is a not-for-profit organisation, any potential loan provider will have to apply the same criteria to its loan request as it would use in assessing a request from a profit-making entity.

The first ratio to look at would be gearing. There will be no share capital, so this would be calculated as the ratio of long-term borrowing to net assets. If the club is already carrying a large amount of borrowing, then a further loan may carry too much risk.

The income and expenditure statement will show whether any interest is currently being paid and interest cover can be calculated by dividing the surplus of income over expenditure by the interest payments. This should then also be done taking into account the projected interest payments from the loan that has been requested.

BPP
LEARNING MEDIA

It will be a good idea to look at the current ratio. As there is presumably very little inventory involved, this will probably be the same as the quick ratio and will give some idea of solvency and of how well the cash is being managed.

These ratios should be calculated for all four years to see any underlying trends, and it will also be useful to look at the sources of income, such as memberships and whether they are increasing or decreasing over the period. If an extension is needed, there should be an increasing number of members.

The accounts will also show what assets the club owns, which could be used as security, and whether there are any prior charges against these assets. It is also possible that the trustees may be able to provide additional security.

75 Mocha

Text references. Chapter 4, 13, 14, 21.

Top tips. Statements of cash flow are popular questions with students. This one has a few complications, but is basically straightforward. As always, get the proforma down and do the standard workings.

Easy marks. There are plenty of easy marks available for dealing with the usual adjustments – working capital, tax, finance lease and share capital and 1½ marks just for showing that interest charged is the same as interest paid.

Examiner's comments. The statement of cash flows was very well answered, with many candidates scoring full marks. The main errors involved the profit on disposal, the warranty provision, the tax calculation, the finance lease and the share issue. The bonus issue is not a cash flow. Many candidates seemed to misinterpret the requirement for (b), which was to explain the discrepancy between reported profit and cash flow. This involved discussing working capital adjustments, product warranties and other non-cash items. Some candidates ignored this and just calculated ratios.

Marking scheme

		Marks
(a)	Profit before tax	½
	Depreciation	1
	Profit on disposal of property	1
	Investment income deducted	½
	Interest expense added back	½
	Working capital items	1½
	Decrease in product warranty	1½
	Interest paid	1
	Income tax paid	2
	Purchase of PPE	1
	Disposal of PPE	1
	Disposal of investment	1
	Dividends received	1
	Share issue	2½
	Payments under finance lease	2
	Cash b/f / c/f	1
		19
(b)	(i) and (ii) 3 marks each	6
Total for question		25

STATEMENT OF CASH FLOWS FOR THE YEAR ENDED 30 SEPTEMBER 20X1

	$'000	$'000
Cash flows from operating activities		
Profit before tax	3,900	
Adjustments for:		
Depreciation	2,500	
Profit on sale of property	(4,100)	
Investment income	(1,100)	
Interest expense	500	
	1,700	
Increase in inventories (10,200 – 7,200)	(3,000)	
Decrease in receivables (3,700 – 3,500)	200	
Decrease in payables (4,600 – 3,200)	(1,400)	
Decrease in warranty provision (4,000 – 1,600)	(2,400)	
Cash used in operations	(4,900)	
Interest paid	(500)	
Income tax paid (W3)	(800)	
Net cash used in operating activities		(6,200)
Cash flows from investing activities		
Sale of property	8,100	
Purchase of plant	(8,300)	
Sale of investment	3,400	
Dividends received	200	
Net cash from investing activities		3,400
Cash flows from financing activities		
Issue of share capital (W1)	2,400	
Payments under finance leases (W2)	(3,900)	
Net cash from financing activities		(1,500)
Decrease in cash and cash equivalents		(4,300)
Cash and cash equivalents b/f		1,400
Cash and cash equivalents c/f		(2,900)

Workings

1

SHARE CAPITAL

	$'000		$'000
		B/f	8,000
		Bonus issue:	
		Share premium	2,000
		Revaluation surplus	1,600
C/f	14,000	Issued for cash (ß)	2,400
	14,000		14,000

2

FINANCE LEASE OBLIGATIONS

	$'000		$'000
Payments (ß)	3,900	B/f – current	2,100
C/f – current	4,800	– non-current	6,900
– non-current	7,000	Additions	6,700
	15,700		15,700

BPP LEARNING MEDIA

INCOME TAX

	$'000		$'000
Paid (ß)	800	B/f – current	1,200
C/f – current	1,000	- deferred	900
- deferred	1,300	Tax charge	1,000
	3,100		3,100

(b) (i) The statement of profit or loss of Mocha shows profit for the year of $3.9m. However this figure includes amounts based on estimates, such as the reduction in product warranties and gains which have not translated into cash, such as the increase in fair value of investments. $4.1m of the profit for the year related to sale of a property – if this was removed there would be a trading loss of $0.2m.

Net cash from operating activities records only those transactions which have resulted in movement of cash, so items which rely on judgement or are unrealised are automatically excluded. It is to this degree a more verifiable amount than profit before tax and many users would consider it more useful.

(ii) Accrual-based financial information spreads the lives of property, plant and equipment over the periods expected to benefit from their use and this can be affected by revaluations, impairment and changes in expected life, which are all issues based on judgement. Also, entities can choose whether or not to transfer back excess depreciation to retained earnings following a revaluation. So there is a lot of subjectivity involved in asset values. In the case of Mocha the carrying amount of property, plant and equipment has increased by $8.5m over the year, but the statement of financial position needs to be properly examined in order to see that $6.7m of the increased plant was obtained under finance leases and therefore carries a corresponding liability.

Net cash from investing activities deals simply in amounts paid to acquire property, plant and equipment and in any proceeds of selling property, plant and equipment. This is valuable and verifiable additional information which is not shown by the statement of financial position.

76 Preparation question: Changing prices

(a) CURRENT COST OPERATING PROFIT FOR 20X6

	$m	$m
Historical cost profit		15
Current cost adjustments:		
Depreciation adjustment	3	
Cost of sales adjustment	5	
		(8)
Current cost profit		7

SUMMARISED CURRENT COST STATEMENT OF FINANCIAL POSITION
AS AT 31 DECEMBER 20X6

	$m	$m
Property, plant & equipment		85
Current assets		
Inventories	21	
Receivables	30	
Bank	2	
		53
		138
Equity		88
Non-current liability		20
Current liabilities		30
		138

(b) (i) **Interest cover**

HC accounts: 15 ÷ 3 = 5 times
CC accounts: 7 ÷ 3 = 2.3 times

(ii) **Return on shareholders' equity**

HC accounts: 12 ÷ 62 = 19.4%
CC accounts: 4 ÷ 88 = 4.5%

(iii) **Debt/equity ratio**

HC accounts: 20 ÷ 62 = 32.3%
CC accounts: 20 ÷ 88 = 22.7%

(c) (i) **Interest cover**

Companies must maintain their capital base if they wish to stay in business. The significance of the interest cover calculation is that it indicates the extent to which profits after tax are being eaten into by payments to finance external capital. The figures calculated above indicate that only one-fifth of historical cost profit is being absorbed in this way, while four-fifths are being retained to finance future growth. On the face of it, this might seem satisfactory; however, the current cost interest cover is only 2.3 times indicating that, after allowing for the impact of rising prices, interest payments absorb nearly half of profits after tax.

(ii) **Return on shareholders' equity**

This is the ratio of profits earned for shareholders (ie profits after interest) to shareholders' equity. Once again, the position disclosed by the historical cost accounts is more favourable than appears from the current cost ratio. The historical cost profit is higher than the current cost profit because no allowance is made for the adverse impact of rising prices, and, at the same time, the denominator in the historical cost fraction is lower because, shareholders' capital is stated at historical values rather than their higher current values.

The significance of the ratio is that it enables shareholders to assess the rate of return on their investment and to compare it with alternative investments that might be available to them.

(iii) **Debt/equity ratio**

The significance of this ratio is as a measure of the extent to which the company's net assets are financed by external borrowing and shareholders' funds respectively.

In times of rising prices it can be beneficial to finance assets from loan capital. While the assets appreciate in value over time (and the gain accrues to shareholders), the liability is fixed in monetary amount. The effect of this is that current cost accounts tend to give a more favourable picture of the debt/equity ratio than historical cost accounts. In the ratios calculated above, the amount of debt is $20m in both statements of financial position. This represents nearly one-third of the historical cost value of shareholders' funds, but only one-fifth of the equity calculated on a current cost basis.

77 Update

(a) *Problems with historical cost*

Although retail price inflation has eased throughout the developed world, it is still a big issue for many businesses.

The carrying values of property and other assets with long useful lives soon become unrealistic if based on historical cost, leading to the following problems:

- Even with modest inflation, the depreciation charge on these assets will be too low in comparison with the revenues that the assets are generating, inflating operating profits.

BPP
LEARNING MEDIA

- The return on capital employed is doubly distorted; not only are operating profits overstated, but the related net assets will be understated, resulting in a flattering and unrealistic return. This makes it difficult to compare two companies with similar assets if those assets were bought at different times.
- Low asset values reduce the net assets of a business. This exaggerates the gearing ratio, which might dissuade banks from advancing loans to the business. It might also cause the stock market to undervalue a business.

The traditional solution to these problems is to revalue certain items. However, this creates a hybrid set of financial statements, with some assets at historical cost others at valuation.

(b) *Alternative methods*

	Historical cost $		CPP $		Current cost $
Cost/Valuation	250,000	(a)	300,000	(b)	280,000
Carrying value based on 2 years depreciation (c)	160,000		192,000		179,200
Carrying value based on 3 years depreciation (d)	128,000		153,600		143,360
Depreciation charge for this year (c − d = e)	32,000		38,400		35,840

(1) The original cost of $250,000 will be indexed up for the change in the retail price index between the date of purchase and the end of the reporting period.

$250,000 \times 216/180 = $300,000

(2) The current cost will be reduced to reflect the lower productivity of the old asset.

$320,000 \times 420/480 = $280,000

(3) The carrying value after two years depreciation at 20% reducing balance will be 64% of the gross amount (0.8×0.8).

(4) The carrying value after three years depreciation at 20% reducing balance will be 51.2% of the gross amount ($0.8 \times 0.8 \times 0.8$).

(5) This years charge will be the difference between (c) and (d).

78 Appraisal

A **not-for-profit organisation** needs funds to operate, just as a profit-making organisation does. It is also required to make good and sensible use of its assets and spend within its budget. To this degree, calculation of certain financial ratios and their comparison to the previous year is valid and would yield information about how well the organisation is run, and how well it manages its funds.

However, there are a number of differences between a profit-making and a not-for-profit organisation. A not-for-profit organisation does not have the basic purpose of increasing the wealth of its shareholders or of achieving a return on capital. Its success or failure is judged by the degree to which it achieves its objectives. These are laid down in a whole different set of parameters. A hospital has many different targets to meet – some of them apparently not that useful. One of its major targets will be to cut the length of its waiting lists for operations. Local government bodies may be judged on the basis of whether they have secured VFM (value for money) in spending local taxes. Schools are judged on their examination passes and their budgets may be affected by issues such as how many of their children are considered to have 'special needs'.

A charity will judge its success by the amount of work it has achieved in line with its mission statement, and by the level of funding and donations it has secured – without which nothing can be achieved.

It is worth pointing out that, just as a profit-making organisation may seek to enhance the picture given by its financial statements, not-for-profit organisations may also be driven in the same direction. It has been found in the UK that some hospitals have brought forward minor operations and delayed major ones in order to secure maximum impact on the waiting list and meet government targets. Some schools have a policy of only entering pupils for exams which they have a good chance of passing. This keeps up their pass rate and their position in the school league tables.

BPP
LEARNING MEDIA

Mock Exams

BPP
LEARNING MEDIA

ACCA
Fundamentals Level
Paper F7
Financial Reporting (Int)

Mock Examination 1

Question Paper	
Time allowed	
Reading and Planning Writing	15 minutes 3 hours
Answer all FIVE questions	

DO NOT OPEN THIS PAPER UNTIL YOU ARE READY TO START UNDER EXAMINATION CONDITIONS

BPP LEARNING MEDIA

BPP
LEARNING MEDIA

1 Hillusion (2.5 6/03)

45 mins

In recent years Hillusion has acquired a reputation for buying modestly performing businesses and selling them at a substantial profit within a period of two to three years of their acquisition. On 1 July 20X2 Hillusion acquired 80% of the ordinary share capital of Skeptik at a cost of $10,280,000. On the same date it also acquired 50% of Skeptik's 10% loan notes at par. The summarised draft financial statements of both companies are:

STATEMENTS OF PROFIT OR LOSS: YEAR TO 31 MARCH 20X3

	Hillusion	Skeptik
	$'000	$'000
Sales revenue	60,000	24,000
Cost of sales	(42,000)	(20,000)
Gross profit	18,000	4,000
Operating expenses	(6,000)	(200)
Loan interest received (paid)	75	(200)
Profit before tax	12,075	3,600
Income tax expense	(3,000)	(600)
Profit for the year	9,075	3,000

STATEMENTS OF FINANCIAL POSITION AS AT 31 MARCH 20X3

	Hillusion	Skeptik
Non-current assets		
Property, plant and equipment	19,320	8,000
Investments	11,280	Nil
	30,600	8,000
Current assets	15,000	8,000
Total assets	45,600	16,000
Equity and liabilities		
Equity		
Ordinary shares of $1 each	10,000	2,000
Retained earnings	25,600	8,400
	35,600	10,400
Non-current liabilities		
10% loan notes	Nil	2,000
Current liabilities	10,000	3,600
Total equity and liabilities	45,600	16,000

The following information is relevant:

(i) The fair values of Skeptik's assets were equal to their book values with the exception of its plant, which had a fair value of $3.2 million in excess of its book value at the date of acquisition. The remaining life of all of Skeptik's plant at the date of its acquisition was four years and this period has not changed as a result of the acquisition. Depreciation of plant is on a straight-line basis and charged to cost of sales. Skeptik has not adjusted the value of its plant as a result of the fair value exercise.

(ii) In the post acquisition period Hillusion sold goods to Skeptik at a price of $12 million. These goods had cost Hillusion $9 million. During the year Skeptik had sold $10 million (at cost to Skeptik) of these goods for $15 million.

(iii) Hillusion bears almost all of the administration costs incurred on behalf of the group (invoicing, credit control etc). It does not charge Skeptik for this service as to do so would not have a material effect on the group profit.

(iv) Revenues and profits should be deemed to accrue evenly throughout the year.

(v) The current accounts of the two companies were reconciled at the year-end with Skeptik owing Hillusion $750,000.

(vi) The goodwill was reviewed for impairment at the end of the reporting period and had suffered an impairment loss of $300,000, which is to be treated as an operating expense.

(vii)   Hillusion's opening retained earnings were $16,525,000 and Skeptik's were $5,400,000. No dividends were
        paid or declared by either entity during the year.

(viii) It is the group policy to value the non-controlling interest at acquisition at fair value. The directors valued the
        non-controlling interest at $2.5m at the date of acquisition.

Required

(a)   Prepare a consolidated statement of profit or loss and statement of financial position for Hillusion for the
        year to 31 March 20X3.   **(20 marks)**

(b)   Explain why it is necessary to eliminate unrealised profits when preparing group financial statements; and
        how reliance on the entity financial statements of Skeptik may mislead a potential purchaser of the company.
                                                                                                   (5 marks)

                                                                                        (Total = 25 marks)

2 Dexon (6/08)   45 mins

Below is the summarised draft statement of financial position of Dexon, a publicly listed company, as at 31 March
20X8.

	$'000	$'000	$'000
Assets			
Non-current assets			
Property at valuation (land $20,000; buildings $165,000 (note (ii))			185,000
Plant (note (ii))			180,500
Financial assets at fair value through profit or loss at 1 April 20X7 (note (iii))			12,500
			378,000
Current assets			
Inventory		84,000	
Trade receivables (note (iv))		52,200	
Bank		3,800	140,000
Total assets			518,000
Equity and liabilities			
Equity			
Ordinary shares of $1 each			250,000
Share premium		40,000	
Revaluation surplus		18,000	
Retained earnings – at 1 April 20X7	12,300		
– for the year ended 31 March 20X8	96,700	109,000	167,000
			417,000
Non-current liabilities			
Deferred tax – at 1 April 20X7 (note (v))			19,200
Current liabilities			81,800
Total equity and liabilities			518,000

The following information is relevant:

(i)   Dexon's statement of profit or loss includes $8 million of revenue for credit sales made on a 'sale or return'
        basis. At 31 March 20X8, customers who had not paid for the goods, had the right to return $2.6 million of
        them. Dexon applied a mark up on cost of 30% on all these sales. In the past, Dexon's customers have
        sometimes returned goods under this type of agreement.

(ii)   The non-current assets have not been depreciated for the year ended 31 March 20X8.

        Dexon has a policy of revaluing its land and buildings at the end of each accounting year. The values in the
        above statement of financial position are as at 1 April 20X7 when the buildings had a remaining life of fifteen
        years. A qualified surveyor has valued the land and buildings at 31 March 20X8 at $180 million.

        Plant is depreciated at 20% on the reducing balance basis.

BPP
LEARNING MEDIA

(iii)   The financial assets at fair value through profit and loss are held in a fund whose value changes directly in proportion to a specified market index. At 1 April 20X7 the relevant index was 1,200 and at 31 March 20X8 it was 1,296.

(iv)   In late March 20X8 the directors of Dexon discovered a material fraud perpetrated by the company's credit controller that had been continuing for some time. Investigations revealed that a total of $4 million of the trade receivables as shown in the statement of financial position at 31 March 20X8 had in fact been paid and the money had been stolen by the credit controller. An analysis revealed that $1.5 million had been stolen in the year to 31 March 20X7 with the rest being stolen in the current year. Dexon is not insured for this loss and it cannot be recovered from the credit controller, nor is it deductible for tax purposes.

(v)   During the year the company's taxable temporary differences increased by $10 million of which $6 million related to the revaluation of the property. The deferred tax relating to the remainder of the increase in the temporary differences should be taken to profit or loss. The applicable income tax rate is 20%.

(vi)   The above figures do not include the estimated provision for income tax on the profit for the year ended 31 March 20X8. After allowing for any adjustments required in items (i) to (iv), the directors have estimated the provision at $11.4 million (this is in addition to the deferred tax effects of item (v)).

(vii)   On 1 September 20X7 there was a fully subscribed rights issue of one new share for every four held at a price of $1.20 each. The proceeds of the issue have been received and the issue of the shares has been correctly accounted for in the above statement of financial position.

(viii)   In May 20X7 a dividend of 4 cents per share was paid. In November 20X7 (after the rights issue in item (vii) above) a further dividend of 3 cents per share was paid. Both dividends have been correctly accounted for in the above statement of financial position.

Required

Taking into account any adjustments required by items (i) to (viii) above

(a)   Prepare a statement showing the recalculation of Dexon's profit for the year ended 31 March 20X8.

(8 marks)

(b)   Prepare the statement of changes in equity of Dexon for the year ended 31 March 20X8.   **(8 marks)**

(c)   Redraft the statement of financial position of Dexon as at 31 March 20X8.   **(9 marks)**

Note. Notes to the financial statements are NOT required.

(Total = 25 marks)

3 Coaltown (6/09)

45 mins

(a) Coaltown is a wholesaler and retailer of office furniture. Extracts from the company's financial statements are set out below:

STATEMENTS OF PROFIT OR LOSS AND OTHER COMPREHENSIVE INCOME FOR THE YEAR ENDED:

	31 March 20X9		31 March 20X8	
	$'000	$'000	$'000	$'000
Revenue – cash	12,800		26,500	
– credit	53,000	65,800	28,500	55,000
Cost of sales		(43,800)		(33,000)
Gross profit		22,000		22,000
Operating expenses		(11,200)		(6,920)
Finance costs– loan notes	(380)		(180)	
– overdraft	(220)	(600)	nil	(180)
Profit before tax		10,200		14,900
Income tax expense		(3,200)		(4,400)
Profit for the year		7,000		10,500
Other comprehensive income				
Gain on property revaluation		5,000		1,200
Total comprehensive income for the year		12,000		11,700

STATEMENT OF CHANGES IN EQUITY FOR THE YEAR ENDED 31 MARCH 20X9

	Equity shares $'000	Share premium $'000	Revaluation surplus $'000	Retained earnings $'000	Total $'000
Balances b/f	8,000	500	2,500	15,800	26,800
Share issue	8,600	4,300			12,900
Comprehensive income			5,000	7,000	12,000
Dividends paid				(4,000)	(4,000)
Balances c/f	16,600	4,800	7,500	18,800	47,700

STATEMENTS OF FINANCIAL POSITION AS AT 31 MARCH:

	20X9		20X8	
	$'000	$'000	$'000	$'000
Assets				
Non-current assets (see note)				
Cost		93,500		80,000
Accumulated depreciation		(43,000)		(48,000)
		50,500		32,000
Current assets				
Inventory	5,200		4,400	
Trade receivables	7,800		2,800	
Bank	nil	13,000	700	7,900
Total assets		63,500		39,900

BPP
LEARNING MEDIA

	$'000	$'000	$'000	$'000
Equity shares of $1 each		16,600		8,000
Share premium		4,800		500
Revaluation surplus		7,500		2,500
Retained earnings		18,800		15,800
		47,700		26,800
Non-current liabilities				
10% loan notes		4,000		3,000
Current liabilities				
Bank overdraft	3,600		nil	
Trade payables	4,200		4,500	
Taxation	3,000		5,300	
Warranty provision	1,000	11,800	300	10,100
		63,500		39,900

Note

Non-current assets

During the year the company redesigned its display areas in all of its outlets. The previous displays had cost $10 million and had been written down by $9 million. There was an unexpected cost of $500,000 for the removal and disposal of the old display areas. Also during the year the company revalued the carrying amount of its property upwards by $5 million, the accumulated depreciation on these properties of $2 million was reset to zero.

All depreciation is charged to operating expenses.

Required

Prepare a statement of cash flows for Coaltown for the year ended 31 March 20X9 in accordance with IAS 7 *Statement of Cash Flows* by the indirect method. **(15 marks)**

(b)   The directors of Coaltown are concerned at the deterioration in its bank balance and are surprised that the amount of gross profit has not increased for the year ended 31 March 20X9. At the beginning of the current accounting period (ie on 1 April 20X8), the company changed to importing its purchases from a foreign supplier because the trade prices quoted by the new supplier were consistently 10% below those of its previous supplier. However, the new supplier offered a shorter period of credit than the previous supplier (all purchases are on credit). In order to encourage higher sales, Coaltown increased its credit period to its customers, and some of the cost savings (on trade purchases) were passed on to customers by reducing selling prices on both cash and credit sales by 5% across all products.

Required

(i)   Calculate the gross profit margin that you would have expected Coaltown to achieve for the year ended 31 March 20X9 based on the selling and purchase price changes described by the directors;
         (2 marks)

(ii)   Comment on the directors' surprise at the unchanged gross profit and suggest what other factors may have affected gross profit for the year ended 31 March 20X9; **(4 marks)**

(iii)   Applying the trade receivables and payables credit periods for the year ended 31 March 20X8 to the credit sales and purchases of the year ended 31 March 20X9, calculate the effect this would have had on the company's bank balance at 31 March 20X9 assuming sales and purchases would have remained unchanged. **(4 marks)**

Note: the inventory at 31 March 20X8 was unchanged from that at 31 March 20X7; assume 365 trading days.

(Total = 25 marks)

4 Tentacle (2.5 6/07)   27 mins

After the end of the reporting period, prior to authorising for issue the financial statements of Tentacle for the year ended 31 March 20X7, the following material information has arisen.

(i)   The notification of the bankruptcy of a customer. The balance of the trade receivable due from the customer at 31 March 20X7 was $23,000 and at the date of the notification it was $25,000. No payment is expected from the bankruptcy proceedings.   **(3 marks)**

(ii)   Sales of some items of product W32 were made at a price of $5·40 each in April and May 20X7. Sales staff receives a commission of 15% of the sales price on this product. At 31 March 20X7 Tentacle had 12,000 units of product W32 in inventory included at cost of $6 each.   **(4 marks)**

(iii)   Tentacle is being sued by an employee who lost a limb in an accident while at work on 15 March 20X7. The company is contesting the claim as the employee was not following the safety procedures that he had been instructed to use. Accordingly the financial statements include a note of a contingent liability of $500,000 for personal injury damages. In a recently decided case where a similar injury was sustained, a settlement figure of $750,000 was awarded by the court. Although the injury was similar, the circumstances of the accident in the decided case are different from those of Tentacle's case.   **(4 marks)**

(iv)   Tentacle is involved in the construction of a residential apartment building. It is being accounted for using the percentage of completion basis in IAS 11 *Construction contracts*. The recognised profit at 31 March 20X7 was $1.2 million based on costs to date of $3 million as a percentage of the total estimated costs of $6 million. Early in May 20X7 Tentacle was informed that due to very recent industry shortages, building materials will cost $1.5 million more than the estimate of total cost used in the calculation of the percentage of completion. Tentacle cannot pass on any additional costs to the customer.   **(4 marks)**

Required

State and quantify how items (i) to (iv) above should be treated when finalising the financial statements of Tentacle for the year ended 31 March 20X7.

Note: The mark allocation is shown against each of the four items above.   **(Total = 15 marks)**

5 Hideaway (2.5 12/05 amended)   18 mins

Related party relationships are a common feature of commercial life. The objective of IAS 24 *Related party disclosures* is to ensure that financial statements contain the necessary disclosures to make users aware of the possibility that financial statements may have been affected by the existence of related parties.

Required

(a)   Explain why the disclosure of related party relationships and transactions may be important.   **(4 marks)**

(b)   Hideaway is a public listed company that owns two subsidiary company investments. It owns 100% of the equity shares of Benedict and 55% of the equity shares of Depret. During the year ended 30 September 20X5 Depret made several sales of goods to Benedict. These sales totaled $15 million and had cost Depret $14 million to manufacture. Depret made these sales on the instruction of the Board of Hideaway. It is known that one of the directors of Depret, who is not a director of Hideaway, is unhappy with the parent company's instruction as he believes the goods could have been sold to other companies outside the group at the far higher price of $20 million. All directors within the group benefit from a profit sharing scheme.

Required

Describe the financial effect that Hideaway's instruction may have on the financial statements of the companies within the group and the implications this may have for other interested parties.   **(6 marks)**

(Total = 10 marks)

BPP
LEARNING MEDIA

Answers

DO NOT TURN THIS PAGE UNTIL YOU HAVE
COMPLETED THE MOCK EXAM

BPP
LEARNING MEDIA

BPP
LEARNING MEDIA

A plan of attack

If this were the real Financial Reporting exam and you had been told to turn over and begin, what would be going through your mind?

Perhaps you're having a panic. You've spent most of your study time on groups and interpretation of accounts (because that's what your tutor/BPP study Text told you to do), plus a selection of other topics, and you're really not sure that you know enough. The good news is that you can always get a solid start by tackling the first question, which is **always on group accounts.** So calm down. Spend the first few moments or so **looking at the paper,** and develop a **plan of attack.**

Looking through the paper

As it will be in the real exam, Question 1 is on group accounts. Here you have a consolidated statement of profit or loss and statement of financial position , together with a discussion of unrealised profit. In **Section B** you have **four questions on a variety of topics**:

- Question 2 requires recalculation of profit and preparing a statement of changes in equity and statement of financial position.

- Question 3 is a statement of cash flows and comment on financial position.

- Question 4 is covers various issues that must be resolved before the financial statements are finalised.

- Question 5 is a discussion question on related parties.

All of these questions are compulsory

Question 1 is straightforward but requires you to work quickly.

Question 2 looks nasty but in fact the numbers are not difficult and you should get marks for detailed workings

Question 3 includes a statement of cash flows.. Remember to set up your pro-forma and work logically through the points.

Question 4 requires good knowledge of IAS 10, IAS 2, IAS 37 and IAS 11

Question 5 requires some thought. All the points you make must be relevant.

Allocating your time

BPP's advice is always allocate your time **according to the marks for the question** in total and for the parts of the question. But **use common sense.** If you're doing Question 4 but haven't a clue how to do Part (b), you might be advised to re-allocate you time and pick up more marks on, say, Question 5, where you can always add something to your discussion.

After the exam...Forget about it!

And don't worry if you found the paper difficult. More than likely other candidates will too. If this were the real thing you would need to **forget** the exam the minute you left the exam hall and **think about the next one**. Or, if it's the last one, **celebrate**!

Question 1 Hillusion

Text references. Chapters 9 and 10.

Top tips. Don't forget **Part (b)** There are five quick and easy marks here, but to score them all you must use numbers from your answer to Part (a). So, do Part (b) as soon as you have calculated the unrealised profit.

Part (a) This is a straightforward consolidation apart from dealing with NCI at fair value. Remember that goodwill impairment also affects NCI in the statement of profit or loss.

(Although Hillusion intends to sell Skeptik within two to three years, Skeptik must still be consolidated. IAS 27 only allows non-consolidation if the subsidiary was acquired with the intention of selling it within twelve months.)

1   Sketch out the group structure, noting percentage holdings and the date of acquisition.

2   Prepare a pro-forma statement of profit or loss and statement of financial position for your answer.

3   Calculate the carrying value of the goodwill in the subsidiary, and the impairment charge in profit or loss.

4   Calculate the group retained earnings.

5   Calculate the profit attributable to the parent and to the non-controlling interest.

6   Calculate the non-controlling interest for the statement of financial position.

7   Note the adjustments for fair valuations, inter-company balances, inter-company trade and unrealised profit.

Easy marks. Part (b) is 5 easy marks.

Examiner's comments This was a fairly straightforward consolidated statement of profit or loss and statement of financial position. The adjustments involved were simpler than if just one statement had been required. The main concern was that a number of candidates used proportional consolidation to account for the subsidiary.

Part (b) was generally well understood and answered. However some candidates chose to answer how such profits arise and how they are eliminated. The question asks **why** they are eliminated. Many candidates either did not answer this question or based their answer on the group statement instead of the entity's statements.

Marking scheme

		Marks
(a)	*Statement of profit or loss*	2
	Sales revenue	3
	Cost of sales	2
	Operating expenses including goodwill	1
	Loan interest	1
	Tax	1
	Non-controlling interest	1
	Retained earnings b/f	1
	Statement of financial position:	
	Goodwill	3
	Property, plant and equipment	2
	Current assets	2
	Retained earnings	1
	Non-controlling interest	2
	10% loan notes	1
	Current liabilities	1
	Available	24
	Maximum	20
(b)	1 mark per relevant point to Maximum	5
	Maximum for question	25

(a)   THE HILLUSION GROUP
      CONSOLIDATED STATEMENT OF PROFIT OR LOSS FOR THE YEAR ENDED 31 MARCH 20X3

	$'000
Sales revenues (60,000 + ($^9/_{12}$ 24,000) – 12,000 (W5))	66,000
Cost of sales (42,000 + ($^9/_{12}$ 20,000) – 12,000 + 500 (W5) + 600 (W4))	(46,100)
Gross profit	19,900
Operating expenses (6,000 + (200 × $^9/_{12}$) + 300 (W3))	(6,450)
Finance costs (200 × $^9/_{12}$ less 75 income)	(75)
Profit before tax	13,375
Income tax expense (3,000 + (600 × $^9/_{12}$))	(3,450)
Profit for the year	9,925
Profit attributable to:	
Owners of the parent	9,655
Non-controlling interest ((3,000 × $^9/_{12}$) – 600 (W6)) × 20% - 60(W3))	270
	9,925

CONSOLIDATED STATEMENT OF FINANCIAL POSITION AS AT 31 MARCH 20X3

	$'000
Assets	
Non-current assets	
Property, plant and equipment (19,320 + 8,000 + 2,600 fair valuation (W6))	29,920
Goodwill (W3)	1,130
Investments (11,280 – 10,280 (W5) – 1,000 loan notes)	–
	31,050
Current assets (15,000 + 8,000 – 500 unrealised profit (W5) – 750 inter-company)	21,750
Total assets	52,800
Equity and liabilities	
Equity attributable to owners of the parent	
Share capital (Parent only)	10,000
Retained earnings (W4)	26,180
	36,180
Non-controlling interest (W7))	2,770
Non-current liabilities (0 + 2,000 – 1,000 loan notes)	1,000
Current liabilities (10,000 + 3,600 – 750 inter-company)	12,850
	52,800

Workings

1   *Group Structure as at 31 March 20X3*

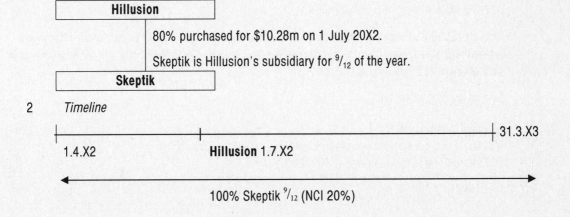

2   *Timeline*

3   *Goodwill in Skeptik*

	$'000	$'000
Consideration transferred		10,280
Non-controlling interests (at 'full' fair value)		2,500
Fair value of net assets at acquisition:		
Share capital	2,000	
Opening retained earnings	5,400	
Time apportioned profits for the year; $3m \times \, ^3/_{12}$	750	
Fair value increase for the plant	3,200	
		(11,350)
		1,430
Impairment losses		(300)
		1,130

4   *Retained earnings attributable to owners of the parent*

| | Hillusion | Skeptik |
	$'000	$'000
Per question	25,600	8,400
Pre-acquisition reserves	–	(6,150)
Provision for unrealised profit (W5)	(500)	–
Depreciation on fair valuation (W6)	–	(600)
	25,100	1,650
Group share (80%)	1,320	
Group share of impairment losses (300 × 80%)	(240)	
	26,180	

5   *Intra group trade and the provision for unrealised profit*

Group revenues and cost of sales are reduced by the $12m of intra-group sales at invoiced value. This adjustment does not affect profits.

An adjustment is made for the unrealised profit on goods sold by Hillusion to Skeptik but still unsold at the year-end. This increases the cost of sales in the statement of profit or loss and reduces the value of the inventories in the statement of financial position. The gross profit margin was 25% ($3m/$12m).

	$'000
Goods unsold at the year-end; $12m - $10m	2,000
Unrealised profit: $2m × 25%	500

6   *Fair valued plant*

	$'000
Fair value at acquisition	3,200
Depreciation over four years for nine months; $3.2m \times \, ^1/_4 \times \, ^9/_{12}$	(600)
Carrying value of licence 31 March 20X3	2,600

The extra $600,000 depreciation is taken into account when apportioning the profit for the year between the parent and the non-controlling interest. It also affects the group's retained earnings in the statement of financial position.

7   *Non-controlling interests*

	$'000
NCI at acquisition (W3)	2,500
NCI share of post acquisition retained earnings ((W4) 1,650 × 20%)	330
NCI share of impairment losses (300 × 20%)	(60)
	2,770

(b)   **Unrealised profits**

Unrealised profits arise when group companies trade with each other. In their own individual company accounts profits and losses will be claimed on these transactions, and goods bought from a fellow group company will be recorded at their invoiced cost by the purchaser.

However, consolidated accounts are drawn up on the principle that a group is a single economic entity. From a group point of view, no transaction occurs when goods are traded between group companies, and no profits or losses arise. Revenue and profits will only be claimed when the goods are sold onto a third party from outside of the group.

In this example, Hillusion sold $12m of goods to Skeptik making a profit of $3m. The sale by Hillusion and the purchase by Skeptik must be eliminated from the group statement of profit or loss. This adjustment will not affect profits because both the sales and the purchases have been reduced by the same amount.

By the year-end Skeptik had sold $10m of these items making a profit of $5m. From a group point of view, the profit on these items, including their share of the profit claimed by Hillusion, has now been realised. However, Skeptik still has $2m of goods bought from Hillusion. This valuation includes an element of profit ($500,000) that has not yet been realised and needs to be eliminated. This will reduce the carrying value of the inventory to the amount originally paid for them by Hillusion. If unrealised profits were not eliminated, then groups could boost their profits and asset values by selling goods to each other at inflated prices.

A future purchaser of Skeptik would obviously review Skeptik's own financial statements. These show a $3.6m profit before tax, which gives a very healthy 15% net profit on revenues. However, over 60% of Skeptik's revenue comes from selling goods supplied by Hillusion. The gross profit earned on these items is $5m, which is more than the $4m gross profit for the company as a whole. A new owner might not get such favourable terms from Hillusion, leaving them with the loss making products. Nobody would be interested in buying such a business, but this information cannot be gleaned from the entity's own financial statements.

Question 2 Dexon

Text references. Chapters 3, 7, 17.

Top tips. It is important to read a question like this carefully. You need to adjust back for the rights issue in order to work out what the dividend payments were. It is also important to notice that the land and buildings need to be adjusted for current year depreciation before the revaluation surplus can be calculated.

Easy marks. This was not an easy question and you would have been unlikely to get it all done. However, easy marks were available for the depreciation calculations and accounting for current tax.

Examiner's comments. The recalculation of profit was quite well done by those who knew how to do it. The most common errors were:
–   failing to add dividends back to the retained earnings
–   adjusting for sales revenue rather than profit on goods on SOR
–   treating the revaluation as having taken place at the beginning of the year
–   not taking part of the deferred tax increase to the revaluation surplus.

These errors were then carried forward to the SOCIE and SFP.

Marking scheme

		Marks
(a)	Adjustments	
	Add back dividends	1
	Balance of fraud loss	1
	Goods on sale or return	1
	Depreciation charges	2

	Investment gain	1
	Taxation provision	1
	Deferred tax	1
		8
(b)	Statement of changes in equity	
	Balances b/f	1
	Restated earnings b/f	1
	Rights issue	2
	Total comprehensive income	3
	Dividends paid	1
		8
(c)	Statement of financial position	
	Property	1
	Plant	1
	Investment	1
	Inventory	1
	Trade receivables	2
	Equity from (b)	1
	Deferred tax	1
	Current liabilities	1
		9
	Total for question	25

(a)

	$'000	$'000
Draft retained profit		96,700
Dividends paid (W6)		15,500
Draft profit for the year		112,200
Profit on goods on sale or return (2,600 × 30/130)		(600)
Depreciation:		
Buildings (165,000/15)	11,000	
Plant (180,500 × 20%)	36,100	
		(47,100)
Gain on investment (W3)		1,000
Current year fraud loss		(2,500)
Increase in deferred tax provision (W5)		(800)
Current year tax		(11,400)
		50,800

(b) DEXON – STATEMENT OF CHANGES IN EQUITY FOR THE YEAR ENDED 31 MARCH 20X8

	Share capital $'000	Share premium $'000	Revaluation surplus $'000	Retained earnings $'000	Total equity $'000
At 1 April 20X7	200,000	30,000	18,000	12,300	260,300
Prior period adjustment	–	–	–	(1,500)	(1,500)
Restated balance	200,000	30,000	18,000	10,800	258,800
Share issue	50,000	10,000			60,000
Dividends paid				(15,500)	(15,500)
Total comprehensive income for the year	–	–	4,800 *	50,800	55,600
At 31 March 20X8	250,000	40,000	22,800	46,100	358,900

BPP LEARNING MEDIA

* Revaluation surplus:

	$
Land and buildings at 31 March 20X7	185,000
Depreciation (165,000 / 15)	(11,000)
	174,000
Valuation at 31 March 20X8	180,000
Surplus	6,000
Deferred tax provision (6,000 × 20%)	(1,200)
Net surplus	4,800

(c)   DEXON – STATEMENT OF FINANCIAL POSITION AS AT 31 MARCH 20X8

	$'000	$'000
Non-current assets		
Property (W1)		180,000
Plant (W1)		144,400
Investments (W3)		13,500
		337,900
Current assets		
Inventory (84,000 + 2,000 (W2))	86,000	
Trade receivables (W7)	45,600	
Bank	3,800	
		135,400
Total assets		473,300
Equity and liabilities		
Share capital		250,000
Share premium		40,000
Revaluation surplus		22,800
Retained earnings		46,100
Total equity		358,900
Non-current liabilities		
Deferred tax (19,200 + 2,000 (W5))		21,200
Current liabilities		
As per draft SFP	81,800	
Tax payable	11,400	
		93,200
Total equity and liabilities		473,300

Workings

1   *Property, plant and equipment*

	Land	Buildings	Plant	Total
	$'000	$'000	$'000	$'000
Per question	20,000	165,000	180,500	365,500
Depreciation	-	(11,000)	(36,100)	(47,100)
	20,000	154,000	144,400	318,400
Revaluation	-	6,000	-	6,000
Balance c/d	20,000	160,000	144,400	324,400

2   *Sale or return*

	$'000	$'000
Cancel sale:		
Dr Sales	2,600	
CR Receivables		2,600
Record inventories:		
DR Inventories (SOFP) 2,600 × 100/130	2,000	
CR Cost of sales (closing inventories)		2,000

3   *Financial assets at FV through profit or loss*

	$'000
FV at year end (12,500 × 1,296/1,200)	13,500
Per draft SOFP	(12,500)
Gain – to profit or loss	1,000

4   *Fraud*

	$'000	$'000
DR Retained earnings re prior year	1,500	
DR Current year profit	2,500	
CR Receivables		4,000

5   *Deferred tax*

	$'000	$'000
DR Revaluation surplus (6,000 × 20%)		1,200
DR Profit or loss (tax charge) (4,000 × 20%)		800
CR Deferred tax liability (10,000 × 20%)		2,000

6   *Dividends paid*

	$'000
May 20X7 (200m* × $0.04)	8,000
November 20X7 (250m × $0.03)	7,500
	15,500

*250m × 4/5 = 200m

7   *Trade receivables*

	$'000
Per draft SFP	52,200
Sale or return	(2,600)
Adjustment re fraud	(4,000)
	45,600

BPP
LEARNING MEDIA

Question 3 Coaltown

Text references. Chapters 19 and 21

Top tips. Note that the statement of cash flows here is only worth 15 marks, so move quickly through it. You cannot afford to neglect (b).

Read all the information carefully. Do not miss the adjustment needed for loss on disposal in (a) or the note regarding opening inventory in (b).

Easy marks. The statement of cash flows is straightforward and you should have been able to score most of the marks. Part (iii) of (b) was quite easy as long as you did not miss the note at the end. Parts (i) and (ii) took a bit of thought.

Examiner's comments. Few candidates earned full marks on the statement of cash flows. Some had trouble distinguishing between cash and non-cash items (reserve movements, warranty provision, loss on disposal). Some had trouble dealing with the revaluation and the effect on depreciation. In part (b) some candidates adjusted the 20X8 figures rather than the 20X9 figures. Part (ii) was very badly answered. Most candidates were unable to identify factors which could have affected the gross profit margin. Very few were unable to compute the effect on the bank balance in Part (iii)

Marking scheme

			Marks
(a)	Operating activities		
	Profit before tax		½
	Add back interest		½
	Depreciation charge		2
	Loss on disposal		1
	Warranty adjustment		½
	Working capital items		1½
	Finance costs		1
	Income tax paid		1
	Purchase of non-current assets		2
	Disposal cost of non-current assets		1
	Issue of equity shares		1
	Issue of 10% loan notes		1
	Dividend paid		1
	Cash and cash equivalents b/f and c/f		1
			15
(b)	(i)	Calculation of expected gross profit margin for 20X9	2
	(ii)	Comments on directors' surprise and other factors	4
	(iii)	Calculate credit periods (receivables and payables) in 20X8	2
		Apply to 2009 credit sales/purchases	1
		Calculate 'savings' and effect on closing bank balance	1
			4
			25

BPP LEARNING MEDIA

(a)   COALTOWN
        STATEMENT OF CASH FLOWS FOR THE YEAR ENDED 31 MARCH 20X9

	$'000	$'000
Cash flows from operating activities		
Profit before tax	10,200	
Depreciation (W2)	6,000	
Loss on disposal of displays (W3)	1,500	
Interest expense	600	
	18,300	
Increase in warranty provision (1,000 – 300)	700	
Increase in inventories (5,200 – 4,400)	(800)	
Increase in receivables (7,800 – 2,800)	(5,000)	
Decrease in trade payables (4,500 – 4,200)	(300)	
Cash generated from operations	12,900	
Interest paid	(600)	
Income tax paid (W4)	(5,500)	
Net cash from operating activities		6,800
Cash flows from investing activities		
Purchase of property, plant and equipment (W1)	(20,500)	
Cost of disposal of property, plant and equipment	(500)	
Net cash used in investing activities		(21,000)
Cash flows from financing activities		
Share issue ((16,600 + 4,800) – (8,000 + 500))	12,900	
Loan note issue	1,000	
Equity dividends paid	(4,000)	
Net cash from financing activities		9,900
Net decrease in cash and cash equivalents		(4,300)
Cash and cash equivalents at beginning of period		700
Cash and cash equivalents at end of period		(3,600)

Workings

1   NON-CURRENT ASSETS – COST

	$'000		$'000
Balance b/f	80,000	W/off old displays	10,000
Revaluation (5,000 – 2,000)	3,000		
Purchases (bal)	20,500	Balance c/f	93,500
	103,500		103,500

2   NON-CURRENT ASSETS – DEPRECIATION

	$'000		$'000
W/off on disposal	9,000	Balance b/f	48,000
Revaluation adjustment	2,000		
Balance c/f	43,000	Charge in year (bal)	6,000
	54,000		54,000

3   NON-CURRENT ASSETS – DISPOSAL

	$'000		$'000
Cost	10,000	Acc depreciation	9,000
Cost of disposal	500	Loss on disposal	1,500
	10,500		10,500

BPP
LEARNING MEDIA

4

	$'000		$'000
Tax paid (bal)	5,500	Balance b/f	5,300
Balance c/f	3,000	Charge for year	3,200
	8,500		8,500

(b)　(i)　Taking the figures for the year ended 31 March 20X8 and applying the 10% reduction in purchase costs and the 5% discount to customers, the directors would have expected the gross profit to be as follows:

	$'000
Revenue (55,000 × 95%)	52,250
Cost of sales (33,000 × 90%)	(29,700)
Gross profit	22,550

Gross profit % (22,550 / 52,250 × 100)　　　　　　　　43.2%

The actual gross profit for the year ended 31 March 20X9 is:

(22,000/65,800 × 100)　　　　　　　　33.4%

(ii)　The directors should not be surprised at the unchanged gross profit as cost of sales has increased by the same amount as revenue, wiping out any possible increase in gross profit. In fact the actual gross profit margin has fallen from 40% in 20X8 to 33.4% in 20X9, so despite the 10% reduction in the cost of purchases the company was trading less profitably.

Possible reasons for this could be:

Shipping costs involved in importing goods having to be borne by the recipient.

Import duties.

Currency exchange losses, perhaps exacerbated by having to pay within a shorter period.

Inventory losses – uninsured damage, obsolescence etc.

Selling a larger proportion of goods on which the gross profit % is lower than the average.

Perhaps sales or special offers to customers, which will have lowered the average mark-up.

The foreign supplier may have increased his prices at some point during the year.

Also there may have been changes in accounting policy during the year – perhaps depreciation or distribution costs which were treated as expenses in 20X8 and have been charged to cost of sales in 20X9. If this has happened it will require retrospective restatement so that 20X8 and 20X9 can be correctly compared.

(iii)　Credit periods year ended 31 March 20X8:

Receivables (2,800 / 28,500 × 365)	35.9 days
Payables (4,500 / 33,000 × 365)	49.8 days

In 20X9 there is a movement in inventory, so we calculate purchases as follows:

43,800 – 4,400 + 5,200 = 44,600

Applying the periods above we get:

Receivables: 53,000/365 × 35.9	5,213
Payables: 44,600/365 × 49.8	6,085

Cash increase:

	$'000
Receivables (7,800 – 5,213)	2,587
Payables (6,085 – 4,200)	1,885
	4,472

Question 4 Tentacle

(i) This is an adjusting event after the reporting period within the terms of IAS 10. $23,000 should be written off to irrecoverable debts at the year end and the trade receivables balance correspondingly reduced.

(ii) In this case sales after the reporting period have demonstrated that the NRV of inventory item W32 is below cost. In accordance with IAS 2, inventories of W32 should now be written down to NRV as follows:

	$
Cost (12,000 × 6)	72,000
NRV (12,000 × (5.4 × 85%))	(55,080)
Write off to profit or loss	16,920

(iii) As it is not yet known whether the employee's legal action will be successful, Tentacle is correct to show it as a contingent liability. However, on the basis of the settlement in the other case, the contingent liability should be increased to $750,000. If the case is settled before the financial statements are authorised for issue, this will be an adjusting event requiring a provision for damages if Tentacle is found liable.

(iv) IAS 11 requires that the profit on the contract be recalculated to take into account these additional costs. Profit is based on costs to date as a percentage of total costs. As costs to date are $3m and total costs $6m, the percentage is currently 50%. This will change when the additional costs are included as follows:

	Costs to date	Total expected costs	%	Total expected profit	Profit to date
	$m	$m		$m	$m
Original	3	6	50%	2.4	1.20
Additional costs	–	1.5		(1.5)	–
Amended	3	7.5	40%	0.9	0.36

Recognised profit for the year to 31 March 20X7 should therefore be restated as $360,000. $840,000 (1.2m − 0.36m) will be written off to profit or loss and adjusted in the statement of financial position against amounts due to/from customers.

BPP
LEARNING MEDIA

Question 5 Hideaway

IAS 24 Related Parties

(a) *Importance of related party disclosures*

Investors invest in a business on the assumption that it aims to maximise its own profits for the benefit of its own shareholders. This means that all transactions have been negotiated at arm's length between willing and informed parties. The existence of related parties may encourage directors to make decisions for the benefit of another entity at the expense of their own shareholders. This can be done actively by selling goods and services cheaply to related parties, or by buying in goods and services at an above market price. It can also happen when directors chose not to compete with a related party, or offer guarantees or collateral for the other party's loans.

Disclosure is particularly important when a business is being sold. It may receive a lot of custom, supplies, services or general help and advice from family or group companies. When the company is sold these benefits may be withdrawn.

Related party transactions are not illegal, nor are they necessarily a bad thing. However shareholders and potential investors need to be informed of material related party transactions in order to make informed investment and stewardship decisions.

(b) *Hideaway, Benedict and Depret*

The directors and shareholders of Hideaway, the parent, will maximise their wealth by diverting profitable trade into wholly owned subsidiaries. They have done this by instructing Depret (a 55% subsidiary) to sell goods to Benedict (a 100% subsidiary) at $5m below fair value. As a result the non-controlling shareholders of Depret have been deprived of their 45% interest in those lost profits, amounting to $2.25m. The non-group directors of Depret will also lose out if their pay is linked to Depret's profits.

Because Depret's profits have been reduced, the non-controlling shareholders might be persuaded to sell their shares to Hideaway for less than their true value. Certainly potential shareholders will not be willing to pay as much for Depret's shares as they would have if Depret's profits had been maximised.

The opposite possibility is that the Directors of Hideaway are boosting Benedict's reported performance with the intention of selling it off for an inflated price.

Depret's non-controlling shareholders might be able to get legal redress because the majority shareholders appear to be using their power to oppress the non-controlling shareholders. This, however, will depend on local law. The tax authorities might also suspect Depret of trying to avoid tax, especially if Benedict is in a different tax jurisdiction.

BPP
LEARNING MEDIA

ACCA

Fundamentals Level

Paper F7

Financial Reporting (Int)

Mock Examination 2

Question Paper	
Time allowed	
Reading and Planning Writing	15 minutes 3 hours
Answer all FIVE questions	

DO NOT OPEN THIS PAPER UNTIL YOU ARE READY TO START UNDER EXAMINATION CONDITIONS

BPP
LEARNING MEDIA

Question 1 Hydan

45 mins

On 1 October 20X5 Hydan, a publicly listed company, acquired a 60% controlling interest in Systan paying $9 per share in cash. Prior to the acquisition Hydan had been experiencing difficulties with the supply of components that it used in its manufacturing process. Systan is one of Hydan's main suppliers and the acquisition was motivated by the need to secure supplies. In order to finance an increase in the production capacity of Systan, Hydan made a non-dated loan at the date of acquisition of $4 million to Systan that carried an actual and effective interest rate of 10% per annum. The interest to 31 March 20X6 on this loan has been paid by Systan and accounted for by both companies. The summarised draft financial statements of the companies are:

STATEMENTS OF PROFIT OR LOSS FOR THE YEAR ENDED 31 MARCH 20X6

	Hydan	Systan Pre-acquisition	Systan Post-acquisition
	$'000	$'000	$'000
Revenue	98,000	24,000	35,200
Cost of sales	(76,000)	(18,000)	(31,000)
Gross profit	22,000	6,000	4,200
Operating expenses	(11,800)	(1,200)	(8,000)
Interest income	350	nil	nil
Finance costs	(420)	nil	(200)
Profit/(loss) before tax	10,130	4,800	(4,000)
Income tax (expense)/relief	(4,200)	(1,200)	1,000
Profit/(loss) for the year	5,930	3,600	(3,000)

STATEMENTS OF FINANCIAL POSITION AS AT 31 MARCH 20X6

	Hydan $'000	Systan $'000
Non-current assets		
Property, plant and equipment	18,400	9,500
Investments (including loan to Systan)	16,000	nil
	34,400	9,500
Current assets	18,000	7,200
Total assets	52,400	16,700
Equity and liabilities		
Ordinary shares of $1 each	10,000	2,000
Share premium	5,000	500
Retained earnings	20,000	6,300
	35,000	8,800
Non-current liabilities		
7% Bank loan	6,000	nil
10% loan from Hydan	nil	4,000
Current liabilities	11,400	3,900
Total equity and liabilities	52,400	16,700

The following information is relevant:

(i)   At the date of acquisition, the fair values of Systan's property, plant and equipment were $1·2 million in excess of their carrying amounts. This will have the effect of creating an additional depreciation charge (to cost of sales) of $300,000 in the consolidated financial statements for the year ended 31 March 20X6. Systan has not adjusted its assets to fair value.

(ii) In the post acquisition period Systan's sales to Hydan were $30 million on which Systan had made a consistent profit of 5% of the selling price. Of these goods, $4 million (at selling price to Hydan) were still in the inventory of Hydan at 31 March 20X6. Prior to its acquisition Systan made all its sales at a uniform gross profit margin.

(iii)   Included in Hydan's current liabilities is $1 million owing to Systan. This agreed with Systan's receivables ledger balance for Hydan at the year end.

(iv)   An impairment review of the consolidated goodwill at 31 March 20X6 revealed that its current value was $375,000 less than its carrying amount.

(v)   Neither company paid a dividend in the year to 31 March 20X6.

(vi)   It is group policy to value the non-controlling interest at acquisition at full (or fair) value. Just prior to acquisition by Hydan, Systan's shares were trading at $7.

Required

(a)   Prepare the consolidated statement of profit or loss for the year ended 31 March 20X6 and the consolidated statement of financial position at that date.   **(20 marks)**

(b)   Discuss the effect that the acquisition of Systan appears to have had on Systan's operating performance.

(5 marks)

(Total = 25 marks)

Question 2 Highwood (6/11)   **45 mins**

The following trial balance relates to Highwood at 31 March 20X6:

	$'000	$'000
Equity shares of 50 cents each		56,000
Retained earnings (note (i))		1,400
8% convertible loan note (note (ii))		30,000
Freehold property – at cost 1 April 20X0 (land element $25 million (note (iii)))	75,000	
Plant and equipment – at cost	74,500	
Accumulated depreciation – 1 April 20X5 – building		10,000
– plant and equipment		24,500
Current tax (note (iv))		800
Deferred tax (note (iv))		2,600
Inventory – 4 April 20X6 (note (v))	36,000	
Trade receivables	47,100	
Bank		11,500
Trade payables		24,500
Revenue		339,650
Cost of sales	207,750	
Distribution costs	27,500	
Administrative expenses (note (vi))	30,700	
Loan interest paid (note (ii))	2,400	
	500,950	500,950

The following notes are relevant:

(i)   An equity dividend of 5 cents per share was paid in November 20X5 and charged to retained earnings.

(ii)   The 8% $30 million convertible loan note was issued on 1 April 20X5 at par. Interest is payable annually in arrears on 31 March each year. The loan note is redeemable at par on 31 March 20X8 or convertible into equity shares at the option of the loan note holders on the basis of 30 equity shares for each $100 of loan note. Highwood's finance director has calculated that to issue an equivalent loan note without the conversion rights it would have to pay an interest rate of 10% per annum to attract investors.

The present value of $1 receivable at the end of each year, based on discount rates of 8% and 10% are:

	8%	10%
End of year 1	0.93	0.91
2	0.86	0.83
3	0.79	0.75

 BPP
LEARNING MEDIA

(iii)   Non-current assets:

On 1 April 20X5 Highwood decided for the first time to value its freehold property at its current value. A qualified property valuer reported that the market value of the freehold property on this date was $80 million, of which $30 million related to the land. At this date the remaining estimated life of the property was 20 years. Highwood does not make a transfer to retained earnings in respect of excess depreciation on the revaluation of its assets.

Plant is depreciated at 20% per annum on the reducing balance method.

All depreciation of non-current assets is charged to cost of sales.

(iv)   The balance on current tax represents the under/over provision of the tax liability for the year ended 31 March 20X5. The required provision for income tax for the year ended 31 March 20X6 is $19.4 million. The difference between the carrying amounts of the net assets of Highwood (including the revaluation of the property in note (iii) above) and their (lower) tax base at 31 March 20X6 is $27 million. Highwood's rate of income tax is 25%.

(v)   The inventory of Highwood was not counted until 4 April 20X6 due to operational reasons. At this date its value at cost was $36 million and this figure has been used in the cost of sales calculation above. Between the year end of 31 March 20X6 and 4 April 20X6, Highwood received a delivery of goods at a cost of $2.7 million and made sales of $7.8 million at a mark-up on cost of 30%. Neither the goods delivered nor the sales made in this period were included in Highwood's purchases (as part of cost of sales) or revenue in the above trial balance.

(vi)   On 31 March 20X6 Highwood factored (sold) trade receivables with a book value of $10 million to Easyfinance. Highwood received an immediate payment of $8.7 million and will pay Easyfinance 2% per month on any uncollected balances. Any of the factored receivables outstanding after six months will be refunded to Easyfinance. Highwood has derecognised the receivables and charged $1.3 million to administrative expenses. If Highwood had not factored these receivables it would have made an allowance of $600,000 against them.

Required

(i)   Prepare the statement of profit or loss and other comprehensive income for Highwood for the year ended 31 March 20X6;   **(11 marks)**

(ii)   Prepare the statement of changes in equity for Highwood for the year ended 31 March 20X6;   **(4 marks)**

(iii)   Prepare the statement of financial position of Highwood as at 31 March 20X6.   **(10 marks)**

(Total = 25 marks)

Note: your answers and workings should be presented to the nearest $1,000; notes to the financial statements are not required.

Question 3 Nedburg

The financial statements of Nedberg for the year to 30 September 20X2, together with the comparative statement of financial position for the year to 30 September 20X1 are shown below:

INCOME STATEMENT – YEAR TO 30 SEPTEMBER 20X2

	$m
Sales revenue	3,820
Cost of sales (note (1))	(2,620)
Gross Profit for the period	1,200
Operating expenses (note (1))	(300)
Interest – Loan note	(30)
Profit before tax	870
Taxation	(270)
Profit for the year	600

STATEMENTS OF FINANCIAL POSITION AS AT 30 SEPTEMBER

		20X2		20X1
Non-current assets	$m	$m	$m	$m
Property, plant and equipment		1,890		1,830
Intangible assets (note (2))		650		300
		2,540		2,130
Current assets				
Inventory	1,420		940	
Trade receivables	990		680	
Cash	70	2,480	nil	1,620
Total assets		5,020		3,750
Equity and liabilities				
Ordinary Shares of $1 each		750		500
Reserves:				
Share premium		350		100
Revaluation surplus		140		nil
Retained earnings		1,890		1,600
Total equity		3,130		2,200
Non-current liabilities (note(3))		870		540
Current liabilities (note(4))		1,020		1,010
Total equity and liabilities		5,020		3,750

Notes to the financial statements

(1)   Cost of sales includes depreciation of property, plant and equipment of $320 million and a loss on the sale of plant of $50 million. It also includes a credit for the amortisation of government grants. Operating expenses include a charge of $20 million for the impairment of goodwill.

(2)   Intangible non-current assets

	20X2	20X1
	$m	$m
Deferred development expenditure	470	100
Goodwill	180	200
	650	300

(3)   Non-current liabilities

	20X2	20X1
10% loan note	300	100
Government grants	260	300
Deferred tax	310	140
	870	540

(4)   Current liabilities

	20X2	20X1
	$m	$m
Trade payables	875	730
Bank overdraft	nil	115
Accrued loan interest	15	5
Taxation	130	160
	1,020	1,010

The following additional information is relevant:

(i)   Intangible non-current assets

The company successfully completed the development of a new product during the current year, capitalising a further $500 million before amortisation charges for the period.

(ii)   Property, plant and equipment/revaluation reserve

–   The company revalued its buildings by $200 million on 1 October 20X1. The surplus was credited to revaluation surplus.

BPP
LEARNING MEDIA

- New plant was acquired during the year at a cost of $250 million and a government grant of $50 million was received for this plant.

- On 1 October 20X1 a bonus issue of 1 new share for every 10 held was made from the revaluation surplus.

- $10 million has been transferred from the revaluation surplus to realised profits as a year-end adjustment in respect of the additional depreciation created by the revaluation.

- The remaining movement on property, plant and equipment was due to the disposal of obsolete plant.

(iii) *Share issues*

In addition to the bonus issue referred to above Nedberg made a further issue of ordinary shares for cash.

(iv) *Dividends*

Dividends paid during the year amounted to $320,000.

Required

(a) A statement of cash flows for Nedberg for the year to 30 September 20X2 prepared in accordance with IAS 7 *Statement of cash flows*. **(20 marks)**

(b) Comment briefly on the financial position of Nedberg as portrayed by the information in your statement of cash flows. **(5 marks)**

(Total = 25 marks)

Question 4 Peterlee II   27 mins

Peterlee is preparing its financial statements for the year ended 31 March 20X6. The following items have been brought to your attention:

(a) Peterlee acquired the entire share capital of Trantor during the year. The acquisition was achieved through a share exchange. The terms of the exchange were based on the relative values of the two companies obtained by capitalising the companies' estimated future cash flows. When the fair value of Trantor's identifiable net assets was deducted from the value of the company as a whole, its goodwill was calculated at $2·5 million. A similar exercise valued the goodwill of Peterlee at $4 million. The directors wish to incorporate both the goodwill values in the companies' consolidated financial statements. **(5 marks)**

(b) During the year Peterlee acquired an iron ore mine at a cost of $6 million. In addition, when all the ore has been extracted (estimated in 10 years time) the company will face estimated costs for landscaping the area affected by the mining that have a present value of $2 million. These costs would still have to be incurred even if no further ore was extracted. The directors have proposed that an accrual of $200,000 per year for the next ten years should be made for the landscaping. **(5 marks)**

(c) On 1 April 20X5 Peterlee issued an 8% $5 million convertible loan at par. The loan is convertible in three years time to ordinary shares or redeemable at par in cash. The directors decided to issue a convertible loan because a non-convertible loan would have required an interest rate of 10%. The directors intend to show the loan at $5 million under non-current liabilities. The following discount rates are available:

	8%	10%
Year 1	0·93	0·91
Year 2	0·86	0·83
Year 3	0·79	0·75

(5 marks)

Required

Describe (and quantify where possible) how Peterlee should treat the items in (a) to (c) in its financial statements for the year ended 31 March 20X6 commenting on the directors' views where appropriate.

The mark allocation is shown against each of the three items above. **(Total = 15 marks)**

Question 5 Errsea

The following is an extract of Errsea's balances of property, plant and equipment and related government grants at 1 April 20X6.

	Cost	Accumulated depreciation	Carrying amount
	$'000	$'000	$'000
Property, plant and equipment	240	180	60
Non-current liabilities			
Government grants			30
Current liabilities			
Government grants			10

Details including purchases and disposals of plant and related government grants during the year are:

(i) Included in the above figures is an item of plant that was disposed of on 1 April 20X6 for $12,000 which had cost $90,000 on 1 April 20X3. The plant was being depreciated on a straight-line basis over four years assuming a residual value of $10,000. A government grant was received on its purchase and was being recognised in profit or loss in equal amounts over four years. In accordance with the terms of the grant, Errsea repaid $3,000 of the grant on the disposal of the related plant.

(ii) An item of plant was acquired on 1 July 20X6 with the following costs:

	$
Base cost	192,000
Modifications specified by Errsea	12,000
Transport and installation	6,000

The plant qualified for a government grant of 25% of the base cost of the plant, but it had not been received by 31 March 20X7. The plant is to be depreciated on a straight-line basis over three years with a nil estimated residual value.

(iii) All other plant is depreciated by 15% per annum on cost

(iv) $11,000 of the $30,000 non-current liability for government grants at 1 April 20X6 should be reclassified as a current liability as at 31 March 20X7.

(v) Depreciation is calculated on a time apportioned basis.

Required

Prepare extracts of Errsea's statement of profit or loss and statement of financial position in respect of the property, plant and equipment and government grants for the year ended 31 March 20X7.

Note: Disclosure notes are not required. **(10 marks)**

BPP LEARNING MEDIA

Answers

**DO NOT TURN THIS PAGE UNTIL YOU HAVE
COMPLETED THE MOCK EXAM**

BPP
LEARNING MEDIA

BPP
LEARNING MEDIA

A plan of attack

Managing your nerves

As you turn the pages to start this mock exam a number of thoughts are likely to cross your mind. At best, examinations cause anxiety so it is important to stay focused on your task for the next three hours! Developing an awareness of what is going on emotionally within you may help you manage your nerves. Remember, you are unlikely to banish the flow of adrenaline, but the key is to harness it to help you work steadily and quickly through your answers.

Working through this mock exam will help you develop the exam stamina you will need to keep going for three hours.

Managing your time

Planning and time management are two of the key skills which complement the technical knowledge you need to succeed. To keep yourself on time, do not be afraid to jot down your target completion times for each question, perhaps next to the title of the question on the paper. As all the questions are **compulsory**, you do not have to spend time wondering which question to answer!

Focusing on scoring marks

When completing written answers, remember to communicate the critical points, which represent marks, and avoid padding and waffle. Sometimes it is possible to analyse a long sentence into more than one point. Always try to maximise the mark potential of what you write.

As you read through the questions, jot down on the question paper, any points you think you might forget. There is nothing more upsetting than coming out of an exam having forgotten to write a point you knew!

Structure and signpost your answers

As you read through the paper, highlight the key words and phrases in the examiner's requirements. This will help you focus precisely on what the examiner wants.

Also, where possible try to use headings and subheadings, to give a logical and easy-to-follow structure to your response. A well structured and sign-posted answer is more likely to convince the examiner that you know your subject.

Doing the exam

Actually doing the exam is a personal experience. There is not a single *right way*. As long as you submit complete answers to five questions after the three hours are up, then your approach obviously works.

Looking through the paper

Question 1, as always, is on **group accounts**. This time it requires a statement of profit or loss for a group and statement of financial position.

*   Question 2 is on **preparing financial statements for an individual company**.
*   Question 3 is a **statement of cash flows and interpretation of accounts**.
*   Question 4 requires good understanding of **goodwill, provisions and convertible loans**.
*   Question 5 is a question on **non-current assets** and **government grants**.

Allocating your time

BPP's advice is to always allocate your time **according to the marks for the question.** However, **use common sense.** If you're doing a question but haven't a clue how to do part (c), you might be better off re-allocating your time and getting more marks on another question, where you can add something you didn't have time for earlier on.

Question 1 Hydan

Text references. Chapters 9 and 10.

Top tips. Note that Systan made a loss in the post-acquisition period – therefore the retained earnings at acquisition were higher than the retained earnings at the year end. This means that, in the statement of profit or loss, the non-controlling interest will be allocated their share of a loss. This is unusual – do not be put off by it.

Easy marks. In this question you had to deal with NCI at fair value and post-acquisition loss in Systan. There were no other major complications. You were told what the additional depreciation was on the fair value adjustment, and the unrealised profit calculation was simple. The rest was straightforward consolidation procedure, with easy marks for issues such as cancelling out the intercompany loan.

The information in the question and your answer will have told you all you needed to know to answer (b), and there were five easy marks available there

Examiner's comments. The most common errors in this question were:

- Incorrect cost of investment. Some candidates included the loan and some were unable to calculate the value of the shares
- Post-acquisition results of subsidiary treated as profits
- Fair value adjustments omitted
- Problems with non-controlling interest
- Errors dealing with intra group transactions, tax relief and unrealised profit

Marking scheme

		Marks
(a)	**Statement of profit or loss**	
	Revenue	2
	Cost of sales	3
	Operating expenses including 1 mark for goodwill	2
	Interest receivable/payable	1
	Income tax	1
	Non-controlling interest	2
	Statement of financial position	
	Goodwill	3
	Property, plant and equipment	2
	Investments	1
	Current assets/current liabilities	2
	7% bank loan	1
	Elimination of 10% intra-group loan	1
	Non-controlling interest	2
	Share capital and share premium	1
	Retained earnings	1
	Available	25
	Maximum	20
(b)	1 mark per relevant point to Maximum	5
	Maximum for question	25

(a) HYDAN CONSOLIDATED STATEMENT OF PROFIT OR LOSS YEAR ENDED 31 MARCH 20X6

	$'000
Revenue (98,000 + 35,200 – 30,000 intra-group)	103,200
Cost of sales (76,000 + 31,000 – 30,000 intra-group + 200 (W6) + 300 (W7))	(77,500)
Gross profit	25,700
Operating expenses (11,800 + 8,000 + 375 (W2))	(20,175)
Interest receivable (350 – 200 intra-group (4,000 × 10% × $^6/_{12}$))	150
Finance costs	(420)
Profit before tax	5,255
Income tax expense (4,200 – 1,000)	(3,200)
Profit for the year	2,055

	$'000
Profit attributable to:	
Owners of the parent	3,605
Non-controlling interest (W4)	(1,550)
	2,055

HYDAN CONSOLIDATED STATEMENT OF FINANCIAL POSITION AT 31 MARCH 20X6

	$'000
Non-current assets	
Property, plant and equipment (18,400 + 9,500 + 1,200 – 300 (W7))	28,800
Goodwill (W2)	3,025
Investments (16,000 – 10,800 (W2) – 4,000)	1,200
Current assets (18,000 + 7,200 – 200 (W6) – 1,000 intra-group)	24,000
Total assets	57,025
Equity and liabilities	
Equity attributable to owners of the parent	
Ordinary shares of $1 each	10,000
Share premium	5,000
Retained earnings (W3)	17,675
	32,675
Non-controlling interest (W5)	4,050
	36,725
Non-current liabilities	
7% bank loan	6,000
Current liabilities (11,400 + 3,900 – 1,000 intra-group)	14,300
Total equity and liabilities	57,025

Workings

1   *Group structure*

Hydan

→ 60% 1.10.X5

Systan

2   *Goodwill in Systan*

	$'000	$'000
Consideration transferred (1,200 × $9)		10,800
Non-controlling interests (at 'full' fair value) (800 × $7)		5,600
Fair value of net assets at acquisition:		
Ordinary shares	2,000	
Share premium	500	
Pre-acquisition reserves (6,300 + 3,000)	9,300	
Fair value adjustment	1,200	
		(13,000)
Goodwill		3,400
Impairment losses		(375)
Carrying amount		3,025

3   *Group retained earnings*

	Hydan $'000	Systan $'000
Per question	20,000	6,300
Pre-acquisition		(9,300)
Unrealised profit in inventory (W6)		(200)
Additional depreciation (W7)		(300)
	20,000	(3,500)
Group share of Systan ((3,500) × 60%)	(2,100)	
Goodwill impairment (375 × 60%)	(225)	
	17,675	

4   *Non controlling interest: statement of profit or loss*

	$'000
Post-acquisition loss	(3,000)
Unrealised profit in inventory (W6)	(200)
Additional depreciation (W7)	(300)
Adjusted loss	(3,500)
Non-controlling share 40%	(1,400)
Goodwill impairment (W5)	(150)
	(1,550)

5   *Non-controlling interest: statement of financial position*

	$'000
At acquisition (W2)	5,600
Share of post acquisition retained earnings ((W3) (3,500) × 40%)	(1,400)
Share of impairment losses (375 × 40%)	(150)
	4,050

6   *Unrealised profit*

	$'000
Goods sold by Systan to Hydan and still in inventory	4,000
Unrealised profit – 5% of selling price to Hydan	200

DEBIT Retained earnings (Systan)	200	
CREDIT Group inventory		200

7   *Fair value adjustment*

	At acquisition date $'000	Movement $'000	At 31.3.X6 $'000
Property, plant and equipment (Note (i))	1,200		1,200
Additional depreciation		(300)	(300)
	1,200	(300)	900
	↓	↓	↓
	Goodwill	Retained earnings	PPE/NCI

(b)   If we look at Systan's pre-acquisition operating performance, we can see a gross profit margin of 25% and a net profit margin of 15%. During the post-acquisition 6-month period revenue is up by 46% but the gross profit margin is only 12% and the company has made a net loss of 8.5%. Clearly this requires some explanation.

Hydan obtained a controlling interest in Systan in order to secure its supplies of components. In the post-acquisition period $30m of Systan's $35m sales were to Hydan and realised 5% gross profit. In order to compensate for this, Systan has substantially increased the price charged to its other customers to give a

BPP LEARNING MEDIA

50% gross profit margin on those sales. The eventual result of this may be that it will no longer have any other customers.

Systan's results for the second half-year have also suffered from a large rise in operating expenses – from $1.2m in the pre-acquisition half year to $8m in the post-acquisition half year. It looks as though Systan has been charged a large share of group operating expenses. Hydan itself has operating expenses for the year of $11.8m on a revenue of $98m, while Systan has expenses of $8m on 6 months revenue of $35m. As there are no current account balances outstanding, Systan has obviously had to pay the intra-group portion of this $8m, facilitated by a loan from Hydan at 10%. At the same time, Hydan owes Systan $1m on which no interest is being paid.

The overall conclusion must be that Systan's position has been adversely affected by the acquisition and by the resulting related party transactions. Hydan has used transfer pricing and inter-company charges to transfer profits from the subsidiary to the parent company, thus benefiting its own shareholders at the expense of the non-controlling shareholders.

Question 2 Highwood

Text reference Chapter 3

Top tips. Start with the proformas for the three financial statements so that you can put in any easy numbers straightaway. Then go through the workings, setting them out very clearly so that the marker can see what you have included. The part you may have found challenging was the convertible loan note. If you have trouble with something like this, don't waste time working over it, just move on.

Easy marks. Property, plant and equipment accounted for quite a few marks here and it required a proper working, but none of it was difficult. Similarly, correcting the inventory was easy and so was dealing with the factored receivables. Once you realised that the accounting treatment had been incorrect, it was only necessary to carefully reverse those entries.

Examiner's comments This question was generally well done. Most errors arose in the statement of [profit or loss and other] comprehensive income. Some candidates got the inventory adjustment the wrong way round and then incorrectly adjusted the sales revenue. Many candidates adjusted for the factored debts but omitted to then recognise a receivables allowance. Many also had difficulty with the finance cost of the convertible loan note. The revaluation gain on the property was generally well done, but most candidates did not include the deferred tax on the gain in other comprehensive income.

Marking scheme

		Marks
(i)	Statement of profit or loss and other comprehensive income	
	Revenue	½
	Cost of sales	4
	Distribution costs	½
	Administrative expenses	1½
	Finance costs	1½
	Income tax expense	1½
	Other comprehensive income	1½
		11
(ii)	Statement of changes in equity	
	Opening balance on retained earnings	1
	Other component of equity (option)	1
	Dividend paid	1
	Comprehensive income	1
		4

(iii)   Statement of financial position

Property, plant and equipment	2½
Inventory	1
Trade receivables	1
Deferred tax	1
Issue of 8% loan note	1½
Liability to Easyfinance	1
Bank overdraft	½
Trade payables	½
Current tax payable	1
	10
	25

(i)

HIGHWOOD
STATEMENT OF PROFIT OR LOSS AND OTHER COMPREHENSIVE INCOME FOR THE YEAR ENDED 31 MARCH 20X6

	$'000
Revenue	339,650
Cost of sales (W1)	(216,950)
Gross profit	122,700
Distribution costs	(27,500)
Administrative expenses (W1)	(30,000)
Finance costs (W3)	(2,848)
Profit before tax	62,352
Income tax expense (19,400 + (W4) 400 – 800)	(19,000)
Profit for the year	43,352
Other comprehensive income:	
Revaluation gain on property (W2)	11,250
Total comprehensive income for the year	54,602

(ii)

HIGHWOOD
STATEMENT OF CHANGES IN EQUITY FOR THE YEAR ENDED 31 MARCH 20X6

	Share capital $'000	Equity option $'000	Retained earnings $'000	Revaluation surplus $'000	Total $'000
Balance 1 April 20X5	56,000	–	7,000	–	63,000
Dividend	-	-	(5,600)	-	(5,600)
Total comprehensive income			43,352	11,250	54,602
Loan note issue (W3)	-	1,524	-	-	1,524
Balance 31 March 20X6	56,000	1,524	44,752	11,250	113,526

BPP
LEARNING MEDIA

(iii)

HIGHWOOD
STATEMENT OF FINANCIAL POSITION AS AT 31 MARCH 20X6

	$'000	$'000
Non-current assets		
Property, plant and equipment (W2)		117,500
Current assets		
Inventory (W5)	39,300	
Receivables (47,100 + 9,400 (W6))	56,500	
		95,800
Total assets		213,300
Equity		
Share capital	56,000	
Other component of equity (W3)	1,524	
Revaluation surplus (W2)	11,250	
Retained earnings	44,752	
		113,526
Non-current liabilities		
Deferred tax (W4)	6,750	
Convertible loan note (W3)	28,924	
Easyfinance loan (W6)	8,700	
		44,374
Current liabilities		
Trade payables	24,500	
Tax payable	19,400	
Overdraft	11,500	
		55,400
Total equity and liabilities		213,300

Workings

1. Expenses

	Cost of sales	Distribution costs	Administrative expenses
	$'000	$'000	$'000
Per question	207,750	27,500	30,700
Depreciation – buildings (W2)	2,500		
- plant (W2)	10,000		
Increase in inventories (W5)	(3,300)		
Reverse factoring charge (W6)			(1,300)
Bad debt (W6)			600
	216,950	27,500	30,000

2. Property, plant and equipment

	Land $'000	Buildings $'000	Plant and equipment $'000	Total $'000
Per TB – cost	25,000	50,000	74,500	149,500
Acc'd depreciation 1.4.20X5		(10,000)	(24,500)	(34,500)
Carrying amount 1.4.20X5	25,000	40,000	50,000	115,000
Revaluation surplus	5,000	10,000	-	15,000
Revalued amount 1.4.20X5	30,000	50,000	50,000	130,000
Depn –bldgs (50,000/20yrs)		(2,500)		(2,500)
- plant (50,000 x 20%)			(10,000)	(10,000)
	30,000	47,500	40,000	117,500

Note that the deferred tax on the revaluation (15,000 x 25%) will be charged to the revaluation surplus, leaving a balance of 11,250 (15,000 – 3,750).

3. *Loan note*

As this is a convertible loan note, it has to be split between debt and equity:

	$'000
Interest years 1-3 (2,400 × (0.91 + 0.83 + 0.75)	5,976
Repayment year 3 (30,000 × 0.75)	22,500
Liability component	28,476
Equity component	1,524
Cash received	30,000

Liability component	28,476
Interest (28,476 × 10%)	2,848
Less interest paid	(2,400)
Balance at 31.3.20X6	28,924

4. *Deferred tax*

	$'000
Balance required at 31.3.X6 (27m × 25%)	6,750
Current balance	(2,600)
Deferred tax on revaluation (15m × 25%)	(3,750)
Charge to current tax	400

5. *Inventory*

	$'000
Per TB	36,000
Received after year end	(2,700)
Sold after year end (7,800 × 100/130)	6,000
Correct balance	39,300

Adjustment required – deduct 3,300 from cost of sales.

6. *Factoring*

The factoring arrangement is in substance a loan of $8.7m. To reflect this, the $10m receivables are reinstated, less the allowance of 600.

	DR	CR
	$'000	$'000
Loan payable		8,700
Receivables	9,400	
Administrative expenses	600	1,300

BPP
LEARNING MEDIA

Question 3 Nedburg

Text reference. Chapter 21.

Top tips. Start by putting down the proforma. Then go methodically through the net cash flow from operating activities calculation. You will have to do the workings for property, plant and equipment and deferred development expenditure in order to complete it.

Easy marks. The statement of cash flows is straightforward and represents 20 easy marks.

Examiner's comments. This question was generally well answered and part (a) in particular was extremely well answered. However candidates still made mistakes in including non-cash items. Part (b) was poorly answered, some candidates making no effort to answer it at all. Most answers were superficial, giving general trends without commenting on them.

Marking scheme

			Marks
(a)	Net cash flows from operating activities		
	1 mark per item		8
	Except – loan interest		2
	– taxation		2
	Capital expenditure – proceeds from the sale of the plant		2
	– other items, 1 mark per component		3
	Financing – equity shares		2
	– loan note		2
	Equity dividends		1
	Movement in cash and cash equivalents		<u>1</u>
		Available	23
		Maximum	20
(b)	1 mark per relevant point to a	Maximum	<u>5</u>
		Total for question	25

(a)   NEDBERG - STATEMENT OF CASH FLOWS FOR THE YEAR ENDED 30 SEPTEMBER 20X2

	$'000	$'000
Cash flows from operating activities		
Net profit before taxation		870
Adjustments for:		
Depreciation		320
Loss on disposal of plant		50
Amortisation of development expenditure (W3)		130
Impairment of goodwill		20
Release of government grants (W4)		(90)
Interest expense		30
		1,330
(Increase) decrease in trade and other receivables (990 – 680)		(310)
(Increase) decrease in inventories (1,420 – 940)		(480)
Increase (decrease) in trade payables (875 – 730)		145
Cash generated from operations		685
Interest paid (30 + 5 – 15)		(20)
Income taxes paid (W5)		(130)
Net cash from operating activities		535
Cash flows from investing activities		
Proceeds from sale of property, plant and equipment (W2)	20	
Purchase of property, plant and equipment	(250)	
Receipt of government grant	50	
Development expenditure capitalised	(500)	
Net cash used in investing activities		(680)
Cash flows from financing activities		
Proceeds from issue of share capital (200 + 250)(W6), (W7)	450	
Proceeds of long term borrowings (300 – 100)	200	
Dividends paid	(320)	
Net cash from financing activities		330
Net increase in cash and cash equivalents		185
Opening cash and cash equivalents		(115)
Closing cash and cash equivalents		70

Workings

1

PROPERTY, PLANT AND EQUIPMENT – CARRYING VALUE

	$m		$m
Bal b/f	1,830	Depreciation	320
		Plant disposal	
Revaluation	200	(balancing figure)	70
Plant acquisition	250	Bal c/f	1,890
	2,280		2,280

2

PROPERTY, PLANT AND EQUIPMENT – DISPOSAL

	$m		$m
Plant disposal (W1)	70	Loss on disposal (from question)	50
		Disposal proceeds (balancing figure)	20
	70		70

BPP
LEARNING MEDIA

3

DEFERRED DEVELOPMENT EXPENDITURE

	$m		$m
Opening	100	Closing	470
Expenditure	500	Amortised	130
	600		600

4

GOVERNMENT GRANTS

	$m		$m
Closing	260	Opening	300
Released during year	90	Cash received	50
	350		350

5

TAX

		$m			$m
Closing liability	Current	130	Opening liability	Current	160
	Deferred	310		Deferred	140
Cash paid		130	Charge for the year		270
		570			570

6

SHARE CAPITAL

	$m		$m
		Bal b/f	500
		Bonus issue (1/10)	50
Bal c/f	750	Issue for cash	200
	750		750

7

SHARE PREMIUM

	$m		$m
		Bal b/f	100
Bal c/f	350	Premium on cash issue	250
	350		350

(b) Nedberg has positive cash flow, generating $685m from operations which is sufficient to cover interest ($20m), tax ($130m) and dividends ($320m).

Unusually, the cash flow from operations is less than the operating profit of $900m. The cause of this appears to be the increase in current assets; inventories have increased by 51% and receivables by 46%. Without the comparative income statement it is impossible to say whether these increases are in line with increased activity or whether it is the result of poor working capital management.

Nedberg has paid out $250m on property plant and equipment and capitalised $500m of development costs. In theory this is a good thing, as these investments will generate profits and cash flows in the future. However, Nedberg has had to raise $650m externally in order to pay for these investments, and this cannot be repeated year after year. Nedberg would be advised to reduce its capital investment for a year or two to enable it to get its finances back in order.

The financing section reveals that Nedberg has paid out in dividends half of the money it has received by issuing loans and shares. This seems pointless; the shareholders are getting back money that they have just invested (and they might have to pay tax on the dividends that they have received). The dividend for the year is also high compared with the profits after tax; Nedberg should reduce its dividends to a more modest and sustainable amount.

Overall, Nedberg has a healthy cash flow from operating activities. However, management need to:

- monitor working capital,
- scale back capital expenditure, and
- practise dividend restraint.

Question 4 Peterlee II

(a) The goodwill in Trantor is purchased goodwill and can be capitalised and shown as an asset in the consolidated statement of financial position at the value calculated. However, the goodwill in Peterlee itself is internally generated goodwill, and per IAS 38 it cannot be capitalised because it cannot be reliably measured. So the directors will be allowed to include the goodwill in Trantor of $2.5 million in the financial statements, but the goodwill estimated to exist in Peterlee cannot be recognised.

(b) Per IAS 37 this treatment is not correct. The $2 million present value of the landscaping cost should be recognised as a provision at 31 March 20X6. The debit will be to the asset account, giving an asset value for the mine of $8 million. This total value will be depreciated over 10 years. In this way the landscaping cost will be charged to profit or loss over the life of the mine. At the same time, the discount to present value will 'unwind' over the 10 year period. This will be credited to the provision and charged as a finance cost. At the end of 10 years, the amount in the provision account should equal the amount due to be paid.

(c) As this is a convertible loan, it must be apportioned between debt and equity. Per IAS 32 this is calculated as follows:

	$'000
Present value of the principal to be repaid: $5 million × 0.75	3,750
Present value of interest: $0.4 million × 2.49 (0.91 + 0.83 + 0.75)	996
Debt element	4,746
Equity element	254
Proceeds of issue	5,000

The statement of profit or loss and statement of financial position amounts will be as follows:

	$'000	$'000
Debt element of loan		4,746
Interest at 10% (profit or loss)	475	
Interest paid	(400)	
Balance due		75
Balance of loan at 31 March 20X6 (statement of financial position)		4,821

Question 5 Errsea

> **Top tips.** This question requires really clear workings, to enable you to work methodically and to show the marker what you have done.

STATEMENT OF PROFIT OR LOSS (EXTRACTS)

	$
Income from government grants (W2)	19,000
Loss on disposal of plant (30,000 – 12,000)	18,000
Depreciation (52,500 + 22,500 (W1))	75,000

BPP LEARNING MEDIA

STATEMENT OF FINANCIAL POSITION (EXTRACTS)

	$
Non-current assets	
Property, plant and equipment (W1)	165,000
Current assets	
Receivable-government grant	48,000
Non-current liabilities	
Government grants	39,000
Current liabilities	
Government grants	27,000

Workings

1 Property, plant and equipment

	Cost $	Accumulated depreciation $	Carrying value $
At 1.4.X6	240,000	(180,000)	60,000
Disposal 1.4. X6	(90,000)	60,000	(30,000)
Acquisition 1.7. X6	210,000		210,000
Depreciation on acquisition ((210/3) × 9/12)		(52,500)	(52,500)
Depreciation on assets on hand at 1.4.X6 ((240 – 90) × 15%)		(22,500)	(22,500)
	360,000	(195,000)	(165,000)

2 Government grants

	Current liability $	Non-current liability $	Income $
At 1.4.X6	10,000	30,000	
Grant repaid	(3,000)		
	7,000		
Transfer to income at 31.3.X7	(7,000)		7,000
Transfer to current liability	11,000	(11,000)	
Grant receivable *	16,000	20,000	12,000
	27,000	39,000	19,000

	$
*	
Total grant (192,000 × 25%)	48,000
Transfer to income ((48,000/3) × 9/12)	12,000
Current liability (48,000/3)	16,000
Non-current liability	20,000
	48,000

BPP
LEARNING MEDIA

ACCA Fundamentals Level

Paper F7

Financial Reporting (Int)

Mock Examination 3
(December 2012 paper)

Question Paper	
Time allowed	
Reading and Planning Writing	15 minutes 3 hours
Answer all FIVE questions	

DO NOT OPEN THIS PAPER UNTIL YOU ARE READY TO START UNDER EXAMINATION CONDITIONS

BPP
LEARNING MEDIA

BPP
LEARNING MEDIA

Question 1 Viagem

On 1 January 2012, Viagem acquired 90% of the equity share capital of Greca in a share exchange in which Viagem issued two new shares for every three shares it acquired in Greca. Additionally, on 31 December 2012, Viagem will pay the shareholders of Greca $1.76 per share acquired. Viagem's cost of capital is 10% per annum.

At the date of acquisition, shares in Viagem and Greca had a stock market value of $6.50 and $2.50 each respectively.

Statements of profit or loss for the year ended 30 September 2012

	Viagem	Greca
	$'000	$'000
Revenue	64,600	38,000
Cost of sales	(51,200)	(26,000)
Gross profit	13,400	12,000
Distribution costs	(1,600)	(1,800)
Administrative expenses	(3,800)	(2,400)
Investment income	500	-
Finance costs	(420)	-
Profit before tax	8,080	7,800
Income tax expense	(2,800)	(1,600)
Profit for the year	5,280	6,200
Equity as at 1 October 2011		
Equity shares of $1 each	30,000	10,000
Retained earnings	54,000	35,000

The following information is relevant:

(i)   At the date of acquisition the fair values of Greca's assets were equal to their carrying amounts with the exception of two items:

      1   An item of plant had a fair value of $1.8 million above its carrying amount. The remaining life of the plant at the date of acquisition was three years. Depreciation is charged to cost of sales.

      2   Greca had a contingent liability which Viagem estimated to have a fair value of $450,000. This has not changed as at 30 September 2012.

Greca has not incorporated these fair value changes into its financial statements.

(ii) Viagem's policy is to value the non-controlling interest at fair value at the date of acquisition. For this purpose, Greca's share price at that date can be deemed to be representative of the fair value of the shares held by the non-controlling interest.

(iii) Sales from Viagem to Greca throughout the year ended 30 September 2012 had consistently been $800,000 per month. Viagem made a mark-up on cost of 25% on these sales. Greca had $1.5 million of these goods in inventory as at 30 September 2012.

(iv) Viagem's investment income is a dividend received from its investment in a 40% owned associate which it has held for several years. The underlying earnings for the associate for the year ended 30 September 2012 were $2 million.

(v) Although Greca has been profitable since its acquisition by Viagem, the market for Greca's products has been badly hit in recent months and Viagem has calculated that the goodwill has been impaired by $2 million as at 30 September 2012.

Required

(a)   Calculate the consolidated goodwill at the date of acquisition of Greca.   **(7 marks)**

(b)   Prepare the consolidated statement of profit or loss for Viagem for the year ended 30 September 2012.

(14 marks)

(c) The carrying amount of a subsidiary's leased property will be subject to review as part of the fair value exercise on acquisition and may be subject to review in subsequent periods.

Required

Explain how a fair value increase of a subsidiary's leased property on acquisition should be treated in the consolidated financial statements and how any subsequent increase in the carrying amount of the leased property might be treated in the consolidated financial statements. **(4 marks)**

(Total = 25 marks)

Question 2 Quincy

The following trial balance relates to Quincy as at 30 September 2012.

	$'000	$'000
Revenue (note (i))		213,500
Cost of sales	136,800	
Distribution costs	12,500	
Administrative expenses (note (ii))	19,000	
Loan note interest and dividend paid (notes (ii) and (iii))	20,700	
Investment income		400
Equity shares of 25 cents each		60,000
6% loan note (note (ii))		25,000
Retained earnings at 1 October 2011		18,500
Land and buildings at cost (land element $10 million) (note (iv))	50,000	
Plant and equipment at cost (note (iv))	83,700	
Accumulated depreciation at 1 October 2011: buildings		8,000
plant and equipment		33,700
Equity financial asset investments (note (v))	17,000	
Inventory at 30 September 2012	24,800	
Trade receivables	28,500	
Bank	2,900	
Current tax (note (vi))	1,100	
Deferred tax (note (vi))		1,200
Trade payables		36,700
	397,000	397,000

The following notes are relevant:

(i) On 1 October 2011 Quincy sold one of its products for $10 million (included in revenue in the trial balance). As part of the sale agreement, Quincy is committed to the ongoing servicing of this product until 30 September 2014 (ie three years from the date of sale). The value of this service has been included in the selling price of $10 million. The estimated cost to Quincy of the servicing is $600,000 per annum and Quincy's normal gross profit margin on this type of servicing is 25%. Ignore discounting.

(ii) Quincy issued a $25 million 6% loan note on 1 October 2011. Issue costs were $1 million and these have been charged to administrative expenses. The loan will be redeemed on 30 September 2014 at a premium which gives an effective interest rate on the loan of 8%.

(iii) Quincy paid an equity dividend of 8 cents per share during the year ended 30 September 2012.

(iv) Non-current assets:

Quincy had been carrying land and buildings at depreciated cost but, due to a recent rise in property prices, it decided to revalue its property on 1 October 2011 to market value. An independent valuer confirmed the value of the property at $60 million (land element $12 million) as at that date and the directors accepted this valuation. The property had a remaining life of 16 years at the date of its revaluation. Quincy will make a transfer from the revaluation surplus to retained earnings in respect of the realisation of the revaluation surplus. Ignore deferred tax on the revaluation.

Plant and equipment is depreciated at 15% per annum using the reducing balance method.

No depreciation has yet been charged on any non-current asset for the year ended 30 September 2012. All depreciation is charged to cost of sales.

(v) The investments had a fair value of $15.7 million as at 30 September 2012. There were no acquisitions or disposals of these investments during the year ended 30 September 2012.

(vi) The balance on current tax represents the under/over provision of the tax liability for the year ended 30 September 2011. A provision for income tax for the year ended 30 September 2012 of $7.4 million is required. At 30 September 2012 Quincy had taxable temporary differences of $5 million, requiring a provision for deferred tax. Any deferred tax adjustment should be reported in profit or loss. The income tax rate of Quincy is 20%.

Required

(a) Prepare the statement of profit or loss and other comprehensive income for Quincy for the year ended 30 September 2012. **(11 marks)**

(b) Prepare the statement of changes in equity for Quincy for the year ended 30 September 2012.

(4 marks)

(c) Prepare the statement of financial position for Quincy as at 30 September 2012. **(10 marks)**

(Total = 25 marks)

Notes to the financial statements are not required.

Question 3   Quartile

Quartile sells jewellery through stores in retail shopping centres throughout the country. Over the last two years it has experienced declining profitability and is wondering if this is related to the sector as a whole. It has recently subscribed to an agency that produces average ratios across many businesses. Below are the ratios that have been provided by the agency for Quartile's business sector based on a year end of 30 June 2012.

Return on year-end capital employed (ROCE)	16.8%
Net asset (total assets less current liabilities) turnover	1.4 times
Gross profit margin	35%
Operating profit margin	12%
Current ratio	1.25:1
Average inventory turnover	3 times
Trade payables' payment period	64 days
Debt to equity	38%

The financial statements of Quartile for the year ended 30 September 2012 are:

STATEMENT OF PROFIT OR LOSS

	$'000	$'000
Revenue		56,000
Opening inventory	8,300	
Purchases	43,900	
Closing inventory	(10,200)	
		(42,000)
Gross profit		14,000
Operating costs		(9,800)
Finance costs		(800)
Profit before tax		3,400
Income tax expense		(1,000)
Profit for the year		2,400

STATEMENT OF FINANCIAL POSITION

	S'000
ASSETS	
Non-current assets	
Property and shop fittings	25,600
Deferred development expenditure	5,000
	30,600
Current assets	
Inventory	10,200
Bank	1,000
	11,200
Total assets	41,800
EQUITY AND LIABILITIES	
Equity	
Equity shares of $1 each	15,000
Property revaluation reserve	3,000
Retained earnings	8600
	26,600
Non-current liabilities	
10% loan notes	8,000
Current liabilities	
Trade payables	5,400
Current tax payable	1,800
	7,200
Total equity and liabilities	41,800

Note. The deferred development expenditure relates to an investment in a process to manufacture artificial precious gems for future sale by Quartile in the retail jewellery market.

Required

a) Prepare for Quartile the equivalent ratios to those provided by the agency. **(9 marks)**

b) Assess the financial and operating performance of Quartile in comparison to its sector averages.

(12 marks)

c) Explain four possible limitations on the usefulness of the above comparison. **(4 marks)**

(Total = 25 marks)

Question 4 Lobden

(a) Two of the qualitative characteristics of information contained in the IASB's *Conceptual Framework for Financial Reporting* are understandability and comparability.

Required

Explain the meaning and purpose of the above characteristics in the context of financial reporting and discuss the role of consistency within the characteristic of comparability in relation to changes in accounting policy.

(6 marks)

(b) Lobden is a construction contract company involved in building commercial properties. Its current policy for determining the percentage of completion of its contracts is based on the proportion of cost incurred to date compared to the total expected cost of the contract.

One of Lobden's contracts has an agreed price of $250 million and estimated total costs of $200 million.

BPP
LEARNING MEDIA

The cumulative progress of this contract is:

Year ended:	30 September 2011	30 September 2012
	$m	$m
Costs incurred	80	145
Work certified and billed	75	160
Billings received	70	150

Based on the above, Lobden prepared and published its financial statements for the year ended 30 September 2011. Relevant extracts are:

STATEMENT OF PROFIT OR LOSS

	$m
Revenue (balance)	100
Cost of sales	(80)
Profit $(50 \times 80/200)$	20

STATEMENT OF FINANCIAL POSITION

	$m
Current assets	
Amounts due from customers	
Contract costs to date	80
Profit recognised	20
	100
Progress billings	(75)
	25
Contract receivables (75 – 70)	5

Lobden has received some adverse publicity in the financial press for taking its profit too early in the contract process, leading to disappointing profits in the later stages of contracts. Most of Lobden's competitors take profit based on the percentage of completion as determined by the work certified compared to the contract price.

Required

(i) Assuming Lobden changes its method of determining the percentage of completion of contracts to that used by its competitors, and that this would represent a change in an accounting estimate, calculate equivalent extracts to the above for the year ended 30 September 2012. **(7 marks)**

(ii) Explain why the above represents a change in accounting estimate rather than a change in accounting policy.

(2 marks)

(Total = 15 marks)

Question 5 Shawler

(a) Shawler is a small manufacturing company specialising in making alloy casings. Its main item of plant is a furnace which was purchased on 1 October 2009. The furnace has two components: the main body (cost $60,000 including the environmental provision – see below) which has a ten-year life, and a replaceable liner (cost $10,000) with a five-year life.

The manufacturing process produces toxic chemicals which pollute the nearby environment. Legislation requires that a clean-up operation must be undertaken by Shawler on 30 September 2019 at the latest.

Shawler received a government grant of $12,000 relating to the cost of the main body of the furnace only.

The following are extracts from Shawler's statement of financial position as at 30 September 2011 (two years after the acquisition of the furnace).

	Carrying amount	
	$	
Non-current assets		
Furnace: main body	48,000	
replaceable liner	6,000	
Current liabilities		
Government grant	1,200	
Non-current liabilities		
Government grant	8,400	
Environmental provision	18,000	(present value discounted at 8% per annum)

Required

(i) Prepare equivalent extracts from Shawler's statement of financial position as at 30 September 2012.

(3 marks)

(ii) Prepare extracts from Shawler's statement of profit or loss for the year ended 30 September 2012 relating to the items in the statement of financial position.

(3 marks)

(b) On 1 April 2012, the government introduced further environmental legislation which had the effect of requiring Shawler to fit anti-pollution filters to its furnace within two years. An environmental consultant has calculated that fitting the filters will reduce Shawler's required environmental costs (and therefore its provision) by 33%. At 30 September 2012 Shawler had not yet fitted the filters.

Required

Advise Shawler as to whether they need to provide for the cost of the filters as at 30 September 2012 and whether they should reduce the environmental provision at this date.

(4 marks)
(Total = 10 marks)

BPP
LEARNING MEDIA

Answers

DO NOT TURN THIS PAGE UNTIL YOU HAVE
COMPLETED THE MOCK EXAM

BPP
LEARNING MEDIA

A plan of attack

What's the worst thing you could be doing right now if this was the actual exam paper? Sharpening your pencil? Wondering how to celebrate the end of the exam in about 3 hours time? Panicking, flapping and generally getting in a right old state?

Well, they're all pretty bad, so turn back to the paper and let's sort out a **plan of attack**!

First things first

You have fifteen minutes of reading time. Spend this looking carefully through the questions and deciding the order in which you will attempt them. As a general rule you should attempt the questions that you find easiest first and leave the hardest until last.

This paper has five compulsory questions. Therefore, you do not have to spend your 15 minutes reading time working out which questions to answer. So you can use it to read the paper and get some idea of what you need to do. At this stage you can make notes on the question paper but not in the answer book. So scribble down anything you feel you might otherwise forget.

It's a good idea to just start with Question 1. Once you have the consolidation question done, you will feel more relaxed. Question 1 will have lots of information and you should read it a second time before you start. Get really clear about % shareholdings and dates on which they were acquired. Get the formats down and then proceed methodically with the workings.

Question 2 is a single company accounts preparation question. This question does not have a lot of complications – deferred income, property revaluation and a financial instrument – but it does require three financial statements. Set the formats out and then tackle the workings. Make it very clear to the marker which workings belong to which question and cross-reference them.

Question 3 is an interpretation question. Remember you do not get marks simply for commenting on a ratio, you must look at why it is up or down.

Question 4 is a discussion and scenario question on construction contracts. Make sure you leave time for the written parts.

Question 5 is on provisions. Read this question twice so you are clear about what's involved.

You've got spare time at the end of the exam.....?

If you have allocated your time properly then you **shouldn't have time on your hands** at the end of the exam. But if you find yourself with five or ten minutes to spare, check over your work to make sure that there are no silly arithmetical errors.

Forget about it!

And don't worry if you found the paper difficult. More than likely other candidates will too. If this were the real thing you would need to **forget** the exam the minute you leave the exam hall and **think about the next one**. Or, if it's the last one, **celebrate**!

Question 1 Viagem

Text references Chapters 9 and 10

Top tips Note that part (a) requires the goodwill at acquisition, not at the year end, so the impairment does not appear, although it will be deducted from the consolidated profit or loss. The subsidiary has been owned for 9 months so revenue and expenses must be apportioned in part (b).

Easy marks 7 marks for the goodwill calculation is quite generous. You just had to take care with the share exchange and the deferred consideration – remember to discount it. Part (b) had plenty of marks available and part (c) was easier than it looked. You only had to make four valid points to get full marks.

Examiner's answer The examiner's answer to this question is at the end of this Kit.

Marking scheme

	Marks
(a) Consolidated goodwill:	
Consideration – share exchange	1½
- deferred consideration	1½
Non-controlling interest	1
Net assets – share capital	½
- retained earnings	1
- fair value adjustments	1½
	7
(b) Consolidated statement of profit or loss:	
Revenue	2
Cost of sales	2½
Distribution costs	1
Administrative expenses	2
Share of profit of associate	1½
Finance costs	1½
Income tax	1
Profit for year – attributable to parent	½
- attributable to NCI	2
	14
(c) One mark per valid point	4
Total for question	25

(a) Consolidated goodwill at acquisition

	$'000	$'000
Consideration transferred:		
Shares (9m x 2/3 x $6.50)		39,000
Deferred consideration ((9m x $1.76) / 1.1)		14,400
		53,400
Non-controlling interest ((10m x $2.50) x 10%)		2,500
		55,900
Fair value of net assets:		
Share capital	10,000	
Retained earnings: b/f	35,000	
three months to 1 Jan 2012 (6,200 × 3/12)	1,550	
FVA on plant (W3)	1,800	
Contingent liability	(450)	
		(47,900)
Goodwill		8,000

(b) VIAGEM GROUP

CONSOLIDATED STATEMENT OF PROFIT OR LOSS FOR THE YEAR ENDED 30 SEPTEMBER 2012

	$'000
Revenue (64,600 + (38,000 × 9/12) − 7,200 (W2))	85,900
Cost of sales (51,200 + (26,000 × 9/12) − 7,200 + 300 (W2) + 450 (W3))	(64,250)
Gross profit	21,650
Distribution costs (1,600 + (1,800 × 9/12))	(2,950)
Administrative expenses (3,800 + (2,400 × 9/12) + 2,000 (goodwill impairment))	(7,600)
Finance costs (W4)	(1,500)
Share of profit of associate (2,000 × 40%)	800
Profit before tax	10,400
Income tax expense (2,800 + (1,600 × 9/12))	(4,000)
Profit for the year	6,400
Profit attributable to	
Owners of the parent (ß)	6,180
Non-controlling interest (W5)	220
	6,400

Workings

1 *Group structure*

      Viagem

1 Jan 2012   ↓   90%   Mid-year acquisition, 9 months before year end.

      Greca

2 *Intragroup trading*

	$'000	$'000
Intragroup trading (800 × 9 months)		
DEBIT Revenue	7,200	
CREDIT Cost of sales		7,200
PURP (1,500 × 25/125)		
DEBIT Cost of sales	300	
CREDIT Group inventory (SFP)		300

3 Fair value adjustment

	Acquisition $'000	Movement $'000	Year end $'000
Plant	1,800	(450)*	1,350

* (1,800/3) × 9/12

4 Finance costs

	$'000
Viagem per statement of profit or loss	420
Unwinding of discount on deferred consideration:	
((14,400 × 10%) x 9/12)	1,080
	1,500

5 Non-controlling interest

	$'000
Profit for the year (6,200 × 9/12)	4,650
Depreciation on fair value adjustment (W3)	(450)
Goodwill impairment	(2,000)
	2,200
Non-controlling share 10%	220

(c)   Property held under a lease by a subsidiary is treated as an **asset of the entity**. A fair value increase at acquisition (assuming it has not been accounted for by the subsidiary) will be added to the fair value of net assets acquired, which will have the effect of **reducing goodwill at acquisition**. In the consolidated financial statements the amount of the fair value uplift will be added to group property plant and equipment, less additional depreciation on the uplift, which will be calculated over the remaining useful life of the property at the date of the fair value exercise.

If the group policy is to apply the revaluation model under IAS 16 *Property, plant and equipment*, then a post-acquisition increase in the value of the subsidiary's property will be added to group property, plant and equipment and to the revaluation surplus and will be shown as 'other comprehensive income'. **Additional depreciation** will be accounted for on the surplus. The non-controlling interest share of the increase in value less the additional depreciation will be shown in the non-controlling interest's equity in the statement of financial position and the non-controlling interest's share of the additional depreciation will be **deducted from the profit attributed to the non-controlling interest** in the statement of profit or loss.

Question 2 Quincy

Text references Chapters 3, 4 and 14

Top tips As so often seems to be the case with Question 2, this is quite a time-pressured question so you need to work fast. Get the proformas down for all three statements and then go methodically through the workings, filling in the proformas as you go.

Easy marks There are some marks available for figures that can be lifted straight from the question and a good, clear PPE working will enable you to fill in several gaps.

Examiner's answer The examiner's answer to this question is at the end of this kit.

BPP
LEARNING MEDIA

Marks

(a) Consolidated statement: of profit or loss and other comprehensive income

Revenue	1½	
Cost of sales	2	
Investment income	½	
Distribution costs	½	
Administrative expenses	1	
Loss on investments	1	
Finance costs	1½	
Income tax	2	
Gain on revaluation of land and buildings	1	11

(b) Statement of changes in equity

Balances b/f	1	
Total comprehensive income	1	
Dividend paid	1	
Transfer to retained earnings	1	4

(c) Statement of financial position

Property, plant and equipment	2½	
Equity investments	1	
Inventory	½	
Trade receivables	½	
Bank	½	
Deferred tax	1	
Deferred revenue	1	
6% loan note	1½	
Trade payables	½	
Current tax payable	1	10
Total for question		25

(a) QUINCY

STATEMENT OF PROFIT OR LOSS AND OTHER COMPREHENSIVE INCOME FOR THE YEAR ENDED 30 SEPTEMBER 2012

	$'000
Revenue (213,500 – 1,600 (W3))	211,900
Cost of sales (W1)	(147,300)
Gross profit	64,600
Investment income	400
Distribution costs	(12,500)
Administrative expenses (W1)	(18,000)
Loss on fair value of equity investments (17,000 – 15,700)	(1,300)
Finance costs (20,700 – 19,200 (SCE) + 420(W4))	(1,920)
Profit before tax	31,280
Income tax expense (1,100 – 200 (W5) + 7,400)	(8,300)
Profit for the year	22,980
Other comprehensive income	
Revaluation gain on property (W2)	18,000
Total comprehensive income for the year	40,980

(b) QUINCY

STATEMENT OF CHANGES IN EQUITY FOR THE YEAR ENDED 30 SEPTEMBER 2012

	Share capital $'000	Retained earnings $'000	Revaluation surplus $'000	Total $'000
B/f 1 October 2011	60,000	18,500	-	78,500
Dividend paid (60m × 4 × 0.08)	-	(19,200)	-	(19,200)
Total comprehensive income	-	22,980	18,000	40,980
Transfer to retained earnings (W2)	-	1,000	(1,000)	-
Balance at 30 September 2012	60,000	23,280	17,000	100,280

(c) QUINCY

STATEMENT OF FINANCIAL POSITION AS AT 30 SEPTEMBER 2012

ASSETS	$'000
Non-current assets	
Property, plant and equipment (W3)	99,500
Equity financial asset investment	15,700
	115,200
Current assets	
Inventory	24,800
Trade receivables	28,500
Cash	2,900
	56,200
Total assets	171,400

EQUITY AND LIABILITIES	
Equity	
Share capital	60,000
Revaluation surplus (part (b))	17,000
Retained earnings (part (b))	23,280
	100,280
Non-current liabilities	
Deferred tax (W5)	1,000
Loan note (W4)	24,420
Deferred income (W3)	800
	26,220
Current liabilities	
Trade payables	36,700
Income tax	7,400
Deferred income (W3)	800
	44,900
Total equity and liabilities	171,400

Workings

1 Expenses

	Cost of sales $'000	Distribution costs $'000	Admin expenses $'000
Per question	136,800	12,500	19,000
Issue costs on loan note (W4)	-	-	(1,000)
Depreciation (W2)	10,500	-	-
	147,300	12,500	18,000

BPP
LEARNING MEDIA

2 Property, plant and equipment

	Land $'000	Buildings $'000	Plant $'000	Total $'000
Cost	10,000	40,000	83,700	133,700
Accumulated depreciation	-	(8,000)	(33,700)	(41,700)
	10,000	32,000	50,000	92,000
Revaluation gain	2,000	16,000	-	18,000
	12,000	48,000	50,000	110,000
Depreciation:				
(48,000 / 16)	-	(3,000)*	-	(3,000)
(50,000 × 15%)	-	-	(7,500)	(7,500)
	12,000	45,000	42,500	99,500

Note

*If no revaluation had taken place the depreciation on the building would have been $2m (32/16 years). Therefore the additional depreciation, which represents the realisation of the revaluation surplus, is $1m and this is transferred back to retained earnings.

3 Deferred income

	$'000	$'000
Two years' maintenance at 'selling price' ((600 × 100/75) × 2)		
DEBIT Revenue	1,600	
CREDIT Deferred income		1,600

The deferred income will be split between non-current and current liabilities.

4 Loan note

	$'000
Proceeds (25,000 – 1,000 (W1))	24,000
Interest at effective interest rate (8%)	1,920
Interest paid at nominal interest rate (6%)	(1,500)
Liability at 30 September 2012	24,420

5 Deferred tax

	$'000
Balance at 30 September 2012 (5,000 × 20%)	1,000
Balance at 30 September 2011	1,200
Reduction in provision – credit to profit or loss	200

Question 3 Quartile

Text references Chapters 19 and 20

Top tips A bit of planning is useful for a question like this and the categories of profitability, liquidity and gearing give you a structure around which to base your analysis. Note that this is a retail business, so this will affect the ratios.

Easy marks Calculation of the ratios is straightforward for nine marks and some useful points on the limitations on usefulness of a sector average comparison could have earned four marks.

Examiner's answer The examiner's answer to this question is at the end of this Kit.

Marks

(a) Ratios:
 ROCE 2 marks, all others 1 mark — 9
(b) 1 mark per valid comment — 12
(c) 1 mark per issue — 4
 Total for question — 25

(a) **Equivalent ratios for Quartile**

	Quartile	Sector average
ROCE (4,200 / (26,600 + 8,000))	12.1%	16.8%
Net asset turnover (56,000 / 34,600)	1.6 times	1.4 times
Gross profit margin (14,000 / 56,000)%	25%	35%
Operating profit margin ((14,000 – 9,800)/ 56,000))%	7.5%	12%
Current ratio (11,200 / 7,200)	1.55:1	1.25:1
Average inventory turnover (42,000 / 9,250)	4.5 times	3 times
Trade payables days ((5,400 / 43,900) x 365)	45 days	64 days
Debt to equity (8,000 / 26,600) %	30%	38%

(b) **Analysis of financial and operating performance of Quartile compared to sector average**

Profitability

Quartile has a **ROCE significantly lower** at 12.1% than the sector average of 16.8%. This is mainly due to the lower than average gross profit margin and consequent **low operating profit margin**. The operating expenses are actually lower (17.5%) as a percentage of revenue than the sector average of 23% (35% - 12%) so the problem lies between revenue and cost of sales. Inventory turnover is quite brisk (4.5 times compared to a sector average of 3 times) but Quartile's mark-up of 33.3% ((25 / 75) × 100) is significantly below the sector average of 54% (35 / 65) × 100). Quartile is **maintaining turnover by keeping prices down**.

The other component of ROCE, net asset turnover, is slightly higher than the sector average. This is due to the buoyant turnover, as the ratio will have been depressed by the property revaluation and the capitalisation of the development expenditure, which have increased the asset base. It is to be hoped that the development expenditure will generate the expected revenue. If it had been necessary to expense it for the year ended 30 September 2012 Quartile would have reported a loss before tax of $1.6m.

Liquidity

Quartile has a current ratio of 1.55:1 compared to the sector average of 1.25:1. Both appear low, but satisfactory for the retail sector as the cash cycle is fairly rapid. Inventory can be turned into immediate cash and this is particularly true for Quartile with its high inventory turnover level. The lower than average payables days (45 compared to 64) and the absence of an overdraft suggest that **Quartile is not suffering liquidity problems**.

Gearing

Quartile's debt to equity ratio is 30%, well below the sector average of 38% and the interest rate on the loan notes is below the ROCE of 12.1%, meaning that the **borrowings are earning a good return** for the business. The interest cover of 5.25 times (4,200 / 800) is satisfactory. Quartile is not having any problems servicing its loan and is unlikely to give lenders any particular concern,

Conclusion

There are no going concern worries for Quartile but it does have an issue with **low profitability**. It appears to be positioned at the bottom end of the jewellery market selling high volume cheap items rather than more valuable

pieces on which there would be significantly higher profit margins. This may or may not be the most advantageous strategy in a period of recession.

(c) The following factors may limit the usefulness of comparisons based on business sector averages:

(i) The companies included in the average may have used different accounting policies. Some may be applying the revaluation basis to their assets and some may not. This will affect asset turnover and ROCE.

(ii) Some companies in the average may have used some form of creative accounting, such as sale and leaseback transactions, which will have boosted both profit for the year and ROCE.

(iii) The average may include a wide variety of entities with different trading methods and risk profiles. Very high-end jewellers may even operate on an invoice rather than a cash basis and will have receivables included in their current assets. Very large chains will probably have more access to cheap borrowing.

(iv) Some ratios, in particular ROCE and gearing, can be calculated in different ways. It is up to the organisation carrying out the comparison to ensure that a standard definition is used, and they may or may not do this.

Question 4 Lobden

Text references Chapters 1 and 12

Top tips Note that more than half of the marks in this question are available for written parts of the answer, so don't spend all the time on the numbers. Remember that construction contracts are accounted for on a cumulative basis and that, as this is a change in accounting estimate, no retrospective restatement is required.

Easy marks The calculations here were straightforward and there were plenty of marks available for the discussion in part (a).

Examiner's answer The examiner's answer to this question is at the end of this Kit.

Marking scheme

		Marks
(a) 1 mark per valid point: understandability	2	
comparability	4	
		6
(b)(i) Revenue	2	
Cost of sales	½	
Recognised profit	2	
Amount due from customers	2	
Contract receivables	½	
		7
(b)(ii) Discussion	1	
Conclusion	1	2
Total for question		15

(a) **Understandability**

Financial information is intended to **assist users in making economic decisions**. For this purpose it is important that financial information is presented in a form which users can understand. However, this does not mean that complex matters which some users may find difficult to understand, and which some **directors may like an excuse to exclude**, should be left out of financial statements. Reports from which data has been excluded could be incomplete and misleading. The *Conceptual Framework* states that users can be assumed to have reasonable knowledge of business and economic activities and be prepared to review and analyse the information diligently.

Comparability

In understanding the financial performance of an entity, users will want to compare its results with those of **other entities in the same sector** and with its own results for previous periods. The concept of comparability is therefore very important. Comparison between entities is made more possible by IFRSs in which most allowed alternatives have been removed and by the requirement to disclose accounting policies. So if two entities have applied different accounting policies users can be aware of that and allow for it.

Comparing an entity's results with its performance in prior years requires the application of consistency. An entity should treat financial items and transactions in a consistent manner from year to year, by applying the same accounting policies. Where there is a change of accounting policy from one year to the next, the comparative information must be restated to show what the results for the previous year would have been if the new accounting policy had been applied. The statement of changes in equity also shows the effect on the previous year's equity balances of the change of accounting policy. The user is therefore able to adjust for the change of accounting policy and observe the changes in underlying performance.

(b) (i) Based on value of work certified, the contract is 64% complete ((160 / 250) x 100) at 30 September 2012. Extracts are:

STATEMENT OF PROFIT OR LOSS

	$ million
Revenue ((250 × 64%) − 100)	60
Cost of sales ((200 × 64%) − 80)	(48)
Profit ((50 × 64%) − 20)	12

STATEMENT OF FINANCIAL POSITION

	$ million
Current assets	
Amounts due from customers	
Contract costs to date	145
Profit recognised (50 × 64%)	32
	177
Progress billings	(160)
	17
Contract receivables (160 − 150)	10

(b) (ii) Accounting policies are the **rules, principles and practices** adopted by an entity in preparing its financial statements. They should be **based upon IFRSs** or other financial reporting standards.

Accounting estimates are the **measurements and valuations** arrived at by an entity in applying accounting policies to specific items and transactions.

In the case of Lobden, the accounting policy is in accordance with IAS 11 *Construction contracts*. Revenue and costs are recognised according to the **stage of completion** of the contract. Lobden's current means of estimating the stage of completion is based on proportion of cost to date to total cost.

Although the question refers to it as Lobden's 'current policy', this is an **accounting estimate**, because it is Lobden's method of applying the accounting policy. A different measurement basis, based on the same accounting policy, is to estimate stage of completion based on the value of work certified. In transferring from one to the other, Lobden is making a **change of accounting estimate**.

BPP
LEARNING MEDIA

Question 5 Shawler

Text references Chapters 4 and 13

Top tips The issues here are the complex asset, the government grant and the environmental provision and it is important not to get them mixed up. Read the question carefully and make a note of the dates.

Easy marks Part (a) was very straightforward, up to six marks for very simple calculations. Part (b) was a bit more challenging, but you should have been able to make enough points for two marks.

Examiner's answer The examiner's answer to this question is at the end of this Kit.

Marking scheme

		Marks
(a) (i) Furnace	1	
Government grant (½ for split)	1	
Environmental provision	<u>1</u>	
		3
(ii) Depreciation	1	
Government grant (credit)	1	
Finance costs	<u>1</u>	
		3
(b) Not an obligating event as legislation not yet in force	1	
Need not provide for filters even when it is in force	1	
May need separate provision for a fine	1	
Cannot reduce the environmental provision	<u>1</u>	
		<u>4</u>
Total for question		<u>10</u>

(a)(i) STATEMENT OF FINANCIAL POSITION EXTRACTS 30 SEPTEMBER 2012

	Carrying amount
	$
Non-current assets	
Furnace: main body (48,000 × 7/8)	42,000
liner (6,000 – 2,000)	4,000
Non-current liabilities	
Government grant (8,400 – 1,200)	7,200
Environmental provision (18,000 × 1.08)	19,440
Current liabilities	
Government grant	1,200

(ii) STATEMENT OF PROFIT OR LOSS EXTRACTS

	$	$
Income: government grant		1,200
Depreciation: furnace/ main body	6,000	
furnace/ liner	<u>2,000</u>	
		(8,000)
Unwinding of discount on provision (19,440 – 18,000)		(1,440)

(b) **No provision** should be made for the filters at this point in time because the **legislation does not come into force for two years**. When Shawler fits the anti-pollution filters, they should be capitalised and depreciated over their useful life. At that point the existing environmental provision should be reviewed, but not before.

It may be expected that a provision will be required in two years time to cover the fitting of the filters. However IAS 37 states that where an entity needs to carry out expenditure in order to operate in a particular way in the future, that expenditure could be avoided by **changing its method of operation**, so **no provision is recognised**. In the case of Shawler, it could be said that it could find some other way of reducing its pollution. If the legislation comes into force without Shawler having fitted the filters, it may recognise a provision for any fines payable.

BPP
LEARNING MEDIA

ACCA examiner's answers:
June and December 2012 papers

BPP
LEARNING MEDIA

1   (a)   Pyramid – Consolidated statement of financial position as at 31 March 2012

	$'000	$'000
Assets		
Non-current assets:		
Property, plant and equipment (38,100 + 28,500 + 3,000 fair value – 600 depreciation)		69,000
Goodwill (w (i))		7,400
Investments – associate (w (ii))	6,600	
– fair value equity investments	2,800	9,400
		85,800
Current assets		
Inventory (13,900 + 10,400 + 1,500 GIT – 500 URP (w (iii)))	25,300	
Trade receivables (11,400 + 5,500 – 1,200 CIT – 3,200 intra group (w (iii)))	12,500	
Bank (900 + 600 + 1,200 CIT (w (iii)))	2,700	40,500
Total assets		126,300
Equity and liabilities		
Equity attributable to owners of the parent		
Equity shares of $1 each		25,000
Reserves:		
Share premium	17,600	
Retained earnings (w (iv))	36,380	53,980
		78,980
Non-controlling interest (w (v))		8,480
Total equity		87,460
Non-current liabilities		
11% loan notes (12,000 + 4,000 – 2,500 intra-group)	13,500	
Deferred tax (4,500 + 1,000)	5,500	19,000
Current liabilities		
Deferred consideration (6,400 + 640 unwinding of discount (w (iv)))	7,040	
Other current liabilities (9,500 + 5,000 + 1,500 GIT – 3,200 intra group (w (iii)))	12,800	19,840
Total equity and liabilities		126,300

Workings (figures in brackets are in $'000)

(i)   Goodwill in Square

	$'000	$'000
Controlling interest		
Share exchange		24,000
Deferred consideration (10,000 x 80% x 0·88/1·1)		6,400
Non-controlling interest (10,000 x 20% x $3·50)		7,000
		37,400
Equity shares	10,000	
Pre-acquisition reserves	18,000	
Fair value adjustments – plant	3,000	
– unrecorded deferred tax	(1,000)	(30,000)
Goodwill arising on acquisition		7,400

(ii)   Carrying amount of Cube at 31 March 2012

	$'000
Cost	6,000
Share post-acquisition profit (2,000 x 30%)	600
	6,600

(iii) Reconciliation of current accounts

	Pyramid $'000	Square $'000
Current account balances per question to eliminate	4,400	1,700
Goods-in-transit (GIT) (16,000 – 14,500)		1,500
Cash-in-transit (CIT) (balance required to reconcile)	(1,200)	
	3,200	3,200

The goods-in-transit sale of $1·5 million includes unrealised profit (URP) of $500,000 (1,500 x 50/150).

(iv) Consolidated retained earnings:

	$'000
Pyramid's retained earnings (16,200 + 14,000)	30,200
Square's post-acquisition profit (7,400 see below x 80%)	5,920
Cube's post-acquisition profit (2,000 x 30%)	600
Interest on deferred consideration (6,400 x 10%)	(640)
URP in inventory (w (iii))	(500)
Gain on equity investments (2,800 – 2,000)	800
	36,380

The adjusted post-acquisition profits of Square are:

	$'000
As reported	8,000
Additional depreciation on plant (3,000/5 years)	(600)
	7,400

(v) Non-controlling interest

	$'000
Fair value on acquisition (w (i))	7,000
Post-acquisition profit (7,400 x 20% (w (iv)))	1,480
	8,480

2 (a) (i) Fresco – Statement of comprehensive income for the year ended 31 March 2012

	$'000
Revenue	350,000
Cost of sales (w (i))	(311,000)
Gross profit	39,000
Distribution costs	(16,100)
Administrative expenses (26,900 + 3,000 re fraud)	(29,900)
Finance costs (300 + 2,300 (w (ii)))	(2,600)
Loss before tax	(9,600)
Income tax relief (2,400 + 200 (w (iii)) – 800)	1,800
Loss for the year	(7,800)
Other comprehensive income	
Revaluation of leased property (w (ii))	4,000
Total comprehensive losses	(3,800)

(ii) Fresco – Statement of changes in equity for the year ended 31 March 2012

	Share capital $'000	Share premium $'000	Revaluation reserve $'000	Retained earnings $'000	Total equity $'000
Balances at 1 April 2011	45,000	5,000	nil	5,100	55,100
Prior period adjustment (re fraud)				(1,000)	(1,000)
Restated balance				4,100	
Rights share issue (see below)	9,000	4,500			13,500
Total comprehensive losses (see (i) above)			4,000	(7,800)	(3,800)
Transfer to retained earnings			(500)	500	
Balances at 31 March 2012	54,000	9,500	3,500	(3,200)	63,800

BPP LEARNING MEDIA

The rights issue was 18 million shares (45,000/50 cents each x 1/5) at 75 cents = $13·5 million. This equates to the balance on the suspense account. This should be recorded as $9 million equity shares (18,000 x 50 cents) and $4·5 million share premium (18,000 x (75 cents – 50 cents)).

The discovery of the fraud represents an error part of which is a prior period adjustment ($1 million) in accordance with IAS 8 *Accounting policies, changes in accounting estimates and errors*.

(iii) Fresco – Statement of financial position as at 31 March 2012

	$'000	$'000
Assets		
Non-current assets		
Property, plant and equipment (w (ii))		62,700
Current assets		
Inventory	25,200	
Trade receivables (28,500 – 4,000 re fraud)	24,500	
Current tax refund	2,400	52,100
Total assets		114,800
Equity and liabilities		
Equity (see (ii) above)		
Equity shares of 50 cents each		54,000
Reserves		
Share premium	9,500	
Revaluation	3,500	
Retained earnings	(3,200)	9,800
		63,800
Non-current liabilities		
Finance lease obligation (w (ii))	15,230	
Deferred tax (w (iii))	3,000	18,230
Current liabilities		
Trade payables	27,300	
Finance lease obligation (19,300 – 15,230 (w (ii)))	4,070	
Bank overdraft	1,400	32,770
Total equity and liabilities		114,800

(b) Fresco – Basic earnings per share for the year ended 31 March 2012

Loss per statement of comprehensive income	$7·8 million
Weighted average number of shares (w (iv))	99 million
Loss per share	7·9 cents

Workings (figures in brackets are in $'000)

	$'000
(i) Cost of sales	
Per question	298,700
Amortisation of – leased property (w (ii))	4,500
Amortisation of – leased plant (w (ii))	5,000
Depreciation of other plant and equipment ((47,500 – 33,500) x 20%)	2,800
	311,000
(ii) Non-current assets	
Carrying amount 1 April 2011 (48,000 – 16,000)	32,000
Revaluation reserve	4,000
Revalued amount 1 April 2011	36,000
Amortisation year to 31 March 2012 (over 8 years)	(4,500)
Carrying amount 31 March 2012	31,500

$500,000 (4,000/8 years) of the revaluation surplus will be transferred to retained earnings (reported in the statement of changes in equity).

BPP
LEARNING MEDIA

Leased plant:

Fair value 1 April 2011	25,000
Deposit	(2,000)
	23,000
Interest at 10%	2,300
Payment 31 March 2012	(6,000)
Lease obligation 31 March 2012	19,300
Interest at 10%	1,930
Payment 31 March 2013	(6,000)
Lease obligation 31 March 2013	15,230

Amortisation for the leased plant for the year ended 31 March 2012 is $5 million (25,000/5 years).

Summarising the carrying amount of property, plant and equipment as at 31 March 2012:

Leased property	31,500
Owned plant (47,500 – 33,500 – 2,800)	11,200
Leased plant (25,000 – 5,000)	20,000
	62,700

(iii) Deferred tax

Provision required at 31 March 2012 (12,000 x 25%)	3,000
Provision at 1 April 2011	(3,200)
Credit (reduction in provision) to income statement	200

(iv) Theoretical ex-rights value:

	Shares	$	$
Holding (say)	100	1·20	120
Rights taken up	20	0·75	15
	120		135

Theoretical ex-rights value   1·125 ($135/120 shares)

Weighted average number of shares:

1 April 2011 to 31 December 2011	90 million x 1·20/1·125 x 9/12 =	72 million
1 January 2012 to 31 March 2012	108 million x 3/12 =	27 million
Weighted average for the year		99 million

3 (a) Tangier – Statement of cash flows for the year ended 31 March 2012

(Note: figures in brackets are in $ million)

	$ m	$ m
Cash flows from operating activities:		
Profit before tax		195
Adjustments for:		
Depreciation/amortisation of non-current assets		140
Finance costs		40
Increase in inventory (200 – 110)		(90)
Increase in trade receivables (195 – 75)		(120)
Increase in trade payables (210 – 160)		50
Cash generated from operations		215
Interest paid		(40)
Income tax paid (w (i))		(90)
Net cash from operating activities		85
Cash flows from investing activities:		
Purchase of property, plant and equipment (w (ii))	(305)	
Purchase of intangibles (300 – 200 + 25)	(125)	
Purchase of investment	(230)	
Net cash used in investing activities		(660)
Cash flows from financing activities:		
Shares issued (350 – 250)	100	
Issue of 10% loan notes	300	
Equity dividends paid (w (iii))	(55)	
Net cash from financing activities		345
Net decrease in cash and cash equivalents		(230)
Cash and cash equivalents at beginning of period		120
Cash and cash equivalents at end of period		(110)

Workings

	$ m
(i) Income tax	
Provision b/f	(110)
Income statement charge	(60)
Tax paid (= balance)	90
Provision c/f	80
(ii) Property, plant and equipment	
Balance b/f	(410)
Depreciation	115
Revaluation	(80)
Acquired during year (= balance)	(305)
Balance c/f	680
(iii) Equity dividends	
Retained earnings b/f	295
Profit for the year	135
Dividends paid (= balance)	(55)
Retained earnings c/f	375

(b) Note: references to '2012' are in respect of the year ended 31 March 2012 and '2011' to the year ended 31 March 2011.

Despite an increase in revenue of 48·4% (880/1,820 x 100) in 2012, the company suffered a dramatic fall in its profitability. This has been caused by a combination of a falling gross profit margin (from 40% in 2011 to only 30% in 2012) and markedly higher operating overheads. An eight-fold increase in finance costs, caused by the increased borrowing at double the interest rate of existing borrowing and some bank overdraft interest, has led to profit before tax more than halving.

This is reflected in the ROCE falling from an impressive 61·7% in 2011 to only 19·5% in 2012 (though even this figure is respectable). The fall in the ROCE is attributable to a dramatic fall in profit margin at the operating level (from 21·9% in 2011 to only 8·7% in 2012) which has been compounded by a reduction in the non-current asset turnover, with only $2·23 being generated from every $1 invested in non-current assets in 2012 (from $2·98 in 2011).

BPP LEARNING MEDIA

The information in the question points strongly to the possibility (even probability) that the new contract may be responsible for much of the deterioration in Tangier's performance. It is likely that the new contract may account for the increased revenue; however, the bidding process was 'competitive' which implies that Tangier had to cut its price (and therefore its profit margin) in order to win the contract.

The costs of fulfilling the contract have also been heavy:

Investment in property, plant and equipment has increased by $270 million (at carrying amount) representing an increase of 66% (though this increase would be 46% on a comparative basis if carrying amounts in 2012 were adjusted for the effect of the property revaluation of $80 million (ignoring its depreciation)).

The licence to manufacture the new engines has cost $125 million (allowing for amortisation as shown in the statement of cash flows).

The investment in Raremetal to secure materials supplies has cost $230 million. There has been no benefit in 2012 from this investment in terms of dividends or capital growth. It is impossible to quantify the benefit of securing material supplies, which was the main reason for the investment, but it has come at a high cost. It is also questionable how the investment has 'secured' the provision of materials as an 8% equity investment does not normally give any meaningful influence over the investee. An alternative (less expensive) strategy might have been to enter into a long-term supply contract with Raremetal.

The finance cost of the additional loan to partly fund the investment in non-current assets has also reduced reported profit and increased debt/equity (one form of gearing measure) from 18·3% in 2011 to 49·7% in 2012. At this level, particularly in view of the large increase from 2011, it may give debt holders (and others) cause for concern. If it could be demonstrated that the overdraft could not be cleared for some time, this would be an argument for including it in the calculation of debt/equity, making the gearing level even worse.

It could be speculated that the 73% increase in administrative expenses may be due to one-off costs associated with the tendering process (consultancy fees, management time, etc) and the 77% increase in distribution costs could be due to additional freight/packing/insurance costs of the engines and delivery distances may also be longer (even abroad).

All of this seems to indicate that the new contact has been very detrimental to Tangier's performance, but more information is needed to be sure. The contract was not signed until June 2011 and there is no information of when production/sales started, but clearly there has not been a full year's revenue from the contract. Also there is no information on how long (or what total value) the contract is for. Unless the contract is for a considerable time, the increased investment in operating assets represents a considerable risk. There are no figures for the separate revenues and costs of the contract, but from 2012's declining performance it does not seem profitable, thus even if the contract does secure work for several years, it is of doubtful benefit if the work is loss-making. An alternative scenario could be that the early costs associated with the contract are part of a 'learning curve' and that future production will be more efficient and therefore the contract may become profitable as a result.

Salient ratios

	2012	2011
Gross profit margin (810/2,700 x 100)	30·0%	40·0%
Profit margin before interest (235/2,700 x 100)	8·7%	21·9%
ROCE (235/(805 + 400))	19·5%	61·7%
Non-current asset turnover (2,700/1,210)	2·23 times	2·98 times
Debt/equity (400/805)	49·7%	18·3%

Tutorial note:
The workings for the 2012 ratio calculations are shown, the ratios for 2011 are calculated equivalently. Alternative ratio calculations and ratios would be acceptable. For example, ROCE and non-current asset turnover for 2012 could exclude the effect of the property revaluation and/or include the bank overdraft as long-term finance. Net asset turnover (revenue/capital employed) and gearing (debt/capital employed) could be given as alternatives.

4 (a) An impairment review is the procedure required by IAS 36 *Impairment of assets* to determine if and by how much an asset may have been impaired. An asset is impaired if its carrying amount is greater than its recoverable amount. In turn the recoverable amount of an asset is defined as the higher of its fair value less costs to sell or its value in use, calculated as the present values of the future net cash flows the asset will generate.

The problem in applying this definition is that assets rarely generate cash flows in isolation; most assets generate cash flows in combination with other assets. IAS 36 introduces the concept of a cash generating unit (CGU) which is the smallest identifiable group of assets that generate cash inflows that are (largely) independent of other assets. Where an asset forms part of a CGU any impairment review must be made on the group of assets as a whole. If impairment losses are then identified, they must be allocated and/or apportioned to the assets of the CGU as prescribed by IAS 36.

(b) (i) The carrying amount of the plant at 31 March 2012, before the impairment review, is $500,000 (800,000 – (150,000 x 2)) where $150,000 is the annual depreciation charge ((800,000 cost – 50,000 residual value)/5 years).

This needs to be compared with the recoverable amount of the plant which must be its value in use as it has no market value at this date.

Value in use:

year ended:		Cash flow $'000	Discount factor at 10%	Present value $'000
	31 March 2013	220	0·91	200
	31 March 2014	180	0·83	149
	31 March 2015	170 + 50	0·75	165
				514

At 31 March 2012, the plant's value in use of $514,000 is greater than its carrying amount of $500,000. This means the plant is not impaired and it should continue to be carried at $500,000.

(ii)

	Per question $'000	Plant write off $'000		Impairment losses $'000
Goodwill	1,800	1,800	write off in full	nil
Patent	1,200	1,200	at realisable value	1,000
Factory	4,000	4,000	pro rata loss of 40%	2,400
Plant	3,500	3,000	pro rata loss of 40%	1,800
Receivables and cash	1,500	1,500	realisable value	1,500
	12,000	11,500	value in use	6,700

The plant with a carrying amount of $500,000 that has been damaged to the point of no further use should be written off (it no longer meets the definition of an asset). The carrying amounts in the second column above are after writing off this plant.

After this, firstly, goodwill is written off in full.

Secondly, any remaining impairment loss should write off the remaining assets pro rata to their carrying amounts, except that no asset should be written down to less than its fair value less costs to sell (net realisable value).

After writing off the damaged plant the remaining impairment loss is $4·8 million (11·5m – 6·7m) of which $1·8 million is applied to the goodwill, $200,000 to the patent (taking it to its realisable value) and the remaining $2·8 million is apportioned pro rata at 40% (2·8m/(4m + 3m)) to the factory and the remaining plant.

The carrying amounts of the assets of Tilda, at 31 March 2012 after the accident, are as shown in the third column above.

5   (a)   A rules-based accounting system is likely to be very descriptive and is generally considered to be a system which relies on a series of detailed rules or accounting requirements that prescribe how financial statements should be prepared. Such a system is considered less flexible, but often more comparable and consistent, than a principles-based system. Some would argue that rules-based systems can lead to looking for 'loopholes'. By contrast, a principles-based system relies on generally accepted accounting principles that are conceptually based and are normally underpinned by a set of key objectives. They are more flexible than a rules-based system, but they do require judgement and interpretation which could lead to inconsistencies between reporting entities and can sometimes lead to the manipulation of financial statements.

Because IFRSs are based on *The Conceptual Framework for Financial Reporting*, they are often regarded as being a principles-based system. Of course IFRSs do contain many rules and requirements (often lengthy and complex), but their critical feature is that IFRS 'rules' are based on underlying concepts. In reality most accounting systems have an element of both rules and principles and their designation as rules-based or principles-based depends on the relative importance and robustness of the principles compared to the volume and manner in which the rules are derived.

(b)   There are several aspects of Baxen's business strategy where adopting IFRS would be advantageous.

It is unclear how sophisticated or developed the 'local' standards which it currently uses are, however, it is widely accepted that IFRS are a set of high quality and transparent global standards that are intended to achieve consistency and comparability across the world. They have been produced in co-operation with other internationally renowned standard setters, with the aspiration of achieving consensus and global convergence. Thus if Baxen does adopt IFRS it is likely that its status and reputation (for example, an improved credit rating) in the eyes of other entities would be enhanced.

Other more specific advantages might be:

Its own financial statements would be comparable with other companies that use IFRS. This would help the company to better assess and rank prospective investments in its foreign trading partners.

Should Baxen acquire (as a subsidiary) any foreign companies, it would make the task of consolidation much simpler as there would be no need to reconcile its foreign subsidiary's financial statements to the local generally accepted accounting principles (GAAP) that Baxen currently uses. The use of IFRSs may make the audit fee less expensive.

If Baxen needs to raise finance in the future (highly likely because of its ambitions), it will find it easier to get a listing on any security exchange that is a member of the International Organisation of Securities Commissions (IOSCO) as they recognise IFRS for listing purposes. This flexibility to raise funding also means that Baxen's financing costs should be lower.

BPP
LEARNING MEDIA

1   (a) Viagem: Consolidated goodwill on acquisition of Greca as at 1 January 2012

	$'000	$'000
Investment at cost		
Shares (10,000 x 90% x 2/3 x $6·50)		39,000
Deferred consideration (9,000 x $1·76/1·1)		14,400
Non-controlling interest (10,000 x 10% x $2·50)		2,500
		55,900
Net assets (based on equity) of Greca as at 1 January 2012		
Equity shares	10,000	
Retained earnings b/f at 1 October 2011	35,000	
Earnings 1 October 2011 to acquisition (6,200 x 3/12)	1,550	
Fair value adjustments: plant	1,800	
contingent liability recognised	(450)	
Net assets at date of acquisition		(47,900)
Consolidated goodwill		8,000

(b) Viagem: Consolidated income statement for the year ended 30 September 2012

	$'000
Revenue (64,600 + (38,000 x 9/12) – 7,200 intra-group sales)	85,900
Cost of sales (working)	(64,250)
Gross profit	21,650
Distribution costs (1,600 + (1,800 x 9/12))	(2,950)
Administrative expenses (3,800 + (2,400 x 9/12) + 2,000 goodwill impairment)	(7,600)
Income from associate (2,000 x 40% based on underlying earnings)	800
Finance costs (420 + (14,400 x 10% x 9/12 re deferred consideration))	(1,500)
Profit before tax	10,400
Income tax expense (2,800 + (1,600 x 9/12))	(4,000)
Profit for the year	6,400
Profit for year attributable to:	
Equity holders of the parent	6,180
Non-controlling interest ((6,200 x 9/12) – 450 depreciation – 2,000 goodwill impairment) x 10%))	220
	6,400

Working in $'000

Cost of sales	
Viagem	51,200
Greca (26,000 x 9/12)	19,500
Intra-group purchases (800 x 9 months)	(7,200)
URP in inventory (1,500 x 25/125)	300
Additional depreciation (1,800/3 years x 9/12)	450
	64,250

(c) A fair value adjustment to the carrying amount of a subsidiary's leased property is usually required where the property has been carried at depreciated historical cost. If it is already carried at a revalued amount, this should be broadly equal to its fair value and no adjustment would normally be required. The pre-acquisition increase should be reflected in the consolidated statement of financial position by including the subsidiary's leased property at its fair value, with the corresponding effect being a fair value adjustment in the calculation of consolidated goodwill. The adjustment has the effect of reducing the amount of the purchase consideration that is allocated to goodwill. The fair value of the leased property need not be reflected in the subsidiary's own entity financial statements, although sometimes this is done to make future consolidation simpler.

Where there is a post-acquisition increase in the value of a subsidiary's leased property, this may or may not be reflected in the consolidated financial statements, depending upon whether the group has a policy of carrying such properties at revalued amounts (current values). If it does, then the increase would be included in 'other comprehensive income' and the non-controlling interest would be shown to have a share of this. The other effect would be that there is likely to be an adjustment in the income statement for additional amortisation based on the increase in value. In the statement of financial position, the group's share of the post-acquisition increase would be added to the group's property revaluation reserve and the non-controlling interest's share of it would be added to the non-controlling interest's part of equity.

2 (a) Quincy – Statement of comprehensive income for the year ended 30 September 2012

	$'000
Revenue (213,500 – 1,600 (w (i)))	211,900
Cost of sales (w (ii))	(147,300)
Gross profit	64,600
Distribution costs	(12,500)
Administrative expenses (19,000 – 1,000 loan issue costs (w (iv)))	(18,000)
Loss on fair value of equity investments (17,000 – 15,700)	(1,300)
Investment income	400
Finance costs (w (iv))	(1,920)
Profit before tax	31,280
Income tax expense (7,400 + 1,100 – 200 (w (v)))	(8,300)
Profit for the year	22,980
Other comprehensive income	
Gain on revaluation of land and buildings (w (iii))	18,000
Total comprehensive income	40,980

(b) Quincy – Statement of changes in equity for the year ended 30 September 2012

	Share capital $'000	Revaluation reserve $'000	Retained earnings $'000	Total equity $'000
Balance at 1 October 2011	60,000	nil	18,500	78,500
Total comprehensive income		18,000	22,980	40,980
Transfer to retained earnings (w (iii))		(1,000)	1,000	nil
Dividend paid (60,000 x 4 x 8 cents)			(19,200)	(19,200)
Balance at 30 September 2012	60,000	17,000	23,280	100,280

(c) Quincy – Statement of financial position as at 30 September 2012

Assets	$'000	$'000
Non-current assets		
Property, plant and equipment (57,000 + 42,500 (w (iii)))		99,500
Equity financial asset investments		15,700
		115,200
Current assets		
Inventory	24,800	
Trade receivables	28,500	
Bank	2,900	56,200
Total assets		171,400
Equity and liabilities		
Equity		
Equity shares of 25 cents each		60,000
Revaluation reserve	17,000	
Retained earnings	23,280	40,280
		100,280
Non-current liabilities		
Deferred tax (w (v))	1,000	
Deferred revenue (w (i))	800	
6% loan note (2014) (w (iv))	24,420	26,220
Current liabilities		
Trade payables	36,700	
Deferred revenue (w (i))	800	
Current tax payable	7,400	44,900
Total equity and liabilities		171,400

BPP
LEARNING MEDIA

Workings (figures in brackets in $'000)

(i) Sales made which include revenue for ongoing servicing work must have part of the revenue deferred. The deferred revenue must include the normal profit margin (25%) for the deferred work. At 30 September 2012, there are two more years of servicing work, thus $1·6 million ((600 x 2) x 100/75) must be treated as deferred revenue, split equally between current and non-current liabilities.

(ii) Cost of sales

	$'000
Per trial balance	136,800
Depreciation of building (w (iii))	3,000
Depreciation of plant (w (iii))	7,500
	147,300

(iii) Non-current assets

Land and buildings:

The gain on revaluation and carrying amount of the land and buildings is:

	Land $'000		Building $'000
Carrying amount as at 1 October 2011	10,000	(40,000 – 8,000)	32,000
Revalued amount as at this date	(12,000)	(60,000 – 12,000)	(48,000)
Gain on revaluation	2,000		16,000
Building depreciation year to 30 September 2012 (48,000/16 years)			3,000

The transfer from the revaluation reserve to retained earnings in respect of 'excess' depreciation (as the revaluation is realised) is $1 million (48,000 – 32,000)/16 years.

The carrying amount at 30 September 2012 is $57 million (60,000 – 3,000).

Plant and equipment:

	$'000
Carrying amount as at 1 October 2011 (83,700 – 33,700)	50,000
Depreciation at 15% per annum	(7,500)
Carrying amount as at 30 September 2012	42,500

(iv) Loan note

The finance cost of the loan note is charged at the effective rate of 8% applied to the carrying amount of the loan. The issue costs of the loan ($1 million) should be deducted from the proceeds of the loan ($25 million) and not treated as an administrative expense. This gives an initial carrying amount of $24 million and a finance cost of $1,920,000 (24,000 x 8%). The interest actually paid is $1·5 million (25,000 x 6%) and the difference between these amounts, of $420,000 (1,920 – 1,500), is accrued and added to the carrying amount of the loan note. This gives $24·42 million (24,000 + 420) for inclusion as a non-current liability in the statement of financial position.

Note: *The loan interest paid of $1·5 million plus the dividend paid of $19·2 million (see (b)) equals the $20·7 million shown in the trial balance for these items.*

(v) Deferred tax

	$'000
Provision required as at 30 September 2012 (5,000 x 20%)	1,000
Less provision b/f	(1,200)
Credit to income statement	200

3 (a) Below are the specified ratios for Quartile and (for comparison) those of the business sector average:

		Quartile	sector average
Return on year-end capital employed	((3,400 + 800)/(26,600 + 8,000) x 100)	12·1%	16·8%
Net asset turnover	(56,000/34,600)	1·6 times	1·4 times
Gross profit margin	(14,000/56,000 x 100)	25%	35%
Operating profit margin	(4,200/56,000 x 100)	7·5%	12%
Current ratio	(11,200:7,200)	1·6:1	1·25:1
Average inventory (8,300 + 10,200/2) = 9,250) turnover	(42,000/9,250)	4·5 times	3 times
Trade payables' payment period	(5,400/43,900 x 365)	45 days	64 days
Debt to equity	(8,000/26,600 x 100)	30%	38%

(b) Assessment of comparative performance

Profitability

The primary measure of profitability is the return on capital employed (ROCE) and this shows that Quartile's 12·1% is considerably underperforming the sector average of 16·8%. Measured as a percentage, this underperformance is 28% ((16·8 − 12·1)/16·8). The main cause of this seems to be a much lower gross profit margin (25% compared to 35%). A possible explanation for this is that Quartile is deliberately charging a lower mark-up in order to increase its sales by undercutting the market. There is supporting evidence for this in that Quartile's average inventory turnover at 4·5 times is 50% better than the sector average of three times. An alternative explanation could be that Quartile has had to cut its margins due to poor sales which have had a knock-on effect of having to write down closing inventory.

Quartile's lower gross profit percentage has fed through to contribute to a lower operating profit margin at 7·5% compared to the sector average of 12%. However, from the above figures, it can be deduced that Quartile's operating costs at 17·5% (25% − 7·5%) of revenue appear to be better controlled than the sector average operating costs of 23% (35% − 12%) of revenue. This may indicate that Quartile has a different classification of costs between cost of sales and operating costs than the companies in the sector average or that other companies may be spending more on advertising/selling commissions in order to support their higher margins.

The other component of ROCE is asset utilisation (measured by net asset turnover). If Quartile's business strategy is indeed to generate more sales to compensate for lower profit margins, a higher net asset turnover would be expected. At 1·6 times, Quartile's net asset turnover is only marginally better than the sector average of 1·4 times. Whilst this may indicate that Quartile's strategy was a poor choice, the ratio could be partly distorted by the property revaluation and also by whether the deferred development expenditure should be included within net assets for this purpose, as the net revenues expected from the development have yet to come on stream. If these two aspects were adjusted for, Quartile's net asset turnover would be 2·1 times (56,000/(34,600 − 5,000 − 3,000)) which is 50% better than the sector average.

In summary, Quartile's overall profitability is below that of its rival companies due to considerably lower profit margins, although this has been partly offset by generating proportionately more sales from its assets.

Liquidity

As measured by the current ratio, Quartile has a higher level of cover for its current liabilities than the sector average (1·6:1 compared to 1·25:1). Quartile's figure is nearer the 'norm' of expected liquidity ratios, often quoted as between 1·5 and 2:1, with the sector average (at 1·25:1) appearing worryingly low. The problem of this 'norm' is that it is generally accepted that it relates to manufacturing companies rather than retail companies, as applies to Quartile (and presumably also to the sector average). In particular, retail companies have very little, if any, trade receivables as is the case with Quartile. This makes a big difference to the current ratio and makes the calculation of a quick ratio largely irrelevant. Consequently, retail companies operate comfortably with much lower current ratios as their inventory is turned directly into cash. Thus, if anything, Quartile has a higher current ratio than might be expected. As Quartile has relatively low inventory levels (deduced from high inventory turnover figures), this means it must also have relatively low levels of trade payables (which can be confirmed from the calculated ratios). The low payables period of 45 days may be an indication of suppliers being cautious with the credit period they extend to Quartile, but there is no real evidence of this (e.g. the company is not struggling with an overdraft). In short, Quartile does not appear to have any liquidity issues.

Gearing

Quartile's debt to equity at 30% is lower than the sector average of 38%. Although the loan note interest rate of 10% might appear quite high, it is lower than the ROCE of 12·1% (which means shareholders are benefiting from the borrowings) and the interest cover of 5·25 times ((3,400 + 800)/800) is acceptable. Quartile also has sufficient tangible assets to give more than adequate security on the borrowings, therefore there appear to be no adverse issues in relation to gearing.

Conclusion

Quartile may be right to be concerned about its declining profitability. From the above analysis, it seems that Quartile may be addressing the wrong market (low margins with high volumes). The information provided about its rival companies would appear to suggest that the current market appears to favour a strategy of higher margins (probably associated with better quality and more expensive goods) as being more profitable. In other aspects of the appraisal, Quartile is doing well compared to other companies in its sector.

(c) Factors which may limit the usefulness of the comparison with business sector averages:

It is unlikely that all the companies that have been included in the sector averages will use the same accounting policies. In the example of Quartile, it is apparent that it has revalued its property; this will increase its capital employed and (probably) lower its ROCE (compared to if it did not revalue). Other companies in the sector may carry their property at historical cost.

The accounting dates may not be the same for all the companies. In this example the sector averages are for the year ended 30 June 2012, whereas Quartile's are for the year ended 30 September 2012. If the sector is exposed to seasonal trading (although this may be unlikely for jewellery), this could have a significant impact on many ratios, in particular working capital based ratios. To allow for this, perhaps Quartile could prepare a form of adjusted financial statements to 30 June 2012.

It may be that the definitions of the ratios have not been consistent across all the companies included in the sector averages (and for Quartile). This may be a particular problem with ratios like ROCE as there is no universally accepted definition. Often agencies issue guidance on how the ratios should be calculated to minimise these possible inconsistencies. Of particular relevance in this example is that it is unlikely that other jewellery retailers will have an intangible asset of deferred development expenditure.

BPP
LEARNING MEDIA

Sector averages are just that: averages. Many of the companies included in the sector may not be a good match to the type of business and strategy of Quartile. 'Jewellery' is a broad category and some companies may adopt a strategy of high-end (expensive) goods which have high mark-ups, but usually lower inventory turnover, whereas other companies may adopt a strategy of selling more affordable jewellery with lower margins in the expectation of higher volumes.

Note: *Other relevant examples may be acceptable, but they must relate to issues of inter-company comparison and not general issues of interpretation such as inflation distorting profit trends.*

4 (a) The main objective of financial statements is to provide information that is useful to a wide range of users for the purpose of making economic decisions. Therefore, it is important that the activities and events of the entity, as expressed within the financial statements, are understood by users, meaning that their usefulness and relevance is maximised. This can present management with a problem because clearly not all users have the same (financial) abilities and knowledge. For the purpose of understandability, management are allowed to assume users do have a reasonable knowledge of accounting and business and are prepared to study the financial statements diligently. Importantly, this characteristic cannot be used by management to avoid disclosing complex information that may be relevant in user decision-making. However, management must recognise that too much or overly complex disclosure can obscure the more important aspects of an entity's performance, i.e. important information should not be 'buried' in the detail of unfathomable information.

Comparability is the main tool by which users can assess the performance of an entity. This can be done through trend analysis of the same entity's financial statements over time (say five years), or by comparing one entity with other (suitable) entities (or business sector averages) for the same time period. This means that the measurement and disclosure (classification) of like transactions should be consistent over time for the same entity, and (ideally) between different entities. Consistency and comparability are facilitated by the existence and disclosure of accounting policies. The above illustrates the close correlation between comparability and consistency. However, it is not always possible for an entity to apply the same accounting policies every year; sometimes they have to change (e.g. because of a new accounting standard or a change in legislation). Similarly, it is not practical for accounting standards to require all entities to adopt the same accounting policies.

Thus, if an entity does change an accounting policy, this breaks the principle of consistency. In such circumstances, IFRSs normally require that any reported comparatives (previous year's financial statements) are restated as if the new policy had been in force when those statements were originally reported. In this way, although there has been a change of policy, comparability has been maintained.

It is more difficult to address the issue of consistency across entities; as already stated, accounting standards cannot prescribe the use of the same policy for all entities (this would be uniformity). However, accounting standards do prohibit certain accounting treatments (considered inappropriate or inferior) and they do require entities to disclose their accounting policies, such that users become aware of differences between entities and this may allow them to make value adjustments when comparing entities using different policies.

(b) (i) Lobden's income statement (extracts) for the year ended:

		30 September 2012 $million
Revenue (based on work certified)	(160 – 100)	60
Cost of sales (balance)		(48)
Profit	((50 x 160/250) – 20)	12

Statement of financial position (extracts) as at:

		30 September 2012 $million
Current assets:		
Amounts due from customers		
Contract costs to date		145
Profit recognised (cumulative 20 + 12)		32
		177
Progress billings (cumulative)		(160)
Amounts due from customers		17
Contract receivables	(160 – 150)	10

(ii) The relevant issue here is what constitutes the accounting policy for construction contracts. Where there is uncertainty in the outcome of a contract, the appropriate accounting policy would be the completed contract basis (i.e. no profit is taken until the contract is completed). Similarly, any expected losses should be recognised immediately. Where the outcome of a contract is reasonably foreseeable, the appropriate accounting policy is to accrue profits by the percentage of completion method. If this is accepted, it becomes clear that the different methods of determining the percentage of completion of construction contracts are different accounting estimates. Thus the change made by Lobden in the year to 30 September 2012 represents a change of accounting estimate. This approach complies with the guidance in IAS 11 *Construction Contracts* paras 30 and 38.

5   (a)   (i)   Shawler statement of financial position (extract) as at 30 September 2012

Carrying amount

	$	
Non-current assets:		
Furnace: main body	42,000	(48,000 – (60,000/10 years))
replaceable liner	4,000	(6,000 – (10,000/5 years))
Current liabilities		
Government grant	1,200	(prior year amount transferred to the income statement)
Non-current liabilities		
Government grant	7,200	(8,400 – 1,200 (12,000/10 years) transferred to current liabilities)
Environmental provision	19,440	(18,000 x 1·08)

(ii)   Income statement (extract) year ended 30 September 2012

	$
Depreciation (6,000 + 2,000)	8,000
Government grant (credited)	(1,200)
Finance costs (18,000 x 8%)	1,440

(b)   Although the legislation requiring the fitting of the filters has been passed, it does not come into force for two years. Even if Shawler has the intention of fitting the filters within this period, this still does not constitute an obligating event; therefore no provision should be made for this future cost. Surprisingly, even if Shawler had not fitted the filters before the date required by the legislation, it would still not require a provision. However, there could be a separate provision required for a liability to a fine.

As it would be the fitting of the filters that directly causes the reduction in the environmental clean-up costs, it follows that until the filters are actually fitted, Shawler could not reduce its environmental provision.

BPP
LEARNING MEDIA

BPP
LEARNING MEDIA

BPP
LEARNING MEDIA

BPP
LEARNING MEDIA

BPP
LEARNING MEDIA

BPP
LEARNING MEDIA

BPP
LEARNING MEDIA

BPP
LEARNING MEDIA

BPP
LEARNING MEDIA

BPP
LEARNING MEDIA

BPP
LEARNING MEDIA

BPP
LEARNING MEDIA

BPP
LEARNING MEDIA

BPP
LEARNING MEDIA